S M P L C T Y

ECOLOGICAL CIVILISATION AND THE WILL TO ART

Samuel Alexander

S M P L C T Y: Ecological Civilisation and the Will to Art
ISBN: 978-0-6488405-7-2

Published by the Simplicity Institute 2023
Essays on the Aesthetics of Existence
Cover design by Andrew Doodson, Copyright © 2023
Cover image by Agim Sulaj, Copyright © 2023
https://www.agimsulaj.com/index.shtml

Acknowledgements: Heartfelt thanks to Professor Brendan Gleeson for critically reviewing these essays. Countless improvements, both substantive and stylistic, were made in response to his feedback. Remaining errors are my own. Thanks also to Agim Sulaj for generously giving permission to use his image on the cover, and to Andrew Doodson for his design of the cover.

‘The bleaker and emptier life becomes under capitalism, the more intense is the yearning after beauty.’

– **Georg Lukács**

CONTENTS

PREFACE

THE APOCALYPTIC SUBLIME

There once lived a philosopher of the future called Zarathustra, who, increasingly aware of his unsettled spirit, left his home by the lakeside and went to live alone in the mountains. For ten years he meditated on his troubled condition and wearied not thereof. But eventually he felt something change in his heart, as if he were a bee that had gathered too much honey – his cup was about to overflow. So, one morning as the sun rose, Zarathustra announced before the great star that he would descend from the mountain, as the sun does at nightfall, and bring light to the underworld. Thus began Zarathustra's descent. On his way down the mountain he happened to cross paths with a saint who had left his hermitage to gather roots in the forest. In the morning mist the aged man was singing and chanting in glorification of God. Could it be possible, Zarathustra spoke in his heart, that this saint had not yet heard that *God is dead?*

Friedrich Nietzsche's parable is well known.[1] Suppose, however, that this philosopher of the future were alive today, cast into the apocalyptic environment of industrial civilisation in the twenty-first century. What life might he lead? He would soon realise that, despite the deepest desire for spiritual retreat, he could no longer exit society to live alone in the mountains, for all the available land had been enclosed and privatised. Instead, he would have to sell his labour simply in order to live within global capitalist society. By accident of fate, he might find himself trying to meet key performance indicators in a corporate university, enduring his unsettled spirit in the polluted and crowded atmosphere of some urban landscape.

Nevertheless, if this philosopher were sufficiently firm of mind – if he were a yea-sayer that affirmed his fate – he could undertake his inner work even in the inhospitable conditions of industrial modernity, living humbly within the wasteland of acquisitive society and yet above it. One day a clown in the ivory tower might summarily cast Zarathustra out of the educational-industrial complex, imposing upon him the precarious freedom to meditate on the human condition without the distractions of academic life. Blessed be the clown, declared Zarathustra, and he continued to love his fate. But what now for this free spirit?

Retiring to his small garden in the suburbs, we can imagine Zarathustra leaping into the depths of his being and writing a book, drafting and redrafting it in a timeless state of poetic frenzy. Eventually, after an indeterminate duration, he would rise with the dawn and realise that his meditations were complete, at which point he would immediately share his learnings with the world, startling the Owl of Minerva as he left.

Zarathustra would be shocked but not surprised by the darkness that lay waiting for him as he reemerged into the world. In the marketplace people were gathered to be entertained by a tightrope walker, but lo and behold the entertainer failed to make the perilous crossing, falling to his death on the busy tarseal below. The people cheered and called out for more entertainment. Could it be possible, Zarathustra wondered, that these people had not yet heard that *capitalism is dying and Earth is being killed*? Verily, he muttered to himself as he looked around the marketplace, this civilisation is still moving, but it is the movement of a falling corpse, the hair and fingernails of which will continue to grow long after death.

♦ ♦ ♦

If God is dead, capitalism is dying, and Earth itself is being killed: how now shall we live? This is the confronting question that consumed me over the last year as I worked on this collection of essays, and I'm happy to admit that I wrote them primarily for myself – not so much as a scholarly exercise but rather as an existential need. It is an anxiety of mine that I never really know my position on an issue until I have attempted to distil my vague musings into words. As my project got underway, this anxiety became unbearably acute regarding a particular matter that I needed to clarify and to which the following pages are dedicated, namely, whether existence can be affirmed while living in a dying civilisation, on a dying planet, situated in what seems to be a godless and absurd universe. If one were to find a way, despite all this, to say 'yes' to life – and for now this remains an open question – in what form or by what process could such an affirmation authentically emerge? What might such an affirmation look like? Perhaps more importantly, what might it feel like? Conversely, perhaps the only reasonable response to an existence such as ours might be a disciplined renunciation of a world that ought not to exist. These are some of the lingering existential uncertainties that have fuelled my inquiries.

Despite the personal motivations for working on this project, it would please me if there were at least a few fragments of these essays that might be of use to others, so I cast them out into the darkness of cyberspace and drop the manuscript down the well of industrial civilisation. I'm now left waiting, listening for any echo as it hits the bottom. My hope is that the themes may reverberate in the soul of some readers, as they have done in mine, in strange, unsettling, but uplifting harmony. The only advice I offer the reader (echoing Henry Thoreau) is that this book, like all books, should be read as deliberately as it was written, for the themes and theses will be easier to digest if they are chewed over slowly.

♦ ♦ ♦

In this preface I will explain why I came to write these essays. My purpose is to state some of the background assumptions, defended in my other publications,[2] that I don't intend to explain or justify in any detail herein. The present work is quite long enough. Fortunately, I feel many of these critical perspectives on contemporary society already reside in the collective unconscious, so most people should accept and understand them intuitively. Every day I see these unsettling realities rising more clearly to the surface of consciousness, like oil in water, ever harder to repress, even if most people have not yet admitted as much to themselves.

We are, it seems, cursed to live in 'interesting' times. For almost two decades I have been studying and writing about industrial civilisation, focussing on the interwoven problems of growth economics, societal complexity, fossil energy dependence, ecosystemic decline, consumerism, and capitalism. During this time a reality has dawned on me that I now believe is inescapable: this civilisation has no future. There are contradictions built into the very nature of the global capitalist system that admit no resolution. Let me briefly restate this critique.

Most starkly, industrial civilisation is fatally dependent on a finite and depleting stock of fossil energy – coal, oil, and gas. It becomes clearer by the day that post-carbon technologies (whether renewables or nuclear) will be unable stop humanity from blowing the 'carbon budget' for a safe climate. That is, it is already too late for 'green tech' to save us from destabilising climatic systems, with existing atmospheric concentrations of carbon having already locked us into a dangerous amount of global heating and extreme weather.[3] Furthermore, as fossil energy supplies eventually peak and decline in coming years, the global economy will be unable to maintain, let alone expand, current energy surpluses, especially in the affluent societies that currently enjoy unprecedented and unsustainable energy abundance. While transitioning to a renewable energy system of moderated production and consumption is both desirable and ultimately necessary – particularly when distributive equity is taken into account – almost nowhere do we hear about the necessity of *planned energy descent*. Instead, the dominant, celebratory message in public discourse is always and everywhere the techno-optimistic fantasy that we will simply 'green' the supply of energy and all socio-ecological contradictions will be resolved. Little do people seem to appreciate that global capitalism would remain grossly unjust and unsustainable, even if it managed to run entirely on solar and wind energy. Energy is indeed the lifeblood of civilisation, but our problems are even more fundamental.

More broadly, the structural demand for infinite economic growth on a finite biosphere is ecocidal, a tragedy unfolding in real time, exacerbated by the wealth-concentrating tendencies of capitalist economies. If once our species lived on a planet relatively empty of human beings, today we live on a planet that is evidently full to overflowing. The human population has grown exponentially to exceed eight billion people, trending towards eleven billion by the end of the century. As this expanding population continues to seek ever-rising material living standards by way of sustained economic growth, the global economy is being driven into gross ecological overshoot, dangerously crossing or threatening to cross a range of planetary boundaries with dire consequences that are already unfolding. Indeed, the metaphor of 'Earth as a Petri dish' has become worryingly apt, given that the dominant colony seems to be consuming all the available resources and is at risk of poisoning itself from its own wastes. This raises questions about whether humanity can muster the intelligence to avoid the fate of common bacteria. Techno-optimists and free marketeers promise ecological salvation via continuous 'green growth', all the while the face of Gaia is vanishing as Empire marches resolutely on.

To add cruel fuel to the fire, the so-called peak of industrial civilisation – consumerist culture – is failing to satisfy the human craving for meaning, and yet the collective response seems to be to dig deeper into the pit in search of something that has not yet been provided. As poet Bertolt Brecht noted with piercing insight, 'What were bad harvests / To the need that ravages us in the midst of plenty?'[4] Too much is never enough. Few consider the option of climbing out of this pit, or avoiding it altogether, through the escape routes of mindful sufficiency and the economics of 'enough'. Admittedly, that's no easy feat in a web of complexity that is conspiring against us, entangling us against our will – by design. Even the affluent societies find themselves in a pit, ensnared in a web. For whom, then, do we destroy the planet?

On top of all this, the threat of nuclear Armageddon remains ever present – the terrifying capacity to destroy ourselves through the 'sophistication' of our weaponry. Such a technological catastrophe could fast-track humanity's demise at any moment, a risk heighted by growing geopolitical tensions over access to the declining stocks of natural resources. I write these words in early 2023, when the global superpowers are rattling their nuclear sabres more loudly than they have for decades. The Doomsday Clock has never been closer to midnight.

These menacing contradictions are intensifying year by year, and I fear that at some point they will lead to the collapse of civilisation as we know it. No one can know for certain whether this great rupture will happen swiftly or unfold agonisingly over multiple decades, and there are many descent pathways that lie before us. But my confident hypothesis – both frightful and hopeful – is that by the end of this century, industrial civilisation will be an *historical phenomenon*. In fact, this process of inevitable descent is already well under way, as evidenced by the range of environmental, social, and political crises competing for our attention today. We need not examine those matters in any detail here, for they are too numerous, and are known well enough – even as we might look away.

The end of *this* civilisation, however, does not imply the end of civilisation, *as such*.[5] Whether some phoenix might one day emerge from the ashes of the Empire is a speculative inquiry to which this collection of essays dedicates some attention. But every day it becomes harder to imagine that there is some door hidden in the wall through which we might escape the Four Horsemen. This imaginative sterility however suggests that any escape will require an imaginative intervention, not merely a technocratic solution. As the Parisian graffiti of 1968 declared: 'those who lack imagination cannot imagine what is lacking'.

♦ ♦ ♦

What might seem surprising about this grim diagnosis is that there is absolutely no shortage of evidence to support it.[6] In fact, it was supportable several decades ago – and nothing has changed, except the mounting of further evidence on the deepening of the human-ecological predicament. Most of my scholarly work has involved reviewing and synthesising that evidence, attempting to draw out its implications, and exploring responses and strategies for transformation. What needs to happen seems clear enough. Lifting the poorest billions out of destitution is obviously a moral imperative, but doing so is likely to place further burdens on an already overburdened ecosystem. This confluence of ecological and social justice imperatives calls radically into question the legitimacy of further economic expansion in the already high-impact, consumerist societies of the so-called developed world. It follows that any resolution to the crisis of ecological overshoot will need to entail 'degrowth' – that is, *planned economic contraction* of the energy and resource demands of the most developed regions of the world. It will also require a reconceptualisation of sustainable development in the Global South, beyond the conventional path of carbon-based industrial growth. This 'limits to growth' position signifies a necessary paradigm shift in the dominant conception of human progress, one that is being explored boldly today within movements associated with degrowth, permaculture, post-development, voluntary simplicity, appropriate technology, and economic re-localisation.

I have summarised the critical perspective – but what about the positive, regenerative alternative? Although the range of post-growth and post-capitalist movements are diverse and defy singular definition, in general terms the alternative paradigm is as clear as the problems. What is needed is a transition beyond the existing order of growthism, building in its place a constellation of highly localised economies of sufficiency, based on renewable sources of energy, appropriate technology, egalitarianism, participatory democracy, and non-affluent but sufficient material cultures of voluntary simplicity. Counter-intuitively, perhaps, advocates for this type of Great Transition also maintain that moving beyond growth economics will increase quality of life, by reshaping cultures and societal structures to promote non-materialistic forms of meaning and wellbeing beyond consumerist conceptions of 'the good life'. Sometimes dismissed as utopian or naive, the obvious rejoinder is that nothing could be more fantastical than the current economic model that assumes the viability of limitless growth on a finite planet. In any case, in an era when it is commonly remarked that it is easier to imagine the end of the world than the end of capitalism, perhaps utopianism is not an indictment but a defence of radical movements today. This is the paradigm shift I have been working on since my doctoral thesis on degrowth (2006-2010), and it is heartening to see these movements expanding and gaining momentum, albeit slowly and despite remaining on the margins of public discourse.

Nevertheless, over time I began to wonder whether I was approaching the transitional question in the wrong way. The scientific evidence for deep change is compelling, supported by basic moral principles of fairness, justice, and sustainability. Yet, these forces of evidence and theory aren't having much practical, real-world impact. As I began contemplating the reasons for this civilisational inertia, I realised that I had been proceeding as if the primary problem was an information deficit, assuming that existing crises were mainly a result of *intellectual* or *scientific* failings of our species. I had assumed with typical academic bias that when more evidence and better theories were available, we would see the error of our ways and steer the ship of civilisation away from the cliff's edge.

Having been struck too often by the ineffectiveness of evidence and argument, I now see that humanity's primary obstacle is not an intellectual or evidential one but an *aesthetic* one, related to our sensibilities, felt needs, communication strategies, and imaginative capacities. I will suggest, consequently, that this obstacle also demands an engagement in aesthetic terms – an approach that will obviously require some explaining and defending. Defined further in the introduction, my use of the term 'aesthetic' will appeal both to the modern usage, pertaining to the philosophies of art, beauty, and taste, as well as to the earlier meaning, pertaining to the realm of sensuous experience. Inspired by and engaging with thinkers such as Friedrich Schiller, William Morris, Friedrich Nietzsche, Michel Foucault, Richard Rorty, and Jane Bennett, I will be proposing that through art and the aesthetic dimensions of life we can move most coherently toward an ecological civilisation in which freedom, flourishing, and justice are open and unfolding realities.

Herein lies one of the points of departure in the following essays. Humanity's fatal problem is not that we do not *know* we have to change in fundamental ways (although some still deny this); nor is there any shortage of assertions about *how* to change (although there are many false paths). My preliminary proposition – a premise of the project – is that to date very few people have acquired a *taste* for the profound changes that are needed. This is partly because so few have developed the imaginative or aesthetic capacities to *envision* those changes, and fewer still have shown the disposition to *desire* them. Taste, vision, imagination, desire – these can be understood as aesthetic categories, and this collection of essays emerged from the hypothesis that those categories would reward aesthetic analysis. For in an age increasingly called the Anthropocene – the age of ecological overshoot driven by human activity – what is needed more than anything is planned contraction of energy and resource demands by overgrown and overconsuming regions of the world. As I have suggested, the evidential case for embracing degrowth is compelling.[7] But *there is no taste for degrowth*, which can be understood as an aesthetic obstacle requiring an aesthetic intervention.

Strangely, this approach implies that if my arguments are ultimately accepted, readers will eventually find themselves needing to throw away the ladder after having climbed up it, given that I am presenting a rational case for an aesthetic response. In other words, reasoning can only take us so far, or rather, it may be that the intellectual shifts that are required may need to be *preceded* by an aesthetic engagement and transformation in the emotional and sensuous capacities of our species. This realisation points to the need for a new politics of art. To paraphrase poet Samuel Taylor Coleridge: we must create the taste by which we will be judged.

Accordingly, my starting point is this: that we know in our heads that there must be more humane, meaningful, and sustainable ways to live, but we do not yet *feel* this in our hearts. For if we did – if a new aesthetic sensibility had already arisen – the emotional energy would be at hand to bring new worlds into existence through creative and sustained collective action. The aesthetic revolution would have already done its work. And yet we wait, as if paralysed before the looming apocalypse. I believe this is due to an aesthetic deficit – a shortage of beauty, meaning, creativity, and pleasure in our lives. But I will argue that this deficit is within our creative hands and minds to resolve.

♦ ♦ ♦

It is good to remember that the term 'apocalypse' has a dual meaning, not simply referring to the 'end of the world' but also signifying a 'great unveiling or disclosure' of knowledge. I confess that I have had fleeting experiences of the sublime when contemplating the apocalyptic unveiling that awaits our species. In the eighteenth century, the pioneering philosopher of the sublime, Edmund Burke, described this notion as the strongest emotion the mind is capable of feeling: 'Whatever is fitted in any sort to excite the ideas of pain, and danger, that is to say, whatever is in any sort terrible, or is conversant about terrible objects, or operates in a manner analogous to terror, is a source of the sublime.'[8]

And yet, Burke explained that the sublime is not exclusively an unpleasant emotion, for the fear and danger we feel can, in certain circumstances, also confer a certain delight. As we observe an ominous storm approaching, watch fierce waves crashing violently against the rocks, or stand upon a majestic mountain ridge and look down upon the vast ravines below, we can be cast into an unsettling state of awe and self-conscious insignificance, at once frightening and pleasurable, restoring a certain perspective to our lives. What is more, Burke suggested that feelings of the sublime can overwhelm our faculties of reason: 'The passion caused by the great and the sublime in *nature*, when those causes operate most powerfully, is Astonishment; and astonishment is the state of the soul, in which all its motions are suspended, with some degree of horror.'[9]

Of course, the delight induced by experiences of the sublime are only possible because of the safe distance one remains from the immense and threatening forces under consideration. I acknowledge the privilege of this distance, for it's obvious that the apocalypse has already arrived for billions of human beings on Earth today, not to mention the broader community of life whose habitats are under ruthless and relentless attack. Thus, I must also acknowledge the perversity of any feelings of awe in relation to a falling civilisation that might end up destroying us all.

But it is for this very reason that prospects of the apocalypse can evoke strangely seductive feelings of uncomfortable pleasure. Such a rupture promises a path of transformative change that has proven unachievable through the mechanisms of activism, politics, or conventional education. Contemplation of such change provides a further source of the sublime in what Burke calls 'infinity', where the eye is not able to 'perceive the bounds'[10] of something, or 'see an object distinctly',[11] and this gives rise to a 'terrible uncertainty of the things described.'[12] For Burke: 'Infinity has a tendency to fill the mind with that sort of delightful horror, which is the most genuine effect, and the truest test of the sublime.'[13]

A recent realisation, however, has come to haunt me: I no longer experience the apocalyptic sublime. My only explanation for this is that I no longer feel I am at a safe distance. One cannot experience sublimity when submerged in great waves that are threatening at any moment to cast one violently into the rocks. And so, my state of perception has shifted, leaving me with a new sense of urgency, and, if I were to speculate, I sense this heightened urgency in other people too, even if we are unsure how to talk about our unsettled condition. I sometimes worry that the intensifying cultural tensions we see in the world today are an indirect and confused manifestation of these anxieties, of which we are still learning to manage and which no one fully understands. Great cultural shifts are often understood only in the rear-view mirror, by which time it is too late to adjust to the fact that the changes perceived were even closer to transpiring than what they appeared to be.

Traditional apocalyptic discourse has always involved the anticipation of some world-disclosing event – the apocalypse 'to come'. I feel time is nigh to deconstruct this linear conception – or rather, the linear conception has deconstructed itself. In other words, we must no longer conceive of the apocalypse as some future event that may or may not arrive. Instead, it should be accepted that we are already living in the End Times – from a geological perspective, the Anthropocene is a blink of the eye. The great unveiling is already underway, even if we remain entrenched in conditions of disorder and disorientation. No longer can we merely 'bear witness'. We are always and already involved in a perpetual state of crisis that is not *imminent* but *immanent*.

This is the soil in which this project was seeded, coming to fruition in the fading light of the apocalyptic sublime. As related above, the thesis I will be presenting is that only by passing through a new aesthetic condition, induced by aesthetic experience and creative activity, can humanity hope to respond adequately or appropriately to our current predicament. That response is going to involve a shift away from ever-expanding materialistic goals and turning to the realm of the spirit to satisfy our hunger for infinity, a monumental task, of which the pioneering underlabourers have already begun. Having had my hopes for salvation exhausted elsewhere, I am now convinced that the aesthetic dimensions of life alone have the capacity to solve the most fundamental problems caused by growth-orientated, technological society, problems which are not themselves related to a lack of technology and which cannot be solved by more or better technology. Thus, in the face of extreme pessimism, which in the past has tempted me to despair, I can now offer readers an aesthetic justification for existence, which I believe is both coherent, compelling, even hopeful – despite everything.

As my friend Mark Burch says: 'When all appeals to reason have failed, tell a new story.'[14]

---

[1] Fredrich Nietzsche, *Thus Spoke Zarathustra* (Cambridge: Cambridge University Press, 2006).

[2] My publications are listed, and mostly freely available, at my website: https://samuelalexander.info/ (accessed 20 April 2023).

[3] For example, see the reports by David Spratt and Ian Dunlop, published by the Breakthrough Institute, which review and analyse the latest climate science. Available at: https://www.breakthroughonline.org.au/publications (accessed 20 April 2023).

[4] Bertolt Brecht, 'On Judging' in Bertolt Brecht, *Poems 1913-1956* (London: Methuen, 1987) p. 308.

[5] Rupert Read and Samuel Alexander, *This Civilisation is Finished: Conversations on the End of Empire and What Lies Beyond* (Melbourne: Simplicity Institute, 2019).

[6] See generally, William Ripple et al, 'World's Scientists' Warning of a Climate Emergency' (2021) *BioScience* 71(9): pp. 894-898; Thomas Wiedmann, Manfred Lenzen, Lorenz Keyber, and Julia Steinberger, 'Scientist' Warning on Affluence' (2020) *Nature Communications* 11: 3107; Thomas Homer-Dixon et al, 'Synchronous Failure: The Emerging Casual Architecture of Global Crisis' (2015) *Ecology and Society* 20(3): 6. See also, note 6.

[7] Useful literature reviews include, Martin Weiss and Claudio Cattaneo, 'Degrowth – Taking Stock and Reviewing an Emerging Academic Paradigm' (2017) *Ecological Economics* 137: pp. 220-230; Giorgos Kallis et al, 'Research on Degrowth' (2018) *Annual Review of Environmental and Resources* 43: 4.1-4.26. See also, note 2.

[8] Edmund Burke, *A Philosophical Enquiry into the Origin of our Ideas of the Sublime and Beautiful* (Oxford: Oxford University Press, 1990), p. 36.

[9] Ibid, p. 53

[10] Ibid, p.67.

[11] Ibid, p. 58

[12] Ibid.

[13] Ibid, p. 67.

[14] Mark Burch, *Euterra Rising: The Last Utopia* (Winnipeg: Mark Burch, 2016).

BOOK ONE

THE WILL TO ART

‘Rising, tram, four hours in the office or factory, meal, tram, four hours of work, meal, sleep and Monday, Tuesday, Wednesday, Thursday, Friday and Saturday, according to the same rhythm – this path is easily followed most of the time. But one day the “why” arises and everything begins in that weariness tinged with amazement.’

– **Albert Camus**

INTRODUCTION

THE AESTHETIC DIMENSION

This collection of essays presents an aesthetics of existence which I call the 'Will to Art'. Readers will be invited to consider the possibility that the universe is fundamentally an aesthetic phenomenon, understood as a process of creative evolution that is moving, albeit agonistically, towards ever-increasing opportunities for artistic expression and aesthetic experience. Art will be defined broadly and openly as the meaningful and pleasurable expression of creative labour, and human experience can be considered 'aesthetic' if it flows from the sensuous engagement with art or nature. To speak of the Will to Art is to interpret the world as having an underlying tendency toward artistic and aesthetic flourishing, even though the outcome of this evolutionary process, due to its indeterminate nature, is unknowable in advance.

From this perspective, the cosmos itself is a sensuous and artful reality that is unfolding in order to *experience itself* through the genesis and diversity of conscious and creative life. This aesthetic universe is not a singular, conscious being, but it attains consciousness through the development of diverse experiential nodes in the fabric of existence. In the case of human beings, these nodes have become reflective, visionary, poetic, and self-aware. Our bodies are composed of elements from dead stars, and now, on starry nights, we can look up at ourselves in wonder. We are the vibrating strings of a strange and sublime cosmological symphony – a collaborative project that we must try to compose, perform, and conduct, together.[1]

The telos or goal of this universe is beauty. This guiding ideal is defined not as mere cosmetic ornamentation, but as the pleasurable experience of art and nature, the meaningful interaction with self, other, and world, and the undertaking and contemplation of aesthetic activity. If we interpret art to include all creative work through which order, form, and meaning are given to existence, then we can say that art is life's highest calling – the truest expression of freedom. Thus all human beings can conceive of themselves as aesthetic agents in an aesthetic universe – as *homo aestheticus* – the art-created art creators.

At the base of this worldview there is a creative force or impulse – the Will to Art – which gives energy, substance, and vitality to all phenomena. This unconscious motive permeates the universe, striving to produce conditions in which art and aesthetic experience can blossom with infinite diversity. But this primordial impulse will remain dissatisfied and restless, in search of harmony, until its energy achieves the free and creative expression it seeks. The Will to Art is experienced in human consciousness as the insatiable drive of desire – a reckless and amoral yearning for beauty, pleasure, freedom, and meaning. It is represented through our sensory apparatus as material or phenomenological reality.

Accordingly, the world we experience is both will and representation – to borrow terminology from German philosopher Arthur Schopenhauer.[2] As I will be using these terms, will and representation are dual aspects of an underlying cosmological art-force manifesting in alternative but mutually dependent ways. In other words, the Will to Art has both internal and external dimensions, even though it is the inner dimension of this reality that we know most directly and intimately, through our own willing natures. Despite being thrown into an existence we never asked for, our capacity to experience beauty shows that human beings have a place in this world, at least potentially, and our capacity to create beauty provides us with a noble, orienting purpose.

Arising out of aesthetic metaphors rather than being grounded in metaphysics, the Will to Art can be understood as a mythopoetic origin story. As such, it is the cause of the cosmological instability which led to the spectacular explosion at the beginning of time, resulting in the universe itself and the perpetual creative drives working in and through all phenomena. It is the internal spark of life, giving consciousness to matter and materiality to consciousness, and the cause of literally unpredictable moments in what French philosopher Henri Bergson called 'creative evolution'.[3] And it is the poetic madness that gives rise to that mysterious feeling or mood which inspires, even compels, the artist to sit down to compose *something out of nothing*. Therein – by creating something out of nothing – humanity is able to commune with the Dionysian impulse from which existence itself has emerged. As philosopher Abraham Kanovitch wrote of essentially this experience:

> They who have not felt it cannot believe it, but once felt, it is marvellous to know that the universe holds such depths of feeling within itself – it is more than words can tell. It satisfies the longing of the heart; all external commotion pales before it. It justifies the existence of the universe.[4]

The history of political society can be interpreted through this lens, as a dialectical process of evolution through which human beings struggle, often unconsciously and indirectly, toward the ideal of beauty. Political progress toward this latent aesthetic ideal need not be linear and its attainment may be forever elusive. Indeed, a true Democracy of Art, in which all people can find meaning and pleasure in creative labour, is still a very distant beacon in the dark of night. Nevertheless, the Will to Art is a passion, a yearning for beauty that seeks its own actualisation through art and aesthetic experience. It is an existential dissonance in search of harmony, through which beauty tends to beget beauty, if only from the perspective of deep time.

Given that the arc of this cosmology bends slowly and inconsistently towards beauty, it follows that sometime in the future – perhaps only in the deep future – an ecological civilisation of artisan-artists could emerge. I state 'could' emerge because nothing is preordained in an aesthetic universe. The dissonance of the world will not necessarily resolve into harmony, but there is a chance, a tendency. Should humanity struggle successfully in the pursuit of beauty, I believe the result would be a society composed of free spirits who have enabled themselves to explore their aesthetic capacities and sensibilities, while living simply in harmony with nature and each other. Such an idealised social order would be defined, not by relations of master and slave, or worker and capitalist, but by the revolving and reciprocal relations of artist and art-lover, a process driven onwards by the Will to Art.

In developing this vision, my two guiding premises are, first, that material sufficiency is all that is *needed* for human beings to live rich, meaningful, and artful lives; and second, that material sufficiency is all that is *possible*, over the long term, on a finite planet in an age of environmental limits. Based on those premises, I will propose and defend a conception of ecological civilisation which I call S M P L C T Y. This is not a utopian prediction about what I think is a likely future for our species. Rather, it is an *orientating vision*, one in which individuals and communities thrive in humble conditions of material sufficiency but cultural richness, meaningfully engaged in pleasurable and creative labour in collaboration with others. According to this vision, life itself would become an aesthetic project, a never-ending process of creative activity, sensuous experience, aesthetic engagement, and spiritual exploration. Such a society would be structured with the aim of sustainably providing opportunities for all people to find meaning and pleasure through creative labour and aesthetic experience.

Of course, the concept of art has no stable or determinate 'essence', so it is a category that is, and ought to be, contested, challenging, and evolving.[5] As stated above, my working definition – inspired by nineteenth-century artist and philosopher William Morris – is to assume that art broadly refers to the meaningful and pleasurable expression of creative labour.[6] This definition encompasses both the 'fine arts' (music, poetry, painting, sculpture, and architecture) and the so-called 'lesser arts' of handcraft (carpentry, sewing, pottery, glassware, carving, etc). Building upon Morris, I will defend a societal vision in which art, as defined, becomes integrated into the necessary labours, rituals, and experiences of everyday life. This intentionally blurs the distinction between artist and artisan. I have described such society in my work of fiction, *Entropia: Life Beyond Industrial Civilisation* (2013), and my four volumes of collected academic essays provide evidential foundations as well as social, political, and economic theories of sufficiency.[7] The present collection of essays seeks to provide philosophical and mythopoetic foundations for the same vision, but through the lens of aesthetics, which I now realise is fundamental.

By removing the 'i' from the conventional spelling, the neologism SMPLCTY is intended to evoke a 'less is more' philosophy – or rather, a philosophy of 'just enough is plenty'. This reflects the ethos of sufficiency underpinning the aestheticised form of ecological civilisation that I am inviting readers to consider. The removal of the 'i' is also meant to imply the achievement of a diminished egoism (or increased communitarianism) compared to the possessive individualism that has come to define globalised industrial capitalism. Paradoxically, it will be seen that this diminished egoism actually increases opportunities for individual self-creation. In essence, I will employ SMPLCTY to signify an anarcho-socialist form of life in which human beings minimise material and energetic demands for reasons of social and ecological justice, while creatively exploring the good life in non-materialistic sources of meaning and happiness, especially through art and aesthetic experience. This is supported by an interpretation of the universe as embodying a primordial energy called the Will to Art, which seeks to experience itself through the aesthetic flourishing that would be cultivated in such an ecological civilisation.

This is no degeneration into naïve romanticism. Despite the telos of this universe being beauty, the harsh struggle for existence that is evident in our early phase of creative evolution easily disguises the Will to Art as a violent and oppressive Will to Power – not in the Nietzschean sense of power over oneself, but in the sense of an insecure grasping for dominance over the external world. This distortion of the universe's primal striving leads willing, desiring, and sensuous creatures to pursue their aesthetic destinies in confused, inefficient, and often counterproductive ways. This is because people who are deprived of the power of aesthetic expression can end up expressing themselves in a drive for power.[8] Unnecessary and meaningless suffering is the result. One only needs to contemplate the profound ugliness of human societies and the many twisted faces that comprise them to see that our collective journey toward beauty and aesthetic freedom is still in its infancy. As I see things, we are creatures that are currently alienated from our inherent nature as an artful species, seeking some form of aesthetic redemption, and my position is that this is the only kind of redemption available to humanity given the death of God and the absence of any alternative metaphysical comforts. As Friedrich Nietzsche declared: it is only as aesthetic phenomena that existence and the world can be justified.[9]

♦ ♦ ♦

The Will to Art, as I have introduced it here, is a grand narrative of our universe and humanity's place in it. Given my sympathies with Nietzschean perspectivism, however, I do not present this vision or cosmodicy as if it were, in any sense, a neutral or objective reading of the world.[10] I believe it to be true, and indeed I experience its truthfulness, but there may be other true theories of existence also – true in the pragmatic sense of being useful for living. Mine is but one interpretation of an infinitely complex cosmological phenomenon, and because reality is infinitely complex, the human situation is liable to various and competing, even contradictory, interpretations.

To be clear, my goal in presenting this collection of essays is certainly not to persuade everyone to think exactly as I do – that would be a grossly authoritarian imposition. Rather, my goal is to tell a plausible, coherent, and engaging story of our place in the universe, in the hope that it may serve the aesthetic values of creativity, freedom, and beauty that my story seeks to describe, evaluate, and uphold. Thus my reasoning is circular, as all reasoning ultimately is – based on premises and values which rest only on themselves. It follows that the Will to Art signifies what American philosopher Richard Rorty called a 'final vocabulary'[11] – the bedrock of one's justificatory project, beneath which one has no further argumentative recourse. But it is a final vocabulary that I will attempt to present in a persuasive way, while acknowledging that this aesthetics of existence does not, and cannot, rest on metaphysical foundations.

To admit that I am engaged in the art of storytelling, however, should not in any way imply that this project resides in the realm of 'mere fantasy' or lacks a critical relationship to reality. Every individual and every society are enactments of a story people tell themselves about the nature and purpose of their existence and of the world they live in. The myths and stories we tell ourselves situate us in space and time, shape our perceptions of the present, and guide us as we move into the future, influencing our interpretations of what is possible, proper, and important. Even though we typically embody cultural myths unconsciously, these shared narratives are influential not only in how we *think* about social and political life but, perhaps more importantly, how we *feel* about it – and thus how we act. This implies that there is a politics of storytelling – and a politics of art and aesthetics more generally. To acknowledge the political function of story is the first step in exposing the blurry distinction between art, life, and politics, suggesting that there is an inherent aesthetic dimension to life and politics, just as there is a political or even revolutionary potential inherent to certain forms of art or aesthetic practice. These are central themes to be explored.

If I am justified in describing human beings as storytelling creatures, then this project can be seen to reflect our creative essence. But it is an offering that also demands a creative interpretation by the reader, not merely a passive absorption. There are certainly gaps in my story, sometimes deliberately so, which I leave for artful and imaginative readers to fill in according to their own political or spiritual disposition. My invitation is simply for you to take the view of existence outlined here seriously, to see what happens to your spirit should you come to look at the world and your life through the aesthetic lens being presented. If you finish this volume identifying as an artist and seeing the world as a canvas we must paint together in mutual support and engagement, then we can be sure that our spirits burn with the same fire – the Will to Art.

The essays to follow defend this mythopoetic perspective and explore what might be the proper modes of social, economic, and political organisation for an aesthetic creature such as ours, in a universe such as this. This orientation does not deny or downplay the gruesome violence, humiliating poverty, ecological devastation, and widespread oppression that shapes the contemporary world in so many ways. On the contrary, I am trying to approach such issues from a new angle, in the hope of shedding light on opportunities for social, political, and ecological progress that currently lie in the shadows of dominant modes of thinking.

At once the spectre of 'aestheticism' is raised: Will taking an aesthetic perspective on politics lead to what critical theorist Walter Benjamin called an aestheticisation of politics (fascism) or the politicisation of aesthetics (Soviet communism)?[12] The question is fair, but ultimately misdirected. I unconditionally place every member of our species, *homo aestheticus*, on an equal and egalitarian footing – each having the same right to fashion their life according to their unique creative capacities and sensibilities. Freedom implies constraint, however, both socially and ecologically, which is the never-ending task of politics to manage. It follows that any concerns that I am at risk of presenting an elitist, fascist, or aestheticised aristocracy (concerns sometimes directed toward Nietzsche) can be dissolved before they arise. For if, as Jacques Rancière asserts, 'politics is aesthetic in principle'[13] – a statement to which we will have to return – then it is no objection to a political vision that it is, at base, aesthetic. Mine is simply self-conscious of this inevitability, and I see no reason to try to disguise this fact. The critical issues to be addressed, then, are how politics is aesthetic, to what ends, and for whose benefit. Before anticipating my answers to these questions, I will attempt to clarify the philosophical context of this project.

The aesthetic dimensions of existence

I wish to speak a word for aestheticism, for aesthetic freedom and wildness, as contrasted with a freedom that is metaphysically constrained. I wish to conceive of the human being as an aesthetic agent in an aesthetic universe, or part and parcel of a work of art that demands creative interpretation and participation, as opposed to a predefined being in a predetermined cosmos. I will make an extreme statement, so that I can make an emphatic one, for there are enough champions of metaphysics who will deny or downplay the aesthetic dimensions of life.[14]

And what might those dimensions be? Aesthetics can be understood as having two primary meanings. The first pertains to the philosophy of art and beauty – exploring issues such as the meaning of art, the nature of beauty, judgements of taste, and the role of the artist in society. The second domain of aesthetic inquiry pertains to the senses – exploring issues related to bodily experience, sensuality, pleasure, perception, feelings, passions, and emotions. The word 'aesthetic' derives from the ancient Greek term *aisthētikós* (meaning 'perceptive, sensitive, pertaining to sensory perception') which in turn derives from *aisthánomai* (meaning 'I perceive, sense, learn'). Accordingly, this second field of aesthetic inquiry addresses matters that extend beyond what would conventionally be called 'art objects' or 'perceptions of beauty' and engages questions related to sensuous human experience in its manifold dimensions. Being in the presence of great art is an aesthetic experience, but so is plunging into the ocean or sauntering through a rainforest.

The aesthetic dimensions of existence are discernible, most fundamentally, at the cosmological level. I have already proposed that the universe itself can be coherently understood as being fundamentally aesthetic – artistic and sensuous to the core. This involves elevating our cosmos to the dignity of a work of art through a bold act of interpretation, and this calls for an aesthetic orientation toward existence. The Big Bang, for example, can be understood as a primordial creative explosion – the Original Aesthetic Event – and throughout this collection of essays I will present both the unfolding of the universe, as well as the historical emergence of the human species, through this aesthetico-evolutionary lens.[15]

The physical matter of the universe evolved, over billions of years, to become conscious. How this occurred, and the relationship between matter and mind, remains one of life's great unsolved mysteries – what scientists and philosophers call the 'hard problem' of consciousness. In the human species, matter has even become self-aware, reflective, and capable of directing its own creative evolution, as opposed to merely being the determinate *product* of physical laws and biological processes and instincts. What if the freedom to seek meaning and pleasure through creativity is the mysterious *purpose* of the universe? What if the outcome of this process is inclined towards beauty, a process through which the universe gets to experience itself through the phenomenon of consciousness? What would a politics of beauty involve? These are some of the guiding questions posed by a cosmology based on the Will to Art. It will be seen in a forthcoming essay that art and aesthetic practices have been central to human evolution throughout our species' history, such that our aesthetic faculties, capacities, and potentials are fundamental components of our malleable nature. It should come as no surprise, then, that art has been universally present in human societies, so much so that it is unclear whether humans created the arts or whether the arts gave birth to humanity.

This conception of humanity has social, ethical, and political implications, to which I will be giving due attention. Evolutionary theorist Ellen Dissanayake contends that 'social systems that disdain or discount beauty, form, mystery, meaning, value, and quality – whether in art or in life – are depriving their members of human requirements as fundamental as those for food, warmth, and shelter.'[16] In line with this basic reasoning, I am inviting readers to consider a normative view of the cosmos as something that embodies an evolutionary purpose – a telos that is moving slowly and unevenly toward forms of life in which self-reflective beings are empowered to shape their own lives as an aesthetic project. Just as the acorn has an oak tree built into its nature, the cosmological narrative I will present holds that the universe itself has 'art' built into its nature, and our goal as creature-creators is to facilitate this aesthetic blossoming through personal, social, and political action. Whereas utilitarianism aims to maximise happiness and liberalism aims to promote freedom, a political economy of art would seek to foster creative engagements with questions of meaning and beauty in ecologically sustainable ways. Such engagements might depend on freedom, and are likely to advance human happiness, but ultimately the

Will to Art aims to foster something more fundamental and substantive: beauty.

The normatively orientating end-state of this evolutionary process would be a society, not of artists, as such, but of creative self-fashioners who are free to author their own stories and perhaps even sing their own songs – to be the poets of their own lives – in honour of the art-force that drives creative evolution onwards. Given that self-creation never takes place in a vacuum, however, it is inevitably a shared endeavour with the entire community of life. This means, paradoxically, that the art of self-creation has necessary social, political, and ecological dimensions which must be acknowledged. Specifically, in the contemporary context, where humanity is evidently making unsustainable demands on the life-support system called Earth, any resolution to this dire ecological predicament must involve a radical downscaling of our collective energy and resource demands. This raises questions about what material or energetic foundations are needed to fulfill our aesthetic natures as self-creators, and how such a political economy of art might be structured and organised. I have addressed some of those material and energetic questions in my other publications on degrowth, permaculture, energy descent futures, low-tech living, and voluntary simplicity.[17] In this work I will focus on the aesthetic dimensions.

Beyond the creative forces underlying the evolution of life, the human condition has an inherently aesthetic dimension, insofar as lived experience is always shaped and mediated by language. Our linguistic concepts and categories give order and form to our experience of the world and even to our conception(s) of self. This feature of existence can be understood aesthetically in the sense that human beings have had to *create* those concepts and categories, and infuse them with meaning, for neither our concepts nor their meanings were given to us in advance. Indeed, the invention of language is one of humanity's earliest and arguably our most significant creative acts. Our concepts and their meanings could have been otherwise, have been otherwise, will be otherwise, and in fact are always and everywhere changing due to the inherent instability of language and the ever-changing contexts in which it is used and interpreted. This makes the ontological nature of ourselves and our universe inherently unstable. Thus, a close reading of our existential condition reminds us that we are freer than we think we are. The very concept of 'humanity' is always and everywhere becoming, forever shifting beneath our feet. We never step into the same river twice, for neither ourselves nor our contexts endure in any static ontological or metaphysical sense.

From this perspective, there is no way for human beings to step outside the mediation of our linguistic apparatus and somehow perceive the world in an unmediated, pre-linguistic form; no way for us to shed our conceptual schemes through which we experience the world and see the world *as it really is*. Instead, reality is experienced through or with the lens of language, and the immediate point is that humans *created* that lens. This is essentially all that is meant when philosophers talk of the linguistic or social 'construction of reality', even if explanations are usually dressed up in impenetrable jargon. Language thus shapes what we *see* and how we *think*, but given language also shapes our experience of reality, it also shapes what and how we *feel*. In other words, the task of creating language through which we experience reality comes to influence the sensory experience of the reality that language has constructed.

There are various levels to this creative process of constructing reality through our linguistic practices. As children we are all educated into a 'language game' that we did not create ourselves. Our education begins upon someone's knee, then is continued through lessons ratified by wider society. But this immersion into a language game is not a purely passive process. Humans both shape and are shaped by language, and this dialectical relationship is an ongoing process of co-creation and co-production. We don't just speak language. In a very real sense, language speaks us.[18]

By inventing new concepts or vocabularies in response to a changing world, or creatively redefining the meanings given to existing concepts and vocabularies, human beings can literally reshape not just their *experience* of reality, but more fundamentally, the *reality* that they experience. This can expand the horizons of what can be thought, said, seen, and even felt. But our words, to function *as words*, have to be able to reoccur in different contexts. This is what Jacques Derrida referred to as 'iterability'.[19] The meaning of a word can never be fully present in one context given that it may need to be applied or interpreted in a different context where the meanings can shift, sometimes without notice or intention. As we attempt to 'read' reality, the text of existence does not announce its meaning to us, from which it follows that interpretation is the only game in town. There is no pre-existing or *literal* truth to the textual reality we inhabit, so no interpretation of it can ever be final. Existence, at base, is indeterminate. It must be given form – which is an aesthetic challenge.

I proceed on this post-metaphysical basis, but it is not the purpose of these essays to present a philosophical critique of metaphysics or a defence of the 'linguistic turn' in philosophy. Rather, my post-metaphysical stance is simply an assumption I begin from, based on the critical literatures variously labelled neo-pragmatism, deconstruction, and social constructionism.

I limit my affiliation with these literatures mainly in relation to the indeterminacy and contingency of language, as just outlined, which is the basis of my aestheticist reading of the world.

Life as literature: are we all aesthetes now?

The capacity to shape and reshape reality with the tool of language can be understood most clearly perhaps through the narratives and myths we tell ourselves about the world and our place in it. The universe, our histories, our relationships, and our lived experience all defy full and complete accounting by virtue of their infinite complexity. There is no way to tell the *whole story*, so to speak, for there is always more that could be said; other perspectives not yet considered; new events and situations that call into question previous interpretations or categorisations of the world, and so forth. We are inherently creatures of perspective. There is no 'view from nowhere' that offers a neutral perspective on reality devoid of values or assumptions. Thus, the very distinction between 'fact' and 'value' collapses, given that our value-laden purposes, goals, interests, and desires inevitably shape how we experience the factual world 'out there'.

Accordingly, when we find ourselves trying to make sense of the world, we are inevitably faced with the creative challenge of selecting which aspects of life to focus on and how to interpret or describe those limited aspects with an imperfect tool (i.e., language). In thus describing the world or our experience, we are effectively giving a *narrative account* of the world and our own lives – we are giving form to content – and in this sense we find ourselves in a position not dissimilar to the author tasked with telling a story.

In his seminal text *Nietzsche: Life as Literature*,[20] philosopher Alexander Nehamas offers an astute reading of Nietzsche's oeuvre which develops this literary interpretation of existence. Nietzsche is shown to engage the world (and indeed his own subjectivity) as if it were an artwork – a literary text, in particular – in need of composition, stylisation, and creative interpretation. Nehamas writes:

> To engage in any activity, and in particular in any inquiry, we must inevitably be selective. We must bring some things into the foreground and distance others into the background. We must assign a greater relative importance to some things than we do to others, and still others we must completely ignore. We do not, and cannot, begin (or end) with 'all the data'. This is an incoherent desire and an impossible goal. 'To grasp everything' would be to do away with all perspective relations, it would mean to grasp nothing, to misapprehend the nature of knowledge. If we

> are ever to begin a practice or an inquiry we must, and must want to, leave unasked indefinitely many questions about the world.[21]

Nehamas later elaborates on this theme by shifting his metaphor from literature to painting:

> There is no sense in which painters, even if we limit our examples to realistic depictions of one's visual field, can ever paint 'everything' that they see. What they 'leave out' is in itself quite indeterminate, and can be specified, if at all, only through other paintings, each of which will be similarly 'partial'. Analogously, Nietzsche believes, there can be no total or final theory or understanding of the world. On his artistic model, the understanding of everything would be like a painting that incorporates all styles or that is painted in no style at all – a true chimera, both impossible and monstrous.[22]

Both quotes suggest that not only does life make editorial demands on us but also that there is no neutral or objective way to undertake that process. As editors of our individual existence, we are burdened with writing the rules and making decisions; or, as the existential slogan states: we are 'condemned to be free.'[23] In due course I will develop Nietzsche's literary model of existence in more detail, including a closer examination of his curious injunction that we should be 'the poets of our life.'[24] I will also consider the nature and responsibilities of 'self-creation', drawing on Michel Foucault's conception of ethics as an 'aesthetics of existence'[25] and Richard Rorty's vision of a 'poeticized culture'.[26] These post-metaphysical philosophers are sometimes categorised as 'aestheticist' (usually in a pejorative sense), on the grounds that they deny, as I do, that there is a metaphysical reality that is stable, knowable, and given to us in advance. They all argue that existence is somehow inescapably aesthetic, in the sense that the answers to many of life's most important questions – questions about the meaning of life, what the good life consists in, how societies should be organised and structured, etc. – can never be *discovered*, as such. They must be *invented*, and if we do not produce answers ourselves, we can be sure the powers-that-be will produce them for us.

If the meaning of life does not announce itself to us or lie 'out there' in external metaphysical reality waiting to be discovered, it follows that *we must create as an aesthetic project the meaning of our own lives.* Not only that, we must also collectively shape as an aesthetic project the societies in which we live, just as that society inevitably shapes us. This aesthetic imperative orients us toward the world and our own lives in a way that resembles the relationship between artists and their raw materials; between sculptors and their clay. Herein lies a source of hope. No matter how ugly our species may have become as a violent, consumptive, and ecologically brutal force, nothing about our past preordains the future. As Jean-Paul Sartre maintained: 'We can always make something out of what we have been made into,'[27] which is to say that human beings are both creatures and creators of our mysterious situation and condition. Let us be like the poets, then, and make things new.

These are some of the aesthetic dimensions of existence to be explored in this collection of essays. As the arguments unfold, I will consider various social, political, and ecological implications of adopting an orientation to life that is uncompromisingly – and unashamedly – aestheticist. Based on the philosophical position outlined above, I am of the view that we are all aesthetes now, whether we like it or not, and the challenge we face involves determining what this means in an age such as our own, which is one way to frame the central undertaking of this project. I believe human beings have a deep existential need both for meaning and beauty in life – a need that resembles the biophysical hunger for food – even if these aesthetic impulses are not always articulated in such grand-sounding terms. Meaning and beauty are more like subconscious, inarticulate yearnings than clearly stated goals. But the more these yearnings for creative expression and aesthetic experience are repressed and denied, the stronger the Will to Art is experienced in our lives, like floodwaters building up behind a dam that is destined to burst. As Marxist philosopher Georg Lukács wrote: 'The bleaker and emptier life becomes under capitalism, the more intense is the yearning after beauty.'[28]

SMPLCTY: The political economy of art

I can now elaborate on some the main conclusions of this project, alluded to earlier in my proposal for a political economy of art. As noted, my two key premises are first, that material sufficiency is all that is *needed* for human beings to live rich, meaningful, and artful lives; and second, that material sufficiency is all that is *possible* on finite planet in an age of environmental limits. As I am using the phrase, a political economy of art refers to a form of ecological civilisation in which the two stated premises guide social, economic, and political action, organisation, and cooperation.

The goal of a political economy of art is to structure and support a society that I have labelled SMPLCTY. Again, this is neither a utopian statement nor a prediction. It is an orienting vision designed to guide prefigurative action in the here and now. After all, in order to know in what direction to move, some understanding is needed regarding the desired destination, even if it turns out that the destination is dauntingly distant. My goal in these collected essays is not to provide details on the specifics of daily living in this type of ecological civilisation, nor will I provide a set of policies or institutions – issues addressed elsewhere.[29] Rather, in the following pages I set out to present a case for SMPLCTY through the lens of aesthetics, specifically in relation to what I am calling the Will to Art. In later essays I will also outline a theory of change, based on what poet-philosopher Friedrich Schiller called 'aesthetic education' and what critical theorist Herbert Marcuse called 'aesthetic revolution'.

According to this vision of ecological civilisation, the good life would be achieved primarily through aesthetic experience, both creatively (making art) and responsively (appreciating art and nature). This is an endless and dialectical process of infinite diversity and stimulation. My central thesis is that art and aesthetic experience – including the making of useful and beautiful things – are promising and available means of 'living more with less' – of flourishing in simplicity. So far as this is true, it would follow that opportunities for low-impact aesthetic practice and experience ought to be expanded as humanity contracts its material and energy demands for reasons of justice, sustainability, and wellbeing. I believe this vision of SMPLCTY is a coherent and perhaps necessary one to embrace if humanity (as a whole) and affluent societies (in particular) are to move toward an equitable form of life that not only avoids ecosystemic collapse but also ensures the flourishing of all life on Earth within environmental limits. This process of prosperous descent could also be framed as an 'aesthetics of degrowth',[30] and in a later essay I explore how such a process could be facilitated by what I will cautiously call an aesthetic state, shaped by an anarcho-socialist theory of governance.

Although the energy and resource flows are constrained within this envisioned form of life, the exploration of the good life remains unlimited, in the same way that a pianist is not limited by the 88 keys of a piano. There will never be a time when all the beautiful sonatas have been written, just as there will never be a time when all possible manifestations of beautiful lives have been lived. Upon sufficient and sustainable material foundations – that is, in a political economy that ensures enough, for everyone, forever – human beings are left to explore the aesthetics of their own existence in imaginative ways. Thus we are burdened with the task of applying our own aesthetic values to the spiritual practice of self-fashioning. This is the bounded infinity of human flourishing in an aesthetic universe. Within biophysical limits, and upon sufficient material foundations, we are limited only by our imaginations.

In the social order of SMPLCTY I am proposing, aesthetic citizens would seek to live simply in a material and energetic sense, while contributing to necessary economic production and community governance in non-alienated and non-hierarchical conditions. Beyond that, people would be free to explore the good life, and manage the tragic elements of the human condition, through creative activity and aesthetic experience. There will of course be artistic 'geniuses' whose work captures and impresses the social imagination more than others, but the aesthetic citizen, who I will characterise as the poet-farmer, is an ordinary creative soul who revels in their aesthetic practices without need or expectation of social recognition. This mode of ecological civilisation seeks to democratise the poet, blurring the distinction between artist and artisan.

Art would not replace religion in this society, but it would answer the same (and perhaps some new) spiritual needs, such that the artist comes to replace the priest as spiritual advisor and existential provocateur. These simple living communities will be bound together by aesthetic rituals and practices that bring art and culture into the realm of everyday living. As the ideal of this ecological civilisation is approached, beauty will beget beauty, and an aesthetic singularity will everywhere threaten to explode in a chain reaction of unfathomable spectacles of creativity and sensuous experience. The nature of this singularity is unknowable in advance, but it should be acknowledged as a possibility, even if we must then pass over it in silence, like all mystical phenomena.

At some distant point – perhaps in hundreds of millions of years – Earth will be swallowed by a black hole, destroyed by a comet, or become uninhabitable due to the heat-death of the sun. Accordingly, the human story is, ultimately, finite. Our cosmological contribution will be our art – our human stories – all of which will one day be dust, blowing in the winds of a dark, cold, silent universe, bereft of music. After an indeterminate duration of cosmological expansion, the universe may implode into the singularity from which it emerged or begin to expand at the speed of light, and the mysterious cosmological process might begin again, repeating this aesthetic cycle an infinite number of times, in eternal recurrence. This mystery needs and allows for no primal explanation. That the Will to Art exists at all is the marvel of all marvels.

To paraphrase T.S. Eliot: we are the music, while the music lasts.[31]

♦ ♦ ♦

Given that this is a large project, composed of essays designed to stand alone as well as form a coherent whole, I will close this introduction by providing an overview of what lies ahead. This should allow readers to jump around the collection of essays as interest and inclination dictate, while also giving some insight into how the argumentation hangs together in the broadest sense. Alternatively, if the suggestive essay titles in the table of contents provide sufficient information, one may of course skip the following overviews and proceed straight to the essays themselves. Essays in Book One are dedicated mainly to excavating the aesthetic foundations of this project. Book Two focuses mainly on detailing the social and political implications. Nevertheless, at the end of the volume many questions will remain unanswered, which just means that this project is incomplete – or rather, ongoing. Book Three is forthcoming.

1. In the opening essay, **'The Cosmos as a "Readymade": Dignifying the Aesthetic Universe'** I engage the French artist, Marcel Duchamp. Duchamp's provocative innovation was to select ordinary, mundane items – something 'readymade', as he would call these manufactured objects – and declare them art. His most famous readymade piece is *Fountain* (1917), which was merely an ordinary, mass-produced urinal. To develop the foundations of my aesthetic position, I wish to extend Duchamp's infamous gesture in two ways. First, by exploring the possibility of adopting his inclusive aesthetic disposition, not merely when presented with an art object, but as a form of life. My project is based upon this thorough-going aestheticism, which, in later essays, I will argue has ethical, political, even spiritual implications. My second extension of Duchamp is to expand the category of the 'readymade' to include the cosmos itself. After all, if Duchamp was able to dignify a urinal by aestheticising it, then I intend to claim the same dignity for the universe as a whole.

2. Having clarified and developed my aesthetic orientation, I then provide more detail on my mythopoetic cosmology in **'Creative Evolution and the Will to Art'**. Contrasting the metaphor of 'universe-as-machine' with the metaphor 'universe-as-artist', I present a case for the latter, developing the preliminary overview of the Will to Art stated at the beginning of this introduction. This transfiguration of the cosmos doesn't involve changing any of the physical characters of the object under consideration but rather changing its ontological character through redescription in ways that call on individuals to engage with the object differently. The *experience* of art, I will argue, is less about an objective encounter

with a physical entity and more about poetic engagement with the possibilities of meaning that surround the entity under aesthetic contemplation – in this case, the universe itself.

3. In the next two essays I acknowledge my debts to Schopenhauer and Nietzsche – a task which also allows me to highlight areas where my own position can be distinguished from theirs. In **'Pessimism without Despair: Suffering, Desire, and the Affirmation of Life'**, I examine Schopenhauer's quasi-Buddhist metaphysics, an extremely gloomy but necessary undertaking. Schopenhauer maintained, not without some plausibility, that suffering lies at the core of existence. He believed suffering was the result of a blind and purposeless 'Will to Live' that is experienced in human consciousness as insatiable and painful desire. After describing this pessimistic worldview – summarised in his grim conclusion that 'life must be some sort of mistake'[32] – I will consider how he responded with an ethic of compassion; I will also summarise his views on art and aesthetics; and I will outline his ultimate orientation toward life, which involves 'denying the will' through ascetic practices of self-renunciation. This philosophy of resignation provides the groundwork for assessing Nietzsche's critical engagement with Schopenhauer; in particular, I will examine how Nietzsche 'revalues the value of suffering' in search of a way to transcend Schopenhauerian pessimism and affirm life, despite the prevalence of suffering.

4. In **'An Aesthetic Justification of Existence: The Redemptive Function of Art'**, I continue my assessment of Nietzschean philosophy by analysing his famous pronouncement, found in *The Birth of Tragedy* (1872), that it is only as an 'aesthetic phenomenon' that existence and the world can be justified.[33] This examination involves distinguishing his notion of an aesthetic justification from religious or rational justifications, which will help to clarify what it might mean to say that existence could be justified as an aesthetic phenomenon. This draws us into Nietzsche's views on art – tragic art in particular – and I will consider whether or how art can provide a redemptive function in a world replete with suffering and where it seems no other religious or metaphysical comforts exist to offer existential consolation.

5. Even if one were to accept Nietzsche's response to the problem of suffering, human beings would still find themselves facing the problem of nihilism or meaninglessness. Confronting this challenge, in **'Camus on Art and Revolt: Overcoming Nihilism in an Absurd Universe'**, I turn to the work of philosopher and novelist Albert Camus, exploring the ways in which he articulated the problem of meaning and how he developed an aesthetic response to it. Rather than resign himself to nihilism – the view that nothing matters in a world without God or objective meaning – Camus would develop an aesthetics of revolt. This view of the human condition burdens us all with the task of creating our own values, which is not a project of rational discovery but rather an aesthetic project of invention and commitment. Given that human beings all suffer the same 'absurd' condition, Camus maintained we can also find in this tragic reality a ground for human solidarity. We will see that Camus argues that art justifies itself not for its own sake but as something that can present a vision of human dignity in a world full of suffering and oppression. Art thus 'rejects the world on account of what it lacks... in the name of what it sometimes is.'[34]

6. The term 'aestheticism', which I am embracing, has acquired a bad name today. It is employed primarily as a pejorative, directed most often toward people or movements associated with Dandyism. The dandy character attempts to make life a work of art through such things as eccentric dress, attention-seeking behaviour, and the hedonistic pursuit of sensory pleasures. If I am to succeed in reclaiming this dubious term – to make it a plausible centre piece of the current project – then further attention must be given to how aestheticism has acquired its contemporary meaning, what that meaning is, and how I intend to employ the term quite differently. Those are my tasks in **'Rescuing Aestheticism from the Dandies: Critical Distinctions'**. Dandyism is a form of aestheticism, albeit a rather crude one, but I will show that aestheticism is far from exhausted by Dandyism. If I can clarify this distinction, I should have advanced the cause of rehabilitating aestheticism in helpful and important ways.

7. Having surveyed, in previous essays, some philosophical territory on the human condition, I turn to questions concerning aesthetics from an evolutionary perspective, in **'*Homo Aestheticus*, the Artful Species: An Evolutionary Perspective'**. Here I examine what role art and aesthetics may have played in evolutionary history. It is easy enough to acknowledge that art could not have existed without the humans who produced it. Few consider the possibility, however, that humans could not have appeared without our arts. In that spirit, I consider the idea that every human being, on account of evolutionary inheritances, can and should be described as part of an 'artful species' – *homo aestheticus*.[35] When looking to the past it will become clear that the arts have helped our species survive, develop, and flourish in often hostile, uncertain, and changing environments. Looking forward, then, it seems plausible that the wise use of the arts may also be central to our own survival in an age of environmental limits, where our aesthetic capacities and sensibilities are currently being dangerously distorted and repressed, resulting in what I will call an aesthetic deficit disorder.

8. One of the philosophical problems I am exploring in this collection of essays concerns the apparent conflict between biology and philosophy when it comes to understanding human beings. On the one hand, there is the view widely held amongst evolutionary biologists and psychologists that humans have a 'common nature' by virtue of our long, shared species' history; on the other hand, there is a philosophical view, widely held by post-Nietzscheans of various schools, that humans have no 'given' nature but are everyday tasked with creating it. In short, the first position holds that there is a common human nature; the second holds that human nature, as such, does not exist. In **'Giving Birth to Oneself: Ethics as an "Aesthetics of Existence"'**, I develop a synthesis of these apparently conflicting literatures, a possibility which was opened up to me by a reading of evolutionary biology through the lens of art and aesthetics. Specifically, I explore a range of philosophical arguments that support the conception of human beings as 'self-creators', drawing primarily on Michel Foucault and Richard Rorty, both of whom have Nietzsche as a prominent influence. I will also begin considering some of the social and political implications of self-creation through a critical examination of Rorty's vision of a 'poeticized culture'.

9. In **'The Politics of Beauty: Schiller on Freedom and Aesthetic Education'** I review some critical perspectives on modernity and the Enlightenment project through the lens of Friedrich Schiller's theory of aesthetic education. Despite always remaining a champion of reason, Schiller was also one of its severest critics, and in a decisive and original move he argued that 'the way to the head must lie through the heart.'[36] This is not an anti-intellectual point, however. He was offering the profound and subtle insight that through beauty – through the works of poets, painters, musicians, and storytellers – we are best able to engage the intellect *having first affected the emotions*. Moreover, he believed that moral, ethical, and political reasoning *must* engage the heart to be effective, for reason and rationality will fail to motivate or transform behaviour without emotional appeal. I engage these ideas through a close reading of Schiller's *Letters on the Aesthetic Education of Man* (1794). This essay concludes Book One.

10. At this stage in the project I need to acknowledge a significant problem regarding my conceptualisation of human beings as *homo aestheticus*. It is a problem that is evident as soon as one turns from theory to the world as it is: if we are an artful species, one that is creative and self-constituting, why is it that the world is so full of oppression, servitude, anxiety, and ugliness? If we are evolutionarily shaped to be aesthetic agents in an aesthetic universe, why do we see cultures – I'm thinking of the 'advanced' affluent cultures in particular – seemingly content to distract themselves with the trinkets and baubles offered by consumer capitalism? In **'Bad Faith and the Fear of Freedom: Can Art Shake Us Awake?'**, I attempt to illuminate aspects of this problematic by drawing on Jean-Paul Sartre's notion of 'bad faith' and Erich Fromm's idea of the 'fear of freedom'. These two ideas help explain the dire state of human freedom and aesthetic activity today, while also showing why this problem is within our power to resolve.

11. In my earlier essay on Schiller I looked at aesthetic education primarily from a philosophical perspective. In **'Banish the Poets! The Power and Politics of Aesthetic Education'** I attempt to ground the analysis more firmly in the socio-political domain. This involves considering aesthetic education from three angles. First, I compare and contrast an 'education for profit' with an 'aesthetic education'. Second, I consider the so-called 'information deficit

model' of change. This theory assumes that human beings are fundamentally rational, evidence-based thinkers and, on that basis, the theory implies that the primary means of societal progress is more evidence and better arguments. I will argue that this is at best a partial and often misleading theory of change, one that marginalises the role of the arts and aesthetic education in social and political transformation. Third, I diagnose an imaginative sterility in contemporary culture, which has left many citizens largely unable to envision forms of life beyond consumer capitalism. Political and cultural theorist Mark Fisher called this enclosing of the imagination 'capitalist realism',[37] often defined as the view that it is easier to imagine the end of the world than the end of capitalism. The purpose of this tripartite analysis is to explore to what extent a reinvigorated aesthetic education might be needed to resolve these obstacles and drive societal trans-formation.

12. Defending the social and political import of the arts, as I have been doing, can invite the rejoinder that art, in fact, is useless; that artists have no political impact; and that aesthetics is either apolitical or politically dangerous. In **'Making Art While the World Weeps: Political Reflections on Aesthetics'** I address these types of objections. I set out to deconstruct any simplistic dismissal of aesthetics by examining the blurry distinction between art, life, and politics, in order to show that there is in fact an inherent aesthetic dimension to life and politics, just as there is a political or even revolutionary potential inherent to certain forms of art or aesthetic practice. In doing so, my analysis is shaped by the emerging 'aesthetic turn'[38] in politics and by various political interpretations of art and aesthetics. To be clear, my position is not that we *should* or *should not* infuse politics with aesthetic considerations, but rather, as Jacques Rancière states, that 'politics is aesthetic in principle.'[39]

13. Having raised questions about the political significance of aesthetics, in **'Art Against Empire: Marcuse on the Aesthetics of Revolt'** I turn to examine the writings of critical theorist Herbert Marcuse. After reviewing his central theses on the potentially transformative role of art in society, I develop the analysis by proposing a categorisation that helps clarify art's diverse political functions. The four categories are: i) aesthetic indictment, which involves using art to help expose the injustices and violence that can be hidden in the political system or dominant cultural values; ii) aesthetic imagination, which involves using art to help expand the imagination so that alternative futures can be envisioned, as well as help expand ethical sympathises so that people previously deemed 'other' can be come to fall within the circle of care and concern; iii) aesthetic revision of 'needs', which involves exploring the ways in which art can help reshape human needs, drives, and hopes in ways that lay the cultural foundations for political change; and finally, iv) aesthetic enchantment, which involves the ways in which art, beauty, and aesthetic value more broadly can give emotional energy to people in ways that have political effects.

14. In **'Answering Estragon: Art, Godot, and Utopia'**, I continue my aesthetic inquiries by considering whether art can not merely be a *means* to creating a good society but also shape our understanding of the *end* of social and political struggle. In other words, I set out to understand to what extent art and aesthetics can provide ultimate values that could inform not just how to transition to a more humane and liberated society but also shape what that society looks like or ought to look like. I take my point of departure from a line in Samuel Beckett's *Waiting for Godot* (1953), where Estragon asks his fellow tramp, Vladimir: 'What do we do now, now that we are happy?' In response I argue for a politics of meaning – to be distinguished from utilitarianism and conventional liberalism – where political struggle is understood as seeking to maximise opportunities for oneself and others to live a meaningful life in harmony with nature. My thesis is that this search for meaning in life is best achieved through art, a living strategy that has the significant benefit of not requiring high levels of material provision.

15. The grand narrative of industrial civilisation is a story of progress in which societies advance by way of continuous economic growth, rising affluence, and technology. In **'Industrial Aesthetics: A Critique of Taste'** I focus on the aesthetics of industrialisation and consumerism, examining various aesthetic dimensions of consumption practices in the affluent capitalist societies. The purpose is to show that transcending consumerism and the growth economy may well depend on first overcoming various aesthetic obstacles, practices, and tastes. These obstacles include the stories and myths we tell about ourselves and societies; the ways we shape

our identities and communicate through consumption; the disaffection and alienation that evidently is widely experienced in consumer societies, even by those who have achieved high consumption lifestyles; and the way dominant conceptions of taste and social legitimation regarding material living standards entrench materialistic conceptions of the good life. We may all have internalised these cultural narratives to some extent, often unconsciously. It follows that ethical and political activity today may require us to engage the self by the self for the purpose of *refusing who we are* – insofar as we are uncritical consumers – and creating new, post-consumerist forms of subjectivity.

16. To this point I have presented a worldview that conceives of the universe as an aesthetic phenomenon and human beings as an artful species. Art and the aesthetic dimensions of life were upheld as being of ultimate value in such a world, and I have also drawn on various intellectual traditions to explain why art is central to the transformative process of bringing about such an aestheticised society of self-creators through aesthetic education and artful interventions in culture and politics. In **'Artful Descent: A Cosmodicy of SMPLCTY'** this vision is developed further, through the lens of energy. I focus on the work of anthropologist and historian, Joseph Tainter, especially his seminal text, *The Collapse of Complex Societies* (1988). Although largely sympathetic with Tainter's theory, I critically engage it in ways that leads me to conclusions he would reject. In doing so I present a defence of 'voluntary simplification' – essentially Tainter's term for degrowth. This term denotes a dynamic process of radical societal evolution which seeks to solve the most essential problems of life while minimising energy and resource demands. I maintain that voluntary simplification may be the *only* means of avoiding the civilisational process of complexity-to-collapse. My main argument is that art and aesthetic experience are promising and available means of 'living more with less' – of flourishing in simplicity. To the extent this is true, it would follow that opportunities for low-impact aesthetic practice and experience ought to be expanded as our material and energy demands contract for reasons of justice, sustainability, and wellbeing.

17. If it is the case, as argued in the previous essay, that civilisational stability depends on forms of societal organisation that reflect voluntary simplification, then questions arise about what such a way of life might look like, and feel like, in terms of daily practice. In **'Poet-Farmer: A Thoreauvian Aesthetics of Sufficiency'**, I turn to the life and philosophy of American philosopher and pioneering environmentalist Henry David Thoreau to highlight the perspective of 'voluntary simplicity' which lies at the heart of SMPLCTY. As a transitional strategy, I will argue that voluntary simplification or degrowth will depend on an aesthetic transformation of *tastes* in relation to material culture. One of the central theses in this volume of essays is that the aesthetic capacities and sensibilities of humankind can be fully explored in rich and satisfying ways, while living 'simply' in a material and energetic sense. On that basis, I am proposing that expanding opportunities for artistic expression and aesthetic experience are among the best ways of moving toward a civilisation that is environmentally sustainable, socially just, and personally fulfilling. In that light I have employed the term SMPLCTY to refer to an ecological civilisation of simple living 'poet-farmers'. Following Thoreau's lead, these citizens would live aesthetically stimulating and diverse lives while mindfully constraining material and energy requirements.

18. The previous essay set out to convey a material culture of sufficiency mainly from Thoreau's individualist perspective. In **'Democratising the Poet: William Morris on the Art of Everyday Life'**, some of the social implications are explored in relation to the aesthetic philosophy of William Morris. I have already acknowledged how my broad definition of art (as the pleasurable and meaningful expression of creative labour) is indebted to Morris, and in this essay, I explore how he developed his aesthetic perspectives into a socio-political vision which he called a Democracy of Art. I begin by discussing his definition of art in more detail, before reviewing how this took social form in his eco-utopian novel, *News from Nowhere* (1890). After that I examine some of the theoretical foundations of that vision, focussing in particular on the relationship between material needs and labour. It will be seen that Morris celebrated the role of self-governed creative activity in everyday life, through which humans skilfully produced things by hand that were necessary for a good life. I conclude by exploring the political significance of Morris's aesthetic views, which will allow me to bring together some of the societal implications of the preceding essays.

19. In the penultimate essay (forthcoming in Book Three) I address more of the political implications of my arguments, in **'The Aesthetic State: Toward an Ecological Democracy of Art'.** This subject was touched on in the essay on Schiller, who wrote that 'the most perfect'[40] of all works of art is the 'construction of true political freedom.'[41] It was seen, however, that he never developed his comments on the aesthetic state into a formal theory. I will attempt to build on this preliminary work, developing some of Schiller's ideas in relation to the arguments and perspectives offered in this collection of essays. (I have deferred the publication of this essay and the next one as they began expanding beyond original expectations and intentions, justifying a separate release).

20. I conclude this collection (forthcoming, see above) by engaging Herman Hesse's novel *The Glass Bead Game*. This book tells the story of a community of artist-monks who live simple yet aesthetically rich lives in a province called Castalia. I will focus on the theme of social and political 'engagement', central to Hesse's book, which provides a fitting capstone to this ongoing project. This extended conclusion also calls for a review and restatement of the greater project. My central theses should take on a sharper focus when considered as a whole through the rear-view mirror.

---

[1] The comment about dead stars is paraphrasing astrophysicist Michelle Thaller. The idea of the universe being a cosmological symphony of vibrating strings comes from 'string theory' physicists, Brian Green and Michio Kaku. See Brian Greene, *The Elegant Universe: Superstrings, Hidden Dimensions, and the Search for the Ultimate Theory* (London: Vintage, 2000), Part III; and Michio Kaku, 'The Universe is a Symphony of Vibrating Strings' *YouTube* (1 June 2011).

[2] See Arthur Schopenhauer, *The World as Will and Representation: Vol. I* (New York: Dover, 1969). See also, John Fredrick Humphrey, 'Friedrich Nietzsche's *Artisten-Metaphysik* (Doctoral thesis, Graduate Faculty of Political and Social Science, New School for Social Research, 1992).

[3] Henri Bergson, *Creative Evolution* (New York: Dover, 1998).

[4] Abraham Kanovitch, *The Will to Beauty: Being a Continuation of the Philosophies of Arthur Schopenhauer and Friedrich Nietzsche* (New York: Gold Rose Printing, 1922), p. 147.

[5] See Morris Weitz, 'The Role of Theory in Aesthetics' *Journal of Aesthetics and Art Criticism* (1956) 15(1): pp. 27-35; George Dickie, 'Defining Art' *American Philosophical*

Quarterly (1969) 6: pp. 253-256; Walter Gallie, 'Essentially Contested Concepts' *Proceedings of the Aristotelian Society* (1955) 56: 167-198.

[6] See generally, William Morris, *News from Nowhere and Other Writings* (London, Penguin, 2004). Influenced by John Ruskin, Morris defined art as 'the expression of man's pleasure in labour.' Ibid, p. 367. I have paraphrased that definition and added 'meaning' to it, given that art need not always be pleasurable. Even when no pleasure flows from producing or contemplating art, it can still be of profound aesthetic value if it is *meaningful*. Of course, art can often be both pleasurable and meaningful.

[7] My publications are listed, and mostly freely available, at my website: https://samuelalexander.info/ (accessed 20 April 2023).

[8] Here I am paraphrasing Jose Arguelles. See Matthew Fox, *Original Blessing* (New York: Tarcher/Putnam, 2000), p. 188.

[9] Friedrich Nietzsche, *The Birth of Tragedy*, trans. Walter Kaufmann (New York: Vintage, 1967), p. 22, p. 143.

[10] See Alexander Nehamas, *Nietzsche: Life as Literature* (Cambridge, MA: Harvard University Press, 1985).

[11] Richard Rorty, *Contingency, Irony, and Solidarity* (New York: Cambridge University Press, 1989).

[12] Walter Benjamin, *The Work of Art in the Age of Mechanical Reproduction* (London: Penguin, 2008).

[13] Jacques Rancière, *Dis-Agreement* (London: University of Minnesota Press, 2006), p. 58.

[14] In this paragraph I'm playing with the opening lines of Thoreau's essay 'Walking'. See Henry Thoreau, 'Walking', in Carl Bode (ed.) *The Portable Thoreau* (New York: Penguin, 1982), p. 592.

[15] See especially, my essays 'Creative Evolution and the Will to Art' and 'Homo Aestheticus, the Artful Species: An Evolutionary Perspective' in the present collection. Available at: https://samuelalexander.info/ (accessed 10 April 2023).

[16] Ellen Dissanayake, *Homo Aestheticus: Where Art Comes from and Why* (Seattle: Washington Press, 1995), pp. xx.

[17] See note 7.

[18] See Rorty, *Contingency, Irony, and Solidarity,* note 11, p. 50.

[19] See generally, Frank Farrell, 'Iterability and Meaning: The Searle-Derrida Debate' (1988) *Metaphilosophy* 19(1): pp. 53-64.

[20] Nehamas, *Nietzsche: Life as Literature*, note 10.

[21] Ibid, p. 49.

[22] Ibid, pp. 50-51.

[23] Jean-Paul Sartre, *Existentialism and Humanism* (London: Methuen and Co, 1970), p. 34.

[24] Fredrich Nietzsche, *The Gay Science*, trans. Walter Kaufmann (New York: Vintage Books, 1974). p. 240.

[25] See Michel Foucault, 'An Aesthetics of Existence' in Lawrence Kritzman (ed.) *Michel Foucault: Politics, Philosophy, Culture: Interviews and Other Writings 1977-1984* (New York: Routledge, 1990), pp. 47-53.

[26] See Rorty, *Contingency, Irony, and Solidarity*, note 11.

[27] See Jean-Paul Sartre, *Situations* (Paris: Gallimard, 1964), p. 101.

---

[28] Georg Lukacs, *Writer and Critic: And Other Essays* (New York: Universal Library, 1971), p. 89.
[29] See note 7.
[30] See Samuel Alexander, *Art Against Empire: Toward an Aesthetics of Degrowth* (Melbourne: Simplicity Institute, 2017).
[31] See T.S. Eliot, 'The Dry Salvages' from *Four Quartets* (1941). Available here: http://www.davidgorman.com/4quartets/3-salvages.htm (accessed 2 January 2023).
[32] Arthur Schopenhauer, *Essays and Aphorisms* (London: Penguin, 2004), p. 53.
[33] See note 9.
[34] Albert Camus, *The Rebel* (London: Penguin, 2000), p. 219.
[35] On this topic, see Robert Joyce, *The Esthetic Animal: Man, the Art-Created Art Creator* (New York: Exposition Press, 1975); Ellen Dissanayake, *Homo Aestheticus: Where Art Comes from and Why* (Seattle: Washington Press, 1995); Dennis Dutton, *The Art Instinct: Beauty, Pleasure, and Human Evolution* (New York: Bloomsbury Press, 2010); Stephen Davies, *The Artful Species* (Oxford: Oxford University Press, 2014); Anjan Chatterjee, *The Aesthetic Brain: How We Evolved to Desire Beauty and Enjoy Art* (Oxford: Oxford University Press, 2015).
[36] Friedrich Schiller, *Letters on the Aesthetic Education of Man*, ed. Reginald Snell (New York: Dover, 2004), p. 50.
[37] Mark Fisher, *Capitalist Realism: Is There No Alternative?* (Winchester: Zero Books, 2009).
[38] See generally, Nikolas Kompridis (ed.) *The Aesthetic Turn in Political Thought* (New York: Bloomsbury, 2014).
[39] See note 13.
[40] Friedrich Schiller, *Letters on the Aesthetic Education of Man*, in Friedrich Shiller, *Essays*, eds. Walter Hinderer and Daniel Dahlstrom (New York: Continuum, 2005), p. 88.
[41] Ibid.

‘For the nature of humanity is art. Everything for which there is a predisposition in our existence can and must in time become art.’

– ***Johann Gottfried von Herder***

ESSAY ONE

THE COSMOS AS A 'READYMADE': DIGNIFYING THE AESTHETIC UNIVERSE

In 1917 a revolution took place that would change the world forever – not in the domain of politics, as one might assume, but in the world of art. The Bolshevik revolution will be remembered for centuries to come, but when Marcel Duchamp anonymously submitted an ordinary, mass-produced urinal to be exhibited by the Society of Independent Artists in New York, he immortalised himself and his provocative gesture. The story is a critical page in twentieth-century history. The Society of Independent Artists, which Duchamp had helped establish, was to hold an exhibition in the spirit of democratising art. Any artist who paid the very modest submission fee could have their work exhibited. The slogan of the exhibition was 'No Jury – No Prizes', alluding to the radically inclusive and non-hierarchical vision of the event. Despite this liberal platform, Duchamp's submission – entitled *Fountain* and signed 'R. Mutt 1917' – was rejected, or, in Duchamp's words, 'supressed'.[1] The board refused to exhibit it on the grounds of it being 'indecent' and 'not art'.[2] Feigning outrage, Duchamp was delighted, resigning from the board in protest.

It is too early to tell whether this event was ultimately a positive intervention in the narrative of art history. But the questions Duchamp raised are unlikely to be forgotten, forever haunting art with a picture of its ambiguous self-image. Merely to call *Fountain* a 'joke' is to do injustice to the profundity of Duchamp's gesture, although by choosing a urinal he was clearly trying to 'take the piss' out of the artworld – or rather, bring it into the artworld. It was an act rivalled only by Piero Manzoni who, in 1961, exhibited cans of his own excrement. In relation to these provocations, Andy Warhol's *Brillo Boxes* of 1964 – which were virtually indistinguishable from the ordinary commercial packaging they copied – were positively tame. Nevertheless, each case raises the niggling question: but is it art?

Duchamp's striking innovation was to select ordinary, mundane items specifically for their aesthetic neutrality or lack of beauty – something 'readymade', as he would call these manufactured objects – and declare them art. His intention was to shatter artistic conventions and traditions in the most fundamental way. By displaying readymade items like bicycle wheels, snow shovels, combs, and urinals, art came to imitate life as never before, such that the very distinction between art and life could no longer be taken for granted. Indeed, the analytical task of answering the question 'What is art?' has never been the same. Although the Society of Independent Artists rejected *Fountain* as 'not art', a replica of the work now resides in the Tate Modern (the original was lost), and in 2004 a panel of five hundred art experts declared it the most influential artwork of the twentieth century.

So is *Fountain* art? The question doesn't seem to get old, even though it has been analysed to death – or eternal life – over the last century. To answer this question, philosopher Ludwig Wittgenstein would have said: 'Don't think, but look!'[3] The point is that our answer to whether something is art will not be found in conceptual analysis, for the concept of art is radically indeterminate;[4] it is an 'essentially contested' term for which necessary and sufficient conditions cannot be provided.[5] As philosopher of art Morris Weitz wrote:

> If we actually look and see what it is that we call 'art', we will also find no common properties – only strands of similarities... 'Art' itself is an open concept. New conditions (cases) have constantly arisen and will doubtless constantly arise; new art forms, new movements, will emerge... Aestheticians may lay down similarity conditions but never necessary and sufficient ones for the correct application of the concept.[6]

From this influential Wittgensteinian perspective, identifying art can only be achieved by observing whether something is actually *treated as art* in social practice and discourse; that is to say, 'whatever convention allows to be an artwork is an artwork.'[7] On those terms – a version of which philosopher George Dickie called the 'institutional theory of art'[8] – the answer is clear: yes, *Fountain* is, or has become, art. It has been thoroughly institutionalised by the collectors, curators, and critics of the 'artworld,'[9] even if the installation remains reviled as often as it is revered. Where some saw sheer arrogance and inanity, others saw a stimulating and revolutionary 'transfiguration of the commonplace'.[10]

Whatever one's personal view may be, Duchamp's provocation caused a crisis within the artworld from which it has never fully recovered, subjecting 'modern art' (in the scariest of scare quotes) to a barrage of mocking critique from those who no longer knew what to think. Is modern art only worth urinating on? The crisis is ruthlessly highlighted by a cartoon from the *New Yorker*, which depicts a gathering of art aficionados staring intently at a gridded square on a museum wall. The punchline is delivered by the security guards, one of whom whispers to the other: 'I'm not going to be the one to tell them it's a heating vent.' To be sure, visiting galleries was easier when the nature of art seemed self-evident, and for most of 'art history' that was the case. Those days, however, are forever gone – a Duchampian rubicon has been crossed. Perhaps it is better to embrace this ambiguous, unsettling reality than to live with regret or contempt about questions having been asked that cannot be unasked.

Duchamp's gesture has enduring significance for two primary reasons. First, it invites us to recognise that there is, or could be, aesthetic or artistic value in literally *anything*. Some people who have viewed the famous urinal have commented on its wonderful, flowing curves, and noticed how beautifully the light is reflected off the white porcelain. Even if this aesthetic reaction was not Duchamp's goal or intention,[11] who could deny people the pleasures of such experiences if *Fountain* happened to induce them? Beauty seems to be in the eye of the beholder, challenging us to explore the possibility that aesthetic value might be more present in our lives than we commonly think, if only we would adopt the aesthetic perspective more readily. Readers might remember the story that went viral on the internet in 2007 about the unassuming violinist who played Bach in a Washington subway one winter morning. People rushed by to get to work on time, occasionally throwing the performer a dollar or two but without slowing down. The individual who paid the most attention was a three-year-old boy, who was quickly tugged along by his mother who impatiently had somewhere to be. The violinist happened to be Joshua Bell, one of the world's most accomplished violinists, who was playing an instrument worth three and half million dollars. A few days before he had sold out a Boston theatre at $100 a seat.

The point is not to compare the beauty of this violinist's music to the aesthetic qualities of *Fountain*, but to remind ourselves that beauty might be almost anywhere, even everywhere, if only we take the time to look for it. It is a call to adopt the aesthetic attitude or disposition and be open to absorbing what the world is waiting to offer us. If we miss a virtuoso performing before our very eyes, on account of being too hurried by the demands of modern life, what else might we be missing? Ralph Waldo Emerson once pondered how people would react if the stars at night only showed themselves once every thousand years.[12] Surely the entire species would gather for such a viewing and be overwhelmed by the 'envoys of beauty'[13] that were on display. And yet, we have access to the sublime vista of the stars every clear night, so easily taken for granted, all the while many of us complain, not without some justification, that the world is all too ugly. Something has gone astray if our modes of existence filter away our ordinary and everyday access to beauty and the sublime. As I will suggest in this collection of essays, perhaps we find ourselves suffering from an 'aesthetic deficit disorder', but without knowing it – for the only evidence is absence.

The second reason *Fountain* caused such a stir was because it contradicted the almost universally held assumption that art had to be, if not beautiful, then at least expressive of some refined aesthetic skill through the act of creation. But in the case of the urinal, it was merely purchased from a manufacturer – 'readymade', as the artist would happily admit. The only thing Duchamp did to the very ordinary piece of plumbing hardware was to place it on its side and sign it. This raised the objection by some that *Fountain* could not be art, and if it was, then Duchamp, who did not make it, was guilty of plagiarism.

In response Duchamp declared that the artistic nature of the piece derived not from the manufacturer but from his own *selection* of that particular object as a readymade. 'An ordinary object,' he insisted, could be 'elevated to the dignity of a work of art by the mere choice of an artist.'[14] So the aesthetic value of *Fountain* arose not because it was beautiful – - although, as noted, some consider it to be – or that the artist showed great skill in its physical creation – Duchamp did not. Rather, *Fountain* is artistically important because of the 'meaning' that the gesture embodied. It was not intended to evoke an affective response so much as an intellectual or philosophical response – not of the body but of the mind or spirit. He was certainly not aiming to gratify the eye with beauty. In this case, and in his other readymades, Duchamp was of course provoking thought about the question: 'What is art?', inducing a radical self-consciousness in the artworld about its own identity. Perhaps it wasn't even a definitional controversy that Duchamp was trying to ignite. He said his readymades were 'neither art nor non-art. It's not the point. The point is that I wanted to go as far as I could in *doing* art.'[15]

This is where things get particularly interesting. If we accept that Duchamp's *Fountain*, Warhol's *Brillo Boxes*, or other famous 'readymades', are art by virtue of their deep institutionalisation in the artworld, then it follows that art cannot be identified merely by examining the object through one's perceptual apparatus. After all, if *Fountain* is art, but the same urinal in the men's restroom would not be art, then something other than physical features must be what makes an artwork 'art'. Perceptual criteria cannot be provided, because two objects can be physically identical in every way, and yet, since Duchamp, we know that one of those things can be art, and the other, not art. As philosopher Arthur Danto noted dryly: 'To mistake an artwork for a real object is no great feat when an artwork is the real object one mistakes it for.'[16] What matters, one might say, is whether the object is *considered from the aesthetic perspective.* If it is – by artist and/or audience – it would seem that *anything* has potential to be art and offer aesthetic value, provided it somehow embodies and expresses meaning.

Like it or not, this expansive understanding of art is Duchamp's immortal legacy, and it is lost on those who too quickly conclude that an unadorned urinal in a museum cannot be art. If, however, a readymade did *not* embody meaning in some way – say, like an ordinary Brillo Box in the supermarket – any interpretation of it as a work of art would be groundless. As Danto explained: 'A flight of birds gets read as a sign from the gods, until one stops believing in the gods, after which a flight of birds is just a flight of birds.'[17] And sometimes a Brillo Box is just a Brillo Box.

The end of art?

It was reflecting upon readymade art and what distinguished these objects from 'mere real things' that led Danto to develop his 'end of art' thesis.[18] This is not a claim about a loss of creative energy in the world (which may or may not be true) or that people have stopped doing art (which is obviously false). Danto's thesis is more profound. It was provoked after attending Warhol's exhibition of *Brillo Boxes* in 1964.[19] To help clarify the foundations of my own position, Danto's thesis about the end of art is worth restating, even if for present purposes I must oversimplify his complex theory.

Influenced by Hegelian philosophy, Danto argued that art had been developing in a dialectical fashion over the course of history but that this process had come to an end in the twentieth century, through the likes of Duchamp and Warhol. The grand narrative can be summarised as follows. Plato offered a 'mimetic theory' of art, whereby art was treated as 'mere representation' or only an imitation of true reality. In fact, art was considered two-steps removed from reality, given that sense experience, for Plato, was merely the appearance of an underlying reality (of Forms). This rendered art a representation of a representation. On this view, what made art 'good art' was how accurately the artist was able to represent or imitate the phenomena being depicted. According to Plato, however, artists could never do that as well as philosophers, given that the latter were able to commune with the true metaphysical reality through the philosophy of Platonic Forms. Danto described this as the original 'philosophical disenfranchisement of art',[20] for the nature of art became defined by philosophers and demoted to the realm of mere appearance or representation. If there was beauty in the world, it lay in truth and goodness, not art. Friedrich Nietzsche would disdainfully label this view 'aesthetic Socraticism',[21] complaining that rationality and morality did not exhaust the category of the beautiful.

Danto perceived in art history a progressive narrative, unfolding over centuries, in which artists (he focussed on painters) increasingly developed the ability to produce visual experiences effectively equivalent to those furnished by actual objects and scenes. That is, artists were getting better at depicting the world with increasing perceptual equivalence. Progress was being made. For example, artists were developing their abilities to accurately employ shadows or show perspective, progressively moving toward optical duplication of visually perceived reality. Eventually, however, this historical process of aesthetic development came to clash with the emergence, first of photography, and then cinema. Painters were also trying to accurately represent reality, but they simply could not compete with these new technologies. According to Danto, this induced a crisis within the world of art, as artists no longer had their traditional purpose to fulfil. After all, with the invention and development of the camera in the early nineteenth century, the goal of accurately representing reality was masterfully achieved, by clicking a button. When the painter Paul Delaroche first heard about this new technology, he is reported to have declared: 'As of today, painting is dead.'[22]

In true dialectical fashion, however, painters reacted by shifting the grounds upon which they stood, producing art movements like impressionism, cubism, and abstract expressionism. Abandoning the goal of accurately representing the world as it is visually perceived, artists like Monet, Picasso, and Kandinsky, began exploring less representational and more impressionistic, expressive, and abstract forms of art. These movements came to prominence because their art did *not* look like a photographed 'mirror image' of visually perceived reality. Monet was more interested in hazy moods and impressions than in the clear depiction of reality, although perhaps he was depicting an inner reality as accurately as possible. Picasso, with his cubist paintings, was not representing but representing reality, through creative acts of aesthetic destruction and reconstruction. Further, Kandinsky, the pioneer of abstract art, and later Rothko, were certainly not trying to depict visually perceived reality, exploring instead what could be expressed in purely abstract statements of shape, colour, and aesthetic configuration. In abstract art, objects, as such, had disappeared entirely from such paintings. Surrealists, like Dali, took this one step further, by painting fantastical images derived purely from the imagination. If Dali was trying to 'represent' anything, it was not anything in material reality but rather, he drew inspiration from the kaleidoscopic territory of his own bizarre unconscious, accessible through dreams.

The world of art had shifted in unrecognisable ways, with artists now doing things which historically would have been unthinkable or, if they were thinkable, would not have been considered art. To oversimplify, art had moved from representation to expression, a shift that also drew more attention to the inner work of the artists. This demanded new forms of aesthetic interpretation as audiences tried to understand the meaning of a work rather than contemplate the quality of its visual representation.

This very selective, Eurocentric, and rather stylised art history leads us back to Duchamp and Warhol. As artists began exploring non-representational, more expressive forms of art, the scope of what counted as art began to expand. To cut a much longer story short, this culminated in Duchamp's readymade art, which, as I have noted, were retinally indiscernible from ordinary objects that were not art. Literally *anything* could now fall within the category of art, provided it was selected to be an art object and infused with some meaning. When Danto attended the exhibition of Warhol's *Brillo Boxes* he had an epiphany of sorts – he felt that he was witnessing the 'end of art', not in the sense that artists would stop producing art, but that art had developed to such a stage that it could not be distinguished, based on any perceptual apparatus, from what was not art. Danto's insight was that art had begun self-consciously raising questions about its philosophical identity *from within* the realm of art. This contrasts with art being defined, as it was historically, by philosophers *from without.* The key point here is that art had begun doing philosophy, only in the medium of art, thus signifying the end of art as a separate domain defined by philosophers. Art had *become* philosophy, because artists like Duchamp and Warhol could no longer be understood aside from a theory of art that sought to make sense of what they were doing. Thus the objects of art, or rather art itself, blurred inextricably into the philosophy of art, fulfilling its Hegelian destiny as a practice that could only be comprehensible and justified in theory.

As well as art transforming itself into philosophy, Danto argued that this development represented the 'end of art' because artists were longer embodying some underlying historical narrative or working toward some ultimate goal (e.g., accurate representation or true expression). From this point on there would still be *change* in the artworld, but not *development* of a grand art-historical narrative. If art could be anything, and the artistic identity of a work of art could only be understood and discerned by a theory of art which gave the work some 'meaning', then artists had become freer than they had ever been before. By becoming philosophy, they had paradoxically freed themselves from philosophy, and this was the culmination of art's development in history. Without a historical narrative to serve any more, artists could go in any direction they wanted – reflected in the prominence of 'conceptual art' or 'performance art' today – and Danto explained that 'if everyone goes off in different directions, there is no longer *a* direction toward which a narrative could point.'[23]

Thus the historical narrative of art's development had been shattered into an uncontainable pluralism – as art became conscious of its own freedom – leading Danto to coin the phrase 'post-historical' art to refer to the pluralistic state of art after the end of art.[24] This phrase is not meant to imply that art will no longer be influenced by historical circumstances, but instead that historical circumstances no longer shape what can and cannot be art, since art could now be anything. The Age of Manifestos that tried to define what was 'true art' had come to an end, signalling the end of art as a world-historical narrative.

♦ ♦ ♦

That end point is where my project begins. My position is based on extending Duchamp in two ways, which I can now outline. Duchamp showed that anything could be art if we adopt the aesthetic attitude when selecting and contemplating it. One might adopt such an attitude, for example, when attending a gallery exhibition, or when a friend shows you their new painting, poetry, or readymade, or when you, the artist, are in the process of creation. Duchamp's innovation was to invite his audiences to adopt such a stance when considering ordinary, readymade objects that were intentionally lacking in beauty. The avant-garde musician John Cage made a similar move in 1952, with his piece *4'33*, during which the performing musicians made no sound at all. The point was not so much to invite the audience to enjoy the eloquence of silence, but to aesthetically contemplate the shuffling feet, coughs, and distant car horns that had the capacity to take the form of 'music' when the musicians themselves were silent. The audience became the art, and life itself was placed under aesthetic contemplation.

In this spirit, my first extension of Duchamp (and Cage) is to explore the possibility of adopting the aesthetic attitude *and not letting it go*; that is, to embrace the aesthetic disposition as a 'form of life', not merely upon entering a gallery or being presented with a work of art. After all, I contend that adopting an aesthetic attitude is a *choice* we make – try it now, you can do it. I am inviting readers to consider what the implications might be of adopting and maintaining such a perspective in ordinary, everyday life. An aesthetic perspective can be easily adopted when one is invited to do so upon the presentation of a readymade, and it is possible to adopt that perspective even when one is not presented with any work of art at all. In forthcoming essays I will argue that this voluntary existential shift has ethical, political, even spiritual implications. To the extent that certain people or movements have already called for a thorough-going aestheticism (e.g., the Dadaists and Dandies), I'll show that their theories and practices of aestheticism, more often than not, were misconceived and misapplied. I believe they've given aestheticism a bad name – a name which I would like to restore.

One might immediately object that there are cases – in relation to acts of cruelty or violence, for example – where it would be wrong or inhumane to take an aesthetic attitude; where it would be wrong to admire them as aesthetic events or consider the ways in which they might be beautiful. I hope that the absurdity of such a reading militates against assuming anyone might hold such a position, even though some Surrealists, Dadaists, and Dandies were naive or reckless enough to invite such readings.[25] In any case, I suspect that it would be both psychologically and morally impossible for any half-decent person to seek, let alone find, beauty in cruelty, violence, or humiliation, so the objection should not have any impact in any practically relevant sense.

Nevertheless, given the absurdity of the objection, one should assume (correctly) that the theory I am putting forward must mean something else. In ways to be developed in due course, I will argue that one can defensibly maintain a particular form of aesthetic attitude, even in relation violence, for reasons of exploring *creative* strategies to stop or avoid such violence; or to consider *imaginative* ways of bringing attention to such violence in order to minimise or eliminate it; or to *redescribe* the situation in ways that highlight how the aesthetic potentials and capacities of human beings are being unjustly constrained; or, in Nietzsche's case, to take one's own suffering and use it creatively to *sculpt* one's life into something noble, despite the suffering – and so forth.[26] These can be understood as aesthetic engagements and my point is there are ways to maintain an aesthetic stance in relation to life without implying that violence and cruelty are beautiful. In fact, in recent decades the 'aesthetic turn' in moral and political philosophy has shown how aesthetic perspectives are not just indispensable to ethical and political thought and practice, but unavoidable, thus blurring the conventional distinction between ethics/politics and aesthetics in ways that need not cause moral concern.[27]

At times I will call this general position an 'aesthetics of existence',[28] a phrase borrowed from Michel Foucault, who developed an aesthetic perspective in relation to his conception of ethics as self-fashioning.[29] It will become clear, however, that my approach covers different territory than Foucault's, in different ways, even as I am attempting to stand on his shoulders in the hope of seeing further. Of course, at this stage my proposition about *maintaining the aesthetic disposition* is too vague to be convincing and its implications too unclear, but I ask readers to trust that it will be given more attention. For now, I will simply return the story of the violinist in the train station. To maintain the aesthetic disposition is to adopt a frame of mind that maximises the chances of accessing beauty and sources of meaning when these aesthetic opportunities are on offer. Additionally, this attitude would minimise the chances of being in the presence of such sources of aesthetic value but not absorbing the experiential enrichment.

My hypothesis is that the world is more beautiful and meaningful than we often appreciate, and so one of my aims in this project is to explore modes of existence that assist with the task of squeezing every drop of aesthetic value out of our lives. To be discussed further in due course, I feel an increased openness to aesthetic value is a way to minimise a society's energy and resource demands without diminishing, and indeed increasingly, quality of life. After all, one is less likely seek meaning, happiness, and beauty in consumerism if one has already found those things outside the marketplace – in the freely available aesthetic dimensions of life. I will argue that if this aesthetic method of living became a widely adopted cultural practice or disposition – that is, if we developed a *taste for degrowth* – it would have beneficial ecological, social, and personal implications. I will also argue that aesthetic experience can help develop that taste. As artist and philosopher William Morris wrote: 'that which most breeds art is art.'[30] This is a thesis to which I will return in later essays.

Accordingly, if you pass by a musician playing beautiful music on the street, make sure you let the experience wash over you. Don't forget that the stars are sublime and of spiritual significance, waiting humbly to enrich our lives. And, with a nod to Duchamp, don't deny the possibility that light might glimmer off the surfaces of ordinary readymade objects in ways that offer aesthetic value. An infinite number of such examples could be provided, because the sources of aesthetic value are infinite, but absorbing them depends on an openness to aesthetic experience, which is a disposition that can be mindfully embraced and refined. Opportunities to experience beauty and meaning are too important to waste. We should adopt and refine the aesthetic perspective, then, and not let it go.

My second extension of Duchamp is not to suggest that *anything* can be art, but that *everything* can be art – including, or especially, the cosmos and our place in it. After all, if Duchamp was able to dignify a urinal by aestheticising it, then I intend to claim, in the spirit of the romantic poets and philosophers, the same dignity for the universe as a whole. And why shouldn't we? Surely, of all things, the spectacle of the universe deserves the honorific 'art'. To the objection that the universe cannot be art because it was not made by the hands of a human artist, we can dissolve that objection by noting that art, since Duchamp, can be readymade.

But what could it mean to treat the cosmos as a readymade work of art? Suppose, for example, that the Society of Independent Artists announced another exhibition where anyone could show their work provided they pay a token submission fee. And suppose further that a neo-Duchampian submitted not *anything* as a readymade, but *everything*. How, you might ask, could one even submit the cosmos as a readymade? Let me borrow an example from Danto and employ it for my purposes.[31] An artist could submit a sculpture of a bronze cat and chain it to the pedestal upon which it is exhibited. If someone asks whether this is a sculpture of a cat that happens to be chained to the pedestal (presumably to forestall theft), the artist might respond in the negative and advise that in fact it is a sculpture of a chained cat. When pressed for further detail, the artist would explain that the chain provides a bridge between art and reality – inviting the question: where does the work of art end and reality begin? At the end of the chain? At the bottom of the pedestal? At the doorway of the gallery? And so forth. The purpose of this neo-Duchampian submission would be to create a metaphysical sandpit that swallows the entire universe, achieving the goal of transfiguring the cosmos into a work of art and thus exhibiting it as a readymade.

This 'chained cat' submission should suffice for my purposes, since, like Duchamp, the work of art is not so much in the object being exhibited but in the gesture of exhibiting it. My goal is to induce an aesthetic singularity of sorts – a transformation of lived experience that, once underway, cannot (and should not) be stopped. But I am not only offering an invitation to adopt an aesthetic stance in relation to a non-aesthetic universe. I wish to present an analysis of an *aesthetic universe* that deserves aesthetic attention and concern, even reverence. The following passage from Danto can be applied to help clarify this point:

> We may, upon learning that an artwork is before us, adopt an attitude of respect and awe. We may treat the object differently, as we may treat differently what we took to be an old derelict upon discovering him to be the pretender to the throne, or treat with respect a piece of wood described as from the true cross when we were about to use it for kindling. These changes indeed are 'institutional' and social in character. Learning something to be an artwork we may, just as Dickie says, attend to its

> gleaning surfaces. But if what we attend to could have been attended to before the transfiguration, the only change will have been the adoption of an aesthetic stance, which we could in principle have struck before. It is a matter of merely of attending to what was there to be perceived... No: learning it is a work of art means that it has qualities to attend to which its untrasfigured counterpart lacks, and that our aesthetic responses will be different. And this is not institutional, it is ontological. We are dealing with an altogether order of things.[32]

I propose that orienting ourselves toward the universe as if it were a readymade work of art is a subversive act of aesthetic defiance in a world where readymades have been imposed upon us in virtually all aspects of our lives by the disenchanting logic of capitalism. As the commodification of life continues to expand, we find ourselves being sold readymade products, readymade experiences, and readymade meanings. In that light, I believe embracing the cosmos as a readymade is potentially a liberating intervention in an unfree world. Duchamp showed that how we respond to a urinal depends on whether we see it as a work of art – and that this aesthetic perspective depends on whether an artist says it is a work of art. On that basis, the same logic surely can apply to the universe as a whole. If we see this cosmos as a readymade, as per my invitation, and that life within this meta-readymade is inherently aesthetic, how might we respond differently to this aesthetic being-in-the-world? I would like to explore the implications of this gesture and take the perspective to its logical extreme, if only to see what might happen by doing so. My bold hypothesis is that this process might help set our species free, and help make the world more beautiful, just, and sustainable, in ways to be explained and explored.

To summarise: in this collection of essays I will adopt an aesthetic stance in relation to the universe and our place in it. I am inviting readers to consider the universe as a readymade in which we are living, thereby bestowing upon it the privileged status of art. My goal is to explore the consequences of doing so. My extensions of Duchamp might be deemed 'absurd', but it will become clear in later essays that it is absurd more in line with the work of Samuel Beckett or Albert Camus than the sense evoked by the Dadaists. This transfiguration of the cosmos doesn't involve changing any of the physical characters of the object under consideration but rather, it involves changing its ontological character through redescription in ways that call on individuals to engage with the object differently. The *experience* of art is less about an objective encounter with a physical entity and more about poetic engagement with the possibilities of meaning that surround the entity under aesthetic contemplation – in this case, the universe itself.

In the next essay I will develop my proposal that our readymade universe is the product of a primordial 'Will to Art' that is always and everywhere at work in the cosmos, like gravity. This is not an institutional claim but an ontological one, albeit one grounded in metaphor rather than metaphysics. Those theses, and many others, will be presented in the essays that follow, as I begin to explore the philosophical, social, and political implications of my neo-Duchampian standpoint. In time I will boldly suggest that this aesthetic perspective might help fulfil the two projects of liberation I acknowledged earlier – the aesthetic revolution and the political revolution – which both took place in 1917. To make this case I will have to merge the domains of aesthetics and political economy in ways that I feel have the potential to transform and transcend both in almost unrecognisable ways. By doing so, I hope to advance the cause of freedom by upholding beauty.

---

[1] See Pierre Cabanne, *Dialogues with Marcel Duchamp* (Boston: Da Capo Press, 1987) p. 74. *Fountain* was hidden behind a partition so it could not be viewed for the duration of the exhibition.

[2] See Unsigned review, 'His Art Too Crude for Independents' *The New York Herald* (14 April 1917). The board or committee concluded that *Fountain* was a very useful object but that its place was not in an art exhibition and that it was 'by no definition, a work of art.'

[3] Ludwig Wittgenstein, *Philosophical Investigations* (Oxford: Basil Blackwell, 1963) p. 31.

[4] Morris Weitz, 'The Role of Theory in Aesthetics' *Journal of Aesthetics and Art Criticism* (1956) 15(1): pp. 27-35.

[5] Walter Gallie, 'Essentially Contested Concepts' *Proceedings of the Aristotelian Society* (1955) 56: pp. 167-198.

[6] Weitz, 'Role of Theory', note 4, pp. 31-2

[7] Arthur Danto, *Transfiguration of the Commonplace: A Philosophy of Art* (Cambridge, MA: Harvard University Press, 1981), p. 31.

[8] See, e.g., George Dickie, 'Defining Art' *American Philosophical Quarterly* (1969) 6: pp. 253-256.

[9] Arthur Danto, 'The Artworld' *Journal of Philosophy* (1964) 61(19): pp. 571-584.

[10] Danto, *Transfiguration*, note 7.

[11] As Danto writes: 'What would have provoked Duchamp to madness or murder, I should think, would be the sight of aesthetes mooning over the gleaming surfaces of the porcelain object he had manhandled into the exhibition space: "How like Kiliman-

jaro! How like the white radiance of Eternity! How Arctically sublime!" (Bitter laughter at the *Club des artistes*).' In Danto, *Transfiguration*, note 7, p. 94.

[12] Ralph Waldo Emerson, 'Nature' in Carl Bode (ed.) *The Portable Emerson* (New York: Penguin, 1981) p. 9.

[13] Ibid.

[14] This statement is found in Andre Breton and Paul Eluard's, *Dictionaire Abrege du Surrealism*, published in 1938. The statement is signed off with the initials M.D. (presumably referring to Marcel Duchamp).

[15] Marcel Duchamp to Don Bell, 'A Conversation with Marcel Duchamp' *Canadian Art* (1987) 4(4): p. 57.

[16] Danto, 'The Artworld', note 9, p. 575.

[17] Arthur Danto, 'The End of Art: A Philosophical Defence' *History and Theory* 37(4): p. 130.

[18] Arthur Danto, 'The End of Art' in Arthur Danto, *The Philosophical Disenfranchisement of Art* (New York: Columbia University Press, 1986) Ch. 5.

[19] Presumably the same epiphany could have been provoked by *Fountain*, since on the issue of presenting an ordinary object of the world as art, Warhol offered no interesting development of Duchamp's readymades.

[20] See Danto, *Philosophical Disenfranchisement*, note 18.

[21] Fredrich Nietzsche, *Birth of Tragedy* and *The Case of Wagner* (New York: Vintage Books, 1967), p. 83 (emphasis removed).

[22] Arthur Danto, *What Art Is* (New Haven: Yale University Press, 2013) p. 101.

[23] Danto, 'The End of Art: A Philosophical Defence', note 17, p. 127.

[24] See Danto, 'The End of Art' note 18. See also, Arthur Danto, *After the End of Art: Contemporary Art and the Pale of History* (Princeton: Princeton University Press, 2014).

[25] To provide two notorious examples, in the 'Second Surrealist Manifesto', Andre Breton would write: 'The simplest Surrealist act consists of dashing down the street, pistol in hand, and firing blindly, as fast as you can pull the trigger, into the crowd.' See Andre Breton, 'Second Surrealist Manifesto' in Andre Breton, *Manifestoes of Surrealism* (Ann Arbor: University of Michigan Press, undated), p.125. Secondly, in the preface to *The Picture of Dorian Gray*, Oscar Wilde would write: 'There is no such thing as a moral or immoral book. Books are well written, or badly written, that is all.' See Oscar Wilde, *The Picture of Dorian Gray* (London: Penguin, 2003), p. 3.

[26] I discuss Nietzsche's views on suffering in my forthcoming essays in this collection. See especially, 'Pessimism without Despair: Suffering, Desire, and the Affirmation of Life' and 'An Aesthetic Justification of Existence: The Redemptive Function of Art'. The essays will be posted here: http://samuelalexander.info/s-m-p-l-c-t-y-ecological-civilisation-and-the-will-to-art/ (accessed 10 May 2023).

[27] See generally, Nikolas Kompridis (ed.) *The Aesthetic Turn in Political Thought* (New York: Bloomsbury, 2014). I discuss these issues in more detail in my essay, 'Making Art While the World Weeps: Political Reflections on Aesthetics'. See link in note 26.

[28] See Michel Foucault, 'An Aesthetics of Existence' in Lawrence Kritzman (ed.) *Michel Foucault: Politics, Philosophy, Culture: Interviews and Other Writings 1977-1984* (New York: Routledge, 1990), pp. 47-53.

[29] I discuss the ethics of self-fashioning in my forthcoming essay 'Giving Birth to Oneself: Ethics as an "Aesthetics of Existence"'. See link in note 26.

---

[30] William Morris, 'The Beauty of Life' in William Morris, *Hopes and Fears for Art: Five Lectures by William Morris*. Available at https://www.marxists.org/archive/morris/works/1882/hopes/chapters/index.htm (accessed 10 May 2023), para. 102.

[31] Danto, *Transfiguration*, note 7, p. 102.

[32] Ibid, p. 99.

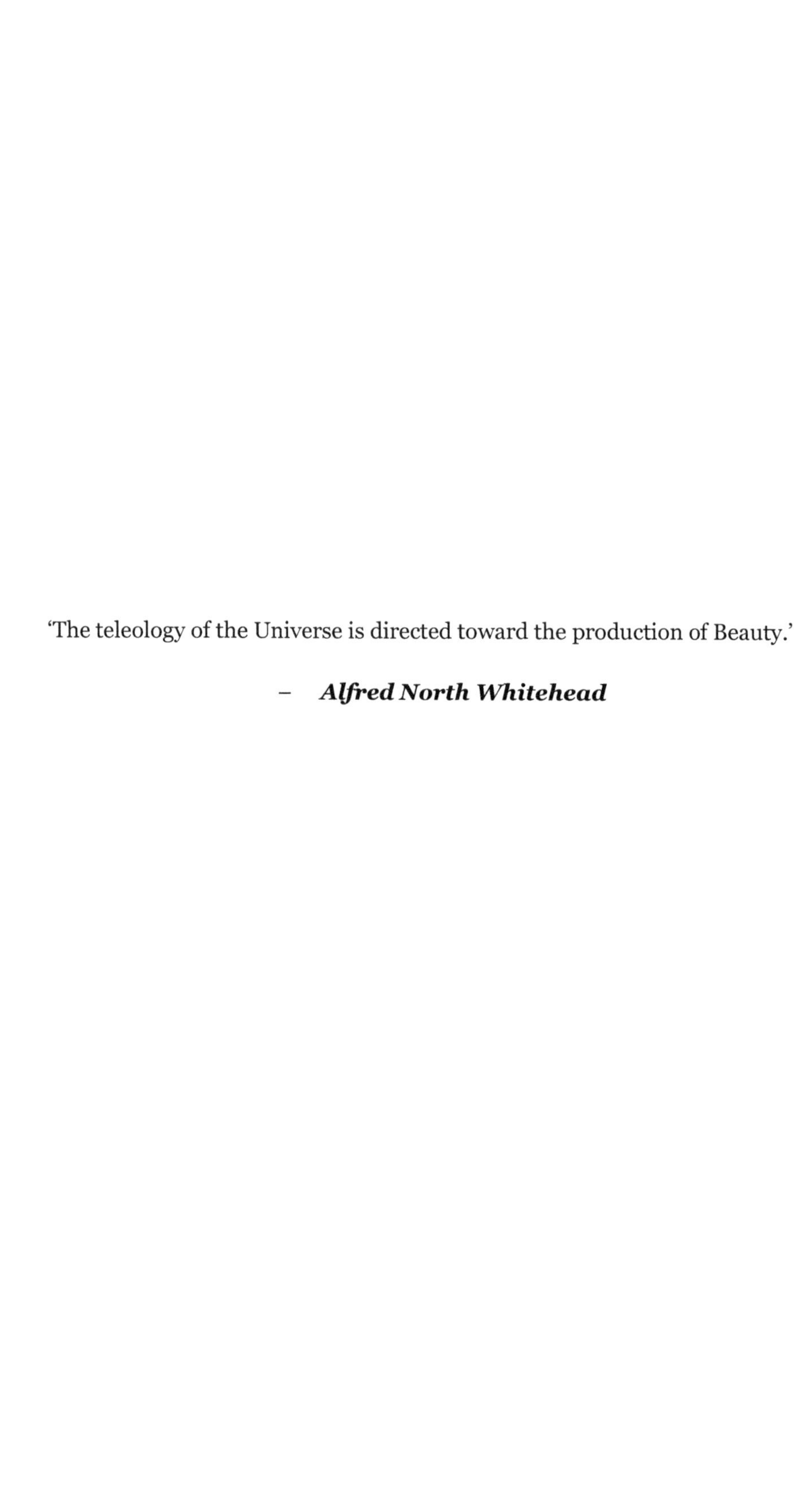

'The teleology of the Universe is directed toward the production of Beauty.'

– ***Alfred North Whitehead***

ESSAY TWO

CREATIVE EVOLUTION AND THE WILL TO ART

The conventional picture of the universe begins by positing an incredibly small, dense, and fiery lump of primordial energy which exploded into existence around 13.8 billion years ago. Thereafter the universe is said to have unfolded mechanically in accordance with the immutable laws of physics. Science is unable to provide any insight into what 'caused' the Big Bang and attributes to the cosmos no purpose or goal. Nevertheless, physicists still hold out hope of one day developing a 'Theory of Everything', which will be able to explain all phenomena, from the cosmological all the way down to the sub-atomic particles of quantum reality. How consciousness arose from and interacts with matter remains one of the 'hard problems' of science, but in time it is assumed that even the inner workings of our brains will be explainable according to determinate physical laws. According to this description of reality – based on the metaphor of a machine – the end of the universe is built into its original state, such that all events that occur along the space-time continuum are simply a result of the machine operating strictly according to its preestablished laws. Many people treat this view as the true, scientific picture of reality, rendering alternative descriptions either false or 'merely poetic'.

Friedrich Nietzsche wrote that 'truth is a mobile army of metaphors.'[1] His point was that our pictures of the world and everything in it, including ourselves, are ultimately metaphorical in nature rather than objective. We can lose sight of this fact when our metaphors have been in place for so long that they are mistaken for 'just the way the world is' rather than one of a variety of potential descriptions. For example, it is easy to forget that the mouth of a river, the eye of a needle, and the face of the clock are descriptions grounded in metaphor. They are so entrenched in our use of language that they have become 'dead metaphors', in the sense that we interpret them literally without needing to think about their meanings. Metaphors come into use not because they reflect reality *in itself* but because they prove useful when communicating or pursuing goals. However, they can also become hindrances if they outlive their usefulness, locking us into a particular way of viewing the world and concealing alternative perspectives and possibilities.

We are living in the Age of the Machine, a product of Enlightenment rationalism. But suppose this mechanical view of the universe is itself a dead metaphor? What if, to borrow a phrase from philosopher Ludwig

Wittgenstein, a picture holds us captive, and we cannot get outside it, for it lies in our language and language seems to repeat it to us inexorably?[2] To ask this question is not to call for the metaphor's rejection, for viewing the universe as a machine that operates according to laws surely serves the useful purpose of helping humanity control and predict nature. But if we were to raise this metaphor from the dead, we might better appreciate its rhetorical and thus contingent nature. We would see that it is only one of a variety of potential 'pictures' of the universe, useful so far as it serves a particular purpose, but also potentially concealing of different ways of knowing and being in the world. To think that the machinic perspective is the one and only right way to view the world is to fall prey to its entrenched, rhetorical value, imbuing it with an objectivity that in reality it lacks.[3]

Metaphors, however, are inherently unstable – even dead ones. Sometimes the mobile army can shift ground in unexpected ways, at which point we can come to see the world and our place in it with fresh eyes. This movement of metaphors would not be a shift toward a clearer or truer picture of a pre-existing reality, rather it would signify a paradigm shift in perspective that helps us see things in new ways. With a new perspective, important problems might be resolved or dissolved, or new possibilities of living might present themselves that were previously unthinkable. A metaphorical shift can never be written off because the universe is infinitely complex, denying humanity the possibility of ever providing a complete or final description of all phenomena. It will always be possible to redescribe our complex world in metaphorically imaginative ways that unveil new insights into the universe, human society, or even our own subjectivities, inviting us to look at life through a different lens. American philosopher Richard Rorty argued that scientists invent descriptions which are designed to help us achieve the goals of prediction and control, just as poets and political thinkers invent other descriptions for other purposes.[4] But there is no chance of ever seeing the world without *any* interpretive 'lens' – no chance, that is, of shedding our conceptual schemes entirely in order to perceive reality as it *really is*.[5]

It follows that there is also no sense in which the vocabularies we create to understand or represent the world can be said to exist 'out there', waiting to be discovered. Instead, poets, philosophers, and scientists must *create* them. Even the notion of 'foundations' of knowledge draws on the spatial metaphors of architecture and therefore is only one way to think about knowledge – a perspective which may be epistemologically revealing of certain insights and concealing of others. As analytic philosopher Donald Davidson wrote, a metaphoric shift can lead us to 'notice what might not otherwise be noticed.'[6] When a new vocabulary catches alight in the social imagination, we call these creative people geniuses, and sometimes bestow upon their perspectives the honorific 'truth'. When new vocabularies are invented that do not catch on, they can be dismissed as uninteresting, false, irrational, or even mad. Of course, a metaphoric shift that at first appears strange can come to be seen, in the fullness of time, as truth, and in the process, the metaphor dies, or at least lies dormant. Thus, the madman can become a poet-philosopher, and old truth-tellers can fall out of fashion as their traditional verities get overturned and replaced by a new generation.

Science teaches no moral lesson, offers no spiritual comfort, and provides no explanation for why there is something rather than nothing. Neither does it confer on the universe any meaning or purpose. And yet, many of us seek insight into these matters out of existential need, even if we discover that answers lie simply in the questioning itself. The great French philosopher Rene Descartes sought to uncover 'first principles' that would lead him to the truth, but his philosophical method of radical doubt was defined by the fear of error – which betrays a value judgement that itself could be false. After all, could a person not be entitled to risk being wrong about the nature of some mystery for the chance of being right? Suppose, for example, that we only allowed ourselves to fall in love or trust people who we knew *for certain* would never hurt us. That strategy might well avoid the pain of heartbreak or betrayal, but mightn't it also result in losing, through lost opportunities, more than we gained? Could there be times when believing *as if* something were true might be a necessary precondition for it becoming true?

The following words from novelist and poet Herman Hesse give me the courage to take such a risk – the risk of falling into error in exchange for the chance to live in some uncertain truth: 'Nothing is harder,' he wrote, 'yet nothing is more necessary, than to speak of certain things whose existence is neither demonstrable nor probable. The very fact that serious and conscientious people treat them as existing things brings them a step closer to existence and to the possibility of being born.'[7] And so, in that spirit, I will now offer readers an alternative cosmology to consider – a grand narrative whose author is perfectly aware of its narrativity.

♦ ♦ ♦

Causation is a temporal concept – an effect always comes after its cause, never before. One never feels the physical vibrations of the note before plucking the string. On that basis, the idea of an uncaused cause – music without a musician – defies our deepest intuitions about physical reality. Yet, to ask what happened 'before' the Big Bang doesn't seem to make literal sense either, given that space-time itself is said to have been created at the moment of that originating explosion. Science negotiates this paradox by refusing to speculate on what cannot be empirically tested or verified, and it is true that there is no direct evidence on what caused the Big Bang. We hear the music of creation but see no musician. This renders the nature of that first cause unknowable and therefore, on this subject, science must forever remain silent.

That is a perfectly coherent position. It assumes, however, that an understanding of the cause of something can only be known directly, whereas I suggest that we can infer an understanding about the nature of something from its effects. This is necessarily a speculative exercise, open to interpretation and contestation, but it is not unscientific, given that all inferences are drawn from experience and must be coherent in light of that experience. Nevertheless, the ambiguity of the evidence in question – regarding the *fundamental* nature of reality – means that there is no way to offer a neutral or objective reading of it; that is, no way to avoid interpretation grounded in a particular perspective. I acknowledge therefore that what follows is an interpretation, not simply the description of a self-evident truth. My opening point, however, is to insist that *not* offering any creation story is itself an interpretation of our place in the cosmos, and to deny this requires making assumptions which are themselves in question.

When the dominant assumptions that hold us captive are suspended, if only for a moment, we are freed to consider the possibility of alternative pictures of the world. What if, for example, in a moment of cosmic madness, the spectacular explosion that originated the universe were interpreted not as a *physical event governed by laws* but rather as the commencement of an *aesthetic unfolding of creative evolution*? My invitation here is to shift the foundational metaphor from universe-as-machine to universe-as-artist, and then see what follows. Again, I am not calling for a rejection of machinic thinking. Rather, I suggest that such thinking conceals as it reveals, and my interest is in exploring what lies behind and beyond the dominant metaphor. As I began to look behind that metaphor and take up residence in its blind field, I found myself writing this essay.

I invite readers to consider the existence of what could be described as a 'aesthetic impulse' or 'creative drive' at the base of reality – a primordial art-force from which everything else follows. I am calling this the Will to Art. This can be understood as the cause of the cosmological instability which led to a mighty explosion at the beginning of time, resulting in the universe itself and the perpetual creative drives working in and through the universe. It is the internal spark of life and the cause of literally unpredictable moments in what French philosopher Henri Bergson called 'creative evolution'.[8] And it is the cause of that mysterious feeling or mood which inspires, even compels, the artist to sit down to compose *something out of nothing*. Therein – by creating something out of nothing – humanity is able to commune with the mysterious aesthetic impulse from which existence itself has emerged.

Although I make the analogy tentatively, the Will to Art, like gravity, is operating everywhere in the universe. Theoretical physicists have no direct observational evidence of 'dark energy' and 'dark matter' but posit the hypothetical existence of such in order to help predict and understand cosmological happenings. So too am I positing an original aesthetic force – a creative impulse that brings the art of life into being – to see if it can help make sense of the world. I believe it can, and I ask readers to indulge me in presenting this creation story before deciding whether to reject it.

To be clear, I am not suggesting there is a conscious, metaphysical 'being' that created the world or governs it. I am not positing a deity – some 'Artist-Creator'. Nietzsche made such a metaphysical claim in his first book, *The Birth of Tragedy* – based on what he called his *Artisten-Metaphysik* or 'artists' metaphysics.'[9] While it will become clear I have a somewhat Nietzschean story to tell, mine is metaphoric not metaphysical, and I have depersonified the cosmos in due regard to the mysteriousness of the entity I am discussing. Nature is more than an 'It' (object) but less than a 'Thou' (subject). Even if there were some 'being' capable of creating a universe out of nothing, it would be crudely anthropomorphic to assume this entity would resemble an old man, with a long white beard, living in the clouds. Any Creator-Being – any god – would surely be so strange to our finite minds as to be utterly incomprehensible. Even without positing a deity, the universe is quite mysterious enough.

As primordial art, the cosmos seems to be unfolding in order to *experience itself*; to experience its underlying creative spirit through the genesis and evolution of conscious life. While I subscribe in most regards to the Darwinian theory of evolution, I realise that one must leave room for the reality that evolution is unpredictably creative not merely mechanistic, and when complex systems emerge and become alive, they become increasingly creative. Creativity begets creativity; art begets art – and here we all are, as living proof. The interpretation I am offering is that there is an originating aesthetic force in the world – the Will to Art – and we are its unfinished products.

Admittedly, we cannot observe this 'first cause' directly – this aesthetic impulse that drives creative activity with unpredictable (non-mechanistic) effects. But we can infer something about the nature of such an impulse or drive from its effects, just as we can know something about the nature of dark matter from its effects, even though this hypothetical substance has no luminosity (i.e., cannot be seen). As Nietzsche maintained: 'it is enough to create new names and valuations... in order to create new "things"'[10] and 'a "thing" is the sum of its effects, synthetically united by a concept.'[11] On that basis, the Will to Art is the sum of its effects – the aesthetic universe itself. Given that its effects can be coherently understood through an aesthetic lens – the fractal lens of art, creativity, beauty, imagination, and sensuality – it requires no interpretative gymnastics to *infer an aesthetic cause from the multiplicity of observable aesthetic effects*. Indeed, one can plausibly claim that a multiplicity of aesthetic effects – the creative universe as we know it – must, in some sense, have a cause that is itself aesthetic. 'The world is a work of art that gives birth to itself,'[12] Nietzsche declared, and through the Dionysian impulse at the heart of reality 'the artistic power of all nature reveals itself.'[13]

Let me present this view another way. The material universe proceeds in accordance with physical laws; matter mysteriously gives rise to life; life becomes conscious; consciousness becomes self-aware; and in the human species – *homo aestheticus* – the cosmos has produced indeterminate nodes of boundless imaginative potential and sensuous capacity. These nodes of sensuous creativity exist within the physical universe – finite souls with infinite poetic potential. There is, however, a creative impulse within each of us that is not itself governed or governable mechanically by physical laws. Indeed, every human begin can affirm the lines from American poet Walt Whitman: 'I am large; I contain multitudes.'[14] The Will to Art is what drives us to explore those multitudes in search of beauty and meaning.

In this way our essentially artistic being is simply a reflection of the restless dynamism of the aesthetic universe itself, a product of the same mysterious, creative drive that knows no inherent closure. As Terry Eagleton writes when discussing the German Idealist Friedrich Schelling: 'The human subject is a form of self-conscious production; but this self-fashioning is also its way of participating in the world's perpetual conjuring of itself into existence... It is the function of the work of art to cast Nature's self-productivity in palpable form, and in doing so permit us a rare insight into the intelligibility of that process.'[15] If we interpret art broadly to include all creative or aesthetic activity through which humans give order, form, and meaning to existence, we can begin to understand what Nietzsche meant when he wrote: 'art is the highest human task'[16] of life.

Moreover, as William Morris wrote: 'that which most breeds art is art.'[17] Beauty and other forms of aesthetic value are often the intended result of creativity and art, and one observes that the contemplation of such aesthetic value propels the expansion and propagation of further aesthetic experience and creativity in new forms. Philosopher Elaine Scarry makes this point by asserting that: 'Beauty brings copies of itself into being... The generation is unceasing.'[18] The poet inspires poetry, just as music gives birth to musicians. In the same vein, Wittgenstein once remarked that when the eye sees something beautiful, the hand wants to draw it.[19] When we are in the presence of beauty, we are naturally inclined to share the experience, to invite others to see the sun setting or to listen to a piece of music we found particularly moving. It is as if there were some aesthetic tendency for beauty to reproduce itself, even as that tendency must fight against ugliness and violence.

On these premises, the aesthetic experiences of beauty and meaning (arising from creative activity or aesthetic contemplation) can be understood as the *telos* of the universe. This universe proceeds toward its telos due to the cosmological impulse I am calling the Will to Art. Just as the acorn has the oak built into its nature, so too does our aesthetic universe have art built into its nature. This mythopoetic account of the world predetermines nothing, however, since art is inherently unpredictable and the evolution of artistic being is unforeseeable. Obviously, the human world is grossly unjust and may remain so. But in an aesthetic universe, hope resides in the possibility of moving towards a more beautiful and humane world, through the exuberant fertility of creative (and destructive) struggle.

What results from imaginative engagement with the world and ourselves is unknowable in advance. Unlike a machine, therefore, the end of creative evolution is not built into its original state. No longer bound exclusively to the physical laws of evolution, *homo aestheticus* is now a co-producer of creative evolution, the results of which are limited only by our imaginations. In line with its nature, the underlying aesthetic impulse of reality has created an artistic species. Through us, the universal aesthetic field in which we exist – the cosmos – is able to experience itself over time as a boundless and evolving work of art. Because the outcome is unknowable, the art-force driving creative evolution seems to be amoral and reckless, existing beyond good and evil. This impulse is defined not so much by what it is but by what it has the capacity to become, through us, for better or for worse.

Within this mythopoetic framework, the Will to Art can be said to lie at the heart of existence and is infused into the fabric of reality. I am inviting readers to consider what would follow if this premise were embraced – even as one must accept that *all premises*, by virtue of their nature, rest on nothing more than their own ground. Consistent with observable data, this aesthetic reading of the universe, as I have said, is not a metaphysical thesis but a metaphorical one – it is, unapologetically, a narrative or interpretation in search of new insight. The universe-as-machine cannot account for the indeterminate phenomena of art – of creativity that cannot be explained merely by what preceded it – and scientists operating within the machinic metaphor dare not speculate about a creation story if the cause cannot be directly observed. But I contend that contemplating the cause of creative elements in the universe and in ourselves might offer insight into the nature of our very existence – of all existence – and so we should hesitate to stay silent on this mystery simply out of fear of being wrong, when doing so ensures that we have no chance of living in some positive but uncertain truth.

The art of nature: reenchanting the machine

The poet-scientist looks to creation itself to know the nature of our cosmos – from which it becomes clear that its *nature is creativity*. When thinking of the origins of the universe, do not imagine you are viewing the Big Bang as a spectator. An external 'view from nowhere' – a position outside of space-time – is incoherent if not contradictory. Rather, imagine the cosmic dawn as a participant, from the internal perspective from where you are being creatively blown out into aesthetic reality. In a sublime moment of poetic frenzy, emerging out of the Will to Art, an unfathomably vast and beautiful expanse of space-time bursts into existence, a canvas painting itself with swirling gases and around two hundred billion trillion stars. Conscious beings emerge sometime later, and occasionally we find ourselves looking up at a night sky, in a universe of breathtaking dimensions, to see the sparkling light from the long dead stars from which we were made. Where did all this come from and where is it going? As one stares into the abyss, this question can induce a shudder between the shoulder blades, ushering in a mystical mood from which one never fully recovers.

Equally, we might think of the creation story of the Big Bang not as an originating physical explosion but rather as an *interior explosion* of the creative spirit in humankind – and then work backwards to see if we can understand how our minds that seek to impose order and meaning on the world came into existence. Some might be tempted to suggest that this aesthetic universe is a very 'inefficient' means of creating merely one (known) planet with the conditions necessary for artistic being, but that is to assume the miracle of life can be weighed against the overwhelming predominance of non-life. Couldn't one just as easily be astounded at how *few* stars were needed to create something as astonishing as life?

As well as imagining what the origin of the universe *looked* like, we might also consider what it *sounded* like. Scientists advise that it would have sounded more like a deep humming bass instrument than a 'bang', the frequency of which would have fallen over time on account of sound waves being stretched as the universe expanded. These ancient soundwaves have left their imprint as temperature variations on the afterglow of the Big Bang – the so-called cosmic microwave background. At the beginning, was not the Word, but the Tone. Mystics of sound have long argued that music and vibration originated the universe and comprise the fabric of reality itself.[20] If the universe can be explained at all, asserts Hazrat Inayat Khan, 'it is by the phases of sound or vibration, which have manifested in different grades in all their various forms of life. Objects and names and forms are but the expression of vibrations in different aspects,'[21] and these vibrations influence 'the tone and rhythm of our being.'[22]

If some readers are concerned that this mystical account has drifted dangerously far from the standards of scientific rigour and is getting frustratingly poetic, let it not be forgotten that contemporary 'string theory' physicists – the controversial but still leading 'Theory of Everything' – employ guiding musical metaphors in precisely the same way. In fact, it is not clear that these physicists are using music as a metaphor at all, for they seem to be trying, just like the mystics, *to be as literal as possible* – even if the tool of language is not fully up to the task. Without attempting any detailed statement, string theorists advance the claim that subnuclear particles – the most fundamental building blocks of reality – are extremely small 'strings' that take on different modes of existence depending on how they vibrate.

One leading proponent of string theory, Brian Greene, describes the universe as a 'cosmic symphony'.[23] In the same spirit, esteemed theoretical physicist Michio Kaku says 'the universe is a symphony of vibrating strings,'[24] so that even human beings are 'nothing but melodies, nothing but cosmic music played on vibrating strings and membranes,'[25] implying that we are ourselves part of the orchestra. In Kaku's view, 'physics is nothing but the laws of harmony that you can write on vibrating strings.'[26]

For now this framing need not be taken any further, but it does serve to counter the perceived objectivity of the disenchanted view of the universe and points to its superficiality. Beneath the mechanistic view of the universe lie alternative possibilities, simmering metaphors of art and music, waiting to be born, to live, and to die. Should these aesthetic metaphors become dead metaphors, we would find ourselves, quite literally, living in a new universe, shaped according to the new but ever-evolving poetic ontology. This would not merely change how we think about everything; it would change everything, forcing us to think differently about it.

As implied above, the process of creative evolution could be understood in stages. First, matter is governed by physical laws that are driven by a 'Will to Life'. For billions of years this process crept onwards, like a cosmological glacier, toward the emergence of life. Eventually, forms of conscious life emerged that were infused with an insecure and confused 'Will to Power' – a harsh struggle for existence driven by a blind striving for something that life did not yet understand.[27] But in the fullness of time, the developed aesthetic consciousness comes to realise the futility or meaninglessness of power in and for itself. With power, one is still left asking: what is power *for*? From which it follows: what are humans *for*? All at once it becomes clear that it is not power but meaning that we seek, and in the absence of external or objective sources of meaning, we are left to explore the poetics of our existence through creative activity and aesthetic experience. Situated delicately on the edge of insanity, the inspired mood, given by grace, is the point of origin for creative expression and experimentation. As always, the cause, however mysterious, precedes the effect. The artist, broadly conceived, is but a medium through which our aesthetic universe can experience itself.

By exercising our imaginative capacities and thereby giving lived expression to the Will to Art, we become who we are, which is a creative force, an aesthetic and affective becoming. We are the art-created art creators, forever tasked with making ourselves and our worlds anew; forever seeking to grant and expand aesthetic opportunities as we explore aesthetic experience. Therein lies the source of human dignity and solidarity – which has social and political implications that will be addressed in due course. In accordance with the telos of the universe, we can honour nature, ourselves, and each other by creating as an aesthetic project the meaning of our own lives; to create and immerse ourselves in beauty so as to propagate it. For it is only as an aesthetic phenomenon, as Nietzsche declared, that existence and the world can be justified.[28] To describe this aesthetic universe merely as a dead, cold empty space in which matter operates according to mechanistic laws, is to do interpretive violence to alternative and equally valid perspectives that see the universe as alive, creative, artistic, mysterious, and full of the affective capacity to enchant. Fortunately, if the mechanistic conception of the universe is *disenchanted*, that implies that it also has the potential to be *reenchanted*.

This collection of essays emerged from my belief that interpreting the world through an aesthetic lens can help us understand the human situation – existentially, socially, and politically. My offering, of course, is merely *one perspective* on an infinitely complex universe. But perspectives and stories are all we have, so it would be imprudent to deny the potential value of a particular story merely because it does not provide a complete, singular, and objective description of all phenomena. The narrative I have offered will resonate more with some people than others. I certainly cannot demonstrate its singular validity. But I am prepared to risk going astray for the chance of uncovering new insights, and this essay has been an invitation for readers to join me on this philosophical journey and dare, if only for a moment, to 'think of things this way'. To invoke the environmental philosopher Henry Thoreau: 'I trust that none will stretch the seams in putting on the coat, for it may do good service to [they] whom it fits.'[29]

---

[1] Friedrich Nietzsche, 'On Truth and Lies in an Extra-Moral Sense' in Walter Kaufmann (ed), *The Portable Nietzsche* (London: Penguin, 1988) p. 46.

[2] See Ludwig Wittgenstein, *Philosophical Investigations* (Oxford: Basil Blackwell, 1963) p. 48.

[3] In an age threatening ecosystemic collapse, we might well ask whether the conventional goal of science as 'control over nature' needs to be rethought – on the grounds of its apparent failure. After all, if climate change burns civilisation to the ground this century, what then could be said of the scientific enterprise? Perhaps only that we rigorously documented civilisation's collapse and understood the causes.

[4] Richard Rorty, *Contingency, Irony, and Solidarity* (New York: Cambridge University Press, 1989) p. 4.

[5] See Donald Davidson, *Inquiries into Truth and Interpretation* (Oxford: Oxford University Press, 1984), p. 185.

[6] Donald Davidson 'What Metaphors Mean' in Sheldon Sacks (ed.), *On Metaphor* (Chicago: Chicago University Press, 1979), p. 39.

[7] Herman Hesse, *The Glass Bead Game* (London: Penguin, 1972), p. 14.

[8] Henri Bergson, *Creative Evolution* (New York: Dover, 1998).

[9] Fredrich Nietzsche, *The Birth of Tragedy* and *The Genealogy of Morals* (New York: Anchor Books, 1956), p. 10.

[10] Friedrich Nietzsche, *The Gay Science* (New York: Vintage, 1974) p. 122.

[11] Friedrich Nietzsche, *The Will to Power* (New York: Vintage, 1968), p. 296.

[12] Ibid, p. 419

[13] See John Fredrick Humphrey, 'Friedrich Nietzsche's *Artisten-Metaphysik* (Doctoral thesis, Graduate Faculty of Political and Social Science, New School for Social Research, 1992), p. 22.

[14] Walt Whitman, 'Song of Myself' in Walt Whitman, *Leaves of Grass* (Toronto: Colonial Press, 1965), p. 79.

[15] Terry Eagleton, *Culture and the Death of God* (New Haven: Yale University Press, 2015), pp. 53-4.

[16] Friedrich Nietzsche, *The Birth of Tragedy* and *The Genealogy of Morals* (New York: Anchor Books, 1956), p. 17.
[17] William Morris, 'The Beauty of Life' in William Morris, *Hopes and Fears for Art: Five Lectures by William Morris*. Available at https://www.marxists.org/archive/morris/works/1882/hopes/chapters/index.htm (accessed 10 May 2023), para. 102.
[18] Elaine Scarry, *On Beauty and Being Just* (Princeton: Princeton University Press, 1999), p. 3-4.
[19] Ibid, p 3.
[20] Hazrat Inayat Khan, *The Mysticism of Sound and Music* (Boulder: Shambhala, 1996), p. 9.
[21] Ibid, p. 18.
[22] Ibid, p. 29.
[23] Brian Greene, *The Elegant Universe: Superstrings, Hidden Dimensions, and the Search for the Ultimate Theory* (London: Vintage, 2000), Part III.
[24] Michio Kaku, 'The Universe is a Symphony of Vibrating Strings' *YouTube* (1 June 2011).
[25] Ibid.
[26] Ibid.
[27] Here I am using the phrase 'will to power' in the conventional or literal sense of power over others, dominance, accumulation of wealth, etc. Nietzsche's very different and more subtle conception (i.e., power over oneself) will be addressed elsewhere in this collection, especially in 'Pessimism without Despair: Suffering, Desire, and the Affirmation of Life'. The full set of essays will be posted here: http://samuelalexander.info/s-m-p-l-c-t-y-ecological-civilisation-and-the-will-to-art/ (accessed 10 May 2023).
[28] Friedrich Nietzsche, *The Birth of Tragedy*, trans. Walter Kaufmann (New York: Vintage, 1967), p. 22, p. 143.
[29] Henry Thoreau, *Walden*, in Carl Bode (ed.) *The Portable Thoreau* (New York: Penguin, 1982), p. 259.

‘Life without music would be a mistake.’

– **Friedrich Nietzsche**

PESSIMISM WITHOUT DESPAIR: SUFFERING, DESIRE, AND THE AFFIRMATION OF LIFE

In the opening essays I offered an interpretation of the universe as an aesthetic phenomenon. By privileging artistic metaphors over machinic metaphors, I proposed a reading of existence based on what I called the Will to Art. This can be understood a process of creative evolution that is moving, albeit agonistically, toward ever-increasing opportunities for artistic expression and aesthetic experience. From this neo-Duchampian perspective, the cosmos is elevated to the dignity of a work of art, one that is unfolding in order to *experience itself* through the genesis and diversity of conscious and creative life. The telos of this universe is beauty, and we are its aesthetic agents – nodes of dissonance in search of harmony. My overarching thesis, developed later in this collection of essays, is that the Will to Art is most likely to realise itself in an ecological civilisation of artisan-artists who privilege 'being' over 'having'.[1] In such a society, which I have labelled SMPLCTY, human communities would live simply but sufficiently in harmony with nature, finding meaning and pleasure through self-directed creative labour and aesthetic experience.

In presenting this vision, however, I cautioned against an overly romantic interpretation. In the introduction it was acknowledged that the Will to Art, in this early phase of creative evolution, often manifests in ways that appear more like a violent and ugly Will to Power, producing unnecessary suffering in the world. Indeed, so vast and pervasive is the reality of suffering that an entire tradition of 'philosophical pessimism' has arisen which concludes that the world, as such, ought not to exist.[2] The reality of suffering cannot be denied or downplayed, and any aesthetic justification of existence, such that I am offering, must give this problem due regard, which is the philosophical task of this essay and the next.

For this undertaking I turn to the work of one of pessimism's most extreme adherents – Arthur Schopenhauer. If a plausible response can be formulated to the 'great pessimist' himself, it may be the problem of suffering can be dealt with in less extreme versions also. Schopenhauer would likely have agreed with the Socratic and Aristotelian dictum that philosophy begins in 'wonder'. But rather than wonder denoting some exhilarating emotion evoked by the mysteries of life, Schopenhauer's philosophical motivation could more accurately be described as 'astonishment' –

astonishment at the horror of existence.[3] Can one digest such a pessimistic outlook without degenerating into despair? Might there be living strategies available that could somehow allow for the affirmation of life – a 'pessimism of strength,'[4] as Friedrich Nietzsche would call it – despite the prevalence of suffering in the world? These are the questions to be considered presently.

After briefly outlining the metaphysical structure of Schopenhauer's bleak and atheistic worldview, I will examine the place of suffering in it and how he responded to this perennial problem. It will be seen that Schopenhauer's worldview has profound similarities to Eastern philosophy – the Buddhist views on suffering and desire, in particular – even though he developed his philosophy independently and in original ways. This engagement with Schopenhauer's thought will require an analysis of his ethics of compassion, his views on art and aesthetics, as well as his case for 'denying the will' through ascetic practices, all articulated in his magnum opus, *The World as Will and Representation* (1818).[5] On that basis I will assess why and in what ways Nietzsche developed, and in many ways reacted against, Schopenhauerian pessimism.

In closing the essay I will link the discussion back to the Will to Art, which can be understood in part as a metaphorical restatement and revision of aspects of Schopenhauer's quasi-Buddhist metaphysics, influenced by Nietzsche's perspective on the aesthetic justification of existence.[6] While I do not want to overstate the influence Buddhism has had on the development of the worldview being presented – I am more Nietzschean than Buddhist, and came to Buddhism through Schopenhauer – the term 'aesthetic Buddhism' will be introduced to help clarify aspects of the cosmology implicit to the Will to Art. This alchemy of philosophies will also allow me to highlight places where both Nietzsche and Schopenhauer misinterpreted aspects of Buddhism and the ascetic practices this tradition may (or may not) imply. While no prior knowledge of Buddhism will be assumed, readers who already have some grasp of this ancient Indian wisdom tradition are well-placed to hear what I have to say about the Will to Art.[7]

Schopenhauer's metaphysics

Any review of Schopenhauer's metaphysics must begin by acknowledging his philosophical debt to Immanuel Kant. Schopenhauer was deeply influenced by Kant's systematic philosophy (often called 'transcendental idealism'), although he claimed to have advanced Kant's view in critically important ways. Schopenhauer began on the Kantian foundations that the world-in-itself – the 'noumenal world', as Kant called it – is unknowable to us. We can only experience and have knowledge of the phenomenal world, given to us through our senses, as sense data. Kant's most significant contribution to philosophy was to explain that this sense data was not raw or unmediated, like earlier empiricists had argued. Instead, the very possibility of experience was dependent on phenomena being *constructed* by our consciousness.

In this view, our experience of reality is shaped by the categories of time, space, and causality, these being some of the categories of the understanding which Kant argued provide the very conditions of thought itself. Our consciousness is like the 'lens' on a pair of spectacles, forever and necessarily colouring or mediating our view of reality. On that basis, Kant concluded that we can never have knowledge of metaphysical reality (the world-in-itself or the thing-in-itself). Rather, the noumenal world is *represented* to us, via our sensory apparatus, as the phenomenal world. Contrary to the view of earlier rationalists, Kant argued that direct access to the underlying metaphysical reality is simply not accessible to creatures such as ourselves. In these ways he was able to merge and at the same time transcend the two major schools of philosophy: rationalism and empiricism.

In Schopenhauer's book *World as Will and Representation*, he developed this view by arguing that Kant, in most regards, accurately delineated the limits of human knowledge, but that he missed one critical element in the philosophical picture. He felt Kant's insistence that we can never know the noumenal world was in one regard a premature defeat. Schopenhauer's definitive theoretical innovation was to argue that we do, in fact, have direct experience of the underlying reality, the thing-in-itself, through what he called the Will (sometimes the 'will-to-live').[8] Granted, we cannot experience the underlying reality of the *external world* represented to us via our senses, given that such experience was necessarily constructed by our sensory apparatus. Agreeing with Kant on this, Schopenhauer wrote: 'In consequence of all this, on the path to *objective knowledge*, thus starting from *representation*, we shall never get beyond the representation, i.e., the phenomenon. We shall therefore remain at the outside of things; we shall never be able to penetrate into their inner nature, and investigate what they are in themselves, in other words, what they may be by themselves.'[9]

Nevertheless, by looking inward rather than outward, Schopenhauer argued that we have direct access to the 'blindly urging force'[10] and 'endless striving'[11] of the Will. Schopenhauer argued that this Will is the thing-in-itself, unmediated, therefore giving us access to the underlying nature of reality. This was not 'representational' knowledge of the external world, hence his distinction (highlighted in his book title) between the world as

Will, and the world as Representation. We can experience our body by touching it, through which we gain representational knowledge of ourselves in the world. But we also have direct, non-representational access to the Will, which he declared was 'the most intimate fact of self-consciousness'.[12]

Schopenhauer argued that this gives us access to reality's 'innermost being, its kernel'.[13] This experience of ourselves as a willing creature was categorically different from touching our own arm, for example, or perceiving an object in nature. 'We must learn to understand nature from ourselves, not ourselves from nature.'[14] For 'we too have absolutely no knowledge of the things-in-themselves... I admit this of everything, but not of the knowledge everyone has of his own *willing*.'[15] Thus, distinguishing his position from Kant's, Schopenhauer said that 'a way *from within* stands open to us to that real inner nature of things... It is, so to speak, a subterranean passage, a secret alliance'[16] between subject and object. Knowledge of the will is not a subject *knowing* the object – it is the subject *as* object, which is to say, a collapsing of that distinction.

At once it must be acknowledged that Schopenhauer employs the term Will in a very unusual sense that can easily mislead. Normally, the term 'will' is associated with a *conscious being*, one that 'wills' or 'desires' something (e.g., the child wilfully jumped into the puddle). Schopenhauer, however, was using it in a far broader sense, referring to the relentless impersonal driving force inherent in *all nature*, of which human consciousness was only a particular, higher-order manifestation. Schopenhauer would argue that the Will is objectified in nature to varying grades – a hierarchy of objectification. At its crudest and most basic level, the hierarchy begins with the forces of nature, such as gravity, then manifests in inanimate objects, like stones and water, moving up through plant life to animal life, and culminating in human consciousness where the Will has become self-aware. This hierarchy also implies increasing degrees of creativity and freedom. Gravity is a constant that does not change. Rocks do not have any agency but change and degrade over time. Plants, as basic life forms, struggle for survival and seek out propitious conditions for life, but lack consciousness. Non-human animals are conscious but seem to act purely on instinct. Then there are self-aware humans, at the top of this hierarchy, who are able to reflect on their situation, show forethought, and act creatively with what is experienced as free will.[17]

In this expanded sense of the Will, a sunflower that follows the sun over the course of the day or pushes its roots deeper into the soil is change brought about by the manifestation of Will – the will-to-live – even though this plant is not conscious. Our own sense of personal experience, our desiring ego or self, is just another, higher-order manifestation of the same underlying, undifferentiated Will. As philosopher Sophia Vasalou writes: 'Willing is not something we do, but something we are, for our embodied condition leaves us no choice as to whether to will or not....'[18] According to Schopenhauer, the Will is the inner nature of reality and everything we experience in nature is a manifestation of its objectification – the Will becoming phenomena.

Schopenhauer's conception of Will, admittedly, seems to strain ordinary language. To place the force of gravity, inanimate objects, life-seeking plants, instinctual animals, and self-conscious human action under the same term seems to gloss over what are the clear differences between these entities. Furthermore, the notion of willing, which is normally associated with a mind or consciousness, implies (or necessitates) no such thing in Schopenhauer's worldview. This jarring usage, however, was no accident. It was intended to unsettle the received understanding of ourselves and the world. The Will is what gives everything in the universe its blind force of energy, striving without purpose: 'Every individual act has a purpose or end; [but] willing as a whole has no end in view.'[19] Schopenhauer warns his readers that 'anyone who is incapable of carrying out the required extension of the concept will remain involved in a permanent misunderstanding.'[20]

Schopenhauerian pessimism: Life is a mistake

The metaphysical system just outlined is the foundation for Schopenhauer's pessimistic outlook, which we can now explore further. Apologies to the reader, things are about to get grim. As individuals, we humans are fundamentally the embodiment of this underlying and insatiable force, the Will. A moment's reflection confirms that we are indeed full of desires – desires which we did not choose to have – and desires that have no end. For as soon as one desire is satisfied, another is there waiting. And unfilled desire implies a state of dissatisfaction, pain, or suffering – for when we desire, presumably something is lacking in our life. As Schopenhauer maintained: 'All willing springs from lack, from deficiency and thus from suffering.'[21]

Any happiness attained by fulfilling a desire is always temporary and fleeting, never lasting. Even when desire seems temporarily satisfied, we nevertheless hope that our satisfied state continues, so we haven't really escaped desire at all. And if such pathological desire is ever tempered for too long, boredom arises, inducing a new form of malaise, as we experience the 'utter bleakness and emptiness of existence.'[22] From a Schopenhauerian perspective, happiness is better understood as the absence of pain rather than anything positive – a passing condition that inevitably returns to the default state of painful lack.[23] 'Thus,' he wrote, 'the subject of willing is constantly lying on the revolving wheel of Ixion, is always drawing water in the sieve of the Danaids and is the eternal thirsting Tantalus.'[24]

Schopenhauer argued that this endless state of discontent lies at the core of the human condition and of existence more generally. 'Every attained end is at the same time the beginning of a new course, and so on *ad infinitum*.'[25] As tormented and agonised beings, we are condemned by nature to suffer. What is more, the balance of pain and pleasure in life is decidedly weighted toward pain: 'Life is a business whose returns are far from covering the cost.'[26] Wanting to ensure people grasped the full bleakness of his conclusions, Schopenhauer elaborated:

> ...for one wish that is fulfilled there remain at least ten that are denied. Further, desiring lasts a long time, demands and requests go on to infinity; fulfilment is short and meted out sparingly. But even the final satisfaction itself is only apparent; the wish fulfilled at once makes way for a new one; the former is a known delusion, the latter a delusion not as yet. No attained object of willing can give a satisfaction that lasts and no longer declines, but it is always like the alms thrown to a beggar, which reprieves him today so that his misery may be prolonged til tomorrow. Therefore, so long as our consciousness is filled by our will... so long as we are the subject of willing, we never obtain lasting happiness or peace.[27]

Readers will be justified in noting the striking resemblance here with the spiritual worldviews of some Eastern philosophies – Hinduism and Buddhism, in particular. These perspectives also posit 'desire' as lying at the root of human existence, through 'tanha', which literally means 'thirst' but is usually translated as 'craving' or 'desire'. Schopenhauer had read the *Upanishads* and the *Bhagavat-Gita,* although he seems to have developed his worldview independently.[28] Nevertheless, he was an avid reader of Eastern philosophy throughout his life, including Buddhist texts. He even had a statue of Buddha on his desk, and is often credited with being the first Western philosopher to have shown the insight to take Eastern philosophy seriously. Like the Buddha's First Noble Truth, Schopenhauer diagnosed existence with piercing simplicity: Life is suffering.[29]

Although Schopenhauer would develop pessimism in unique ways, his perspective shares very similar premises with Eastern philosophy. This overlap with such revered spiritual traditions arguably adds weight to Schopenhauer's position, even if aspects of his metaphysical framing are questionable. It is a defining feature of the human condition that we desire, we suffer because we desire, and since we are forever desiring, we suffer relentlessly, in ways ranging from the modest to the agonal. Desire for food, sex, sleep, warmth, the sensuous pleasures, material possessions, or even desires for personal development or social achievement, will keep on emerging. Any satisfactions of such are, at best, only temporary. We should have no hope or expectation of happiness or satisfaction. '[E]verything in life,' Schopenhauer suggested gloomily, 'is certainly calculated to bring us back from that original error [of expecting happiness], and to convince us that the purpose of our existence is not to be happy.'[30] The desiring Will, at base, is the underlying cause of misery and dissatisfaction in human existence. (Some decades later, Sigmund Freud would present a similarly grim vision of the human condition, albeit framed by psychoanalytic theory.)

This fundamental insight about the insatiable nature of human desire is the first step in Schopenhauer's pessimism – but by no means is it the last. The second step, anticipated above, flows from his position that the Will is blind and purposeless: 'the absence of all aim, of all limits, belongs to the essential nature of the will in itself, which is an endless striving.'[31] We spend our lives chasing vain goals that ultimately lack any objective meaning, made all the worse by the fact that the process of pursuing those goals fills our lives with pain, disappointment, loss, failure, and an underlying sense of futility. Our deepest loves will one day die; our hope for finding meaning in life through fame or wealth is a vain joke; we will all get sick, as will our loved ones, often without personal fault; freak accidents and meaningless violence occur to torment us, and if they don't happen to us personally, the mere possibility that they will colours existence with an underlying sense of anxiety and fear.

This occurs no matter how privileged a person may be. Lying on one's deathbed, all the wealth in the world will not matter much, as one proceeds, inevitability, toward the endless sleep of death, often in pain. Reading Schopenhauer, to be sure, can be rather depressing. This is especially so, as Marxist philosopher and literary critic Terry Eagleton acknowledges, given that the 'appalling vision is accurate in many of its essentials.'[32] Eagleton adds that it 'is remarkable how formally coherent utter futility can be made to appear.'[33]

There are also social injustices that seem to permeate any moral evaluation of the world. The distribution of suffering in the world certainly doesn't seem to be based on merit or fairness. Schopenhauer would also remind us that we are often more selfish than we should be, privileging our own desires over the more pressing needs of others. Some people seem positively cruel and sadistic. Looking around the world, we see great multitudes in humiliating destitution, despite living in a world of unprecedented affluence and capacity. In most if not all societies people are oppressed arbitrarily in one way or another by cultural, religious, or racial prejudices, often in contexts ravaged by war, disease, famine, natural disasters, or ecological degradation. Beyond human societies lies a natural world, red in tooth and claw, where the principle of life is kill or be killed. Schopenhauer's view is that everything in nature 'possesses only what it has wrested from another',[34] such that a 'constant struggle is carried on between life and death.'[35]

Even more troublesome, Schopenhauer continued, is that we live meaningless, painful lives with foreknowledge that we will inevitably die – and die in a universe without God or any metaphysical comfort (raising the issue of nihilism which will be considered in more detail in a forthcoming essay).[36] This is a 'spiritual pain'[37] that washes over the incessant physical suffering, a dread unique to humans who can imagine and contemplate their own demise. Death lies waiting for us, an abyss of nothingness without any higher purpose, reminding us every moment that our lives are finite and forgettable, even as we spend most of our lives trying to forget this gloomy reality. One day our existence will be extinguished, permanently so. But do not take any solace in the finite suffering of our individual lives, because we can be sure the suffering will continue after we are gone, as our illusory egos dissolve back into the relentless striving of the Will upon death. So even suicide is an option that for Schopenhauer 'affords no escape'.[38]

Perhaps a few geniuses – the likes of Plato, Newton, Shakespeare, Bach, Beethoven, and so forth – might be culturally remembered across centuries or in very rare cases millennia; perhaps, for more ordinary folks, our family members might remember us for a generation or two, at most. But ultimately, we will all end up as rotting corpses and be forgotten, at which point, if not before, our vain worldly strivings and achievements will not seem like much. As David Holbrook writes: 'In the end, even the creative achievements of Shakespeare and Bach must be eradicated by death and nothingness, when the earth is burnt up in the sun.'[39]

In summary, Schopenhauer maintained that 'we have not to be pleased but rather sorry about the existence of the world; that its non-existence would be preferable to its existence; that it is something which at bottom ought not to be...'[40] Or, more starkly still, the great pessimist concluded: 'life must be some sort of mistake.'[41]

Schopenhauer's response to suffering: Compassion, aesthetics, and asceticism

Schopenhauer thus concluded that existence cannot be justified. The prospect of an aesthetic justification of existence will be touched on below (and developed in the next essay), where I examine Nietzsche's attempt to grapple with Schopenhauer's pessimism. Before getting to Nietzsche, however, I wish to review how Schopenhauer responded to his own pessimistic conclusions. There are three main themes to address here, related to his views on compassion, aesthetic experience, and asceticism, which will now be considered in turn.

Compassion

If one were to accept the basics of Schopenhauer's worldview, what might the ethical implications be? With a logic similar to Buddhist thought, Schopenhauer made a coherent case for an ethic of compassion. His key premise is that our existence as individuals is just an objectification of an underlying Will that is undifferentiated in its fundamental nature. That is, our sense of 'ego' is really just an illusion and that, at base, all human beings, and indeed, all phenomena of nature, are essentially manifestations of one and the same blind Will.

Two things arguably follow from this. First, Schopenhauer calls on us to recognise the vanity of our personal hopes and ambitions. We experience such things as important in our lives, but according to the grand metaphysical scheme he outlined, they are not. Our strivings are ultimately meaningless in any objective sense, there is no God to judge us or heaven awaiting us – and hell is already here! Everything, including our personal experience, is transitory and ultimately will be extinguished. If the ego can be transcended in this way – by seeing our individuality as illusory – some of our own suffering might be reduced, given that we would come to see our goals as meaningless and, in the greater scheme of things, trivial. Should such a perspective be adopted, we might become less selfish and egotistical, leaving more room for compassion.

Furthermore, Schopenhauer tells us that the suffering we experience as individuals, horrible though it can be, is actually only a partial, limited sense of the full extent of suffering. After all, if, from a metaphysical perspective, we are all the same insatiable Will, then it would follow that our individualities dissolve. It would mean that the suffering of all human beings and everything throughout nature is, in fact, the suffering of the very same Will that constitutes our inner essence – the essence of reality itself.

Upon that basis, Schopenhauer developed an ethic of compassion. Not only does he invite us to put ourselves in the position of other people and infer their suffering from our own, but more fundamentally, when it is grasped that we are all the same underlying Will, the suffering of others can be seen as our own, and our suffering, theirs. In order to motivate our compassion, we somehow need to understand the object of compassion, and this can be achieved by a proper understanding of the indivisibility of the Will, for 'to a certain extent I have identified myself with the other person.'[42] This approach to ethics is grounded to some extent in 'affect' rather than reason. Schopenhauer was acknowledging that, as moral agents, we cannot merely *know* what the right thing to do is. We must also feel some *impetus to act* on that basis. When the self identifies with the whole world, one sees that love of others is self-love, and self-love is at once love of others.

Paradoxically, there is a risk that the compassionate person might actually increase overall suffering in the world, given that their own anguish might deepen as they come to see the pain in the world as their own. This could lead to an increase in the overall economy of unhappiness in the world.[43] On the other hand, that increase in suffering could well be balanced out or outweighed by compassionate acts that reduce pain in the world, and presumably that was Schopenhauer's view.

In this way Schopenhauer developed a morality based on alleviating the suffering of life: 'Injure no-one; rather help all as far as you can.'[44] Again, it is remarkable how close this worldview is to Indian philosophy, notably the Buddhist notion that the 'self' is really just an illusion and that ultimately, we are all One. The self (Atman) and the Absolute Reality (Brahman) are identical at base, in the sense that the self dissolves into that reality upon Enlightenment. This perspective overcomes one of the primary obstacles to ethical practice – that is, the self-interested question: what is in it for me? Buddhist perspectives, as with Schopenhauer's, insist that there is no 'me', and to the extent there is an ego in lived experience, the 'I' is not distinct from the 'other'. The self thereby vanishes into insignificance, making room for compassion as the self-interested ego dissolves.

It is sometimes said that there are two main threads to Buddhism – wisdom and compassion. Wisdom involves seeing the world as it is; compassion involves minimising suffering in that world. This grounds Buddhist ethics of compassion according to a logic similar to Schopenhauer's. Interestingly, Schopenhauer was an early defender of animal rights, and he commended the British for being ahead of Germany in terms of decent treatment of animals. He saw suffering as suffering, and he hoped and advocated for its reduction in all its diverse manifestations. On this issue, at least, he was practising what he preached. In other regards, however, Schopenhauer may not have walked the talk of his ethics so consistently. By all accounts he was not a very nice man. For instance, in a most un-Buddhist act, it is said that he once pushed an old lady down a set of stairs for chatting too loudly outside his door. She was injured and Schopenhauer had to pay compensation until her death, which he deeply resented. Nevertheless, the logic of his ethics of compassion is not undermined just because he was not always able to live up to its demands.

Schopenhauer did not believe that compassion could ever eliminate suffering. Instead, he suggested that approaching life in the spirit of compassion could make a terrible existence slightly less terrible – and that is a respite worth taking, even if it provides little by way of consolation. What is clear, however, is that this provides no 'justification' for existence – it arguably makes the extent of suffering even more profound than it already was, as a consequence of sympathy and empathy. At most, an ethic of compassion offers guidance on how a 'self' that does not exist could live in a world that ought not exist.

Aesthetic contemplation

The second strategy Schopenhauer employed to manage life in a world based on suffering was to turn to art. In fact, his defence of art and aesthetic experience is so powerfully and eloquently presented that he is often referred to as "the artists' philosopher" and, indeed, he has arguably had more influence on the arts than any other philosopher (with Nietzsche or Marx probably being his only competitors). Schopenhauer does not believe art or aesthetic contemplation provides a *justification* for existence, or even any permanent or long-term relief. But he does suggest aesthetic experience leads to a psychological or existential state where, in some sense, we 'lose ourselves' in art and thereby, if only momentarily, transcend the world of suffering. In this way art offers a certain spiritual therapy, a temporary redemption, where we are freed from the service to the Will and attain 'that peace that is higher than reason; that ocean-like calmness of the spirit, that deep tranquillity, that unshakeable confidence and serenity'.[45]

Linking his analysis to some of the language of Kantian aesthetics, Schopenhauer believed that aesthetic experience induces a state of 'disinterestedness' where we contemplate things without any reflection on our own personal desires or attachments. As we experience a work of art, we can find ourselves somehow suspended, as if in another world or dimension, where our sense of self fades into the background of experience; sometimes the self completely disappears, if only for a short time. This brings peace and serenity, since it is the self, with its incessant will, that is the source of all our sorrows and sufferings. He explained: 'we are no longer able to separate the perceiver from the perception, but the two have become one, since the entire consciousness is filled and occupied by a single image of perception.'[46]

Through aesthetic experience, Schopenhauer argued, we are left to experience beauty in quiet, will-less contemplation. We can become so deeply absorbed in art or the aesthetic appreciation of nature that the painful character of existence disappears. We 'no longer consider the where, the when, the why, and the whither of things, but simply and solely the *what*.'[47] Elaborating on this position, he asserted that 'the person who is involved in this perception is no longer an individual, for in such perception the individual has lost himself; he is now a *pure* will-less, painless, timeless *subject of knowledge*.'[48] It's a temporary state of tranquillity, undisturbed by the relentless strivings and impulses of the blind will:

> [A]ll at once the peace, always sought but always escaping us on that first path of willing, comes to us of its own accord, and all is well with us... [F]or that moment we are delivered from the miserable pressure of the will. We celebrate the Sabbath of the penal servitude of willing; the wheel of Ixion stands still.[49]

There is a second element to Schopenhauer's discussion of aesthetic experience which I will note briefly, referring not so much to the therapeutic value of art but rather its cognitive value. Schopenhauer develops his analysis of aesthetic experience by arguing that, when the Will is transcended through art, in such a state our perception of the world is *least distorted*. Schopenhauer argued, on that basis, that the artist can depict representational reality as accurately as possible, by evoking a state where we are able to have access to it. True art is created *in* this aesthetic state, for the purpose of *inducing* that state.

Here Schopenhauer used Platonic terminology, contending that during aesthetic experience we have access to the Platonic Ideas that represent timeless reality. He is careful, however, not to contradict his earlier position, outlined above. We saw that he adopted from Kant the view that phenomena of the world can never be known 'in themselves'. But he did argue that aesthetic experience can offer us an 'adequate objectivity'[50] – that is, the closest thing we will get to knowing the reality underlying representations.[51] If we drop some of the philosophical terminology, it might simply be said that there are truths about reality that are best represented through art and best received in a state of aesthetic experience. Indeed, art might be able to express truths that cannot be expressed or paraphrased through conceptual language.[52]

What is somewhat strange about this presentation however is that it seems to privilege the cognitive aspects of aesthetic experience and diminish, or even remove, the emotional content. This is because a state of disinterestedness would presumably exclude the propriety of an emotional response to art. To the extent emotions are part of genuine aesthetic experience, Schopenhauer suggested that it was not personal emotions being experienced (e.g., sorrow about this or that specific loss) but sorrow *in general*, or rather, Sorrow as a Platonic Idea.

A further word is also due on Schopenhauer's view on the hierarchy of the arts, since this links to his broader worldview. (This cursory review will also clarify Nietzsche's position on tragic art, to be discussed in the next essay, mainly with respect to the privileged role given to music). We have seen that the varying grades of the Will's objectification in the world proceeds from the lower forms of natural forces and inanimate objects, through plants, to animal life and culminating in humanity. So too does Schopenhauer create a hierarchy of the arts that mirrors this. In his view, architecture is the lowest of the arts, since it deals with hard matter (gravity, rigidity, hardness, weight) and has a utilitarian or practical use in a way that a certain conception of 'pure art' is assumed to lack. He then maintains that next in the hierarchy of the arts is horticulture and landscaping, which is akin to the plant life in the world.

Painting and sculpture come next, followed up by poetry and tragedy, reflecting the place of animal life in the Will's objectification. To offer a brief note on tragedy, Schopenhauer argued that the best tragedies are those where something catastrophic happens to a protagonist who did little or nothing wrong. In a rather morbid defence of this genre, he felt tragic narratives were important because they show us 'those powers that destroy happiness and life, and in such a way that the path to them is at any moment open even to us... Then, shuddering, we feel ourselves already in the midst of hell.'[53] Drawing on the notion of the sublime, Schopenhauer argued that tragedy can evoke a strange pleasure as we contemplate something threatening or destructive from a position of safety and distance. 'What gives to everything tragic... the characteristic tendency to the sublime, is the dawning of the knowledge that the world and life can afford us no true satisfaction, and are therefore not worth our attachment to them.'[54]

But Schopenhauer held up music as the highest of the arts, because it is not a representation of anything but is instead a 'copy of the Will itself.'[55] Music, therefore, can draw us closer to the nature of reality more effectively than any of the plastic or representational arts. By doing so, it tends to have the most powerful and universal effect on human beings, calibrating our souls and cultivating our emotions in unique ways. Schopenhauer believed that in music, 'the deepest recesses of our nature find expression.'[56] He particularly admired what he called 'absolute music' (i.e., music without words), because he believed words tend to bring the listener back into conceptual thought, whereas absolute music 'is an unconscious exercise in metaphysics in which the mind does not know it is philosophizing.'[57]

Contemporary philosopher of music Roger Scruton makes a similar point when he states: 'In some way [a great musical work] is setting an example of the higher life, inviting you to live and feel in a purer way, to free yourself from everyday pretenses. That is why it seems to speak with such authority: it is inviting you into another and higher world, a world in which life finds its fulfillment and its goals.'[58] Going further than Schopenhauer did, Scruton adds: 'We single out great works of art generally, and great works of music in particular, because they make a difference to our lives. They grant us an intimation of the depth and worthwhileness of things. Great works of art are the remedy for our metaphysical loneliness.'[59]

Even though Schopenhauer's hierarchy of the arts is rather strange, if not plainly dubious, he nevertheless provided an eloquent and sophisticated defence for the existential importance of art. As noted above, this is certainly no 'aesthetic justification' for existence. For him, art is, at best, a short-term palliative that eases the pains of life, and is vitally important for that reason as well as for the cognitive insights art can provide. But he never held up art as a solution to the problem of pessimism or a cure for the anguish of existence.

Asceticism

Schopenhauer's ethic of compassion, we have seen, doesn't offer much consolation (and can even result in an expanded sense of life's suffering); and aesthetic experience, while always welcome, is only ever fleeting. It follows that the problem of suffering remains the dominant problem of life with nothing so far suggesting that it could be overcome. On these grounds, Schopenhauer offered his defining response to the problem of suffering, which was, to embrace a life of resignation and renunciation. He asserted that the best thing we can do in a world that ought not exist is to negate life as far as possible, through ascetic practices. This is the only path, he claimed, 'if salvation is to be attained from an existence like ours.'[60]

What's more, through aesthetic experience we can gain some glimpse into what this overcoming might feel like if we were successful (i.e., a state without suffering). Like certain interpretations of Indian philosophy, Schopenhauer's fundamental response to the problem of suffering is *denial of the will*, that is, an attempt to overcome desire through renunciation and resignation – a turning away from bodily pleasures and material cravings. 'Thus [the ascetic] resorts to fasting, and even to self-castigation and self-torture, in order that, by constant privation and suffering, he may more and more break down and *kill the will* that he recognises and abhors as the source of his own suffering existence and of the world's'.[61] This hardly sounds uplifting, but in Schopenhauer's poetic way, he describes the spiritual state of the ascetic in terms that invite comparison (perhaps intentionally) to the state of nirvana achieved by the Buddha:

> we can infer how blessed must be the life of a man whose will is silenced for a few moments, as in the enjoyment of the beautiful, but for ever, indeed completely extinguished, except for the last glimmering spark that maintains the body and is extinguished with it. Such a man who, after many bitter struggles with his own nature, has at last completely conquered, is then left only as pure knowing being, as the undimmed mirror of the world. Nothing can distress or alarm him anymore; nothing can any longer move him; for he has cut all the thousand threads of willing which hold us bound to the world, and which as craving, fear, envy, and anger drag us here and there in constant pain.
>
> Then, instead of the restless pressure and effort; instead of the constant transition from desire to apprehension and from joy to sorrow; instead of the never-satisfied and never-dying hope that constitutes the life-dream of the man who wills, we see that peace that is higher than all reason, that ocean-like calmness of the spirit, that deep tranquillity, that unshakable confidence and serenity, whose mere reflection in the countenance, as depicted by Raphael and Correggio, is a complete and certain gospel. Only knowledge remains; the will has vanished.[62]

Schopenhauer's ethics of compassion highlights how the suffering of all is one's own suffering, and this provides an incentive to turn away from the world, since no mortal could possibly endure that insight. By negating life, one arrives at the only redemption. This helps propel the 'transition from virtue to asceticism'.[63] Born out of ethical outrage, one is left only to deny the Will and negate life. The agonal nature of existence must be overcome through ascesis. That is, one ought to abolish desire as a way of life.

Schopenhauer is correct to acknowledge that ascetic practices are evidently very hard to endure and only manageable, it seems, by unusually determined saints, mystics, and monks. Schopenhauer could not manage it himself (e.g., he liked to dine out most nights), nor did he live a particularly compassionate life, as noted earlier. He did, however, spend a lot of his time indulging in the arts, so it could be said that he conceded in practice what he could not grant in theory: an aesthetic justification for life.[64] Still, as if undertaking a pre-emptive attack on any charge of moral hypocrisy, he wrote:

> It is just as little necessary for the saint to be a philosopher as for the philosopher to be a saint; just as it is not necessary for a perfectly beautiful person to be a great sculptor, or for a great sculptor to be himself a beautiful person. In general, it is a strange demand on a moralist that he should commend no other virtue than that which he himself possesses.[65]

This concludes the outline of Schopenhauer's case for pessimism and his main responses to it. He felt that the best we can do in this world that ought not to exist is to negate life as far as possible: by denying the Will. However, he felt that almost everyone is too weak to do this. And so, we go on striving and suffering for what can never bring us happiness, trying to be compassionate, and otherwise simply enduring a life without value, punctuated with rare moments of aesthetic experience.

Can life be affirmed? Revaluing the value of suffering

The purpose of reviewing the full bleakness of Schopenhauer's thoroughgoing pessimism, as well as his main responses, was to gain a foothold for understanding Nietzsche's attempt to seek an 'affirmation of life'. Nietzsche's perspective builds upon Schopenhauer's position while reacting against it in important ways. In fact, it is no overstatement to say that Nietzsche's life project was to find a way of living with Schopenhauer's pessimistic diagnosis of life and the reality of unavoidable suffering. This was not merely a philosophical problem for Nietzsche. Ever since childhood, he was burdened with a range of health problems, including regular, severe migraines. His life was painful and difficult, he eventually went insane, and yet giving in to pessimism did not seem to be an option for him. Somehow, he wanted to find a way to embrace life, to be what he called a 'yea-sayer'.

To be clear, Nietzsche more or less accepted Schopenhauer's existential diagnosis and bleak portrait of the world, even though he would come to reject its metaphysics. He felt that pessimism was an unflinchingly honest and largely accurate perspective on existence. He acknowledged that 'the truth is terrible'[66] and that we are condemned to live in 'this horrible constellation of things'[67] which threatens to induce a 'nausea'[68] – a view starkly presented in his first book *The Birth of Tragedy* (1872).[69] He took seriously, and sat on the brink of accepting, the 'Wisdom of Silenus' – that 'What is best of all is... not to be born, not to *be*, to be *nothing*. But the second best... is – die soon.'[70] Nietzsche first read *World as Will and Representation* as a young man and deeply sympathised with its scathing indictment of life, seeing in Schopenhauer's book a 'mirror'[71] which reflected his own temperament in 'dreadful magnificence.'[72]

But, anticipating his critical stance, Nietzsche would assert that '[o]ne repays a teacher badly if one always remains nothing but a pupil.'[73] He ultimately refused to accept Schopenhauer's life-negating or life-denying conclusions, which Nietzsche would later characterise as a kind of nihilism – as the evaluation of the world as unworthy of being lived in. A note written in 1887 shows how he conceived of life-negating pessimism: 'A nihilist is a man who judges of the world as it is that it ought *not* to be, and of the world as it ought to be, that it does not exist. According to this view, existence (action, suffering, willing, feeling) has no meaning...'[74] This is precisely the view of nihilism that Nietzsche would reject.

If Nietzsche sometimes still retained the language of pessimism in his work, he would insist on 'a pessimism of strength.'[75] In short, he set out to explore whether, or to what extent, he could arrive at an alternative, *affirmative* prescription to Schopenhauer's pessimistic diagnosis. Nietzsche's central philosophical problem, which consumed him throughout his life, was whether life could be affirmed.[76] And Nietzsche did find a way for him to do this in what he called his aesthetic justification of existence. But how was he able to affirm a life, and a world, so full of suffering?

The clearest introduction to Nietzsche's philosophical strategy here is to ask a question: is suffering necessarily an evil? In characteristically provocative ways, he would come to answer this question in the negative, in surprising yet highly illuminating ways. Nietzsche had uncovered an unstated normative assumption in Schopenhauer's work, namely, that suffering was always and everywhere to be valued negatively. By seeing suffering everywhere, Schopenhauer inferred that existence itself was of negative value.

But Nietzsche did not grant Schopenhauer his premise, which meant the conclusions were now in question. When later in his life Nietzsche would come to speak of his philosophical project as being a 'revaluation of all values',[77] a prime focus of this revaluation was the place of suffering in life. Whereas it was convention, then and now, to treat suffering as necessarily of negative value, Nietzsche would invert this received assessment. If life was to be affirmed – if he was to somehow transcend Schopenhauer's world-negating conclusions – Nietzsche would need to find a new way of living with suffering.

Philosopher Bernard Reginster describes Nietzsche's approach to life in terms of 'overcoming resistance.'[78] If we define suffering as something that presents 'resistance' in our life – an impediment that makes us struggle for our highest values or an obstacle that must be overcome – then we can understand how Nietzsche came to place a positive value on suffering. Whereas Schopenhauer had posited a 'will to live' as the basis of existence, Nietzsche came to posit a 'will to power',[79] which should be understood as the will to overcome resistance on the path to achieving one's highest values. Nietzsche does not tell us *what* to value in our lives – other than proposing this second-order value of overcoming resistance. As Reginster explains:

> The doctrine of the will to power radically alters our conception of the role and significance of suffering in human existence. If, in particular, we take power – the overcoming of resistance – to be of value, then we can see easily how it can be the principle behind a revaluation of suffering. Indeed, if we value the overcoming of resistance, we must also value that resistance that is an ingredient of it. Since suffering is defined as resistance, we must also value suffering.[80]

This position should not be interpreted as merely the result of clever wordsmithing or sophistic philosophising by Nietzsche. It should be understood, in part, with reference to one of his most famous aphorisms: 'what does not kill me, makes me stronger'[81] – or in common parlance, 'no pain, no gain.' But Nietzsche's point goes deeper than this and revaluates suffering in a way that makes it a necessary and unavoidable part of the good. It can even be part of the beautiful, insofar as beauty implies giving form to the content of one's life through self-conscious stylisation of existence.

Nietzsche, therefore, seems to be undercutting Schopenhauer at the root. The latter's assumption was that desire – which is insatiable – is always and necessarily a 'lack', something regrettable, painful, an absence. It follows that the fulfillment of desire is always only temporarily satisfying. But are there other ways to frame our condition? Can there be an *affirmative* conception of desire? Nietzsche seems to be suggesting that, at least sometimes, desire should not be seen to imply a painful absence but rather a never-ending process of becoming.

The desire to make excellent music, for example, could be defined, from one perspective, as a painful lack, or, from another perspective, as the unfolding of life's meaning itself. Desire may not even desire the satisfaction of this type of longing, since being fully content with one's musical compositions might quench the thirst, kill the muse, dissolve the meaning and purpose in one's life. Perhaps the artist *should* remain dissatisfied as a part of being an artist. Or the lovers who ache in the chest at being apart – is that not the sweet stuff of life, such that it would be a category mistake to include such desires alongside the painful hunger of someone starving? The desire for a lover can be a pleasure so intense the body aches. Should we consider this a pain that always ought to be avoided? Might there be other desires that do not fit Schopenhauer's framework and thereby undercut his all-embracing pessimism?

Note that Nietzsche's perspective is a distinctly non-utilitarian one. He openly despised the British utilitarians (although, to be fair, he was contemptuous of most people and most schools of thought).[82] In *Thus Spake Zarathustra* (1883) the protagonist declares: 'Of what worth is happiness?... I ceased long since to strive for happiness'.[83] And in *Twilight of the Idols* (1889) he is even more explicit: 'Man does *not* strive for pleasure; only the Englishman does that.'[84] Nevertheless, in only an apparent contradiction he also noted that 'What is happiness? – The feeling that power *increases* – that a resistance is being overcome.'[85] I interpret this last comment in terms of 'meaning' rather than 'happiness'. Nietzsche was not really interested in organising life around the pursuit of happiness in terms of pleasure – perhaps because he felt happiness was so rarely achieved, and if so, only fleetingly. Instead, he wanted to live a passionate and meaningful life, and he argued that that involved creatively interpreting the struggles and sufferings of life in meaningful, even beautiful ways. In one of Nietzsche's most celebrated aphorisms, he declared: 'If we have our own *why* of life, we shall get along with almost any *how*.'[86] Meaningless suffering is the worst thing. But meaningful suffering – that, according to Nietzsche, is a large part of what the good life is composed of. Again, this does not imply a life of happiness. 'What do we long for at the sight of beauty?' Nietzsche asked. 'To be beautiful ourselves: we imagine we would be very happy if we were beautiful. – But that is an error.'[87]

Given that suffering cannot be avoided, there will always be resistances that must be overcome, so Nietzsche came to regard the affirmation of life in terms of *becoming*. Since the Will is insatiable (as per Schopenhauer's diagnosis), the correlative will to power knows no endpoint or consummation either, meaning that life is and ought to be a constant, ongoing process of valuation and revaluation in response to the diverse and ever-new resistances life throws in our way. On this point, the reasons why Nietzsche admired Heraclitus become evident – he who famously declared that 'all is flux.' Indeed, it is the constant overcoming of resistance in which life's meaning resides – and through that process of overcoming one can even *overcome oneself*, which encapsulates Nietzsche's idea of the *Übermensch*.

This line of reasoning ultimately led Nietzsche to develop a concept that neatly summarises his sought-after affirmation of life – the concept of *amor fati*. This is typically translated as 'love thy fate'.[88] Through the love of fate and by embracing rather than regretting the hardships of life, Nietzsche was able to announce a resounding 'yes' to life that abstained from all negation. 'Amor fati: Let that be my love henceforth. I do not want to wage war against what is ugly. I do not want to accuse;... someday I wish to be only a Yes-sayer!'[89] This attitude to life, he maintained, is the 'highest state that a philosopher can attain',[90] and represents the overcoming of life-negating pessimism. 'My formula for greatness in a human being is *amor fati*: that one wants nothing to be different, not forward, nor backward, not in all eternity. Not merely to bear what is necessary, still less conceal it... but *love* it.'[91]

Nietzsche, it seems, was calling on us to live without regrets (or, to use the term he employed, without *ressentiment*). What has happened has happened; what is, is. We should not let what cannot be avoided diminish our lives, for there is no 'after world' where we get a second chance at life. This is certainly not a recommendation to accept everything in life as it is, for some things, many things, can and should be changed. It is only what is *necessary* that ought to be embraced. We only have this one life to live, and there will necessarily be suffering, hard times, setbacks, disappointments, loss, pain, and eventually death. That is the human condition. We should learn how to say yes to life, warts and all, so to speak, which may require practice.[92] It may involve developing a new 'art of living' (a topic explored in later essays).[93]

Suppose, for example, you were wanting to go outside for a walk, but discover it is pouring with rain. Nietzsche would insist: do not waste your life regretting this unchangeable fact. Show the imagination to do something even better, overcome this obstacle – or alternatively, go for your walk despite the rain and embrace the exhilarating experience of the wild elements on your face and body. Love your fate, he implored. Creatively interpret and arrange the events of your life according to your chosen style – both in the smallest and most significant aspects of life. He reflected on his own situation: 'I want to learn more and more to see as beautiful what is necessary in things; then I shall be one of those who makes things beautiful.'[94] This can give rise to a process, as philosopher Guy Elgat argues, 'whereby the two arcs – loving the beautiful and beautifying out of love –

converge and reinforce each other, generating an ever deepening circle of learning and beautification.'[95]

Nietzsche would come to argue that we should embrace life *as if* we must live it eternally, over and over again, *in exactly the same way*. This is the meaning of Nietzsche's doctrine of the 'eternal recurrence' which was central to his worldview, dating from *Thus Spake Zarathustra*.[96] This is not, to be clear, a metaphysical doctrine – he didn't think we are *actually* going to live our lives over and over again. Rather it was a thought experiment designed to ensure we value life – our *only* life – even in its humble moments, and shape something good out of the suffering and resistances we inevitably face. We should seek to become powerful, Nietzsche maintained, not in the sense of leading armies, conquering territories, or accumulating material riches. He was urging us to become creators – artists of life who show the courage to give form or style to our suffering in our own, unique ways. This, in sum, is Nietzsche's fundamental existential-philosophical orientation, his 'pessimism of strength.' It is his main strategy for overcoming Schopenhauerian pessimism, thereby being able to affirm life and, perhaps, even see it as beautiful, by giving it a form of one's own.

Towards an aesthetic Buddhism? Life without music would be a mistake

To close this essay I wish to resituate the discussion in the context of the Will to Art. In doing so I will highlight a few places where there might be a nuanced and fruitful 'middle way' between some of the perspectives offered by Schopenhauer, Nietzsche, and Buddhism. I will introduce the term 'aesthetic Buddhism' to try to explain some of the intricacies of the position that I am developing in relation to the Will to Art. Whereas Schopenhauer summarised his life-negating pessimism with the assertion that 'life must be some form of mistake', the position I am offering is closer to Nietzsche's 'pessimism of strength' – exemplified by his poetic refinement of Schopenhauer: 'Life without music would be a mistake.'[97]

The Will to Art is an outlook that shares significant premises with Schopenhauer and Buddhism. At base, suffering lies at the heart of existence. Indeed, suffering is everywhere, internally and externally. On that basis, dealing with the problem of suffering is a primary task of living in the world. Furthermore, both Schopenhauer and Buddhism present a coherent defence of an ethics of compassion that derives from this view of suffering and desire. Buddhism is attractive to many people because it posits no 'creator being', no deity that demands worship, and instead it calls on individuals to critically explore their own spiritual condition with the tools of philosophical thought and critical inquiry. The same could be said of Schopenhauer.

But whereas Schopenhauer posited a will-to-live as the most fundamental aspect to nature – a blindly driving force without purpose or direction – I am exploring an interpretation that sees the underlying cosmological energy as *having* a purpose or telos. The Will to Art, as I have defined it, seeks beauty. This guiding ideal should be understood broadly, not as mere cosmetic ornamentation, but as the pleasurable experience of art and nature, the meaningful interaction with self, other, and world, and the undertaking and contemplation of aesthetic activity. Suffering is a consequence of the latent ideal of beauty struggling to realise itself through the Will to Art. According to this view, the universe is unfolding according to an aesthetic process of creative evolution, where matter becomes conscious and creative so that the cosmos is able to experience itself through art and aesthetic experience. In these early essays I am attempting to describe and defend this worldview. In later essays I will explore what implications might flow from it, in terms of personal existence as well as social, economic, and political organisation.[98]

I use the term 'aesthetic' in relation to this Buddhist-influenced outlook to make it clear that the Will to Art is not a metaphysical thesis in the spirit of Schopenhauer and Buddhism. I do not believe there is any *single* right way to view the cosmos and our place in it. Rather, there are only perspectives and interpretations that can both reveal and conceal certain insights about our complex situation and condition. This makes discourse and humility key features in philosophical and spiritual exploration – such that any answers to life's deepest mysteries lie only in the questioning itself. As I have noted before, I am offering the Will to Art as a grand narrative, but I acknowledge its narrativity – its roots in story. My motivation is not to arrive at a final truth of things. Instead, I am attempting a redescription of aspects of existence in ways that I hope reveal insights or provide useful tools for living.

One area where Schopenhauer ought to be challenged is in relation to his understanding of the ascetic negation of life. First of all, he misinterprets the spirit and practice of Buddhism here, and because Nietzsche seems to uncritically adopt Schopenhauer's view of Eastern philosophy, Nietzsche makes the same mistake. Schopenhauer defended extreme practices of self-denial, even self-torture, as means of breaking or denying the will. While there is certainly a place for practices of self-discipline in Buddhism, it is a mistake to treat such practices as life-negating. Without even turning to philosophy, one need only 'look and see' (as Wittgenstein would recommend) to discover that Buddhists seem to be some of the happiest and contented people around: warm, loving, compassionate, and thoroughly life affirming. So, Schopenhauer was wrong to move from the premise, 'existence is suffering', to the conclusion, 'life must be denied'.

Furthermore, the Buddhist philosophy of the 'middle way' suggests that asceticism need not imply any extreme or tortuous renunciation of all things good in the world, but instead calls for a practice of mindfulness. This is the delicate art of finding balance between too little of something and too much. Again, given that Nietzsche just adopted the Schopenhauerian view of asceticism, Nietzsche sometimes failed to see how practices of self-discipline and mindfulness, far from being life-negating, are in fact the most direct path to flourishing. I will undertake a critical examination of Nietzsche's view of asceticism in later essays, as well as his very limited embrace (if not outright denial) of any ethics of compassion.

Nevertheless, where Nietzsche clearly made an advance on Schopenhauer, and perhaps even on Buddhism, was in relation to desire. Whereas Schopenhauer treated desire as an inherently negative feature of life – the primary cause of suffering in the world – Nietzsche viewed desire as a necessary part of living a life of value and meaning. Desire is a form of resistance in our life, and overcoming resistance is positive if it is part of moving toward our highest values. Thus, Nietzsche was able to affirm life, even in a world where desire – the Will – is a cause of suffering. Acknowledging that there is such a thing as meaningful suffering is an important aspect of the Nietzschean affirmation of life. There are lessons here for us all.

This last point also draws us back into the realm of the aesthetic, in two central ways. First, Nietzsche looked at life as a sort of aesthetic project, something fundamentally indeterminate and malleable and therefore in need of shaping and stylisation. Through this aesthetic process we are called on to 'make the best' of our individual circumstances through conscious and deliberate endeavour. We should love our fate (*amor fati*), which means living creatively and without regrets. Indeed, Nietzsche urged us all to 'be the poet of our life'[99] – a perspective on self-creation to be explored further in due course. Secondly, Nietzsche held that art and aesthetic experience were amongst the most important ways of justifying existence and the world as aesthetic phenomena. This approach to life is not just about seeking temporary consolation through the nirvana of aesthetic contemplation, as Schopenhauer contended. It also involves the pursuit of a deeper and more enduring means of embracing life, even affirming life, in the face of everything. It is to such an aesthetic justification of existence that I will now turn for closer examination.

[1] On 'being' over 'having', see Erich Fromm, *To Have or to Be?* (New York: Continuum, 2007).
[2] For an excellent survey of pessimism, see Joshua Foa Dienstag, *Pessimism: Philosophy, Ethic, Spirit* (Princeton: Princeton University Press, 2006).
[3] See Sophia Vasalou, *Schopenhauer and the Aesthetic Standpoint: Philosophy as a Practice of the Sublime* (Cambridge: Cambridge University Press, 2015) pp.1-2.
[4] Friedrich Nietzsche, *The Birth of Tragedy*, trans. Walter Kaufmann (New York: Vintage, 1967), p. 17 (emphasis removed).
[5] Arthur Schopenhauer, *The World as Will and Representation: Vol. I* (New York: Dover, 1969).
[6] See Samuel Alexander, 'Creative Evolution and the "Will to Art"', in this collection of essays. The full set will be posted here: http://samuelalexander.info/s-m-p-l-c-t-y-ecological-civilisation-and-the-will-to-art/ (accessed 10 May 2023).
[7] Here I am paraphrasing what Schopenhauer said about interpreting his own work. See Schopenhauer, *The World as Will and Representation*, note 5, p. xv.
[8] I have chosen to capitalise 'Will' to emphasise the Schopenhauerian reading of this term and clarify any distinction, when necessary, between 'willing' in the conventional sense.
[9] Schopenhauer, *The World as Will and Representation*, note 5, p. 195.
[10] Ibid, p. 117.
[11] Ibid, p. 164.
[12] Ibid, p. 183.
[13] Ibid, p. 31.
[14] Ibid, p. 196.
[15] Ibid.
[16] Ibid, p. 195.
[17] Schopenhauer's understanding of the Will's objectification in nature can be interpreted as an early version of what today is called panpsychism.
[18] Vasalou, *Schopenhauer*, note 3, p. 16.
[19] Schopenhauer, *The World as Will and Representation*, note 5, p. 165.
[20] Ibid, p. 111.
[21] Ibid, p. 196 (emphasis removed).
[22] Quoted in Eike Brock, 'Life is Suffering: On Schopenhauer's and Nietzsche's Philosophical Engagement with Suffering' in Katia Hay and Leonel Ribeiro dos Santos (eds) *Nietzsche, German Idealism, and its Critics* (Berlin: De Gruyter, 2015), p. 196.
[23] Schopenhauer, *The World as Will and Representation*, note 5, p. 319.
[24] Ibid, p. 196.
[25] Ibid, p. 164.
[26] Ibid, p. 353
[27] Ibid, p. 196.
[28] See generally, Stephen Cross, *Schopenhauer's Encounter with Indian Thought: Representation and Will and Their Indian Parallels* (Honolulu: University of Hawai'i Press, 2013). With respect to the *Upanishads*, Schopenhauer noted 'it is the most profitable and sublime reading that is possible in the world; it has been the consolation of my life and will be that of my death.' Cross, *Schopenhauer's Encounter,* note 28, p. 2.

[29] Although Schopenhauer and Nietzsche were no fans of Christianity, it is worth pointing out that the central image of the Christian religion is the crucifix – an image of suffering that is arguably unrivalled.
[30] Schopenhauer, *The World as Will and Representation*, note 5, p. 635.
[31] Ibid, p. 164.
[32] Terry Eagleton, *Ideology of the Aesthetic* (Oxford: Blackwell, 1990), p. 158.
[33] See Terry Eagleton, *Culture and the Death of God* (New Haven: Yale University Press, 2015), p. 154.
[34] Schopenhauer, *The World as Will and Representation*, note 5, p. 309.
[35] Ibid.
[36] See Samuel Alexander, 'Camus on Art and Revolt: Overcoming Nihilism in an Absurd Universe', in this collection of essays. See link in note 6.
[37] Quoted in Brock, 'Life is Suffering', note 22, p. 196.
[38] Schopenhauer, *The World as Will and Representation*, note 5, p. 366.
[39] David Holbrook, *Gustav Mahler and the Courage to Be* (Plymouth: Clarke, Doble, and Brendon, 1975), p. 29.
[40] Schopenhauer, *The World as Will and Representation*, note 5, p. 576.
[41] Arthur Schopenhauer, *Essays and Aphorisms* (London: Penguin, 2004), p. 53.
[42] Arthur Schopenhauer, *On the Basis of Morality* (Indianapolis: Bobbs-Merrill, 1965), p. 166.
[43] See Brock, 'Life is Suffering', note 22, p. 200.
[44] Ibid, p. 197.
[45] Schopenhauer, *The World as Will and Representation*, note 5, p. 411.
[46] Ibid, p. 178-9.
[47] Ibid, p. 178.
[48] Ibid, p. 179.
[49] Ibid, p. 198.
[50] Ibid, p. 364.
[51] Note that this deconstructs and inverts Plato's critique of art. Plato had argued that art was dangerous because it was illusory, mere representation of a representation, and could lead people to erroneous thinking. Here, on the other hand, Schopenhauer argues that this was 'one of the best known errors of that great man'. Art does not lead to falsity but gives us the clearest and most direct access to the true reality. Schopenhauer, *The World as Will and Representation*, note 5, p. 212.
[52] See Samuel Alexander, 'Art Against Empire: Marcuse on the Aesthetics of Revolt' in this collection of essays. See link in note 6.
[53] Schopenhauer, *The World as Will and Representation*, note 5, p. 255.
[54] Ibid, pp. 433-4.
[55] Ibid, p. 257.
[56] Ibid, p. 256.
[57] Ibid, p. 264.
[58] Roger Scruton, *The Soul of the World* (Princeton: Princeton University Press, 2016), p 167.
[59] Ibid, p. 173.
[60] Schopenhauer, *The World as Will and Representation*, note 5, p. 405.
[61] Ibid, p. 382 (my emphasis).
[62] Ibid, p. 411.
[63] Ibid, p. 380 (emphasis removed).

[64] See Brock, 'Life is Suffering', note 22, p. 201.
[65] Schopenhauer, *The World as Will and Representation*, note 5, p. 383.
[66] Friedrich Nietzsche, *The Anti-Christ, Ecce Homo, Twilight of the Idols, and Other Writings*, edited by Aaron Ridley and Judith Norman (Cambridge: Cambridge University Press, 2005) p. 144 (emphasis removed). See also, Brian Leiter, 'Truth is Terrible' (2018) *Journal of Nietzsche Studies* 49(2): pp. 151-173.
[67] See Brock, 'Life is Suffering', note 22, p. 198.
[68] Nietzsche, *The Birth of Tragedy*, note 4, p. 60.
[69] Nietzsche, *The Birth of Tragedy*, note 4.
[70] Ibid, p. 42.
[71] See Brock, 'Life is Suffering', note 22, p. 190.
[72] Ibid.
[73] Friedrich Nietzsche, *Basic Writings of Nietzsche* (edited by Walter Kaufmann) (New York: Modern Library, 2000), p. 676. See also, Friedrich Nietzsche, *The Will to Power* (New York: Vintage, 1968), p. 521, where Nietzsche wrote: 'I grasped that my instinct went in the opposite direction from Schopenhauer's: toward a *justification of life*' (emphasis in original).
[74] Nietzsche, *Will to Power*, note 73, p. 318.
[75] See Nietzsche, *Birth*, note 4, p. 17.
[76] Bernard Reginster, *The Affirmation of Life* (Cambridge, MA: Harvard University Press, 2006).
[77] Nietzsche, *Will to Power*, note 73.
[78] Reginster, *Affirmation of Life*, note 76, p. 132.
[79] Nietzsche, *Will to Power*, note 73.
[80] Reginster, *Affirmation of Life*, note 76, p. 177.
[81] Friedrich Nietzsche, *Why I Am So Wise* (London: Penguin, 2004), p. 73.
[82] See generally, Jonny Anomaly 'Nietzsche's Critique of Utilitarianism' *Journal of Nietzsche Studies* (2005) 29: pp. 1-15.
[83] Friedrich Nietzsche, *Thus Spake Zarathustra* (Herron Books, undated edition), p. 209.
[84] Friedrich Nietzsche, 'Twilight of the Idols', in Walter Kaufmann (ed), *The Portable Nietzsche* (London: Penguin, 1988) p. 468.
[85] Quoted in Reginster, *Affirmation*, note 76, p. 195.
[86] Nietzsche, 'Twilight', note 84, p. 468.
[87] Quoted in Aaron Ridley, *Nietzsche on Art and Literature* (New York: Routledge, 2007) p. 58.
[88] See Friedrich Nietzsche, *The Gay Science*, trans. Walter Kaufmann (New York: Vintage Books, 1974). p. 223.
[89] Ibid.
[90] See Brock, 'Life is Suffering', note 22, pp. 205-6.
[91] Nietzsche, 'Ecce Homo', in *Basic Writing*, note 73, p. 714.
[92] See Guy Elgat, '*Amor* Fati as Practice: How to Love Fate' *Southern Journal of Philosophy* (2016) 54(2): pp. 174-188.
[93] See Samuel Alexander, 'Giving Birth to Oneself: Ethics as an "Aesthetics of Existence"', in this collection of essays. See link in note 6.
[94] Nietzsche, *Gay Science*, note 88, p. 223.
[95] See Elgat, *Amor Fati*, note 92, p. 187.

[96] For a discussion, see Alexander Nehamas, *Nietzsche: Life as Literature* (Cambridge, MA: Harvard University Press, 1985), Ch.5.
[97] Nietzsche, *Why I Am So Wise*, note 81, p. 76.
[98] While my arguments hereafter make most sense in relation to the grounding concept of the Will to Art, I should also note that the essays do not stand or fall on that basis. That is, one could reject the grand narrative of the aesthetic universe I am presenting and still accept the specific aesthetic arguments of each essay.
[99] Nietzsche, *Gay Science*, note 88, p. 240.

‘We possess *art* lest we *perish of the truth*.’

– **Friedrich Nietzsche**

ESSAY FOUR

AN AESTHETIC JUSTIFICATION OF EXISTENCE: THE REDEMPTIVE FUNCTION OF ART

In *The Birth of Tragedy*, published in 1872, Friedrich Nietzsche made his intriguing but ambiguous claim that it is only as an 'aesthetic phenomenon' that existence and the world could be justified.[1] Given that the Will to Art can be understood as a perspective offering such an aesthetic justification, in this essay I offer a close reading of Nietzsche's strange pronouncement. Indeed, several of these collected essays can be understood as an attempt to grapple, directly or indirectly, with Nietzsche's aestheticism, even though I will end up traversing territories where Nietzsche himself never roamed and often drawing conclusions with which he would not have agreed.

A number of perplexing issues immediately present themselves. What does it mean to interpret life as an 'aesthetic phenomenon'? As opposed to what? Who said that existence and the world needed to be justified? And what might 'justification' in this context mean?[2] The short answer is simply that Nietzsche would turn to art and aesthetics as a strategy for resolving the problems of personal existence – but that raises more questions than answers. The first task is to understand *what is meant* by an aesthetic justification, after which this justificatory approach can be assessed.

I begin with the question of justification itself – which will also serve as a brief review of the previous essay. Nietzsche, like so many before him and since, felt that the world was in need of justification because, overall, existence is horrible and the 'truth is terrible'.[3] Writing at this stage under the heavy influence of the 'great pessimist', Arthur Schopenhauer, Nietzsche saw that suffering lay at the molten core of the human condition and that our species had no prospect of obtaining lasting happiness. Our desires are insatiable, leaving us forever dissatisfied and blindly striving, and all around us we see creatures living in conditions of pain and anxiety, engaged in a violent struggle for existence. The pessimist wonders whether it would be better if the world did not exist at all.

Schopenhauer's philosophical response to the human situation was to turn away from life, to try to deny the desiring Will in every way possible and live a life of extreme asceticism (a strategy Schopenhauer was never able to practice successfully). Contra Schopenhauer, Nietzsche was not willing to negate life in world-denying resignation. Instead, he spent his intellectual energies pursuing strategies of life affirmation,[4] which drew him toward art and the aesthetic. 'Truth is ugly,' he admitted in a famous unpublished note of 1888. 'We possess *art* lest we *perish of the truth*.'[5] This is a perspective that rewards close examination.

Religious justification of existence

To suffer without understanding why renders life cruel and absurd. It demands an explanation. Historically, the most prominent way of answering these existential questions involved turning to religion – what could be called the *religious justification* of existence. From this perspective, God created the universe and all that is in it, including human beings, and so our purpose on Earth is to live our lives in glorification of our benevolent Creator. But here we are still faced with the so-called 'problem of evil'.[6] Human existence is full of tragic elements, often caused by deliberate human action, and the question arises why an omnipotent and benevolent God would create such a universe and allow such horrible things to happen, often to seemingly innocent beings.

This has led to various 'theodicies' that seek to justify the existence of evil and suffering in a world allegedly created by a loving God. Either God could have created a different world, but did not, in which case he is not good; or else God was unable to create a better universe, in which case he is not omnipotent. To resolve these tensions, some theologians argue that the gift of 'free will' implies that humans must have the *freedom to be evil* (otherwise we would not be truly free). In other words, God must have determined in his infinite wisdom that the full range of freedoms was worth the suffering that such unconstrained freedom of the will could produce. Some might respond, blasphemously, that this infinitely wise reasoning is contestable – couldn't God have made us *mostly free* but incapable of extreme evil? But assuming for argument's sake that the justification of evil on the grounds of free will is sound, it still does not explain or justify why evils exist that are *not* a result of free and deliberate human action (e.g., why some children are born with cancer or why natural disasters occur that are beyond human cause or responsibility).

Some theologians deal with these issues simply by asserting that God has a divine plan, and that he works in mysterious ways. Seemingly inexplicable evils could be understood as God 'testing' human beings in ways that build moral character, even if we may not fully understand or appreciate the subtle benefits of this spiritual process. We are called to have faith. What we perceive as evil, is not really evil. Seventeenth-century philosopher Gottfried Leibniz offered one of the most famous examples of this line of reasoning when he argued that 'God would not permit evil unless he could procure a greater good from evil',[7] concluding that the world that exists must be the best of all possible worlds, because God made it. '[A]ll the imperfections we think we find in the world only originate from our ignorance.'[8]

Another argument in the same vein maintains that earthly suffering is justifiable because, in the end, the good and the chaste will enjoy eternal peace and happiness in the blissful Kingdom of God. This would render our finite, worldly suffering negligible in the grand scheme of things. Without going further into the intricacies of religious apologetics, the basic nature of a religious justification of existence is clear enough. The justification is God – and God is good. For believers, at least, this view can offer some existential consolation.

Of course, the rather significant problem with this line of reasoning, according to Nietzsche, is that 'God is dead'.[9] The existential implications of this will be explored in the next essay. For now, I simply note that, in an increasingly secular age, many people will not find the religious justification of existence plausible – and even theists might doubt specific arguments given in response to the problem of evil. Inexplicable and seemingly meaningless suffering exists in a world without God, and those people who are philosophically inclined are left trying to determine whether there are any good reasons why this might be so. In the absence of such reasons, one might be tempted to despair, concluding that there is no justification for existence.

Rational justification of existence

Religion, however, does not exhaust our options. Another approach is to seek a justification grounded in *human reason*. From this perspective, we may not be God's creatures, but we do seem to be rational animals, and it is conceivable that we might be able to deduce a rational or metaphysical justification of existence, even in the absence of God. This could be called the *rational justification* of existence.

Although there are various forms of this philosophical endeavour, the analytical approach is based on the assumption that humans ordinarily live in an ever-changing world of 'appearance', but if we apply our rational faculties correctly, we can discern an underlying metaphysical 'reality'. The paradigmatic example is given by Plato in his Myth of the Cave.[10] In this allegory, prisoners are in a cave, chained up with their backs to the light, such that they can only see shadows dancing on the wall in front of them. To these prisoners, the shadows constitute their entire experienced reality, but little do they know it is all an illusion. They are deceived, merely living in a world of appearance. Fortunately, so the argument goes, sound philosophical reasoning can break us free from the chains of such illusions, whereupon we can leave the cave and begin to see the world as it *really is*.

According to Plato, the true metaphysical reality that underlies appearances is composed of 'Ideas' (or 'Forms') that are eternal and unchanging. For example, all worldly examples of horses are mere imperfect representations of the Platonic Idea of a Horse. Or a rose might provide a particular example of beauty, but this is an imperfect and transitory example of Beauty itself. Through careful philosophical analysis humans can come to know this reality, and thereby commune, in a sense, with the eternal world. Not only that, understanding the metaphysical structure of reality can provide insight into moral questions about how we ought to live our lives. In doing so we might discover that life has meaning and purpose, despite the suffering it entails. Through the mouthpiece of Socrates – the 'prototype of the theoretical optimist'[11] – we are advised that no one *willingly* does wrong, given that wrongdoing only hurts the soul of the perpetrator, and only people living in ignorance would willingly hurt themselves. It could be said, then, that before the Christian had 'sin', the rationalist had 'error'. On that basis, the injunction to 'know thyself' could guide human beings toward a meaningful life of truth, goodness, and beauty. Similarly, the Stoics declared that nothing can hurt the soul of the wise person, for it is the interpretation of events that cause harm, not the events themselves. The purpose of life is to live virtuously, and this can be done even in harsh conditions. This led many ancient philosophers to conclude that existence is justified on rational grounds.

Around two thousand years later the attempt to grasp ultimate reality can be found in most of the Enlightenment philosophers too, who variously professed to have discovered 'first principles' or 'philosophical foundations' upon which the edifice of human knowledge could be based. Like Plato, these rationalistic philosophers attempted to offer worldly insight, consolation, and orientation by grounding an understanding of existence in human reason. Immanuel Kant, for instance, claimed that he had rationally derived the 'moral law', putting forth his 'categorical imperative' as the guiding principle of ethical action. He assumed this principle would be accepted by all human beings who correctly exercised their rational faculties.[12] It is no coincidence, perhaps, that Kant's categorical imperative functions in a remarkably similar way to Christianity's 'golden rule' (love thy neighbour as thyself). This suggests that both religious and Enlightenment thinkers were searching for guidance of some form – or at least some metaphysical comfort.[13]

It is scarcely necessary to point out that Nietzsche was as scornful of the metaphysicians as he was of the theologians. In his inimitable way, he sought to undermine the confidence that Plato and the Enlightenment philosophers had in reason, by exposing the ways their rationalistic hopes and metaphysical aspirations had fallen short. Not only had they failed historically, but Nietzsche would assert that the nature of the human condition is such that we will forever be denied access to eternal or objectively verifiable truths – and it is sheer hubris to think otherwise. Truth is but a 'mobile army of metaphors,'[14] by which he meant that our outlooks or perspectives on the world are always partial, value-laden, and inevitably shaped by contestable and unstable assumptions. Even the meanings of the words used to philosophise are inclined to shift and change over time, making the notion of static, objective, and eternal 'truths' highly problematic from an epistemological perspective.

I will not rehearse Nietzsche's complex epistemological or moral critiques, other than to note that he sparked a crisis of confidence in the Western philosophic tradition which endures to this day. Contemporary philosophical literatures on deconstruction, neo-pragmatism, anti-realism, social constructionism, literary theory, and post-structuralism, among others, point to the profound influence that he has had over the last century in intellectual and cultural domains well beyond philosophy departments. Pejoratively dismissed as 'postmodernism' by those who don't like the conclusions, metaphysicians today are a dying species and hopes for objective foundations for knowledge seem to be fading. Although there are, and always have been, counter-Nietzscheans who are desperate to avoid his unsettling conclusions, in my view there does not seem to be any antidote to his critique of rationalistic metaphysics. I will be proceeding on that basis.

Aesthetic justification of existence

So where does all this leave us? For post-Nietzscheans, we are left without either religious or rational-metaphysical justifications for suffering. It is on this basis that Nietzsche offered his *aesthetic justification* of existence. This gives rise to questions about what it could mean to describe existence as an aesthetic phenomenon and in what sense this could be said to 'justify' an existence that is full of suffering.

At once it should be clear that an aesthetic justification of existence could not be objectively demonstrable by way of reason or founded upon 'first principles', for that is precisely the rationalistic or metaphysical strategy that Nietzsche forcefully rejected as implausible. He was not claiming to have uncovered eternal truths about an underlying metaphysical or religious reality, for he did not believe reason could penetrate to the depths of being in that way. Instead, we can assume he was offering a justification in a different sense – but what sense was that?

The best way to understand Nietzsche here is to see that he was not offering a rationalistic justification but a psychological or existential one. That is, he was trying to describe or engage existence and the world in ways that might *induce a positive evaluation towards life* – an affective attachment – despite the prevalence of suffering.[15] In this sense, an aesthetic justification is not a proposition of truth or a cognitive evaluation but is instead, as philosopher Daniel Came argues, 'epistemologically neutral'.[16] The success or failure of an aesthetic justification does not depend on whether it can be shown to be based on objective philosophical foundations. Rather, it depends on whether it can induce a subjective affirmation of life in ways that religious and metaphysical justifications, which are no longer credible for post-Nietzscheans, cannot. After all, having a positive affective attitude toward something (e.g., life) does not necessitate being able to cognitively demonstrate that it has *objectively demonstrable value*.[17] It just needs to work psychologically or existentially – which is to say, it needs to induce life affirmation, *in fact*.

As noted above, Nietzsche's defining strategy here is to hold up art and the aesthetic dimensions of existence as the means for affirming life in a godless world, despite the suffering life inevitably entails. He does not suggest, however, that art has objective value. Art has value because it 'makes life possible and worth living,'[18] through its capacity to transform the 'eternal suffering'[19] and 'horror and absurdity of existence'[20] into 'notions with which one can live.'[21] Indeed, Nietzsche seems to suggest that, in the absence of other forms of justification, the contemplation or creation of art, and the imposition of aesthetic form on one's life, are the best means available for keeping despair or resignation at bay. Rejecting an aesthetic justification risks inviting despair, for one could find oneself in a world of suffering but without tools for negotiating or managing such an absurd existence.

Nietzsche-scholars have interpreted the meaning of this strategy in various ways. An aesthetic justification could involve arguing that art offers *therapeutic* consolation or catharsis that makes life bearable. In this light, suffering is mitigated or dissolved as we lose ourselves in aesthetic experience.[22] Furthermore, just as 'roses burst from thorny bushes,'[23] art can provide something of a middle world between human beings and the terrors of existence, transfiguring the original chaos of nature into something humanly digestible. That chaos can be rendered tolerable, more comprehensible, meaningful, perhaps even beautiful. Through the drive for beauty

– or what I am calling the Will to Art – Nietzsche claimed human beings are able to 'develop uniquely from within, to transform and assimilate the past and the alien, to recover completely from wounds, to redeem loses, and to refashion broken forms.'[24] From this perspective, art is a uniquely powerful form of existential medicine.[25]

Moreover, art promises to be somehow redemptive and healing, driven by a 'primordial desire for *Schein*,'[26] (i.e., for illusion, dreaming, veiling, etc.), even if Nietzsche stated that any aesthetic redemption through *Schein* must be a continuous process rather than a final destination. Philosopher Aaron Ridley interprets Nietzsche as suggesting that 'art can present us with truth in such a manner that we do not perish of it,'[27] a position that Nietzsche developed in his theory of tragic art (to be considered in the next section). Schopenhauer also presented a version of this aesthetic response to suffering, but concluded that, at best, aesthetic experience could provide temporary relief from the onslaught of life and could not, in the end, provide any sort of justification. Nietzsche's approach to aesthetic experience was not so fleeting or transitory in its significance. He argued that art can actually have permanent effects on how we see the world and live within it. As Daniel Came writes:

> We do not value works of art only for the experience they induce while we are in direct contact with them. Rather, we value art in some measure because we are able to take something of the aesthetic mindset embodied in the work into our lives. In this way, art is capable of placing our existence in a new and different light.[28]

God may be dead for many people today and objective truths may be inaccessible to creatures like ourselves, but for some people the spiritual needs to which religion and metaphysics catered might remain. Is it only a matter of time before we abandon such needs as the out-dated relic of an untenable worldview? Or are those spiritual needs somehow reflective of our condition as self-creating agents who are in search of meaning in an ambiguous and absurd universe? Artistic creation and aesthetic experience, Nietzsche suggested, may offer the only form of redemption available.

This approach, however, has not been without its critics. T.S. Eliot, for example, rejected as a mere conjuring trick any attempt to find a substitute for religious faith in art: '[N]othing in this world or the next is a substitute for anything else; and if you find that you must do without something, such as religious faith or philosophic belief, then you must just do without it.'[29] Similarly, Gordon Graham writes that 'the abandonment of religion, it seems, must mean the permanent disenchantment of the world, and any ambition on the part of art to remedy this is doomed to failure.'[30]

In his book *Culture and the Death of God* (2015), Terry Eagleton reviews the various historical attempts to find a substitute for God in art and culture and finds them all, in various ways, inadequate.[31]

But Nietzsche demonstrated through his own life and outlook that an aesthetic remedy was not doomed to failure, and others since Nietzsche have discovered the same existential possibility. In the words of celebrated American poet Wallace Stevens: 'After one has abandoned a belief in God, poetry is the essence which takes its place as life's redemption.'[32] And even if art is not a perfect or exact substitute, one might be inclined to agree with philosopher Andrew Huddleston that '[a]n art without God may be better than a conventional religion with a dead God.'[33] The early theorist of aestheticism, Walter Pater, described human beings as 'under the sentence of death but with a sort of indefinite reprieve':

> Some spend this interval in listlessness, some in high passions, the wisest, at least among 'the children of this world', in art and song. For our one chance lies in expanding that interval, in getting as many pulsations as possible into the given time... For art comes to you proposing frankly to give nothing but the highest quality to your moments as they pass, and simply for those moment's sake.[34]

Beyond consolation or therapy, Nietzsche also recognised that great art could induce an *energising* or *intoxicating* affect, one that could inspire an affirmation of life by giving us courage, motivation, or determination to persevere – despite everything. Like Schopenhauer, Nietzsche gave special pride of place to music in the hierarchy of the arts: 'Has it been noticed that music liberates the spirit? gives wing to thought? That one becomes more a philosopher the more one becomes a musician?'[35] There is a dual aspect to this type of aesthetic affect: it can justify the struggle of existence through its energising, intoxicating effects, but it can also inspire the artist to be creative, thus potentially creating more art objects that can justify existence. 'For art to exist...' Nietzsche wrote, 'a certain physiological precondition is indispensable: *intoxication*... The essence of intoxication is the feeling of plenitude and increased energy.'[36] In a later essay it will be seen that poet-philosopher Friedrich Schiller posited two categories of beauty – 'melting beauty' and 'energising beauty' – which can be understood as reflecting different ways art can impact on our condition and for different purposes.[37]

Elsewhere Nietzsche asserted that the condition of aesthetic intoxication 'release[s] artistic powers in us',[38] which enables us to 'infuse a transfiguration and fullness into things.'[39] Walter Pater would celebrate aesthetic experience with similar zeal, maintaining that '[t]o burn always with this hard, gemlike flame, to maintain this ecstasy, is success in life.'[40] This language clearly reflects a spiritual or even mystical orientation toward aesthetic experience. But again, even if art cannot provide an exact substitute for religion, which is true, perhaps it is nevertheless fair to draw a strong analogy here between art and religion, especially if, as Nietzsche himself would say, 'a "thing" is the sum of its effects, synthetically united by a concept.'[41] In other words, if the intoxicating or consolatory effects of art and religion can be similar, then the analogy is not entirely misplaced.

Nietzsche believed that art can even make us aware of, or shape, our deepest values and interests in life,[42] placing a heavy responsibility both on artists and on those who wish to engage art authentically. The intoxicating effects of aesthetic experience, as well as being rapturous and exhilarating, can also be threatening and terrifying. This is because art can bring us in touch with what Nietzsche would call the primordial oneness or *Ur-Eine*, which is the foundational principle of the *Artisten-Metaphysik* presented in *The Birth of Tragedy*.[43] The *Ur-Eine* can be understood as Nietzsche's aesthetic restatement of Schopenhauer's concept of the Will. But being in touch with this underlying cosmic force through art can be a painful and contradictory experience. Because of this possibility – 'which could destroy us' or lead to a 'state of mystical self-abnegation and oneness'[44] – the consolatory and redemptive requirement for *Schein* remains a necessary part of aesthetic justification. Any mystical insight that is attained, however, cannot be described or communicated through words, concepts, or the plastic and representational arts. At best, it can be conveyed through the non-representational medium of music, a point to which we will return when discussing Nietzsche's theory of tragedy.[45]

The therapeutic and energising approaches to aesthetic experience can also be interpreted from either the spectator view (contemplating art can justify existence) or from a creator-artist perspective (creating works of art can justify existence). Philosopher Bernard Reginster argues that, for Nietzsche, the significance of art lies 'less in its *products* than in the *creative activity* by which they are produced.'[46] Through art and creative activity, Nietzsche suggests we have the tools with which human beings can find meaning in our suffering, rendering life, if not rationally justifiable, then at least bearable, perhaps even fulfilling. Another interpretation of the aesthetic justification has been offered by Nietzsche-scholar Jeffery Church, who contends that Nietzsche was calling on us to reverentially hold up great artists as exemplars. This reverence is deserved, Church proposes, on the grounds that the beauty of their creative lives can inspire us to embrace the challenge of living creatively, provoking us to consider whether we, ourselves, might have unfilled creative potentials still to be realised.[47]

The underlying feature in all these approaches involves viewing the world, ourselves included, as aesthetic phenomena – as artworks. From this perspective, we have the capacity and perhaps responsibility to give style or form to the content of our lives and to interpret existence according to certain aesthetic (as opposed to religious or rational) criteria. Nietzsche is inviting us to see if, in doing so, we can affirm life, and I contend his invitation is worth accepting. This would justify art not for the sake of art, but for the sake of life.

The various approaches to aesthetic justification outlined above are not mutually exclusive and indeed can be seen as mutually supportive. If what matters is 'what works' (i.e., what induces a love of life) then it may be that one strategy is effective for one person and a different strategy for another. In this sense, Nietzsche's aesthetic living strategy need not be judged in terms of right or wrong but simply in terms of effectiveness or ineffectiveness. In any case, I am not seeking to defend a *particular interpretation* of Nietzsche, but instead to draw on Nietzsche's work to explore the question of whether life can or cannot be justified in aesthetic terms. It will also be clear that I have not yet attempted to *evaluate* the aesthetic justifications outlined above. Rather, I have simply attempted to *define* what type of justification I am talking about.

Apollo vs. Dionysus: Nietzsche's theory of tragic art

According to Nietzsche, an aesthetic justification of existence, if successful, can affirm existence and thereby the world, thus avoiding Schopenhauer's pessimistic negation of life. But what is the *process* by which this affirmation might present itself to us as a live option? How can we actually live in a world of suffering without degenerating into pessimistic resignation and withdrawal? Not, I have suggested, by looking to religion or relying on pure reason. But even from a post-religious and post-metaphysical standpoint, the suffering and absurdity of life still needs a response or justification. Nietzsche felt that the ancient Greeks had found such a solution in art and the aesthetic interpretation of life – especially in and through the works of the great tragedians. Let us consider this view in more detail.

The Birth of Tragedy celebrated Greek tragedy as the highest and most important art form. In ways to be discussed below, Nietzsche held that tragic art offered a supreme synthesis of the two fundamental, yet opposed, aesthetic forces or art-drives in the world – the Apollonian and the Dionysian. After making (or rather asserting) that case as an historical thesis, he turned his attention to Europe of the nineteenth century. His contemporary thesis was to suggest that, in the cultural abyss created by a dying Christianity, and given the loss of faith in Enlightenment rationalism, the modern age, like ancient Greece, could only hope to find redemption in the aesthetic realm. At this stage, writing in 1872, Nietzsche looked to the operas of Richard Wagner as promising the 'rebirth of tragedy' – as being on the cusp of provoking a regeneration of German culture. The last third of *The Birth of Tragedy* is essentially a gushing celebration of Wagner's music, a celebration, it should be noted, that Nietzsche would eventually regret as he came to see Wagner as being unable to fulfill Germany's hopes.[48]

But even as his infatuation with Wagner waned and soured, Nietzsche remained of the view that tragedy, and great art more generally, ought to be judged according to the extent to which it helped affirm life and regenerate culture. This was a position that Nietzsche held throughout his life, except for an ambiguous, temporary departure in his 'positivistic' book, *Human, All-Too-Human* (1878), in which he tended toward seeing any hope for humanity residing in science. But he returned to his aestheticism thereafter. In an unpublished note that neatly captures his perspective, Nietzsche writes: 'There is no such thing as pessimistic art – Art affirms.'[49]

A key question that has troubled many philosophers of art is why human beings would voluntarily sit through the dark and catastrophic narratives of tragic theatre. More perplexing still is how we could possibly *enjoy* a tragedy that depicts such profound pain and suffering. Tragedies almost always involve a protagonist becoming embroiled in ghastly and violent circumstances, often without any moral culpability, and usually leading to death or at least demise. Real life is grim enough, so why choose to be a spectator on life's harsh realities via tragic theatre? Wouldn't that just invite a debilitating gloom if not despair? On the contrary, far from inducing despair, resignation, or withdrawal, Nietzsche saw tragic art as offering a mixture of therapy, consolation, education, and, at its best, it even an intoxicating energy for life. Tragic art has value, as noted earlier, because it 'makes life possible and worth living,'[50] through its capacity to transform the 'eternal suffering'[51] and the 'horror and absurdity of existence'[52] into 'notions with which one can live.'[53]

How can it achieve this? Nietzsche worried that if we looked at life too *directly,* we would see that suffering was so pervasive that we would risk being destroyed by the ugliness and horror of the truth; by the terrors of existence and the primordial pain that lies at the base of reality. We would be tempted, as Schopenhauer was, to degenerate into a 'longing for a Buddhist negation of the will'[54] or even contemplate suicide as a practical escape.[55] Seeking to avoid precisely those conclusions, and indeed searching for a way to affirm life, Nietzsche explored how art and aesthetic devices and techniques could somehow shield us from the full impact and harshness of reality, somehow blunting the sharp the edge of the truth. In a phrase already quoted, Nietzsche held: 'We possess *art* lest we *perish of the truth*.'[56]

Does this reduce art merely to palliative fantasies, distractions, and illusions? There might be room for a purely *therapeutic* role for art in some contexts – e.g., distracting ourselves with beauty in the darkest of moods just to get through the day. Generally, however, Nietzsche did not justify tragic art merely on palliative grounds and we should beware of the risks of such escapist aestheticism.[57] In his boldest moods, Nietzsche insisted that we should be able to look at the truth, face to face. In his very rare critiques of art, he even suggested that art might be something human beings might need to grow out of as we better learn to manage the full and nasty realities of the human situation. There was some risk, he felt, that arts merely 'soothe and heal' and this 'only provisionally, only for a moment; they even hinder [people] from working for a real improvement in their conditions by suspending and discharging in a palliative way the very passion which impels the discontented to action.'[58] However, Nietzsche did not maintain that critical position for long. His prevailing view was that the profound suffering inherent to the human condition could not be avoided and instead had to be managed. While the unavoidability of suffering reflects a view many Christians and Buddhists, for example, would also accept, Nietzsche believed the only way from 'no' to 'yes' was via the aesthetic. Art and beauty were the only means sufficient to the task.

Thus, Nietzsche found in Greek tragedy the energising power of affirmation, an aesthetic justification for existence. To understand the intricacies of his reasoning here we need to return to the figures of Apollo and Dionysus – the Greek gods that Nietzsche used throughout his work to symbolise two aspects of reality as well as two distinct categories of art.[59] He sometimes used these signifiers loosely, and not always clearly or consistently. Apollo is variously used to signify illusion, appearance, dreaming, beauty, individuation, order, and reason. Apollonian art is exemplified by sculpture, which seeks to represent the world by shaping materials into significant form. On the other hand, Dionysus is variously used to signify underlying or primordial reality, desire, the sublime, unity, intoxication, and chaos. Dionysian art is exemplified by music, which is a medium through which the inner world or fundamental reality can be expressed and experienced most directly, in ways the 'plastic arts' cannot achieve through representation.

Although there is some risk of misrepresentation, it is tempting to roughly translate Apollo into Schopenhauer's notion of 'representation' (the phenomenal world) and Dionysus into Schopenhauer's 'Will' (the primal reality underlying appearances). In the end, however, Nietzsche offered us an original theory, and so *The Birth of Tragedy* should be read on its own terms and not merely as a restatement of Schopenhauer. Most importantly, these two thinkers can be distinguished by noting that the first principle of Nietzsche's *Artisten-Metaphysics* – the 'primordial oneness' or the *Ur-Eine* – is an aesthetic principle, whereas Schopenhauer's 'Will' is a non-aesthetic foundation.[60] This is of some importance because Nietzsche's aesthetic justification of existence can only be derived from an aesthetic foundation – a foundation that permits an affective transition from a 'no' to 'yes' in life. In contrast, one might argue that an aesthetic justification cannot be derived from Schopenhauer's non-aesthetic grounding.

Nietzsche held that Apollonian art belonged to the Homeric period of Greek culture, through which the Greeks overcame or at any rate greatly 'veiled'[61] the horrors of life. Their myths and stories were used as a 'prophylactic'[62] medium through which the agonal character of life could be 'transfigured'[63] in such a way that seduced the Greeks to embrace life: 'existence under the bright light of such gods is regarded as desirable in itself.'[64] He often referred to this form of art – 'the Apollonian impulse to beauty'[65] – as embodying 'illusion' or even a 'lie', and linked it thematically to the symbolism of Apollo as dreaming, sooth-saying, and wish-fulfillment. Dream images presented through art offer 'the aesthetically sensitive [person]... an interpretation of life, and by reflecting on those processes [we] train ourselves for life.'[66] Indeed, 'art saves [us], and through art – life'.[67]

Nevertheless, it would be wrong to interpret Nietzsche here as suggesting that the Greeks overcame pessimism through sentimental fantasy or by merely *looking away* from the harsh side of life. Instead, he spoke of Apollonian art as 'transform[ing] the most terrible things by the joy in mere appearance and in redemption through mere appearance.'[68] Art is able to do this by giving 'significant form' to suffering in ways that can render it, if not beautiful, then at least tolerable. As philosopher Julian Young writes in his book on Nietzsche's aesthetics, 'we may say that beauty lies not in *what* is represented but the *way* it is represented,'[69] which reflects Nietzsche's statement that art is able to move us because it can induce 'delight in beautiful forms.'[70] Young goes on to explain that it is in this way that beauty can co-exist with the terrible, since the content of art can be transfigured by its form.

This aesthetic redemption, then, is not about looking away, which would be a merely cosmetic, escapist, or cowardly 'solution' – that is, no solution at all. Instead, Apollonian art involves looking at the harsh side of life, albeit through the mitigating lens of art. This casts something of an illusory veil over suffering in order to make it digestible and stop us from being paralysed by it. Thus, we are able to learn from and live with the truth, without perishing from it. Nietzsche insisted that in Apollonian art, 'beauty triumphs over the suffering inherent in life.'[71]

In this context, Young believes that the appropriate way to transition from the analysis of art to that of life is to infer, in the shadow of pessimism, that Nietzsche reinterpreted life through an Apollonian lens as something that is terrible but magnificent. 'Such an outlook,' Young adds, 'while not flinching from acknowledging that Hector suffered a terrible fate at the hands of Achilles, nonetheless focuses upon the beauty of its heroes, their powerfulness, courage, the sheen of their armour, their "style."'[72] We might each have our own books, poems, songs, or films that have given noble form to bleak content, and yet, despite the bleakness, we somehow come away from such artistic depictions edified, humbled, more compassionate, and perhaps with a new energy or courage to meet one's own challenges in life. '[E]ven misery,' Nietzsche proclaimed, 'could become a source of enjoyment solely through art.'[73] But the only way this aesthetic process can work is if we are sufficiently distanced from the inner reality of the suffering being depicted. Without the Apollonian veil, we might be at risk of perishing from the truth.

Although this form of art did not look away from the terrible side of life, it did, as we have seen, place a veil over it. For this reason Nietzsche was inclined to describe it as a form of 'lying.'[74] On the one hand, the content required aesthetic stylisation or falsification – a degree of self-deception – in order to render it existentially digestible. On the other hand, the Greeks *knew* that they were not being presented with direct access to the full truth of things, such that an element of self-deception lay at the heart of the Apollonian solution to pessimism. Only through this illusory or fictional veil could we ever enjoy tragic theatre, because this veil is what gives us the necessary distance to view the tragic narrative and events in aesthetic terms. Indeed, Nietzsche worried that the Greeks were 'so plagued by a delight in telling stories that it was hard for them to desist from lies and deception in the course of everyday life – just as all poetical people take delight in lying, a delight that is moreover quiet innocent.'[75]

Young is surely right to see that the Apollonian 'veiling' of the horrors of life as a rather fragile prophylactic against pessimism: 'Though it may seduce one into a general valuing of life, it's "superficiality" appears to leave one unprotected against suffering that thrusts itself upon one in a personal and unavoidable way.'[76] Furthermore, if the necessary element in the Apollonian is transfiguration of the truth in some way, this doesn't seem to deal with the problem of Schopenhauerian pessimism – which holds that the truth of existence is so horrible that it requires life negation. From a purely Apollonian perspective, therefore, it would seem that, in truth, life is not worth living and the only way of making it bearable is through aesthetic or artistic 'lies'.

On this basis, Nietzsche turned to the Dionysian element, as presented in Greek tragedy. If we return to the loose parallels here between Schopenhauerian representation and Will, we can say that Apollonian art re-presents the world of phenomena in a stylised way, whereas the Dionysian form seeks to get at what lies behind phenomena – the Will – giving rise to the 'tragic effect', the sublime – 'the artistic taming of the horrible...'[77] Nietzsche argued that, in tragic theatre, we feel most connected to the chorus – the music that accompanied the acting on stage. And recall from the previous essay that, in Schopenhauerian terms, music was a 'copy of the Will itself',[78] a view with which Nietzsche was broadly sympathetic. We somehow derive pleasure out of voluntarily subjecting ourselves to the ghastly nature of things through tragedy. So, whereas the Apollonian disguised the truth, the Dionysian gives more direct access, but we find it tolerable partly due to the tragic effect of the sublime.

If the Dionysian process brings the audience closer to reality, why didn't the Greeks degenerate into unmanageable psychic gloom or perish from being exposed to the tragic truths of existence? Nietzsche's response was that the Dionysian elements of tragic art deliver us from individuation, as we lose ourselves in the intoxicated state of aesthetic experience and find ourselves communing with the 'primordial oneness' or the *Ur-Eine*. 'We really are for a brief moment primordial being itself, feeling its raging desire for existence and joy in existence'[79] He adds: 'In spite of fear and pity, we are the happy living beings, not as individuals, but as the *one* living being, with whose creative joy we are united.'[80] And again, it is music – the chorus – that Nietzsche argues brings us most effectively into that rapturous or exuberant condition. Through this Dionysian element in tragic art, we are exposed to a higher state of existence, and find that life is not only bearable but enlivening, even intoxicating. Through deep, ecstatic if also unsettling aesthetic experiences, we can be given the energy and courage to go on living. In short: 'Life without music would be a mistake.'[81]

Nevertheless, we must then call on the soothsaying Apollo to provide the veil, or else we might be destroyed by our communion with the suffering inherent in primordial reality. '[H]ere the *Apollonian* power erupts to restore the almost shattered individual with the healing balm of blissful illusion.'[82] Although Nietzsche clearly identifies with the Dionysian, he ultimately accepts that human beings need both the Dionysian and the Apollonian elements in art, in a form of unstable synthesis, in order to find existence and the world 'justifiable'.

The redemptive function of art

This analysis has attempted to explain why the Apollonian can help transfigure suffering by giving 'significant form' the content of life, beautifying it to make it bearable. Further, the Dionysian can intoxicate in ways that can lead us to 'lose ourselves', such that the egotistical perspective which seems to privilege our personal suffering gets transcended as we identify with the *Ur-Eine*. Nietzsche's aesthetic justification of existence, however, is not merely about addressing the problem of suffering through the contemplation of art. As noted earlier, his other perspective on the problem, and probably his most fundamental perspective, is to consider the prospects of an aesthetic justification not as a spectator but as an active creator – and a creator not so much of a work of art, but as a creator or producer of *oneself*. In an important passage, Nietzsche wrote:

> Art is above and before all supposed to *beautify* life, thus make *us* ourselves endurable, if possible pleasing to others... Then, art is supposed to *conceal* or *reinterpret* everything ugly, those painful, dreadful, disgusting things which, all efforts notwithstanding, in accord with the origin of human nature again and again insist on breaking forth.... After this great, indeed immense task of art, what is usually termed art, *that of the work of art,* is merely an *appendage.* A man who feels within himself an excess of such beautifying, concealing and reinterpreting powers will in the end seek to discharge this excess in works of art as well; so, under the right circumstances, will an entire people. – Now, however, we usually start with art where we should end with it, cling hold of it by its tail and believe that the art of the work of art is the true art out of which life is to be improved and transformed – fools that we are![83]

What Nietzsche is saying here is that the real project of the artist is not a physical or external work of art (e.g., a painting, a sculpture, an opera, etc) but the shaping and reshaping of oneself, with the raw materials of one's life. The external work of art can emerge out of this, but the primary and preceding project is, or ought to be, the work of artists on their own subjectivities. Nietzsche noted with disapproval that 'the ceaseless desire to create on the part of the artist, together with his ceaseless observation of the world outside of himself, prevent him from becoming better and more beautiful as a person, that is to say from creating *himself*.'[84] And the most important element in self-fashioning is the revaluation of suffering, which is needed for the affirmation of life.

For these reasons, Nietzsche concluded that it is only as an aesthetic phenomenon that existence and the world can be justified. The passage from *The Birth of Tragedy* where this statement is found is worth quoting in full:

> Insofar as the subject is the artist, however, he has already been released from his individual will, and has become, as it were, the medium through which the one truly existent subject celebrates his release in appearance. For to our humiliation and exaltation, one thing above all must be clear to us. The entire comedy of art is neither performed for our betterment or education nor are we the true authors of this art world. On the contrary, we may assume that we are merely images and artistic projections for the true author, and that we have our highest dignity in our significance as works of art – for it is only as an *aesthetic phenomenon* that existence and the world are eternally *justified* – while of course our consciousness of our own significance hardly differs from that which the soldiers painted on canvas have of the battle represented on it. Thus all our knowledge of art is basically quite illusory, because as knowing beings we are not one and identical with that being which, as the sole author and spectator of this comedy of art, prepares a perpetual entertainment for itself.[85]

We see, then, that Nietzsche's defining position on the human condition was that art and the aesthetic present us with a revitalising antidote to the life-negating implications of Schopenhauer's pessimism, but only by leaving us with the terrifying but exhilarating burden of self-creation.

---

[1] Friedrich Nietzsche, *The Birth of Tragedy*, trans. Walter Kaufmann (New York: Vintage, 1967), p. 22, p. 143.

[2] Further examinations of these questions include, Daniel Came, 'The Aesthetic Justification of Existence' in K. Ansell-Pearson (ed.) *A Companion to Nietzsche* (Oxford: Blackwell, 2006), pp. 41-57; Jeffery Church, 'The Aesthetic Justification of Existence: Nietzsche on the Beauty of Exemplary Lives' *Journal of Nietzsche Studies* (2015) 46(3): pp. 289-307; Brian Leiter, 'Truth is Terrible' (2018) *Journal of Nietzsche Studies* 49(2): pp. 151-173; Stephen Halliwell, 'Justifying the World as an Aesthetic Phenomenon' (2018) *The Cambridge Classical Journal* 64: pp. 91-112. Book length treatments exploring Nietzsche's aesthetics and aestheticism, include Alexander Nehamas, *Nietzsche:*

Life as Literature (Cambridge, MA: Harvard University Press, 1985); Bernard Reginster, *The Affirmation of Life* (Cambridge, MA: Harvard University Press, 2006); Aaron Ridley, *Nietzsche on Art and Literature* (New York: Routledge, 2007); Julian Young, *Nietzsche's Philosophy of Art* (Cambridge: Cambridge University Press, 2009); Daniel Came (ed.), *Nietzsche on Art and Life* (Oxford: Oxford University Press, 2014).

[3] Friedrich Nietzsche, *The Anti-Christ, Ecce Homo, Twilight of the Idols, and Other Writings*, edited by Aaron Ridley and Judith Norman (Cambridge: Cambridge University Press, 2005) p. 144 (emphasis removed). See also, Leiter, note 2. The terribleness of truth was both a philosophical problem for Nietzsche and a very personal one, since from a young age he suffered regular and acute migraines that plagued him throughout his life. That said, the distinction between a philosophical problem and a problem of lived existence was, for Nietzsche, a distinction he sought to undermine.

[4] Reginster, *Affirmation*, note 2.

[5] Friedrich Nietzsche, *The Will to Power* (New York: Vintage, 1968), p. 435.

[6] See Marilyn McCord Adams and Robert Merrihew Adams (eds) *The Problem of Evil* (Oxford: Oxford University Press, 1990).

[7] Cited in Robert Weninger, *Sublime Conclusions: Last Man Narratives from Apocalypse to the Death of God* (Cambridge: Legenda, 2017), p. 11.

[8] Ibid. Voltaire famously mocked this line of reasoning in his novelette, *Candide*.

[9] Friedrich Nietzsche, *The Gay Science*, trans. Walter Kaufmann (New York: Vintage Books, 1974). p. 108

[10] Plato, *The Republic* (London: Penguin, 1955), Book VII.

[11] Nietzsche, *Birth*, note 1, Sect. 15.

[12] Immanuel Kant, *The Metaphysics of Morals* (Cambridge: Cambridge University Press, 1996).

[13] It should be noted that many Enlightenment thinkers also identified as Christian, using reason not to reject religion but to challenge how it was traditionally understood. Often the goal was more about limiting the role of religion in politics than rejecting it in culture. See Terry Eagleton, *Culture and the Death of God* (New Haven: Yale University Press, 2015).

[14] Friedrich Nietzsche, 'On Truth and Lies in an Extra-Moral Sense' in Walter Kaufmann (ed), *The Portable Nietzsche* (London: Penguin, 1988) p. 46.

[15] See Came, 'The Aesthetic Justification', note 2.

[16] Came, note 2, p. 42 (emphasis removed).

[17] Ibid, p. 47.

[18] Nietzsche, *Birth*, note 1, Sect. 1.

[19] Ibid, Sect. 9.

[20] Ibid, Sect. 7.

[21] Ibid.

[22] As Freud wrote: 'This life imposed on us is too hard for us to bear: it brings too much pain, too many disappointments, too many insoluble problems. If we are to ensure it, we cannot do without palliative measures... Of such measures there are perhaps three kinds: powerful distractions, which can cause us to make light of our misery, substitutive satisfactions, which diminish it, and intoxicants, which anesthetize us to it. Something of this sort is indispensable.' Sigmund Freud, *Civilization and its Discontents* (London: Penguin, 2004), pp. 14-15. Freud added that 'Voltaire has distractions in mind when he ends *Candide* with the advice that one should cultivate

one's garden; another such distraction is scholarly activity.' Ibid, *Civilization*, p. 15. With respect to the present discussion of art, Freud made the following relevant remark: 'Substitutive satisfactions, such as art affords, are illusions that contrast with reality, but they are not, for this reason, any less effective psychically, thanks to the tole that the imagination has assumed in mental life.' Ibid, *Civilization,* p.15.

[23] Nietzsche, *Birth*, note 1, Sect. 3.

[24] Ibid, pp. 79-80. See also, Alain de Botton and John Armstrong, *Art as Therapy* (London: Phaidon, 2016).

[25] See Shaun McNiff, *Art as Medicine: Creating a Therapy of the Imagination* (Boulder: Shambhala, 1992).

[26] Quoted in John Fredrick Humphrey, 'Friedrich Nietzsche's *Artisten-Metaphysik* (Doctoral thesis, Graduate Faculty of Political and Social Science, New School for Social Research, 1992) p. 10.

[27]Aaron Ridley, 'Perishing of the Truth: Nietzsche's Aesthetic Prophylactics' *British Journal of Aesthetics* 50(4): p. 427.

[28] Came, The Aesthetic Justification', note 2, p. 50

[29] T.S. Eliot, 'Arnold and Pater' in T.S Eliot, *Selected* Essays (Faber and Faber, 1932).

[30] Gordon Graham, *The Re-Enchantment of the World: Art versus Religion* (Oxford: Oxford University Press, 2007) p. 186.

[31] See Eagleton, *Culture and the Death of God*, note 13, p.13.

[32] Wallace Stevens, *Opus Posthumous* (Vintage, 1990 [1957]).

[33] Andrew Huddleston, 'Introduction' to Andrew Huddleston, *Art's Highest Calling: The Religion of Art in a Secular Age* (forthcoming). I am also indebted to Huddleston for the quotes from Eliot and Stevens above.

[34] Walter Pater, *The Renaissance: Studies in Art and Poetry* (Oxford: Oxford University Press, 1986), p. 153.

[35] Friedrich Nietzsche, 'The Case of Wagner' in *Basic Writings of Nietzsche* (edited by Walter Kaufmann) (New York: Modern Library, 2000), p.614.

[36] Fredrich Nietzsche, *Twilight of the Idols* (Harmondsworth: Penguin, 1990), Sect. 8.

[37] See Friedrich Schiller, *Letters on the Aesthetic Education of Man*, in Friedrich Shiller, *Essays*, eds. Walter Hinderer and Daniel Dahlstrom (New York: Continuum, 2005), p. 133.

[38] Nietzsche, *The Will to Power*, note 5, p. 420.

[39] Ibid, p. 421.

[40] In Huddleston, ch2 p17

[41] Nietzsche, *The Will to Power*, note 5, p. 296.

[42] See Raymond Guess, 'Art and Theodicy' in Raymond Guess, *Morality, Culture, and History* (Cambridge: Cambridge University Press, 199) p. 87.

[43] See Humphrey, 'Friedrich Nietzsche's *Artisten-Metaphysik*', note 26.

[44] Nietzsche, *Birth*, note 1, Sect. 5.

[45] Nietzsche described Schopenhauer's distinction between the plastic arts and the musical arts as 'the most important insight of aesthetics'. See Humphrey, 'Fredrich Nietzsche', note 26, p. 235.

[46] Bernard Reginster, 'Art and Affirmation' in Came (ed.), *Nietzsche on Art and Life*, note 2, p. 25.

[47] See Church, 'The Aesthetic Justification', note 2.

[48] See the new preface to the *Birth of Tragedy*, called 'An Attempt at Self-Criticism', which Nietzsche wrote in 1886. See Nietzsche, note 1.

[49] Nietzsche, *Will to Power*, note 5, p. 435.
[50] See note 18.
[51] See note 19.
[52] See note 20.
[53] See note 21.
[54] Nietzsche, *Birth*, note 1, p. 59.
[55] Ibid, Sect. 15.
[56] Nietzsche, *The Will to Power*, note 5.
[57] See, e.g., Joris-Karl Huysmans, *Against Nature* (London: Penguin, 2022). See my essay, 'Making Art While the World Weeps: Political Reflections on Aesthetics' in this collection of essays. The full set will be posted here: http://samuelalexander.info/s-m-p-l-c-t-y-ecological-civilisation-and-the-will-to-art/ (accessed 10 May 2023).
[58] Friedrich Nietzsche, *Human, All-Too-Human* (Cambridge: Cambridge University Press, 1996), I.148.
[59] The following discussion is indebted to the illuminating analyses offered in the literature referenced in note 2, especially Young, *Nietzsche's Philosophy of Art*; Ridley, *Nietzsche on Art and Literature*; and Came (ed), *Nietzsche on Art and Life*.
[60] See Humphrey, 'Fredrich Nietzsche', note 26.
[61] Nietzsche, *Birth*, note 1, Sect. 3
[62] Ibid, Sect. 21.
[63] Ibid, Sect. 22.
[64] Ibid, Sect. 3.
[65] Ibid, Sect. 4.
[66] Ibid, Sect. 1.
[67] Ibid, Sect. 7.
[68] Ibid, Sect. 4.
[69] Young, *Nietzsche's Philosophy of Art*, note 2, p. 43.
[70] Nietzsche, *Birth*, note 1, Sect. 16.
[71] Young, *Nietzsche's Philosophy of Art*, note 2, p. 43.
[72] Ibid.
[73] Nietzsche, *Human*, note 44, I: 154.
[74] Nietzsche, *Birth*, note 1, Sect. 16.
[75] Nietzsche, *Human*, note 44, I: 154.
[76] Young, *Nietzsche's Philosophy of Art*, note 2, p. 45.
[77] Nietzsche, *Birth*, note 1, Sect. 7
[78] Arthur Schopenhauer, *The World as Will and Representation: Vol. I* (New York: Dover, 1969), p. 257.
[79] Nietzsche, *Birth*, note 1, Sect. 17.
[80] Ibid.
[81] Friedrich Nietzsche, 'Twilight of the Idols' in Walter Kaufmann (ed), *The Portable Nietzsche* (London: Penguin, 1988) p. 471. I've amended the translation to accord with the most common one. Kaufmann's translation reads: 'Without music, life would be an error.'
[82] Nietzsche, *Birth*, note 1, Sect. 21.
[83] Nietzsche, *Human*, note 44, I: 174.
[84] Ibid, II: 102.
[85] Nietzsche, *Birth*, note 1, Sect. 6.

‘The demands of rebellion are really, in part, aesthetic demands.’

‘I *rebel* – therefore we *exist*.’

– **Albert Camus**

ESSAY FIVE

CAMUS ON ART AND REVOLT: OVERCOMING NIHILISM IN AN ABSURD UNIVERSE

In the last two essays I addressed the problem of suffering face to face, exploring the prospect of justifying existence as an aesthetic phenomenon. I did this by engaging the philosophies of Arthur Schopenhauer and Friedrich Nietzsche. Even if an aesthetic justification were deemed plausible, however, one might still object that the case offered so far remains very incomplete. The problem of suffering may have been mitigated through the Nietzschean strategy of 'revaluation', but the spectre of nihilism remains – preliminarily defined as the threat of meaninglessness. This problem emerges in the void left by an absent God and in epistemological conditions where 'reason' is unable to provide any objective or transcendental purpose to our lives.

Here we see another aspect of philosophical pessimism that calls into question any affirmation of life. Schopenhauer framed this in terms of the 'blind striving' and 'purposelessness' of the Will, but in previous essays this point was passed over rather too quickly, as I focussed on the problem of insatiable desire and the pain this brings. To suffer is bad enough; to suffer incessantly is worse; but to suffer without meaning or purpose presents us with a spiritual or existential burden that threatens to be unbearable.

In this essay I will grapple with these issues by drawing on the writings of Algerian-born, French philosopher, Albert Camus. I begin by exploring how Camus formulated the problem of nihilism (drawing on Nietzsche), and how he suggested we could respond to our 'absurd' condition with an aesthetics of revolt.[1] After laying these foundations, I examine how Camus developed the themes of absurdity, rebellion, and solidarity in his novel *The Plague* (1947). We will see that Camus, like Nietzsche, concluded that the human condition was something that could *only* be justified as an aesthetic phenomenon. Nevertheless, Camus developed Nietzsche's position in unique and insightful ways, most notably by highlighting an aesthetic justification for human solidarity. This communitarian ethic was, of course, rather starkly absent (or at least very obscure) in Nietzsche.

Nihilism and the death of God

First stated in his book *The Gay Science,* Nietzsche's proclamation that 'God is dead'[2] was voiced through the character of a 'madman', an outsider to polite society who was brave enough to say what most people were not even prepared to think. God is dead and we have killed him – or rather, Nietzsche found God dead in the hearts and minds of his contemporaries. People were suffering from this lost faith, from a spiritual malady the nature of which was difficult to grasp. For those of us today who are living in the cultures shaped by the Christian tradition, it is fair to wonder whether this metaphysical rupture has still not been fully understood. It represents a Copernican revolution in Western culture, with theological implications that are increasingly hard to deny but which seem so difficult for many people to accept. Even when a post-religious perspective on the human situation is embraced, it can leave one disoriented in a universe that is now empty of transcendental value.

Nietzsche saw this fundamental shift in the spiritual orientation of Europeans as something that was both 'terrible'[3] but also 'hopeful'.[4] Secularisation was a shift that he declared would unfold over coming centuries, as Western civilisation came to discover or accept that it no longer found religious belief credible. This cataclysmic change meant that the moral and cultural foundations of European society were undercut, such that the norms, values, and constitutive myths which had maintained the fabric of society for two thousand years started unravelling. Because of this, Nietzsche saw that the edifice of Western civilisation lay on the precipice of a degeneration into nihilism.

Managing this civilisational trauma involved trying to come to terms with the loss of a meaningful cosmological narrative to structure human existence. This induced a spiritual malaise that Nietzsche diagnosed so bluntly, and which still presents modernity with a problem in need of a response. As frightful as this problem may have been, I noted that Nietzsche also found it 'hopeful'. Rather than living our lives in the shadow of a non-existent Christian 'after world' – a situation Nietzsche found life-negating – he saw the death of God as an opportunity to reorientate our finite selves toward the world in which we actually find ourselves living. According to Nietzsche, this was part of what any genuine affirmation of life required, a complete commitment to living well in *this* life, in *this* world.

In the wake of God's death, however, Camus claimed that we find ourselves in a universe that is 'absurd'. Or rather, our *condition* is absurd, in the sense that we demand a meaning or purpose to our lives but find the universe wholly indifferent to this demand. Unsure of how to live, it is tempting to seek metaphysical guidance 'out there', beyond ourselves. This represents an inarticulate yearning for some external or transcendent justification that would validate our lives and give them significance and order.

In Camus' play *Caligula,* the character Cherea expresses this spiritual need in the following terms:

> To lose one's life is no great matter; when the time comes I'll have the courage to lose mine. But what's intolerable is to see one's life being drained of meaning, to be told there's no reason for existing. A man can't live without some reason for living... all I wish is to regain some peace of mind in a world that has regained a meaning. What spurs me on is not ambition but fear, my very reasonable fear of that inhuman vision in which my life means no more than a speck of dust.[5]

As the existentialists of the twentieth century were fond of highlighting, this threat of meaninglessness can be experienced as a dread. It can be all the more terrible because, as dread settles upon the human consciousness, one worries that the desolate mood will never pass. It is quite understandable that, in the face of death, humans seek some explanation for their existence – some theodicy to justify lives that so often are full of suffering. Historically our species has turned to religion in an attempt to deal with this existential problem, and with respect to Europe, this strategy now has two thousand years of Judeo-Christian legacy. In the affluent West today, faith in God continues to fade, even as socio-religious practices remain. But questions about death, suffering, and the meaning of life re-emerge ever more acutely. We want our lives to make sense in the face of death and suffering, but Camus' point was that they do not make sense.

How are we to live, then, in a universe that seems to be fundamentally indifferent to our very existence? Camus maintained that '[t]he absurd is born of this confrontation between the human need [for meaning, happiness, understanding] and the unreasonable silence of the world.'[6] We find ourselves in a universe without purpose or inherent meaning, of brute 'facticity' to use Martin Heidegger's term, from which the existentialist philosophers inferred that the world-in-itself is irredeemably pointless. If there is to be a purpose to our lives, we should not expect the world to provide it.

This realisation provokes the question of how, or even whether, to keep on living in a world without any transcendental value. Like Sisyphus in Ancient Greek myth, every day human beings are condemned to roll the rock up the hill, only to see it roll down the other side, whereupon our meaningless labours and struggles must begin again. We don't know why we have been cursed with a life governed by accident, chance, and finitude. Our situation is absurd, and we suffer because of it. Despair looms on the horizon. Indeed, if the spiritual condition of modernity could be summarised in a sentence, one might say that we moderns have come to a lucid sense of desolation, of being abandoned by a God that was never there in the first place. In the words of cultural anthropologist Ernest Becker, human beings must feel like 'a locus of value in a world of meaning'[7] or suffer the most profound despair.

In the twentieth century, this existential angst was expressed powerfully in the works of writers like Sartre, Beckett, and Kafka. Camus made his own contributions to this literature, especially in his landmark essay *The Myth of Sisyphus* (1942), addressing what he considered philosophy's most serious problem: the problem of suicide.[8] Is a life without transcendental appeal even worth living? Note how this question can be raised irrespective of the answer given to the problem of suffering discussed in the last two essays. We might be able to 'revalue' the place of suffering in our lives, and affirm life despite or even because of that suffering, only to find that the problem of meaning – or meaninglessness – remains.

Of course, many people still go through the motions, engaging themselves in the mundane rituals of daily life as if their lives had some cosmic, religious significance. The implausibility of religion can be too much to bear, too threatening to one's self-image as a child of God. Some people simply deny the death of God or look away in metaphysical hope. Others are driven to make a 'leap of faith', remaining in the ruts of religious belief in fear of breaking free. They live in accordance with some religious code that was invented by other people, in a different time. In this way the individual responsibility for *choosing* how to live is deferred or abandoned. One might certainly recognise the *appeal* of metaphysical comfort – to see religious guidance and justification as *desirable*. But Camus maintained that this was ultimately a dishonest orientation toward life. There is an unbridgeable gulf between our desires for transcendent values and the universe as it is.

Nevertheless, even as Christianity in the West continues its fall, there remains a temptation to leap into some new faith, some surrogate form of transcendence. Camus saw humanity being easily seduced by dogmatic forms of rationalism, which he considered 'the most widespread spiritual attitude of our enlightened age.'[9] Industrial capitalism can be understood as the economics of rationalism, and perhaps it is no surprise that the materialistic search for meaning through consumption and accumulation coincided with the emergence of the nihilistic threat that began crawling across Europe from around 1800. The Newtonian universe of matter governed by physical laws had become the dominant worldview, and Darwin would explain why human beings were not creatures of God but descendants of the great apes, distinguished from other animals by our ability to be aware of and imagine our own death. In a post-Darwinian cosmological order, there was no longer any need for a religious hypothesis, given that science and reason were providing some of the answers that humans were seeking.

But Camus considered the metaphysical faith in reason, like religious faith, to be a form of 'philosophical suicide'.[10] He wrote: 'During the last century, man cast off the fetters of religion', but 'hardly was he free... when he created new and utterly intolerable chains.'[11] In Camus' view, to have faith in rationality – faith in the ability of reason to answer life's most pressing questions – was little more than religiosity in a new guise. This was not in any way an 'irrationalist' position that rejected argument, logic, and evidence. It was simply an acknowledgement that Reason – with a capital R – was unable to provide objective truths about the human condition or guidance on how to live. Camus believed that to suggest otherwise was either deceitful or deluded – or both.

So what if someone were to give up *all* hope in metaphysical comfort? This was the unsettling question Camus explored throughout his life with unusual eloquence and insight. By giving up any hope for an objective justification for our lives and the promise of some future, 'other-worldly' redemption, Camus believed that we are returned to the eternally present, here and now, and yet we now find ourselves transcendentally homeless and alone:

> A world that can be defended even with bad reasons is a familiar world... On the other hand, in a universe suddenly divested of illusions and lights, man feels an alien, a stranger. His exile is without remedy since he is deprived of the memory of a lost home or the hope of a promised land. This divorce between man and his life, the actor and his setting, is properly the feeling of absurdity.[12]

Living without absolute values

In a world without God or objective truth, it follows that there are no 'absolute values' – at least, none that are rationally knowable or demonstrable to human beings. Upon that premise, Fyodor Dostoyevsky's character Ivan, in *The Brothers Karamazov* (1880), notoriously inferred that 'everything is permitted' and that nothing really matters. Conversely, French psychoanalyst Jacques Lacan would suggest a counter-thesis, that 'nothing is permitted', given that there is no external authority to grant such permission.[13] This is the problem of nihilism concisely defined. Nietzsche foresaw that humanity would not deal well with becoming unmoored from traditional moralities grounded in religion or metaphysics. For people had not yet come to terms with the abyss of nothingness that seemed to have been left in the wake of God's death and reason's demise. But in the absence of any orientating metanarrative, people had become so free, metaphysically speaking, that they were at risk disintegrating. The modern soul was at risk of being torn apart. Thus European culture began its descent into nihilism. This was the frightful warning Nietzsche offered. He saw it as a spiritual reorientation that modern civilisation would have to pass through, although he was uncertain how the transition would play out.

In the time Camus was writing – the mid twentieth century – these themes had to be grappled with in the shadows of Nazism and Stalinism. If excessive reason had led to the 'reign of terror' after the French Revolution, in the twentieth century the same dogmatic faith led to the murder of millions of people, justified by absolutist ideologies across the political spectrum. Camus highlighted how the vanity and hubris of reason or religion could end up justifying the violence one might have assumed reason or religion ought to have condemned. He clashed with Sartre over the way the Communist Party in Russia was justifying death as a means of advancing the march of freedom, something regrettable but permissible. Under Stalin, murder became rational, disguised as the handmaiden of human emancipation. 'One can kill for all sorts of motives,' notes philosopher and literary theorist Terry Eagleton, 'but killing on a spectacular scale is almost always the consequence of ideas.'[14] Having lost faith in God, Western culture turned to finding salvation either in ecocidal capitalist consumption or socialist revolution.

Camus explored the problem of holding absolute values in his play *The Just*.[15] One of the lead characters, Stephan, places his reasoned faith in revolution above all else, whereby 'nothing that can serve our cause should be ruled out'. He castigates his revolutionary colleagues for 'sentimentalizing' about not killing children. 'I do not love life,' he says, 'I love something higher than mere life... I love justice.'[16] Camus' concern was that when you have transcendent belief in your cause – whether rational or religious – the end can be used to justify the means, any means, however violent and deadly. 'You begin by wanting justice, and in the end you set up a police force.'[17] Perhaps what is needed is what philosopher Richard Rorty called the 'liberal ironist'. This is a citizen who recognises that there is no way reason can present a deductive proof of political ideologies, meaning that one's deepest values should always be held 'ironically,' in the sense of maintaining a certain degree of doubt about them and always being open to dialogue and revision. Camus, it seems, was a sort of liberal ironist before the term was invented.

To maintain these doubts about human rationality, however, raises problems with which we are now familiar. Life is cruel and full of arbitrary suffering, it always has been, but in an increasingly post-metaphysical age, there seems to be no transcendent standard by which to condemn this situation. In a state of spiritual exhaustion, we abide, we permit, we wait for Godot who never arrives. The spectre of nihilism has never been so present. Do we have an answer to the murderous Caligula, who, having transcended morality in order to live without any ethical constraints, sought meaning and pleasure in oppression and murder? In a post-metaphysical age, do we have a way to object to the Holocaust and the gulags?

Of course, people might *want* to be able to provide an objective argument for condemning unfathomable violence and cruelty, whether we base such a response on reason or religion. So committed are human beings to finding an answer that we easily make a leap of faith into rationality or religion simply to have an answer – any answer. This is quite understandable, for some might suggest that it is better to hold on to an implausible 'faith' if that meant avoiding what might seem to be the greater problem: having no answer to Caligula, Stalin, or the Nazis.

Serious though this problem obviously is, Camus refused to base his moral outlook upon anything outside ourselves, whether that be objective reason or God. For him, the need to find and sustain meaning in life is humanity's deepest existential source of action. 'This is civilisation's problem,' Camus asserted. 'We must know if man, solely by himself, can create his own values, without the help of rationalist thought or of the eternal.'[18] As Camus-scholar David Sprintzen writes: 'death is the only limit; beyond that all else is possibility.'[19] This places a creative burden on humankind. In an indifferent universe, there is no meaning to 'discover', no transcendent values 'out there'. We are, as Sartre famously declared, 'condemned to be free.'[20]

The language of condemnation is appropriate here. It is intended to convey the heaviness of our task, the responsibility of living on our own terms without metaphysical guidance. It is a call to accept the absolute indifference of the universe, the inevitability of death, the absence of transcendent values, and the lack of hope in any chance of redemption in some after life. These are the characteristics of life with absurd freedom after the death of God. Camus called on us to look at these facts of our condition squarely in the face and to accept the implications of this metaphysical situation. 'The important thing... is not to be cured, but to live with one's ailments.'[21]

But the problem remains: we find ourselves without external or metaphysical guidance. In a so-called postmodern age, humans are dislocated and disorientated, having lost the map and compass provided by religion and rationalism. How to decide what to do or how to live? Has not absurd reasoning cast us into a maelstrom where we are necessarily lost? If we have no reason to die, have we any reason to live? Are values, hopes, and dreams always arbitrary? This is the aesthetic moment which both Nietzsche and Camus isolate so lucidly. In the absence of something external to rely on, what's left? Their answer: our own imaginations and creativity; our aesthetic capacities; our art. Ultimately, they argued, there are no 'philosophical' or 'religious' justifications that can guide our lives. But still, we must live, somehow. This is our aesthetic burden, the burden of living in the face of the absurd – of living in creative revolt, of deciding our own fate, of finding a way to affirm it, perhaps even love it, despite everything.

Camus recognised, therefore, that the absurdity of life is not an end but a beginning.[22] It is an opportunity to take personal responsibility for ourselves without deferring to self-imposed metaphysical constraints. There may be no meaning *of* life, but meaning can be created *in* life. This, in essence, was Camus' strategy for avoiding the nihilistic conclusion that everything is meaningless and that nothing really matters. Our first act of revolt, according to Camus, is simply to continue living, to choose not to commit suicide, for suicide would merely be a Schopenhauerian renunciation or negation of life.[23] This might seem like a very small step, but it was enough for Camus to develop a more comprehensive theory of existential revolt and rebellion.

Metaphysical rebellion is a refusal to submit to the temptations of religion, metaphysics, or nihilism, while also refusing to submit to unjust living conditions or accept the degradation of human life. Camus wanted to face existence on its own terms and to explore the possibility of a meaningful life, even in an absurd condition. He explored for himself, and offered for us, 'a lucid invitation to live and to create, in the very midst of the desert.'[24] In the absence of external sources of meaning, Camus insisted that we find ourselves at a crossroads: nihilism – or the creation of values.

We are not, therefore, locked into nihilism. We are faced with choices – choices about where and how to *invest* reality with a sense of meaning. Camus found within the problem of nihilism a means of going beyond it, of finding solidarity amongst humankind on account of the absurd existence we share. And in this shared absurdity Camus posits a dignity of the individual which leads to a dignity of the species. This creates an aesthetic universe where values can be found not in religion or metaphysics 'out there' but in recognition of our shared condition. It is an absurd situation, in which we should embrace a self-imposed duty to create, not alone, but together. In his essay 'Art and Revolt' Camus quotes Van Gogh, who once wrote: 'I can very well, in life and in painting also, do without God. But I cannot, suffering creature that I am, do without something greater than myself, something that is my life, the power to create.'[25]

To accept this is to accept there is a threshold beyond which the violation of human dignity demands rebellion, revolt. The rebel 'affirms that there are limits and also that he suspects – and wishes to preserve – the existence of certain things beyond those limits'[26] – things such as human dignity and the liberty to create. We are all burdened with the task of creating as an aesthetic project the meaning of our own lives, but we must undertake this task in a world of other life-artists, and just as we expect freedom and dignity ourselves, it is only a small step to grant that same liberty to others. 'In absurdist experience,' Camus wrote:

> suffering is individual. But from the moment when a movement of rebellion begins, suffering is seen as a collective experience – as the experience of everyone. Therefore the first progressive step for a mind overwhelmed by the strangeness of things is to realise that this feeling of strangeness is shared with all men and that the entire human race suffers from the division between itself and the rest of the world... this clue lures the individual from his solitude. Rebellion is the common ground on which every man bases his first values. I *rebel* – therefore we *exist*.[27]

Camus saw that the dominant political ideologies of his time were denying people their dignity by repressing their capacities to create. This denial of dignity was especially present in Nazism and Stalinism, but also, in different ways, in the decaying bourgeois cultures of post-Christian capitalism. Indeed, he saw that the world was dominated by humanity's equally powerful capacity to destroy. Camus claimed that a reinvigorated drive to create, to be artful in life, to search for the beauty amongst the destruction, was the only antidote to the nihilism of contemporary society. Our dignity as creators, as artists, needed to be restored, and through art and aesthetics our dignity could be restored. 'Beauty,' Camus maintained, 'cannot serve any party; it cannot serve, in the long or the short run, anything but men's liberty.'[28] Moreover, 'there is not a single true work of art that has not in the end added to the inner freedom of each person who has known and loved it.' Like Nietzsche, Camus evaluates the worth of 'art' according to its capacity to enrich and energise 'life', and certain hope resides in the fact that the human story is forever unfinished, always in the process of recreating itself.

We see, then, that art justifies itself not for its own sake but as something that can present a vision of human dignity in a world full of suffering and oppression. Through that art, which rejects the world that is, a vision can arise of a world that could yet be. Art, Camus asserts, 'rejects the world on account of what it lacks and in the name of what it sometimes is.'[29] It is therefore an aesthetics of commitment, solidarity, and resistance, and it can be read both from the perspective of the artist creator and with respect to the effects of art on the audience or spectator. In accepting his Noble prize in 1957, Camus said:

> I cannot live without my art. And yet I have never set that art above everything else. It is essential to me, on the contrary, because it excludes no one and allows me to live, just as I am, on a footing with all. To me, art is not a solitary delight. It is a means of stirring the greatest number of [human beings] by providing them with a privileged image of our common joys and woes.[30]

What is important to note is that Camus' response to our absurd situation was neither rationalist nor religious. In *The Myth of Sisyphus*, he offered no 'demonstration' of humanity's ability to affirm our absurd condition, because, like Nietzsche, he felt that reason was not up to the task. However, Camus would argue that while lucid awareness of our situation 'implies a total absence of hope'[31] in any metaphysical salvation, he insisted that this 'has nothing to do with despair'.[32] In a curious and ambiguous phrase, he claimed that the absurd emerges in 'that odd state of the soul in which the void becomes eloquent.'[33]

This is not a rational or religious claim, but an aesthetic one, grounded in feeling and sensual connection with others. 'When you have once seen the glow of happiness on the face of a beloved person,' Camus explained, 'you know that man can have no vocation but to awaken the light on the faces surrounding him.' In another well-known passage, Camus wrote: 'In the depth of the winter, I finally learned that within me there lay an invincible summer.'[34] His position was that we do not so much need to transform our thoughts as our sensibilities. This can be understood as an aesthetic challenge requiring aesthetic means, even if he felt that a certain shift in thinking must precede or coincide with that shift in sensibility. 'Having started from an anguished awareness of the inhuman, the meditation on the absurd returns at the end of its itinerary to the very heart of the passionate flames of human revolt.'[35]

Like Nietzsche, Camus saw an aesthetic justification of existence as primarily about inducing, in the life that we must lead, a positive, affective evaluation of life. As seen in an earlier essay, an aesthetic justification is not a proposition of truth about the objective value of life, but is instead, as philosopher Daniel Came argues, 'epistemologically neutral.'[36] The success or failure of an aesthetic justification thus depends not on whether it can be shown to be based on objective philosophical foundations but whether it can induce a subjective affirmation of life in ways that religious and metaphysical justifications, which are no longer credible for post-Nietzscheans, cannot.

This metaphysical rebellion has its origins in outrage, but it does not confine itself to outrage. Camus held the horrors of life in dialectical tension with the possibilities of joy in life. Even in joy, he advised, one can rebel. The existentialists (broadly defined to include Camus who rejected the label), are often, with good cause, accused of focussing exclusively on the dark side of life. Central themes reoccur, related to human angst, dread, anxiety, nausea, and so forth. But this myopia simply does not apply to Camus, who celebrated the joys of life, however fleeting and tenuous they may be. 'This heart within me I can feel, and I judge that it exists. This world I can touch, and I likewise judge that it exists. There ends all my knowledge, and the rest is construction.'[37] He could just as well have said, the rest is creation – art. 'The absurd joy *par excellence,*' Camus wrote, 'is creation.'[38]

Thus creation of art 'constitutes an *ascesis*',[39] a term that begins to point toward the spiritual character of aesthetic practices of self-creation (an issue to be explored in a forthcoming essay).[40] 'To create is... to give a shape to one's fate.'[41] It is a yearning from within for creative expression and upon which Camus was able to construct a case for the dignity of human existence. He claimed that these are the grounds of a liberating transformation of consciousness and sensibility through personal revolt and defiant acts of creative solidarity. Camus saw *solidarity* as being the outcome of *creativity* because it was something to be achieved rather than a value-base that is somehow discovered or exists independently of human thought and action. From this perspective, it is through art that we are most able to develop a sense of solidarity, without which human community cannot maintain dignity. An artist, Camus maintained, '...if he can tell himself that finally, as a result of his long effort, he has eased or decreased the various forms of bondage weighing upon men, then in a sense he is justified...'[42] This reflects Nietzsche's point that 'the profound Greek, so uniquely susceptible to the subtlest and deepest sufferings... was saved by art, and through art life reclaimed him...'[43] The aim of art, according to

Camus, and the aim of life, 'can only be to increase the sum of freedom and responsibility to be found in every [human being] and in the world.'[44] Art is not for art's sake, therefore, but for life's sake.

To exalt certain aspects of the world is precisely the task of giving aesthetic form to content of existence. That is a task both for the artist as conventionally understood as well as the artists of life – all of us – who are tasked with creating meaning in an objectively meaningless universe. Art is an inherently creative process that gives rise to something – a connection, a feeling, a negation, or affirmation – that was absent before. 'Rebellion, from this point of view, is a fabricator of universes. This also defines art. The demands of rebellion are really, in part, aesthetic demands.'[45]

Accordingly, Camus argued that it is the role of the artist to give form to this world in ways that leaves room for or demands an affirmation too: 'revolt is creative.'[46] 'No form of art,' he insisted, 'can survive on total denial alone... To create beauty, [the artist] must simultaneously reject reality and exalt certain aspects of it. Art disputes reality but does not hide from it.'[47] Given that art was Camus' primary method of communication, it makes sense to give due regard to that aesthetic method by trying to understand his outlook on the human condition via his art. In that spirit, I now turn to consider his great novel *The Plague*, one with strikingly pertinent overtones in the era of COVID-19.[48]

Absurdity, revolt, and solidarity in 'The Plague'

The story begins at a time 'before plague'. The city of Oran is described by the narrator as a large French port on the Algerian coast, a colonial settlement distinguished only by its ordinariness. So ordinary, in fact, that everyone agreed that the extraordinary events that took place there seemed, as it were, out of place. It could be any city of industry and trade around the world, increasingly without birds, gardens, or even the rustle of leaves. In short, Oran was an ugly, thoroughly negative place. Disenchantment came naturally within its gates.

We are told that the citizens work hard, 'but solely with the object of getting rich.' Their chief interest is in commerce, and their chief aim in life is, as they call it, 'doing business.' With a modest qualification the narrator admits that the people of Oran 'don't eschew such simpler pleasures as love-making, sea-bathing, and going to the pictures.' But we are told they reserve these pastimes for the weekend, and employ the rest of the week 'in making money, as much of it as possible.'

These pursuits, practised with a feverish yet casual air, are not peculiar to the city of Oran, of course. It could be any contemporary industrial settlement. In other words, the city was 'completely modern', and after a while, the narrator warns, 'you go complacently to sleep there.' In the rush for material riches and accumulation, one gets the sense that the forces of capitalist dehumanisation had crept into the town well before the plague arrived. It is little wonder that the city itself is sometimes described as one of the book's central characters, along with the narrator and the plague itself.

We know that pestilences have a way of recurring in the world, yet the narrator accurately notes that 'somehow we find it hard to believe in ones that crash down on our heads from a blue sky.' They always take people by surprise. And so the story begins. Dr Bernard Rieux, a central figure in *The Plague*, stepped out of his surgery only to discover a dead rat underfoot in the middle of the landing. Without giving it further thought he kicked it to one side, but as he was leaving the building the doctor mentioned the incident to the door-porter and kindly asked that he see to the rat's removal. 'There weren't no rats here', the door-porter replied.

In vain Dr Rieux assured the door-porter that there *was* a rat, presumably dead, but the man's conviction wasn't to be shaken. 'There weren't no rats here', the door-porter repeated, with a closed mind. But if there was a rat, he added, it was brought in from the outside. Sadly, the reader soon discovers that the door-porter is the first person to die of the plague, despite there being no rats.

What began with one dead rat soon became a disturbing nuisance as numbers multiplied by the day, gutters and dustbins full of them, blood spurting from their mouths. The rats became a great topic of conversation, and 'wild rumours' of the cause and meaning of the phenomenon abounded. People began to die, especially the poor, in tortuous ways and in growing numbers. In usual classist fashion, when people who were *not* poor also began to get ill and die, it was then that fear truly set in. 'A wave of something like panic swept the town,' and after the disease was named 'there was a demand for drastic measures' and 'the authorities were accused of slackness.'

As the infection rate and death count both rose in 'geometrical progression', emergency measures were contemplated. The townspeople were advised to 'practice extreme cleanliness' and 'households were ordered to promptly report any fever diagnosed by their doctors and to permit the isolation of sick members of their families in special wards.' Furthermore, all those who had been in contact with patients 'were advised to consult the sanitary inspector and strictly follow advice.' The people of Oran didn't have the technological capacity to develop surveillance apps, but they did their best to monitor the 'strange malady' – the danger of which still seemed 'fantastically unreal.'

Such efforts, however, were unable to stem the flow of infections and there was no vaccine. Medical supplies became scarce and often insufficient. Before long the hospital wards reached capacity, then the cemeteries, and even the crematoriums were struggling to keep up with the influx of plague-ridden bodies. The formalities at funerals were whittled down and of necessity conducted at lightning speeds, often without families present, to minimise risk. At first this was a cause of social outrage, but in time, as more pressing needs for survival emerged, 'people had no time to think of the manner in which others were dying around them.'

Dr Rieux, who was a prime adviser to the government on medical questions, became conscious that 'the slightly dazed feeling which came over him when he thought about the plague was growing more pronounced.' Finally he realised what he meant: 'simply that he was afraid.' The doctor worked extremely long hours combating the disease, distancing himself emotionally from the pain and suffering of its victims so he could continue his work. 'There's not a question of heroism in all this,' he tells his friend. 'It's a matter of common decency.' That's an idea which he thinks might make some people smile or scoff, but it's the only thing he believes can combat the plague: common decency; helping each other out; doing what one can, even or especially if one is facing a 'never-ending defeat.'

Occasionally there were days when only a few deaths were reported and people began to wonder whether perhaps the spread of infection was beginning to wane. But then the death count shot up vertically. Finally, the authorities got alarmed and jolted into action. An official telegram read: '*Proclaim a state of plague Stop close the town.*' Suddenly citizens woke to discover that the city was in lockdown. The borders were closed and 'commercial activity ceased abruptly' and 'no vehicle had entered since the gates closed.' Traffic thinned out progressively until few vehicles were on the roads or in the air; most shops were closed, and others began to put up '*Sold out*' notices while crowds of buyers stood waiting at their door. Naturally, the epidemic 'spelt the ruin of the tourist trade,' and more generally everyone testified that commerce itself 'had died of the plague.' All this will sound rather familiar to contemporary readers who lived through the COVID-19 pandemic, and the similarities do not end there.

The authorities soon became anxious about food supply, and profiteers were offering, at enormous prices, various essential foodstuffs and products not found in the shops. The result was that 'poor families were in great straits, while the rich were short of practically nothing.' That said, 'the plague was no respecter of persons and under its despotic rule everyone, from the Governor down to the humblest delinquent, was under sentence and, perhaps for the first time, impartial justice reigned in the prison.' There was a story of a grocer who had laid by masses of tinned provisions 'with the idea of selling them later on at a big profit.' When the ambulance arrived to take him to the morgue, several dozen tins of meat were found under his bed. A rather unpoetic justice. In a similar vein, peppermint lozenges had vanished from the chemists' shops, 'because there was a popular belief that when sucking them you were proof against contagion.' Better still, as the citizens of Oran would try to show: 'The best protection against infection is a good bottle of wine, which confirmed an already prevalent opinion that alcohol is a safeguard against infectious disease.'

♦ ♦ ♦

One of the principal themes of *The Plague* – both Camus' story and its contemporary retelling in the Coronaverse – is the torment of human separation. Dr. Rieux's wife had left the city for (unrelated) health reasons only days before the city gates were shut, keeping them apart during the epidemic. Similarly, a journalist called Raymond Rambert had been visiting Oran to gather information for a story just as the city went into quarantine. He was now desperate to find a way out to reunite with his love, although his repeated pleas to the authorities proved ineffective. Such separations might feel like a 'special case', he was told, but they rarely are, and the authorities politely but firmly advised that no exceptions were to be made. Rambert, for the time being, was stuck in Oran's sick bubble.

The citizens of Oran were all 'prisoners of the plague' and in exile, but an 'exile in one's own home.' People came to see so many of life's simplest and richest of pleasures had been taken for granted. As one citizen of Oran was to admit: 'We'll all be nuts before long, unless I'm much mistaken.' Burdensome though the disruption was for the citizens of Oran, in this separation people were not alone. Or, if they were alone, they were alone, *together*. The narrator notes: 'a feeling normally as individual as the ache of separation from those one loves suddenly became a feeling in which all shared alike and – together with fear – the greatest affliction of the long period of exile that lay ahead.'

The world may be cruel and repugnant, but we should live in solidarity with those who suffer in it. That, fundamentally, was Camus' ethic. His most famous existentialist novel, *The Outsider*,[49] did not uphold such an ethic, and so *The Plague* represents an evolution in the direction of solidarity and participation. Whether it is the plague or COVID-19, a common tragedy makes our collective predicament evident to all, thereby establishing, in the words of one commentator, 'the minimal conditions for bringing humans together in a collective effort.'

We see this in how several characters responded to the ambiguous challenge of the plague. The journalist Rambert, after losing his battle with the authorities to gain permission to leave, is introduced to some smugglers who organise for his escape (at a hefty fee). But on the evening when the escape was supposed to take place, Rambert goes to Dr Rieux and explains that he cannot leave. 'I always thought that I was a stranger in this town and that I had nothing to do with you. But now that I have seen what I have seen I know that I belong in this place whether I like it or not. This business concerns us all.'

The doctor asks about Rambert's need to reunite with his lover and the journalist responds that he'd feel ashamed if he left. Dr Rieux counters saying that there is nothing wrong with pursuing happiness – at least, he has no arguments against it. 'Certainly,' Rambert says, 'but it may be shameful to be happy by oneself.' Here we see one of the most powerful symbolic moments in the book, where a person chooses meaning and struggle over personal happiness, only to discover – promisingly – that a life of meaning and purpose can make one happy, albeit in a different sort of way.

Inspiring but also challenging in a different way is the character of Jean Tarrou, a good-natured man who arrived in Oran some weeks before the plague and who became a close friend of Dr Rieux. One of Tarrou's central contributions to the novel is to organise a grassroots assistance (resistance) movement, working with Dr Rieux to combat the spread of the infection and help communities in need. We come to understand Tarrou's driving force later in the book when we learn that his father was a prosecuting attorney who tried death penalty cases. After attending one of those trials as a boy, the young Tarrou recognised in himself an innate disgust for the death penalty, which he regarded as state-sponsored murder. Ever since then his moral orientation in the world involved fighting against unnecessary suffering and killing. 'There is something lacking in my mental make-up', he says, 'and its lack prevents me from being a rational murderer.' He even gave up revolutionary activism when he saw the same urge to violence amongst his fellow political agitators. He interprets the plague metaphorically, as much a spiritual disease as a physical one.

'I've drawn up a plan for voluntary groups of helpers,' Tarrou tells the doctor. 'Get me empowered to try out my plan, and then let's sidetrack officialdom. In any case, the authorities have their hands full already.' In this engaged spirit, Tarrou forms what come to be called 'sanitary squads', which can be understood as small self-organising activist communities that did what needed to be done to help minimise suffering amidst the crisis. They proved to be effective, necessary even, especially given an overwhelmed bureaucracy.

Tarrou accuses the authorities of a lack of imagination in their response to the plague. 'Officialdom can never cope with something really catastrophic.' Fiercely moralistic, Tarrou says he is seeking peace by trying to become a 'saint without God.' Less ambitious but equally committed is Dr Rieux, who works tirelessly to reduce suffering where he can, just because it is the decent thing to do.

Neither Tarrou nor the doctor subscribe to the Christian response to the health crisis, which involved organising a 'Week of Prayer'. Father Paneloux is a well-respected Jesuit priest, known for giving powerful and chastising lectures. In his first sermon after the plague arrives he berates his congregation for their laxity and declares that the plague is a just punishment. 'Calamity has come on you, my brethren, and you deserved it.'

Later in the book Father Paneloux delivers a second sermon, but by this time his message has shifted. The priest had been present at the death of a small child who suffered violently before dying, and this suffering of an innocent child casts his faith into question. He no longer sees the plague as punishment. But rather than give up his faith he only embraces it more fervently, insisting that, while the child's suffering has no rational explanation, that simply means people need to throw themselves unquestioningly into their faith. This is despite the apparent contradiction of a loving God allowing the suffering of innocents to occur. Soon after this sermon, Father Paneloux develops a condition that, without quite being the plague, shares many of its symptoms. Consistent with his own conception of faith, the priest refuses medical treatment and dies.

Perhaps the simplest and most inspiring expression of solidarity in the novel comes from the old government clerk, Joseph Grand. When a neighbour, Cottard, attempts to commit suicide, Dr Rieux looks around for someone to keep an eye on him. Without thinking twice, Grand is there to lend a hand. 'I can't really say I know him, but one's got to help a neighbour, hasn't one?' If citizens in crisis begin with that ethic of mutual aid, then the community will survive a plague, no matter how bad it gets. The suicidal Cottard represents the opposite sort of character. Before the plague he was ready to kill himself, but he is somehow uplifted by the onset of the plague and the suffering it causes others. He is happier during the epidemic, because it has made him feel part of the group.

Grand's significance in the novel, however, goes deeper still, beyond his noble assumption of mutual obligation and care. Despite needing to earn his livelihood as a poorly paid government clerk, and being of old age, he eagerly commits with 'quiet courage' to assist in the fight against the plague at every opportunity. Given work commitments, he tells Tarrou he can assist from six till eight every evening. Beyond his activism, this humble bureaucrat spends any spare time and energy he has working on a novel. As it turns out, he is also a literary perfectionist (but one without much ability), and for a long time he has merely been writing and endlessly re-writing the first sentence, unwilling to move on until he is sure he has sufficiently polished the opening line. This process is absurd, but upliftingly absurd, for it is clear that life, for Grand, is enchanted. He is animated to participate in a troubled world. He does not seek meaning 'out there'. He creates it by living it into existence, here and now, refusing to be dominated by the plague's dehumanising power.

Contrast this with Dr Rieux's elderly asthma patient, who is convinced that life has no meaning, and so decides the best way to live is to do as little as possible. He chooses to spend his time in bed, mindlessly transferring dried peas from one pot to another, a mechanical activity which happens to tell him when it's time to eat. It is the bare minimum needed to survive. This fellow is also absurd, but decidedly in a less uplifting sort of way. It would be better to call this form of life silly, shallow, or even cowardly. Life in a universe without metaphysical foundations is inherently absurd, according to Camus. What matters then is what we do with our absurd existence.

One afternoon Tarrou and Rieux go swimming together. Even this can be read as an act of rebellion, in the midst of struggle – a means of seeking regeneration in sensuous experience as a path on which the struggle can be continued. Friends swimming together in the ocean allowed for happiness, however momentary, even during the grim struggle against the disease. 'For some minutes they swam side by side, with the same zest, in the same rhythm, isolated from the world, at last free of the town and of the plague... They dressed and started back. Neither had said a word, but they were conscious of being perfectly at one, and that the memory of this night would be cherished by them both.'

♦ ♦ ♦

At a superficial level, *The Plague* is simply a well-crafted and aesthetically satisfying story. But such literal interpretations are rarely what an author intends. Beneath the surface Camus is also pointing to the plague as a symbol for the Nazi occupation of Paris during the war – he began writing the book in the early 1940s. In some regards this is a problematic storytelling metaphor, for by 'naturalising' the Nazis into a disease, the manifestation of fascism became the workings of nature rather than deliberate human choices. It also sidesteps a central theme in Camus' work: the philosophical problem of whether it is ever justified to use violence to resist evil. Given that nobody has an ethical problem with killing viruses, this metaphor doesn't entirely work.

This problem is highlighted in Dr Rieux's own words: 'What is natural is the microbe. All the rest, health, integrity, purity, if you like, is an act of will.' There are various ways to respond to crisis situations, whether those crises be health, environmental, financial, political, or spiritual. Human societies may not always be able to avoid diseases and natural disasters. It follows that the social and political challenge is to manage those crises with compassion and solidarity when they arrive, knowing that 'no longer [are there] individual destinies, only a collective destiny.' This is the solidarity that flows, or ought to flow, from separation under lockdown.

In true existentialist fashion, Camus also makes it clear that he is commenting more broadly on the human condition, summed up best perhaps in the words of Tarrou: 'I had plague already, long before I came to this town and encountered it here. Which is tantamount to saying I'm like everybody else.' As the novel concludes we learn that Dr Rieux's wife has died from her illness outside the city walls. Just as tragically, Tarrou is one of the last people to die from the plague, although he doesn't leave the world without a heroic fight. These deaths are Camus' way of saying that, even after beating the plague, suffering is part of the human condition and will ever remain so.

Nevertheless, what makes Camus' work so edifying and surprisingly uplifting is that one closes the book somehow more cognisant of the simple joys of ordinary existence – joys like swimming in the sea or having dinner with friends. And one becomes more cognisant of the sublime responsibility of personal freedom, heavy though it weighs on us in an absurd universe. After reading *The Plague* – or living in the Coronaverse – one is less likely to take such things for granted. The simple things, the human connections, are the fabric of life and give it meaning. And they are worth fighting for – together.

As to be expected, the plague eventually passes, and the gates of Oran are reopened. The city bursts into festivities and celebration. People discover, however, that 'destruction is an easier, speedier process than reconstruction,' but this task was made easier to the extent people were enchanted by 'an inkling of something different.' And even though the fight for a new world probably meant a 'never-ending defeat', Dr Rieux insisted that this is 'no reason for giving up the struggle.'

Why did Dr Rieux (who is finally revealed as the narrator) continue to struggle? 'So as not to be one of those who are silent, so as to testify in favour of these victims of the plague, so as to leave at least a memory of the injustice and the violence which was done to them and so as to tell simply what one learns amongst scourges, that there are in men more things to be admired than despised.' Resistance was offered not because people had expectations of succeeding but because the plague was robbing people of their dignity and life. Camus concludes: '[r]evolt gives life its value.'[50]

The Plague ends, however, with a warning: the bacillus of the plague can lie dormant for years 'in furniture and linen-chests' and may again one day awaken its rats and 'send them to die in a happy city.' It follows that overcoming the plague can never be one of final victory. It merely points to what might need to be done again 'in the never ending fight against terror and its relentless onslaughts... by all who, while unable to be saints but refusing to bow down to pestilences, strive their utmost to be healers.'

Conclusion

In this essay I have considered Camus' framing of the human condition and outlined how he responded with an aesthetics of revolt. He described the human condition as 'absurd' on the basis that we seem to have an innate urge for meaning in our lives, and yet upon philosophical reflection, we find the universe wholly indifferent to this demand. No objective or rationally demonstrable meaning can be discerned from the world, and to make a 'leap of faith' into religion is to deny one's own freedom by deferring to a foundationless code of living that lies outside of oneself.

Modern, secular humanity thus finds itself at a crossroads – nihilism or the creation of values. Camus' life project – which ended in a tragic car accident in 1960 when he was only 46 – was to see if it were possible for human beings to live only by their own values. This remains an open question, especially in an age when nihilism seems to be threatening to overwhelm the dominant culture of global capitalist society as never before. But Camus held that human solidarity could emerge from our shared absurd condition. This recognition was not grounded in reason, as such, but in our affective capacity to feel pain, suffering, and humiliation, and to recognise that there is a limit beyond which the loss of dignity in life demands revolt. Through rebellion solidarity is born: 'I *rebel* – therefore *we exist*.' Nevertheless, this is not a truth to be discovered but rather an orientation of values that must be created and *felt*. As we have seen, Camus highlighted the role of art and aesthetics in rebellion, showing how the task of choosing one's values makes aesthetic demands on us, and moreover, how art and creativity can help expose the injustices of the world and evoke images of a better, more humane, and liberated world.

I wish to close this essay by briefly anticipating a point of criticism about this strategy of holding up art and the aesthetic as viable substitutes for religious or metaphysical faith. In his book *Culture and the Death of God* (2015),[51] Terry Eagleton provides an erudite examination of this strategy, critically reviewing the historical attempts to place art and culture in the void created by the death of God and the loss of faith in pure reason. Despite acknowledging the power of the critiques provided by Nietzsche and others in the diverse post-religious and post-metaphysical traditions, Eagleton argues that the various attempts to find a substitute for religion have, to date, largely failed. Even the Enlightenment philosophers, Eagleton writes:

> paid too little heed to the fact that local customs, pieties and affections are the places where power must embed itself if it is to flourish. Otherwise, it will appear too abstract and remote to be assured of its subjects' allegiance. There can be no effective sovereignty without a foundation in lived experience, which is one reason why Reason feels the need for a kind of supplement or prosthesis known as the aesthetic. For the most part, Enlightenment Reason lacked a corporeal presence, which the German Idealists and Romantics would seek to restore.[52]

Nevertheless, in his critical assessment of the German Idealists and Romantics, Eagleton saw that they essentially made the same error as the rationalists who sought to find answers in 'reason' rather than 'faith'. The case for art and culture, Eagleton maintains, has always been 'too cerebral',[53] at most a plausible substitute in the eyes of some philosophers and elite practitioners of the fine arts, but something unable to replace the daily practices, experiences, and rituals that are required to bind a community together. It is precisely those daily practices, experiences, and rituals that have made religion so hard to replace from a social perspective, even in so-called secular societies.

As I mulled over Eagleton's thesis, I found myself drawn to the aesthetics and politics of William Morris (a thinker to which Eagleton only makes passing reference in his analysis). In ways I will explore in detail in a later essay, Morris brings art into 'the everyday' in ways that I believe sidesteps the critique Eagleton made of the German Idealists and Romantics. For post-Nietzscheans who have lost faith in religious and rational sources of guidance in life, art and culture can present themselves as coherent and compelling alternatives, and yet, as Eagleton highlights, the aesthetic can easily remain too cerebral and abstract to be translated into everyday social practices. That critique simply does not apply to William Morris, who sought to blur the distinction between artist and artisan, by defining art as the expression of pleasure (and I would add meaning) in creative labour.[54] Eagleton is surely correct to state that '[n]o symbolic force in history has matched religion's ability to link the most exalted of truths to the daily existence of countless men and woman.'[55] That may be so historically, but I will argue, drawing on Morris, that the past has not exhausted the range of options available. If a society were able to bring art into the practices and rituals of everyday living, then there is no reason that the aesthetic could not bind a community together in ways that to date only religion has been able to do. I plant the seed of this argument presently, but there is still a fair way to go before I am ready to develop or reconstruct Morris' aesthetic politics in more detail. In the next essay I address a different criticism of aestheticism, one that emerges in relation to the tradition of Dandyism.

---

[1] I will draw mainly from Camus' two major philosophical works. See Albert Camus, *The Myth of Sisyphus* (London: Penguin, 2000); and Albert Camus, *The Rebel* (London: Penguin, 2000).

[2] Fredrich Nietzsche, *The Gay Science*, trans. Walter Kaufmann (New York: Vintage Books, 1974). p. 108.

[3] Friedrich Nietzsche, *On the Genealogy of Morals* (New York: Vintage Books, 1969), Essay III, 27.

[4] Ibid.

[5] Albert Camus, *Caligula,* in Albert Camus, *The Collected Plays of Albert Camus* (London: Hamish Hamilton, 1965), p. 21.

[6] Camus, *Myth*, note 1, pp. 31-2.

[7] Quoted in David Sprintzen, *Camus: A Critical Examination* (Philadelphia: Temple University Press, 1988), p. 17.

[8] Camus, *Myth*, note 1, p. 11.

[9] Ibid, p. 43.

[10] Ibid, p. 32.

[11] Camus, *Rebel*, note 1, p. 243.

[12] Camus, *Myth*, note 1, p. 13.

[13] See Jacques Lacan, *The Ego in Freud's Theory and in the Technique of Psychoanalysis* (New York: Norton, 1998), p. 128.

[14] Terry Eagleton, *Culture and the Death of God* (New Haven: Yale University Press, 2015) p. 32.

[15] Albert Camus, *The Just,* in Albert Camus, *The Collected Plays of Albert Camus* (London: Hamish Hamilton, 1965).
[16] Ibid, p. 130.
[17] Ibid, p.160.
[18] Quoted in Sprintzen, *Camus,* note 7, p. 17.
[19] Ibid, p. 20.
[20] Jean-Paul Sartre, *Existentialism and Humanism* (London: Methuen and Co, 1970), p. 34.
[21] Camus, *Myth*, note 1, pp. 40-1.
[22] See Sprintzen, *Camus,* note 7, p. 47.
[23] Camus, *Rebel*, note 1, p. 19.
[24] Camus, *Myth*, note 1, p. 7.
[25] Albert Camus, 'Art and Revolt' (1952) *Partisan Review* 29:3: p. 272.
[26] Camus, *Rebel*, note 1, p. 19.
[27] Ibid, p. 28.
[28] Albert Camus, *Resistance, Rebellion, and Death* (New York: Knopf, 1961), p. 267.
[29] Camus, *Rebel*, note 1, p. 219.
[30] Albert Camus, 'Nobel Prize Speech' (1957). Available at: https://www.nobelprize.org/prizes/literature/1957/camus/speech/ (accessed 18 April 2023).
[31] Camus, *Myth*, note 1, p. 34.
[32] Ibid.
[33] Ibid, p 19.
[34] Camus, *Myth*, note 1, p. 7. Minor amendment to translation to accord with the better-known version.
[35] Ibid, p. 62.
[36] Daniel Came (ed.), *Nietzsche on Art and Life* (Oxford: Oxford University Press, 2014) p. 42 (emphasis removed).
[37] Camus, *Myth*, note 1, p. 24.
[38] Ibid, p. 86.
[39] Ibid, p. 104.
[40] Camus wrote: 'Thus we make these lives into works of art. In an elementary fashion we turn them into novels. In this sense, everyone tries to make his life into a work of art.' Camus, *Rebel*, note 1, p. 227.
[41] Camus, *Myth*, note 1, p. 106.
[42] Quoted in Sprintzen, *Camus,* note 7, p. 240.
[43] Fredrich Nietzsche, *The Birth of Tragedy*, trans. Walter Kaufmann (New York: Vintage, 1967), Sect. 7.
[44] Albert Camus, *Resistance, Rebellion, and Death* (New York: Vintage Books, 1960), p. 240.
[45] Camus, *Rebel*, note 1, p. 221.
[46] Camus, 'Art and Revolt', note 25, p. 281.
[47] Camus, *Rebel*, note 1, p. 223-4.
[48] The following review draws on Samuel Alexander and Brendan Gleeson, *Urban Awakenings: Disturbance and Enchantment in the Industrial City* (Singapore: Palgrave, 2021), Ch. 17. Given the large number of quotations drawn from *The Plague*, I will not reference each one, so as not to clutter the text. Unless otherwise referenced, they

are all from Albert Camus, *The Plague*. In Stuart Gilbert (ed., trans.) *The Collected Fiction of Albert Camus* (London: Hamish Hamilton, 1960).
[49] Albert Camus, 1960. *The Outsider*, In Camus, *The Collected Fiction*, note 48.
[50] Camus, *Myth*, note 1, p. 54.
[51] Eagleton, *Culture and the Death of God*, note 14.
[52] Ibid, pp. 32-3.
[53] Ibid, p. 56.
[54] See William Morris, 'Preface to the Nature of Gothic' in William Morris, *News from Nowhere and Other Writings* (London, Penguin, 2004), p. 367 ('the lesson which Ruskin here teaches us is that art is the expression of man's pleasure in labour').
[55] Eagleton, *Culture and the Death of God*, note 14, p. 122.

‘All art is quite useless.’

– **Oscar Wilde**

ESSAY SIX

RESCUING AESTHETICISM FROM THE DANDIES: CRITICAL DISTINCTIONS

The term 'aestheticism', which I am embracing, has acquired a bad name today, employed primarily as a pejorative. It is often directed towards people or movements associated with 'Dandyism' – to be defined below. If I am to succeed in reclaiming this dubious term and make aestheticism a plausible centrepiece of a political cosmology, then further attention must be given to how this term acquired its contemporary meaning, what that meaning is, and how I intend to employ it quite differently. Taking form in the hazy space between life and art, my aesthetic position lies in sharp contrast to Dandyism, which raises similar questions about the unstable distinction between life and art, only to offer very different responses. The following critical examination need not entail a comprehensive review of the territory. Rather, I will only aim to clarify the nature of my own undertaking by way of contrast.

Dandyism is associated most prominently with literary figures like Oscar Wilde, Charles Baudelaire, Beau Brummell, and Joris-Karl Huysmans. Pioneering theoretical work on the underlying aestheticism was undertaken by sympathetic critics likes Barbey d'Aurevilly and Walter Pater.[1] These great writers deserve credit for actively and deliberately blurring the distinction between art and life – an aspiration which I share – but the dandies embodied and theorised the aesthetic perspective in ways that I contend were often regrettably superficial, taking aestheticism in many wrong directions, sometimes dangerously so. We should hesitate, however, to reject the task of interpreting life through an aesthetic lens just because some pioneering aesthetes offered a flawed original attempt. Dandyism is a form of aestheticism, albeit a crude one, but aestheticism is far from exhausted by Dandyism. By clarifying this distinction in what follows, I seek to advance the cause of rehabilitating aestheticism in helpful and important ways.

What is a dandy?

The dandy is an eccentric, often one of aristocratic lineage, who is preeminently concerned with making a striking social impression, first and foremost through carefully crafted and flamboyant attire. It is said that dandies would sometimes spend four hours getting ready – beautifying themselves – for a twenty-minute excursion out in public. Being noticed, and noticed in the right way, is of the highest importance. The dandy enters a social gathering with the intention of doing or saying something memorable, witty, or provocative, then promptly departs with the goal of maintaining intrigue and keeping society wanting more. Life, according to the dandy, is always performative, and pleasure, beauty in appearance, and social admiration, are held up as the highest values and goals. Consciously or unconsciously, a strong element of narcissism and self-absorption defines the lifestyle of a dandy.

Legend has it that the nineteenth-century poet Gerard de Nerval would walk a lobster through the Palais Royal Gardens of Paris, using a blue silk ribbon as a leash. Similarly, Walter Benjamin would report that it was fashionable for *flâneurs* (i.e., urban wanderers) to walk through the arcades of nineteenth-century Paris with a turtle on a leash.[2] Whether or not these stories are apocryphal, they are indicative of the type of conduct a dandy would embrace in order to attract sufficient attention to himself – and historically the dandy was always a male character. He was also usually one of sufficient wealth and class to maintain a life of leisure and high fashion (even though some dandies, such a Baudelaire, knew poverty very well). From the dandy's perspective, who one 'is' is little more or less than how one is 'perceived' by others, and since social impressions could be crafted and designed to form a stylistic whole, life itself was seen as a form of art, with an intended audience. It was important to be talked about and to maintain the right appearances in society, suggesting life was to be treated as an aesthetic performance, albeit in rather cosmetic and affected ways.

The Picture of Dorian Gray

I will now delve a little deeper into the ethos and practice of Dandyism, to provide sufficient contrast to the form of aestheticism I will be defending. To do this I will briefly consider how the aestheticised life of the dandy is represented in one of its leading texts, namely, Oscar Wilde's novel, *The Picture of Dorian Gray* (1891).[3] This book is both illustrative of the defining philosophy while also conveying a cautionary note.

The protagonist, Dorian Gray, begins as an innocent, moralistic, and naive young man, one naturally gifted with extraordinary beauty. He is having his portrait painted by one Basil Hallward, who believes the picture to be his finest work, somehow capturing the spectacular aura of this handsome, young Adonis who was 'made to be worshipped'.[4] Into the studio walks Lord Henry Wotton, who, lighting a heavily opium-tainted cigarette, is to be the mouthpiece of Dandyism in the book and soon to have a profound influence on the posing model.

The plot that structures the book is relatively straightforward. Lord Henry easily convinces the impressionable Dorian that the life and values of a dandy are to be pursued to the fullest, a vocation particularly suited to Dorian given his magnificent beauty and youth. 'We are punished for our refusals,' advises Lord Henry. 'Every impulse that we strive to strangle broods in the mind, and poisons us... The only way to get rid of a temptation is to yield to it.'[5] Thus begins Dorian's unrestrained life as a libertine dandy, where any pretensions of propriety and decency take backstage to the amoral exploration of sensuous experience in all its richness, whatever the consequences.

But as Basil reasons: 'Sin is a thing that writes itself across a man's face. It cannot be concealed... [showing] itself in the lines of his mouth, the droop of his eyelids, the moulding of his hands...'[6] Reflecting on this reality, Dorian begins to envy the pure and youthful image of himself in the painting, which he knew would never age. Wanting to live the hedonistic life of sin and debauchery while also maintaining his youthful vitality, Dorian makes a passionate plea: 'If only it were the other way! If it were I who was to be always young, and the picture that was to grow old!... I would give my soul for that!'[7] Little did he know that this wish was to come true – signifying the plot's central twist. As Dorian's life experiences unfold over the course of the novel, the picture would come to change in hideous and frightful ways, reflecting the degeneration of Dorian's soul, while the real Dorian would maintain his youth and beauty, no matter the immorality of his licentious and decadent behaviour. And so, the central theme of *Dorian Gray* emerges: a man exchanges his soul for eternal youth – but at what cost?

Dorian soon falls in love with an actress called Sibyl Vane. They are to marry. It becomes clear, however, that he is in love with the actress, *as an actress*, rather than the young woman herself. 'Tonight she is Imogen...' he tells Lord Henry, 'and tomorrow night she will be Juliet.'[8] When Sibyl remains in the sphere of art, Dorian finds her exciting and interesting. But one night, after a very ordinary performance on stage, Sibyl confesses to Dorian that she cannot be a great actress anymore now that she has known real love. Dorian's heartless response reflects the cruelty of the dandy's aesthetic code: 'Without your art you are nothing... A third-rate actress with a pretty face.'[9] That evening the heart-broken actress commits suicide, and later that night Dorian notices the first changes in his portrait, a cruel curling of the lips that had not been there the day before. Shocked by these bestial differences in expression, he decides to lock the portrait in the attic where the degeneration of his soul would be safe from prying eyes. This allows Dorian to keep on with the business of life, 'hungers that grew more ravenous as he fed them.'[10]

How might a dandy respond to the tragic death of his fiancé? When discussing the suicide with Lord Henry, Dorian exclaims: 'How extraordinarily dramatic life is! If I had read all this in a book, Harry, I think I would have wept over it. Somehow, now that it has happened actually, and to me, it seems far too wonderful for tears.'[11] Lord Henry offers a similarly callous interpretation of the situation, offering consolation to Dorian by saying 'The girl never really lived, and so she never really died.... Mourn for Ophelia, if you like. Put your ashes on your head because Cordelia was strangled... But don't waste your tears over Sibyl Vane. She was less real than they are.'[12]

One evening Basil visits Dorian and asks to see the portrait. With some hesitation Dorian eventually agrees, and the two men enter the attic and the painting is unveiled. We are informed by the narrator that '[a]n exclamation of horror broke from the painter's lips as he saw in the dim light the hideous face on the canvas grinning at him. There was something in the expression that filled him with disgust and loathing.'[13] It seemed to the painter that 'the leprosies of sin were slowly eating [the painting] away. The rotting of a corpse in a watery grave was not so fearful.'[14]

After Dorian confesses to having received the painting's eternal youthfulness in exchange for his soul, Basil lambasts his friend for the life he must be leading. Dorian takes exception to such moralising and he is overcome with an uncontrollable feeling of hatred toward Basil. Dorian notices a knife glimmering nearby and without ceremony or delay he stabs his friend behind the ear, 'crushing the man's head down on the table, and stabbing again and again.'[15] At a social gathering not twenty-four hours after committing this ghastly murder, we are told that Dorian 'felt keenly the terrible pleasure of a double life.'[16] Dorian soon blackmails an associate to get rid of the body, and the mystery of Basil's demise is never resolved, even as the act comes to haunt the murderous dandy.

Over time, Dorian 'grew more and more enamoured of his own beauty, more and more interested in the corruption of his own soul.'[17] Nevertheless, he still found the painting disturbing. Given that it represented his own conscience, why hadn't he already destroyed it? He resolved to do so at once, returning to the locked room where the portrait was hidden away. Lifting the same knife which murdered his friend, Dorian thrust the weapon toward the painting. A scream was heard, so horrible in its agony that the servants woke. Eventually Dorian's dead body is discovered, withered and wrinkled, lying in a pool of his own blood before the unblemished painting, which had returned to its original state of youthfulness and beauty.

♦ ♦ ♦

Even from this brief review, there are several features of Dandyism that must be distinguished from the form of aestheticism I wish to defend; features that I should clarify so that my own project can avoid unnecessary misunderstandings. One can sympathise with Wilde's statement that 'Life itself was the first, the greatest, of the arts, and for it all the other arts seemed to be but a preparation.'[18] But a critical reading of *Dorian Grey* shows how questionable this philosophy of life can become in the hands of an amoral, hedonistic dandy. Examining the flaws and missteps should prove instructive.

First of all, if aestheticism is to be taken seriously, the dandy's all-embracing concern with fashion, cosmetic appearance, and social perception must be rejected. There is something rather facile about defining a well-lived life according to how elegantly one's scarf matches one's shoes or top hat; or by how many types of exotic flowers or antiques are purchased for interior decorating. 'When one loses one's good looks,' remarks Dorian, 'one loses everything.... When I find that I am growing old, I shall kill myself.'[19] Perhaps this first point of critique is merely destroying a caricature of Dandyism that few people would ever take seriously, but given its prominence, this feature deserves cursory attention.

The history of our species may well be richer for having colourful characters like Oscar Wilde. His main orientation toward life was to *become* a work of art, not merely *produce* art. But the idea of Dandyism becoming a broad cultural influence that reaches beyond a small circle of self-centred aesthetes is a terrifying prospect. Perhaps the self-absorption of social media personalities today suggests that a performative and highly choreographed Dandyism has actually made significant inroads into the cultural logic of late capitalism. This is not, however, a puritanical critique that categorically rejects the values of pleasure, beauty, or performance. It is simply to acknowledge that the dandy's materialistic hedonism is evidence only of a shallow and extravagant excess which the world could clearly do without. This critique weighs particularly heavily in an age of ecological decline and where poverty exists amidst such plenty.

There is, to be sure, nothing necessarily illegitimate or unethical about a concern over outward style. Nevertheless, the dandy's craving for social attention is crudely, even embarrassingly, self-indulgent and narcissistic. Surely there is a substance to one's character that ought to matter more than merely how one's outfit and social engagements are perceived by others. If these aspects of the traditional conception of aestheticism are not overcome, all hope for redeeming the term is lost. Fortunately, on this point at least, there should be few objections.

My second point of critique – related to the first – is that Dandyism's 'cult of beauty' ought to be treated with caution purely on ethical grounds. Lord Henry proudly admitted to choosing his friends 'because of their good looks'[20] and insisted that Dorian was 'too charming'[21] get involved in any philanthropic endeavours. When asked to elaborate on his reasons for rejecting philanthropy, Lord Henry said that he would not do so because the subject was too 'tedious'.[22] Moreover, he would declare: 'I like persons better than principles, and I like persons with no principles better than anything else in the world,'[23] claiming unashamedly that '[s]in is the only real colour-element left in modern life.'[24] For this type of amoral aesthete, why give money to the poor when one could purchase a splendid new hat?

If human beings only have a limited amount of attention to direct in life, it follows that the more an individual is concerned with cosmetics and appearance, the less attention one can give to matters of genuine personal, social, or political concern. 'I can sympathise with everything, except suffering,' admits Lord Henry. 'It is too ugly, too horrible, too distressing.... The less said about life's sores the better.'[25] This is doubtless an easier philosophy of life to embrace when one is born into the nobility. 'One's own life –' Lord Henry proclaims, 'that is the important thing.'[26] The self-centredness of Dandyism as presented in Wilde's novel is stark. In one of Wilde's essays we find the phrase: 'Aesthetics are higher than ethics.'[27]

At its extreme, the fetishisation of cosmetic beauty at the expense of ethics could even lead to perverse situations where suffering, cruelty, and violence are appreciated or admired for their aesthetic characteristics. Wilde's novel provides numerous piercing examples to highlight this point. Dorian only loved Sibyl in the realm of art and treated her cruelly and without remorse when that aesthetic fascination waned. Even her suicide was celebrated as an alluring aesthetic phenomenon – 'a wonderful ending to a wonderful play'.[28] Lord Henry was similarly dismissive of any need to shed tears over the death of a woman who had 'never really lived.'[29] He even confessed to Dorian that 'there is something to me quite beautiful about her death.'[30] On a visit to Paris in 1891, Wilde is even reported to have said: 'When Benvenuto Cellini crucified a living man to study the play of muscles in his death agony, a pope was right to grant him absolution. What is the death of a vague individual if it enables an immortal word to blossom and to create, in Keats' words, an eternal source of ecstasy?'[31] The present point is to highlight how aestheticism – at least as it is represented by Dandyism – presents profound risks from an ethical perspective, which I highlight now in order to avoid these perils later.

Readers might fairly assume I am about to insist, contra Wilde, that ethics must take precedence over aesthetics. In forthcoming essays in this volume, however, it will be seen that my position is a different, more nuanced one: that there is a necessary aesthetic dimension to ethics, just as there is, or ought to be, an ethical dimension to aesthetics. Neither *should* take precedence because neither *can* take precedence, at least in the sense that these domains are, as Michel Foucault showed so powerfully, inextricably intertwined and mutually dependent.[32] Even the arch-theorist of aestheticism himself, Walter Pater, became concerned that Wilde and others had propagated interpretations of his aesthetic philosophy in ethically questionable ways, as merely an amoral aesthetic hedonism. Pater even removed the famous 'conclusion' to his book *The Renaissance: Studies in Art and Poetry* (1877) to minimise such a reading of his work (although the original conclusion was later added back in).[33] When Pater was asked: 'Why be moral?', it is said that he responded: 'Because it is beautiful.' While this interaction may well be legend, it properly implies that aesthetics can have, and ought to have, an ethical dimension that must not be lost sight of. For now, however, I merely expose the ethical dangers that are so plainly displayed by Dandyism.

Wilde himself presented an ambiguous moral in *Dorian Gray*. On the one hand, he clearly set out to present the philosophy of Dandyism in an extreme, eloquent, and powerful literary form, through the words of Lord Henry and the actions of Dorian. Life was to be treated as a work of art, to be lived aesthetically rather than morally, with beauty, pleasure, and self-development being the highest values. On the other hand, Wilde chose to portray a character whose pursuit of beauty for the sake of beauty only made his life uglier than ever, and whose immoral aestheticism tragically led to the death of others and ultimately his own. So even Wilde recognised that unbridled Dandyism posed a social and ethical problem, which means his celebration of the aesthetic lifestyle might not be as unqualified as it might have first appeared. Wilde's essay 'The Soul of Man Under Socialism' also calls for a moment's pause, as our aesthete explored a political vision that criticised industrial capitalism. He called for deep structural changes that would enable and empower everyone, not merely the rich, to become genuine, self-determining individuals.[34] Still, despite the grim downfall of his most famous dandy character, Wilde was still prepared to admit that of all the characters in his literary works, Dorian Gray was the individual he would most like to have been.[35]

My third critical note on Dandyism – related to the second – concerns Oscar Wilde's famous declaration in the preface to *Dorian Gray* that 'all art is quite useless.'[36] Not only did he believe art was useless, he also believed that all art *ought to be* useless, in the sense that it was not the role of artists to use their art to advance an ethical or political vision. Art need only be for art's sake, as the aestheticist creed goes,[37] and it was mere high-mindedness to think art ought to serve any moral or didactic purpose. The job of the artist, according to Wilde's aesthetic philosophy, is simply to create beautiful things: 'There is no such thing as a moral or immoral book,' he wrote. 'Books are well written or badly written. That is all.'[38] In the same vein, and in the same preface, he would write: 'No artist has [by which he means, 'ought to have'] ethical sympathies. An ethical sympathy in an artist is an unpardonable mannerism of style.'[39] More directly still he would assert: 'The sphere of art and the sphere of ethics are absolutely distinct and separate.'[40]

This conception of what art is and ought to be is internally consistent, implying that stylistic 'form' is the sole benchmark of beauty. This suggests that the purpose of art is make something beautiful that induces pleasurable aesthetic experience, irrespective of any ethical or political implications a work of art might have. In contrast, the view I will be detailing in these essays is categorically opposed to Wilde's apolitical philosophy of art. Far from being 'useless', it will be shown (if it is not already too obvious a thesis) that art can justifiably be crafted and evaluated according to its existential, social, and political effects. Contra Wilde, it is far more accurate to say, I believe, that *all artforms are useful*, at least potentially, such that the aesthetic question becomes one of consequences and potential consequences. To what use is art being put and to what ends does it serve?

The idea of a politically neutral or 'useless' art is both implausible and misconceived. Art *can never* be neutral, because it will always have some impact on artist or audience, for better or for worse, which will inevitably have social or political implications to some degree. Moreover, art *should never* be neutral, because it is a tool that has social and political impacts, and those impacts deserve critical evaluation. This is not to say that art must always wear its politics on the surface, or even that artists must be conscious of the socio-political effects of their art. The most effective art often works indirectly on the consciousness of its audience, leaving its influence unknown. Furthermore, the creative interpretation of art can also have a life of its own, beyond what the artist ever intended. In any case, it is an impoverished and decadent aesthetic philosophy that treats as useless something as socially and politically potent as art – as something limited purely to the pleasurable but functionless aesthetic experience of beauty. That, in a word, is what Marxists would decry as 'bourgeois' aesthetics.[41]

My fourth point of critical departure concerns the dandy's relation to nature. If Dandyism celebrates beauty in appearance as an ultimate value, it clearly (and perhaps surprisingly) marginalises the natural environment as an important source of beauty and aesthetic value. In his essay 'The Decay of Lying', Wilde would write:

> The more we study Art, the less we care for Nature. What Art really reveals to us is Nature's lack of design, her curious crudities, her extraordinary monotony, her absolutely unfinished condition... If Nature had been comfortable, mankind would never have invented architecture, and I prefer houses to the open air. In a house we feel all the proper proportions.[42]

This derisive attitude toward nature is portrayed in an extreme form by Huysmans' novel *Against Nature* (1884),[43] (a book which is alluded to in Wilde's story as having a profound influence on Dorian Gray). In Huysmans' novel, the aristocratic protagonist, Jean des Esseintes, retreats to his country house to live a reclusive and decadent life of art, aesthetic experience, sensory pleasure, and self-indulgent hedonism. This aesthete did not want to be bothered by the ordinary concerns of the world, wanting instead to craft a life dedicated entirely to aesthetic sensations, absorbed through all the five senses. Des Esseintes' preference for the artificial over the natural is illustrated when he decorates his manor with real flowers chosen specifically because they imitate artificial ones. In another incident, the aesthete sets gemstones into the shell of a tortoise so that it matches the carpet, a procedure that eventually results in the poor creature's death. If aestheticism is to be taken seriously, Dandyism's rejection of nature as a source of aesthetic value must be overturned. The position I am developing is closer to the tradition of the nature-loving romantic poets, a perspective captured in these lines from William Blake: 'To see a World in a Grain of Sand / And Heaven in a Wild Flower / Hold Infinity in the palm of your hand / And Eternity in an hour.'[44]

Finally – and this point returns us to philosophical territory – treating life as a work of art in Dandyism is portrayed as a *choice* one makes. In one sense this framing can be disputed. In previous essays I presented a case for embracing an aesthetic perspective, in the sense of life having *inherent* aesthetic dimensions. I believe this is simply the way things are, for creatures such as ourselves. While Dandyism represents a call *to embrace* the life of an aesthete, I have argued that aestheticism, whether we like it or not, *embraces us*, by virtue of the human condition. It is not a choice. On the other hand, I accept Wilde's position that we should choose to look upon life from the aesthetic perspective, but disagree with him, in most regards, about what that involves and implies.

In the end, however, I am suggesting that we are all aesthetes now, whether we like it or not, and the important challenge is determining what this means in an age such as our own. That is one way to frame the central project of this collection of essays.

---

[1] See generally, Len Gutkin, *Dandyism: Forming Fiction from Modernism to the Present* (Charlottesville: University of Virginia Press, 2020).
[2] Walter Benjamin, *The Arcades Project* (Boston: Harvard University Press, 2002).
[3] Oscar Wilde *The Picture of Dorian Gray* (London: Penguin, 2003).
[4] Ibid, p. 111.
[5] Ibid, p. 21.
[6] Ibid, p. 143.
[7] Ibid, p. 28.
[8] Ibid, p. 54.
[9] Ibid, p. 85.
[10] Ibid, p. 124.
[11] Ibid, p. 96.
[12] Ibid, p. 100.
[13] Ibid, p. 149.
[14] Ibid, p. 150.
[15] Ibid, p. 151.
[16] Ibid, p. 15.
[17] Ibid, p. 124.
[18] Ibid, p. 125.
[19] Ibid, p. 28.
[20] Ibid, p. 11.
[21] Ibid, p. 19.
[22] Ibid.
[23] Ibid, p. 12.
[24] Ibid, p. 30.
[25] Ibid, p. 41.
[26] Ibid, p. 76.
[27] Oscar Wilde, 'The Critic as Artist' (1891). Available at: https://www.wilde-online.info/the-critic-as-artist-page45.html (accessed 15 April 2023).
[28] Wilde, *Dorian Gray*, note 3, p. 98.
[29] Ibid, p. 100.
[30] Ibid, p. 99.
[31] As quoted in Martin Jay, '"The Aesthetic Ideology" as Ideology: Or, What Does it Mean to Aestheticize Politics?' (1992) *Cultural Critique* 21: p. 43. Another notorious

example of how ethics can be marginalised by an improper aestheticism is given by the poet Laurent Tailhade to a deadly anarchist bomb thrown into the French Chamber of Deputies in 1893: 'What do the victims matter if the gesture is beautiful?' See Jay, '"The Aesthetic Ideology" as Ideology' note 31, pp. 43-4. As Jay (p. 44) writes: 'The aestheticization of politics in these cases repels not merely because of the grotesque impropriety of applying criteria of beauty to the deaths of human beings, but also because of the chilling way in which nonaesthetic criteria are deliberately and provocatively excluded from consideration.'

[32] See, e.g., Michel Foucault, 'An Aesthetics of Existence' in Lawrence Kritzman (ed.) *Michel Foucault: Politics, Philosophy, Culture: Interviews and Other Writings 1977-1984* (New York: Routledge, 1990), p. 49. I explore Foucault's 'aesthetics of existence' in the essay [Giving Birth to Oneself – to be confirmed].

[33] Walter Pater, *The Renaissance: Studies in Art and Poetry* (Oxford: Oxford University Press, 1986).

[34] Oscar Wilde, 'The Soul of Man under Socialism' (1891). Available at: https://www.marxists.org/reference/archive/wilde-oscar/soul-man/ (accessed 10 March 2023).

[35] In his published letters, Wilde wrote: 'Basil Hallward is what I think I am: Lord Henry what the world thinks me: Dorian what I would like to be — in other ages, perhaps.' See Oscar Wilde, *The Letters of Oscar Wilde* (London: Hart-Davis, 1962), p. 352.

[36] Wilde, *Dorian Gray*, note 3, p. 4.

[37] See, e.g., Stephen Cheeke, 'The Religion of Art, *Art For Art's Sake:* Dante Gabriel Rossetti and Walter Pater' *RaVoN* (2011) 59-60. Available at: https://www.erudit.org/en/journals/ravon/2011-n59-60-ravon0382/1013271ar/ (accessed 12 March 2023).

[38] Ibid, p. 3.

[39] Ibid.

[40] Wilde wrote this line in response to a critical reviewer of *Dorian Gray*. See the introduction to *Dorian Gray*, note 3, p. xxv.

[41] For a discussion, see Herbert Marcuse, *The Aesthetic Dimension: Toward a Critique of Marxist Aesthetics* (London: MacMillan Education, 1979), p. 62.

[42] Oscar Wilde, 'The Decay of Lying' (1905). Available at: http://virgil.org/dswo/courses/novel/wilde-lying.pdf (accessed 10 March 2023).

[43] Joris-Karl Huysmans, *Against Nature* (London: Penguin, 2003).

[44] William Blake, 'Auguries of Innocence' (1863).

‘What are humans *for*?’

– **Wendell Berry**

ESSAY SEVEN

HOMO AESTHETICUS, THE ARTFUL SPECIES: AN EVOLUTIONARY PERSPECTIVE

In this book I am presenting the universe as something that is fundamentally aesthetic, a vision arising out of the metaphor of 'cosmos-as-artist' as opposed to the dominant paradigm of 'cosmos-as-machine'. As an interpretative and explanatory tool, I have posited an underlying creative force in the universe – a primordial Will to Art – that seeks to explore its creative and sensuous nature through the evolution of conscious life. From this perspective, matter is driven to self-awareness over billions of years, in order to produce and experience art and the beauty it can bring forth. Inspired by William Morris, I have defined art broadly and openly as the pleasurable and meaningful expression of creative labour, a theoretical move intended to blur the distinction between artist and artisan.

According to this poetic ontology, the ultimate *telos* of the universe is beauty, providing a latent purpose to the world and our human struggles within it. This guiding ideal should be understood not as mere cosmetic ornamentation, but as the pleasurable experience of art and nature, the meaningful interaction with self, other, and world, and the undertaking and contemplation of aesthetic activity. Our capacity to experience beauty shows that human beings have a place in this world, at least potentially, and our capacity to create beauty provides us with a noble, orientating purpose. The history of political society can be interpreted through this lens, as a dialectical process of evolution through which human beings struggle, often unconsciously and indirectly, toward the ideal of beauty.

Later in this collection of essays I will propose and defend a political economy of art, being a mode of societal organisation that would structure and support an ecological civilisation of artisan-artists. Such an aestheticised society would be composed of people living materially simple but sufficient lives in harmony with nature, seeking meaning and pleasure in life primarily through self-directed creative labour and aesthetic experience. In developing this orientating vision, my two guiding premises are, first, that material sufficiency is all that is *needed* for human beings to live rich, meaningful, and artful lives; and second, that material sufficiency is all that is *possible*, over the long term, on a finite planet in an age of environmental limits.

In what follows I continue providing foundations for this vision of an ecological civilisation by exploring how human consciousness is presently the most sophisticated evolutionary outcome of the universe's creative unfolding.[1] On that basis I propose that our species is best described, not as *homo sapiens*, but as *homo aestheticus* – that is, artistic or aesthetic human.[2] It is easy enough to acknowledge that art could not have existed without the humans who produced it. Few consider the possibility, however, that humans could not have appeared without our arts.[3]

In that spirit, I will present a case for why every human being, on account of evolutionary inheritances, can (and should) be described and self-identify as being part of an 'artful species',[4] as an aesthetic agent in an aesthetic universe. This account can be derived from our powerfully creative natures and innate aesthetic sensibilities, which are found universally among human societies and which have an origin in biological evolution. In fact, it will be seen that the development of our aesthetic practices and rituals throughout history, including the earliest forms of art, were what made us who we are, such that it is accurate to describe us as an art-created art creator – the aesthetic animal.[5] This isn't something one can simply declare, however. It calls for the presentation of a plausible evolutionary framework.

Furthermore, today it is self-evident that our species has evolved to such a state whereby we can now cooperate with physical evolution in order to shape or co-produce that evolutionary process through deliberative action; that is, through creative evolution.[6] We can cooperate with physical evolution because we are at least partially in control of our own actions and can shape the societies and cultures of which we are a part. Our aesthetic capacities and potentials, therefore, are more powerful than ever. At the same time, we are living in a world where self-realisation through creative expression is being stifled if not extinguished by the seductive emptiness of consumerist cultures and today's profit-centred politics of unsustainable growth. In short, our species seems to be suffering an aesthetic deficit, leaving us alienated from our creative natures. My overarching argument in this collection of essays is that this deficit must be resolved if we are to achieve political and ecological hopes for a more humane, sustainable, and artful social order. Not only that, I will present a theory of change based on the view that art and aesthetic activity are the best tools for producing this new society.

I want to make clear, again, that this narrative of the aesthetic universe is not being presented as the One and Only Right Way to understand evolution in general or humanity in particular. I acknowledge that both the universe and humanity are infinitely complex and, as such, are liable to an infinite number of interpretations. This acknowledgement, however, supports my aesthetic reading of existence, given that it implies that interpretation, an aesthetic practice, cannot be avoided in constructing a view of reality.[7] It follows that my reading – evidenced and coherent through it may be – is only one of many plausible interpretations. Accordingly, rather than claiming a metaphysical grounding or presenting an evidential 'proof', I simply invite people to 'think of things this way' and see where the aesthetic metaphoric leads and what it might reveal. In doing so I present a Grand Narrative of the universe and humanity's place in it, one that is self-consciously a narrative, but which is not, for that reason, untrue.[8]

Overview

After presenting a brief history of life on Earth by way of context, my examination will briefly restate the core elements of evolutionary theory, concerning natural and sexual selection. I then consider what role art and aesthetics may have played in evolutionary history and whether, or to what extent, art can be considered an adaptive strategy that helped our species survive and thrive. Ultimately, however, the question of whether art should be considered an adaptive strategy or 'merely' a cultural innovation is not as important as trying to get a sense of what type of creature we are. This understanding can be enriched by looking to our evolutionary history, irrespective of whether our aesthetic nature is a result of biological inheritances or cultural traditions and practices. It's clear to me that our species is a product of biology *and* culture, and my evolutionary focus herein should not be interpreted otherwise.

Anticipating issues discussed further in later essays, I will also consider whether the future of our species depends on our aesthetic and artistic natures, especially given the present context of intensifying environmental and social pressures. When looking to the past it becomes clear that the arts have helped our species survive, develop, and flourish in often hostile, uncertain, and changing environments. It seems plausible, then, that the wise use of the arts may also be required to assist us through the turbulent present and into unknown futures.[9] Hence this is ultimately a forward-looking analysis, even if this essay resides predominantly in the past.

Over the course of this project, I will seek to show that the human capacity for art and our aesthetic sensibilities may prove to be necessary tools for adapting to, and managing, forthcoming crises – both at the individual and group levels. This will be especially so as biophysical limits begin to impact more deeply on the viability and stability of industrial civilisation (or any growth-orientated civilisation for that matter). Whether we adapt aesthetically or not will, in large part, determine whether we are 'fit to survive' in an increasingly resource and energy constrained and inhospitable ecological era. Just as the fastest deer are more fit to survive in an environment of speedy predators, humanity's aesthetic capacities and sensibilities might be central to our own survival in an age of environmental limits and planetary tipping points. After all, our aesthetic capacities and sensibilities are currently being dangerously repressed, distorted, and underutilised. This has resulted in what I have called an aesthetic deficit disorder – a lack of beauty, sensuality, meaning, and creativity in our lives. Put bluntly, the choice we face is: art or extinction. Fortunately, the choice is ours.

Deep history and the emergence of life

Let me begin at the beginning – literally. Physicists advise that the universe burst into existence approximately 13.8 billion years ago and that Earth formed around 4.5 billion years ago.[10] From that point it is estimated that it took almost one billion years for the earliest forms of microbial life to emerge.[11] Within another billion years cyanobacteria had evolved, which were Earth's first photo-synthesizers, sustaining themselves using water and the sun's energy and releasing oxygen as a result. This 'Great Oxidation Event' set the stage for a remarkable transformation of Earth's atmosphere, as oxygen levels increased dramatically. Eventually, multicellular life developed, and around 600-800 million years ago the earliest forms of plant life, and then animal life, emerged. Over the next few hundred million years, the ecosystems of Earth continued to change and the conditions for more complex life forms developed. This point on the geological timescale is sometimes called the 'Cambrian explosion' (approximately 500 million years ago), when nearly all existing animal types, or phyla (mollusks, arthropods, annelids, etc), were established.

To cut a very long story short, animal life continued to evolve until there came a point, around six million years ago, when the earliest hominins emerged in Africa (ongoing technical debates over precise dates need not concern us – rough estimates are good enough). Hominins were descendants of the great apes – of which human beings are *all* descendants. These proto-humans initiated the transition to walking erect on two legs and developed larger brains, amongst other physiological changes. These were evolutionary adaptations that assisted with surviving in competitive natural environments.

Over the next five million years or so a variety of hominin species lived, evolved, and died out. As environmental conditions changed and as some interbreeding amongst human species occurred, the genetic and cultural variety of these species continued to evolve. *Homo habilis* is thought to have emerged around 2.5 million years ago; *homo erectus* around 1.8 million years ago; and Neanderthals around 400,000 years ago. It is thought the Neanderthals went extinct around 30,000 years ago, being the last species of the *homo* genus to exist besides our own. Stone tools, such as handaxes, were being used at least 2.5 million years ago, giving birth to what is sometimes called *homo faber* ('tool-making human').

The oldest fossils of *homo sapiens* date back to around 300,000 years ago, and fossils from around 160-200,000 years ago look remarkably similar to our own. Although humans living today are in most regards anatomically indistinguishable from these early *homo sapiens,* it would be wrong to suggest that the processes of evolutionary biology have stopped.[12] These early humans *looked* like us, but it is not clear to what extent they *thought* like us, an inevitably speculative inquiry to which I will return. Throughout this long history, hominins typically lived in small hunter-gatherer tribes. It was only with the transition to agriculture around 10,000 years ago did humankind begin to settle in villages and develop more sedentary ways of life with increased socio-technical complexity.[13]

For present purposes this brief historical sketch suffices to lay the groundwork for an inquiry into the relationship between evolution and our artistic or aesthetic sensibilities. The next step in the analysis requires a brief statement of evolutionary theory, the nature of which is well known and, beyond the Creationists, is rarely disputed in any fundamental way (even as technical debates continue).

The theory of evolution

The theory of evolution by 'natural selection' is associated famously with Charles Darwin, who published *The Origin of Species* in 1859. It should be noted that the theory was also independently and concurrently conceived by Alfred Russel Wallace, who publicly presented a paper on the same subject with Darwin in 1858. In essence, this theory begins by acknowledging that environmental pressures placed on plants, insects, and animals lead to a 'struggle for existence'. Each individual in a species has slightly different characteristics (size, speed, other physical attributes, resilience, etc), and when an entire population cannot survive under specific environmental pressures – such as scarcity of food, an inhospitable climate, too many predators, and so forth – only the fittest survive. (The well-known phrase 'survival of the fittest' did not appear in *The Origin of Species* until the 5th edition, borrowed from Herbert Spencer, who coined the apt phrase after reading Darwin).

The result of these dynamics is that the surviving population will have a greater proportion of a particular set of heritable characteristics (e.g., longer necks in giraffes) that help the species adapt to a specific environment (e.g., insufficient food) and those with characteristics less useful in adaptation to the competitive environment (e.g., shorter necks) are more likely to die off. A process that typically occurs over countless generations, species evolve as natural selection leads to usually small incremental adaptations that overtime can provide significant competitive advantage in the prevailing environmental conditions. In more recent times, dating from the work of Gregor Mendel, these adaptations are understood and explained with more precision via modern genetics. Darwin and Wallace knew *that* certain characteristics were heritable; Mendel, and those who advanced this work on genetic transmission, explained *how*.

The process above has come to be known as evolution by 'natural selection'. However, Darwin later introduced a second evolutionary dynamic called 'sexual selection', originally outlined in his 1871 book, *The Descent of Man and Selection in Relation to Sex*. Darwin had noticed that some evolutionary advantages emerged not because of their ability to help a species better negotiate a difficult physical environment, but rather to increase chances of attracting mates and thereby increasing the chances of passing on genes by other means.

This alternative evolutionary dynamic can be clarified by considering the most well-known example of sexual selection – and the one that helped Darwin to develop this sub-theory. The elaborate feathers of a peacock seem to have no competitive advantage in terms of mere survival in a hostile environment, and indeed, would seem to provide a sizeable disadvantage in terms of either fighting or fleeing. With respect to evolution by 'natural selection', the tail doesn't make sense, and it was this incongruity that got Darwin rethinking aspects of his earlier theory. He came to realise that the tail of the peacock can be explained evolutionarily as a feature that is genetically passed on, not because it helped in the struggle for existence, but because it increases the chances of attracting female mates by distinguishing the male from competitors. That is, this physical feature evolves through 'sexual selection' rather than 'natural selection'. Beyond the peacock, this sexual dynamic is seen throughout the animal kingdom (including in humans), where sexual selection clearly plays a role in genetic transmission as individuals select mates after visually assessing their attributes (e.g., perceived health, dominance, fertility, beauty, etc.) and making decisions accordingly.[14]

Consequently, natural selection and sexual selection evoke different notions of 'fitness' and therefore function differently, but concurrently, on evolutionary processes. Genes may have a higher chance of being passed on (and thereby shaping evolution) due to either explanation. Many theorists today, however, place sexual selection under the broader category of natural selection. Either way, for present purposes both processes need to be borne in mind as the discussion proceeds.

Today it can be hard to imagine quite how radical and unsettling the theory of evolution was to many people (even though, to be clear, many aspects of evolutionary theory predated the work of Darwin and Wallace). In nineteenth-century England, the dominant worldview was Christian, and the diversity of species was explained essentially in relation to the Book of Genesis. God created the world in six days, and even if interpreted metaphorically, the received view was that it was God who created the spectacular variety of species on Earth. Most notably, God created humankind in his own image, set apart from the other species. But the main point is that all species were thought to exist because of divine creation not biological evolution.

Evolutionary theory, however, was able to explain scientifically how the variety of species could have emerged *without* the need for positing a Creator. Human beings, although clearly the most sophisticated evolution of animal consciousness, were, in fact, just another animal, descended from the great apes. This nineteenth-century shift in thinking – from Genesis to evolution – was truly a Copernican revolution through which humankind's self-image shifted from 'creature of God' to 'talking ape'. In the absence of religious assumptions, of course, this ought not to imply any loss of dignity.

Art and aesthetics in evolution

With the basic theory outlined, I can begin assessing the evolutionary case for whether, or to what extent, it might be fair to describe the human being as an aesthetic animal – *homo aestheticus*. In particular, I want to enquire into whether art and aesthetics played any adaptive role shaping our biological attributes in evolutionary history, in the sense of providing competitive advantage in the struggle for existence.

First, it must be acknowledged that the human animal is not *uniquely aesthetic* amongst the community of life forms, if we use the term aesthetic broadly and inclusively. Above I gave the example (in relation to sexual selection) of how the extravagant plumage of the peacock's tail is used to 'signal fitness' and attract mates. It follows that the peahen must be impressed by the *visual spectacle* of the tail, which can fairly be described as an aesthetic response based on a particular aesthetic sensibility. Darwin argued that 'it is impossible to deny [the female bird] admires the beauty of her male partner.'[15] We might want to qualify this as being proto-aesthetic, rather than aesthetic proper, especially given that there is probably no conscious aesthetic reflection or strategy at play but rather an instinctive response to stimuli. In any case, here we can at least acknowledge the emergence of aesthetic or proto-aesthetic practice and sensibility in the animal kingdom.

The same could be said of birdsong or the songs of whales. Not only can these be aesthetically beautiful, akin to music, but like the peacock's tail, they are aesthetic products often designed to attract mates or otherwise communicate through melodic rituals. Both the product (the beautiful tail or song) and the ability to be receptive to the spectacle (the aesthetic sensibility) are significant traits that provide competitive advantages. They are advantageous either because they help communicate or because they attract mates, or both. Thus, these aesthetic attributes and characteristics are more likely to be genetically passed on. Darwin and later theorists saw that the elaborate products of human artists resemble the displays of birds and peacocks, even speculating that the origins and functions of artmaking might be attributable to sexual selection.[16] Both the ritual of showing off the peacock's tail and birdsong, however, are instinctive behaviours or genetically conditioned reflexes, presumably lacking in the creative reflection we would normally associate with the production of a work of art. Whether whales, having far greater intelligence than birds, deserve to have their songs understood differently, is an interesting question but one that presently need not be explored further.

Perhaps the closest thing akin to 'art' in the animal kingdom is the decorative practices of the bowerbird. Again, the male of the species will engage in a ritual designed to court females, gathering bright and pretty things, and arranging them in what seems to be a decorative endeavour. This aesthetic practice is arguably more elaborate than what is undertaken by any other animal – except humans. Again, however, this arrangement of pretty things seems categorically distinct from, say, the thoughtful organisation of objects into a sculpture, or the curation of art pieces in a museum. Or rather, with due respect to the bowerbird, perhaps it is rather just a matter of degree, although at different ends of the spectrum. The depth of consciousness in the practices are presumably so different as to be only dubiously classify as the same thing – 'art' – a definitional conundrum to which we will have to return.

The same definitional haze arises with respect to so-called 'animal art', whereby a chimp or an elephant, for example, is provided with a paintbrush and canvas. Is the outcome art? Do we want to call this art? Even if the chimp produces a brush stroke or two that could loosely be described as having some aesthetic value, such experiments tend to show that if the canvas is not taken away, the animal will keep on painting until it is a complete mess, and thereafter show little or no interest in it.[17] One cannot really say these animals are consciously giving 'form' to a creative product in any aesthetic sense. A chimp waving its hand with a brush over canvas is of such a rudimentary, unsophisticated creative act that it cannot be placed in the same category as a Rembrandt or Picasso. As noted, if the result does happen to show a semblance of 'form', it is usually a consequence of a human removing the canvas at a suitable time. So again, the presence of 'art' in the non-human animal kingdom arguably lacks plausibility, even if we should accept that proto-aesthetic sensibilities are certainly present.

Some may want to object here, and insist that these non-human examples are indeed art, and that my analysis is betraying anthropocentric biases. Perhaps. My hunch, however, is that there will be many more sympathisers than detractors in taking this modest theoretical stance. We can easily accept that the peahen has a basic aesthetic sensibility, the capacity to appreciate the beauty of the peacock's tail, and that birds and whales create sounds that resemble the art of music. But I believe it is not unreasonable to proceed on the basis that these are very rudimentary *precursors* to art, but not art itself. At least, that will be my philosophical assumption, which I state to make sure my position is clear, even though someone might reasonably insist on an alternative reading.

The 'origins of art' in human history

Having provided examples of rudimentary or precursory examples of art and the aesthetic sensibility in the non-human animal kingdom, it should come as no surprise that those features exist in human evolution too. Moreover, it would be fair to say that they emerge in more developed or sophisticated forms. Just as the peahen developed an aesthetic sensibility in history, so too have evolutionary theorists and researchers argued that such a sensibility exists in early hominins, albeit in ways specific to our species.

For example, philosopher of art and evolutionary theorist Dennis Dutton argues that the near-universal judgement of beauty when humans contemplate a lush landscape with flowing water can be considered an ancestral aesthetic inheritance.[18] Those humans drawn to such landscapes were more likely to find food and water, being an example of how aesthetic sensibility could provide an adaptive advantage and increase chances of survival and thus reproductive success. Below I will also consider examples of sexual selection, whereby, in ways similar to the peahen and peacock, human beings have always engaged in aesthetic activity, presentation, and evaluation in mating rituals with evolutionary consequences. Archaeological evidence also indicates that ancestral hominins, as early as one million years ago or more,[19] may have collected artefacts made of unusual materials or displaying unusual markings and carried these with them to their dwelling sites. This suggests that these collectors must have somehow been aesthetically attracted to these unusual or 'special' artefacts.[20] To borrow the words of art theorist Arthur Danto, these ancestral practices – as with some contemporary art practices – can be understood as an impulse to 'transfigure the commonplace'.[21]

Beyond mere aesthetic sensibility, however, what about the vexed archaeological question concerning the 'origins of art' itself? This framing risks getting us bogged down in the intractable debate over the definition or meaning of art, for it is certainly the case that answering the question of 'origins' here depends on what counts as 'art'. How, then, should we proceed?

The debate could be easily conceded to John Carey, who argues, with some persuasive force, that the most we can say, by way of definition, is that art is anything that someone has ever considered to be art, even if only one person has considered it to be so.[22] This is the logical consequence of accepting that art is an 'essentially contested' term; a term which, as Morris Weitz argued, has no essence and so will forever be disputed without hope of analytical resolution.[23] Or, as Theodor Adorno wrote: 'It is self-evident that nothing concerning art is self evident anymore, not its inner life, not its relation to the world, not even its right to exist.'[24] This radical anti-essentialism, though theoretically compelling, doesn't much help us determine the origins of art, for if something is indefinable, one cannot be sure when the indefinable thing originated, since it cannot be easily or uncontroversially identified.

In response to these challenges, some theorists offer a 'cluster definition' of art, listing properties widely considered characteristic of art without suggesting that any single characteristic is necessary or sufficient. This approach avoids black and white conceptual statements (e.g., 'this and only this is art'), and it recognises that art objects or practices, at most, share what Wittgenstein called 'family resemblances'.[25] This position implies that examples of art can share overlapping features, without there being a common essence which *all* examples share. Below I list four prominent cluster definitions of art in an attempt to advance the discussion without falling into essentialism. These definitions, which themselves share family resemblances, proceed on the Wittgensteinian assumption that the concept of art is indeterminate.

- Denis Dutton's proposes that art typically: (i) provides immediate experiential pleasure not utility; (ii) displays skill and virtuosity; (iii) exhibits style; (iv) has novelty and demonstrates creativity; (v) is subject to critical judgements and appreciation; (vi) involves representation; (vii) attracts special focus and is bracketed off from the everyday; (viii) expresses individuality; (ix) is emotionally saturated; (x) offers intellectual challenges; (xi) is associated with art traditions and institutions; (xii) evokes imaginative experience.[26]

- Bery Gaut's cluster definition of art is: (i) possessing positive aesthetic properties; (ii) being expressive of emotion; (iii) being intellectually challenging; (iv) being formally complex and coherent; (v) having a capacity to convey complex meanings; (vi) exhibiting an individual point of view; (vii) being an exercise of creative imagination; (viii) being an artifact or performance that is the product of high skill; (ix) belong to an established art form; (x) being the product of an intention to make a work of art.[27]

- Elle Dissanayake makes a list of qualities and characteristics that pervade ideas about art, including: (i) *artifice* (something contrived, 'artificial' rather than natural); (ii) *beauty and pleasure* (admiration and enjoyment); (iii) the *sensual quality of things* (colour, shape, sound); (iv) the *immediate fullness of sense experience* (as contrasted with habituated, unregulated experience); (v) *order* or *harmony* (shaping, pattern-making, achieving unity or wholeness); (vi) *innovation* (exploration, originality, creativity, invention, seeing things a new way, surprise); (vii) *adornment* (decoration, display); (viii) *self-expression* (presenting one's personal view of the world); (ix) *a special kind of communication* (conveying information in a special kind of language, symbolising); (x) *nonutilitarian* (made for its own sake, having no function); (xi) *serious and important concerns* (significance, meaning); (xii) *make-believe* (fantasy, play, wish-fulfilment, illusion, imagination); (xiii) *heightened existence* (exalted emotion, ecstasy, self-transcendence).[28]

- Finally, Stephen Davies, who adopts a different and more concise approach, contends that something is art: (i) if it falls under an established, publicly recognised category of art or within an established art tradition; or (ii) if it is intended by its maker/presenter to be art and its maker/presenter does what is necessary and appropriate to realising that intention; or (iii) if it shows excellence of skill and achievement in realising significant aesthetic or artistic goals.[29]

Without evaluating or trying to choose between them, I list these various attempts in order to provide non-essentialist ways of giving *some* content to the concept of art under discussion. But given they are all non-essentialist, the problem of how to identify art's 'origins' remains, since non-essentialist cluster definitions are inherently fuzzy around the conceptual edges, and so early forms of art might (and do) remain difficult to identify.

There is another way to approach this definitional challenge, however, and that is to accept the blurry boundary between art and non-art by creating a concept that accommodates the *gradual emergence* of art practices along a spectrum. In that spirit, I'll proceed with the cautious but coherent definitional work offered by evolutionary theorist Ellen Dissanayake, who introduced the term 'artification' to resolve the problem under consideration.[30] This concept can be preliminarily understood to refer to behaviours of 'making things special'[31], or of somehow making the ordinary extraordinary by means of artistic/aesthetic operations (e.g., formalisation, repetition, exaggeration, and elaboration).[32] Artification can include features typically associated with art (beauty, imagination, creativity, skill, personal expression, sensory experience, and emotion). These are 'ingredients that artifiers use as they make ordinary things... *extra*ordinary.'[33] In this light, art can be seen as a subset of a broader notion of artification, and through this broader notion, it will be argued that we can come to a deeper understanding of an evolutionary understanding of both the making of, and the responses to, the arts.

The notion of artification proves to be very useful, then, especially in historical analysis, because it can side-step the thorny conceptual challenge of trying to determine whether something either is, or is not, art. Rather than having to make such a controversial theoretical judgement, which can be merely distracting, the notion of artification implies a gradual movement along a creative spectrum, whereby the bowerbird can be said to be engaging in a basic form of 'artification', without the result being art, as such. In the same way, we might say that the shaping of early handaxes or spears in aesthetic yet non-utilitarian ways could be examples of artification without these artefacts being art. The second benefit of Dissanayake's term is that it turns art (as a product) into artification or the verb to 'artify' (as a behaviour). This distinction will bear fruit as the discussion proceeds.

Consider the history of artification in human evolution. Dissanayake argues that the earliest proto-aesthetic behaviour in human beings emerged from ancestral mother-infant relations.[34] As hominin's rose to walk on two legs, the female pelvis contracted, narrowing the birth canal, while at the same time the human brain was growing. Among other adaptations, this led to a reduction in the gestation period to accommodate these changes, meaning that babies with smaller neonate skulls were delivered in a more immature state compared to other primates.[35] This left the hominin newborns more reliant than ever, and for a longer time, on the mother for feeding.[36] Although it can sound crude to express it in evolutionary terms, a behavioural adaptation was needed to ensure the mother would voluntarily care for a helpless baby.

Dissanayake contends that a behavioural adaptation emerged from these physiological changes: the universally observable vocal and gestural interactions between mother and infant that are sometimes called 'motherese':

> Although mother and baby are simply enjoying each other's company, suffused with pleasure and love, these signals are, unknown to a mother, flooding her brain with the prosocial hormones that foster maternal behaviour in all mammals... [This] reinforces her brain's neural circuits for affiliation and development, ensuring that she will be motivated to care for her demanding, helpless baby.[37]

The consequence is that these interactions, which promote bonding between mother and baby, have evolutionary advantages, contributing to infant survival and maternal reproductive success by reinforcing pathways for caretaking and emotional attachment. What is more, Dissanayake notes that '[l]ocating the roots of human artifying in the earliest social interactions of infants with their caretakers reveals that the art impulse is far more deeply dyed and consequential to the evolution and psychology of humans than heretofore suspected by philosophers and scientists alike.'[38] The discovery of such aesthetic sensitivity at the beginning of life 'suggests that emotional response to aesthetic manipulations has been critical to human survival.'[39] It is not surprising, she adds, 'that these operations should become powerful sources of emotion.'[40] While Dissanayake does not argue that this was 'artification', she does describe this ritualised engagement as amongst the earliest, and perhaps *the* earliest, proto-aesthetic behaviour in our species.[41]

Dissanayake then proposes that there were various transitional evolutionary steps that led from the sing-song vocalisations of 'motherese', to more developed examples of artification and ritual, which led coherently over time to what we today call 'the arts'. She provides the example of imaginative play in children. This typically requires the child to take a stance that is different from reality, creating 'another dimension' of experience. (I will consider the concept of 'play' in more detail in a later essay on Friedrich Schiller, but here its origins are evident). There also seems to be a 'mark marking' instinct in children to scribble and draw – which emerges from what some researchers call an 'inner imperative'.[42] Pleasure seems to be derived from using our flexible and dexterous hands, and 'meaning' seems to emerge not merely from the outcome but from the process.

Dissanayake reports that the earliest known human-made marks – the making of 'ordinary rock surfaces extraordinary'[43] – date from around 250kya (thousand years ago). Specifically, 'ancestral hominins hammered cupules (cup-shaped indentations) on horizontal and vertical surfaces, often in rows or ranks, in tens, hundreds, or even thousands at one site.'[44] It is interesting to wonder: what were these people doing by making these indentations? They were often created on vertical surfaces, which suggests that they cannot have been to collect water. By not having any clear utilitarian purpose, they acquire a special mystique. The 'time and physical effort required to make a deeply carved cupules call for an evolutionary explanation, since a biological organism does not regularly engage in such costly or labor-intensive behaviour without gaining some adaptive advantage.'[45] Other geometric or abstract (non-representational) markings have similarly deep history, with some being made by our remote ancestors in the Lower Palaeolithic era (ending about 180 kya).[46]

It is possible and likely, however, that even before this time the earliest artifications were to the human body, self-adornments, altering hair or skin with paint, feathers, bones, or shells, or through permanent changes like tattooing. These body modifications do not leave archaeological evidence, meaning that dating these practices precisely is impossible. Nevertheless, perforated beads fashioned from shell or ivory date from around 200kya, which would have 'artified' those who wore them, making them special or extraordinary in some way.

Moving from 'motherese' and play, through 'making marks', to self-adornment, Dissanayake then considers the role of ceremonial or ritual practices in ancestral societies. These practices differentiate between 'an ordinary or mundane order, realm, mood, or state of being and one that is unusual, extraordinary, or supernatural.'[47] Notably, rituals and ceremonies, apparently universal among human societies, bring together various 'arts' as we know them today, including self-adornment, dance, song, storytelling, decorated or embellished environments, or imbibing a ritual drink. The role or function of these and other artifications or arts are considered further below, but for now it can be noted that ritual and ceremony presumably arose along with, or *were*, religious or spiritual in nature. It is believed ritual and ceremony would have enhanced group bonding and/or provided some form of consolation, guidance, or assumed protection from the uncertainties or dangers of human existence. If art was able to induce altered states of consciousness, as we know to be true, perhaps religion was, in part, an attempt to give meaning to those altered states.

Another contender for the so-called 'origin of art' has been tentatively provided by philosopher and evolutionary theorist Gregory Currie.[48] Acknowledging that people who disagree about what counts as art will answer this question in different ways, he nevertheless makes a strong case for early handaxes as being amongst the earliest forms of art. Such handaxes date back to 'around half a million years ago' (a timespan he accepts is massively imprecise but still usefully suggestive).

Currie notes that most people find his answer unattractive, given that a handaxe is typically understood as a primitive technology, not an early artistic creation. Furthermore, the hominins making such tools so long ago presumably had limited social intelligence, no articulated language or symbolic imagination, and theorists might resist the thesis that art could arise in so 'thin' a cultural and cognitive setting. One assumption he makes, however, is that these early handaxes were examples of 'pure, unmeaningful beauty'.[49] From this he suggests that contemporary analyses of art in terms of 'meaning' can function to marginalise artefacts made simply to 'beautify' without deeper significance.

Currie cites historian J. Desmond Clark who notes that 'The symmetry and refinement of some of the earlier Acheulean handaxes, which surely go beyond utilitarian need, may reflect the first appearance of an aesthetic appreciation of form.'[50] Currie reviews a range of archaeological evidence and analyses that support this conclusion. These 'visually arresting'[51] Acheulean handaxes are distinguished from earlier examples, dating from around 2.5 million years ago, which appear to be tools designed purely for utilitarian purposes, such as simple digging or cutting tasks. Here, again, the value in Dissanayake's notion of artification is apparent. We need not settle on a view about whether the Acheulean handaxes are 'art', as such, while still being able to confidently conclude that they signify some of the earliest examples of artification; that is, of making things special and taking aesthetic issues into consideration.[52]

The most prominent contender for the 'origin of art' in human history is the exquisite, representational cave drawings and carved statues dating from the Upper Palaeolithic period, dating from around 30-40 kya.[53] There are the Chauvet and Lascaux caves in France, and comparable ones in Spain, Germany, and elsewhere.[54] When Pablo Picasso visited the Altamira cave in Spain and assessed the drawings therein, he reportedly confessed that 'we have learned nothing'[55] and that 'after Altamira, all is decadence.'[56] The implication here is that the images were unambiguously 'art', clearly anticipating the so-called 'high art' celebrated by classical and modernist sensibilities. Recently a discovery of cave art on the island of Sulawesi, in Indonesia, has scholars wondering if this site might now be the earliest known example of figurative art (dating from around 35 kya),[57] although the research and scholarly debate continue. Also in the Palaeolithic era there is evidence of carved statutes and musical instruments, such as a vulture-bone flute, which is one of humanity's earliest known artefacts.[58] What did humans do when they first developed the mental and technological capacities to create complex items? It seems we made a musical instrument.

To present cave paintings as the origin story of art is arguably too reductive or narrow a view, for art need not be limited to painting or sculpting an object as opposed to singing, self-adornment, or dance. But, of course, a song or a dance does not physically endure and so archaeologists cannot discover these art forms, leading to their marginalisation in the story of origins. There is also a risk of ethnocentrism, with analysts consciously or unconsciously pointing to Europe as the birth of 'high culture'. How convenient and self-supporting! Whatever the case, these types of representational paintings are widely interpreted as the 'origin of art' and as signalling the birth of the 'modern mind', a higher level of consciousness in our species. Cave art could also represent an early form of human activity that connected religious or spiritual exploration with aesthetic expression – two dimensions of life that ever since have been deeply intertwined.

Prehistorian John E Pfeiffer coined the phrase the 'creative explosion'[59] to refer to this period in the Upper Palaeolithic era. During this period there did seem to be a new aesthetic shift into representational art practices and symbolic culture. Whether this should be described as a leap or a gradual development continues to be debated. Unsurprisingly, perhaps, this is contested theoretical and evidential space, which necessarily involves speculative assumptions about a 'state of mind' in early humankind and about which conclusions will forever remain uncertain and unclear.

My intention in reviewing this literature is not to draw firm or new conclusions. Rather, my goal is to provoke thought about the diverse ways in which, throughout our long species' history, human practices of art and artification have evolved alongside our developing aesthetic sensibilities. More than that, however, art and aesthetics can be understood as being essential to humankind and the understanding of our species. By becoming more aware that our cultures and cultivated feelings are intimately and often fundamentally shaped by art practices and products, we can come to see ourselves as interdependent self-creators of personal and social realities. We create ourselves as we create our arts, such that without our arts, we would never have become who we are. This anticipates the question, central to this collection of essays: how might art shape who we might yet become?[60]

Why was technological development so slow?

At this point I'd like to address a question that affords no straightforward answer but which may reward speculative consideration. Archaeologists confirm that, as the brains of hominins enlarged, tool-making humans (*homo faber*) emerged around 2.5 million years ago. And yet, what is perhaps most striking about the archaeological record thereafter is how slowly technology and toolmaking progressed. Can we say, then, that we owe our survival to our rational intelligence and technological prowess? Evolutionary theorist Robert Joyce argued against this view.[61] He suggested that the most striking thing about human history from more than 500,000 to 10,000 years ago was the 'slower-than-glacial advance'[62] of technological progress. Where, he asked, during this time was the 'rational' or 'tool-making' animal? Indeed, if representational and symbolic cave art is understood as indicating the birth of the 'modern mind' – implying a capacity similar to our own – what was this developed consciousness occupied with? This question is especially interesting when we discover that anthropologists report that hunter-gatherer societies were the most leisure-rich that have ever existed, only needing to work two or three hours a day to meet basic material needs.[63]

Joyce's speculative but coherent answer was that the early advances in toolmaking were carried no further, or only extremely slowly, because, as such, they were satisfactory. His thesis was that the human interest in technology did not point toward the control of nature but toward the development of social relations and consciousness. These fundamental concerns were developed through the production of the arts, satisfied merely to 'get by' as technologists and scientists.[64] This suggests that, for ancestral humanity at least, technological advancement had very fast diminishing returns. After acquiring minimal equipment for survival – a few simple tools and fire – humans seem to have invested less energy toward objective experimentation in the world and instead refined their means of subjective control and exploration. Perhaps the true problems of early humankind were less about threats from our own kind or other animals, but more about the dire necessity of developing supportive existential conditions and sensibilities to replace our lost animal environment.[65] This type of problem is arguably better resolved (back then as today) with the arts than the sciences.

So far as toolmaking did develop, it was primarily in the direction of implements to paint, tattoo, model, play music, carve, and engrave. Moreover, the attention early humans directed toward materials – clay, pigments, gold, copper, and other metals – was largely 'an artists' interest.'[66] Joyce concluded that if we do not credit the arts as having a decisive role in human evolution, 'the physical drift of that evolution makes no sense.'[67] The large brains of these early humans must have been engaged 'in creating and receiving the arts'[68], which led to 'cultural organisation and man's freedom to begin making himself.'[69] Moreover, according to evolutionary scientist Ian Cross, 'more or less the first thing we [humans] did when we developed the capacity and desire to produce diverse and technologically complex objects (probably between 40,000 and 30,000 years BP) was to produce musical instruments (bone pipes).'[70] This has led some writers to describe human beings not merely as an aesthetic animal, but a musical one.[71]

For these reasons Joyce believed that human survival and multiplication in history are owed more to the aesthetic utilisation of the enlarging brain than the rational application. Moreover, as a means of effecting emotional responses, Joyce suggested that 'the arts of the Palaeolithic, the Neolithic, and the twentieth centuries are essentially the same.'[72]

But what is art *for*? And what, if anything, is it *good* for?

There is a remaining conundrum in the history of art and artification which I have yet to consider in any detail, but will now give further attention. If carving cupules into rock, collecting shiny stones, or marking walls on a cave, etc, did not provide food or protect against predators, why did early humans engage in these behaviours? At first interpretation, the theory of evolution would suggest that these are wasteful, inefficient behaviours that would give people a competitive *dis*advantage. They seem to involve investing time and energy in non-utilitarian projects that could draw attention away from direct, survivalist tasks, such as securing food sources or defending against predators. One might assume that over time the instinct for art and artification might have faded out as other traits proved to be more effective in the struggle for existence.

And yet, paradoxically, the opposite seems to be the case. Such practices have evidently developed and expanded over time, to the extent that they are now considered universal traits in human societies. Dutton calls this our 'art instinct'.[73] This counter-intuitively suggests that, from an evolutionary perspective, art and aesthetics are significant and consequential. It is worth delving further into why this might be so.

As discussed earlier, the earliest proto-aesthetic behaviour in humans emerged in mother-infant interaction. Specifically, such behaviour emerged from the sing-song and gestural interactions of so-called 'motherese'. This is a near-universal instinct and one that often reaches beyond the mother and emerges in many who interact with infants. It was seen that this 'ritual' can be coherently explained as providing an adaptive advantage, reinforcing pathways for caretaking and emotional attachment, thereby maximising chances of infant survival and reproductive success for the mother.

Some hypothesise that the origins of music emerge from this early proto-aesthetic behaviour.[74] Darwin himself speculated that, prior to the development of language, men may have begun producing melodic sounds and sequences as a mating ritual to attract females, akin to the signalling of a peacock's tail.[75] In contrast to the process of natural selection, this would suggest that music may have its origins in sexual selection. Other analysts offer an alternative but not mutually exclusive argument that the act of singing or making tonal noises (even in advance of language) is an easier way to project the voice across distances. These melodic forms of communication could have been effective ways to warn tribespeople of dangers or more efficiently communicate one's location. If so, these early forms of music making would have provided competitive advantages that assisted with survival and thus would have been traits that were more likely to be passed on. Perhaps, as suggested above, we are not merely an aesthetic animal, but specifically a musical animal[76] – a view supported by the fact that there are no known human societies that do not practise the art of music.[77]

If music-making was the earliest form of vocal communication, then it is only a small step further to assume that language itself grew out of early musical interactions and behaviours.[78] This flips the conventionally assumed process back-to-front: language emerged out of song, rather than song emerging only after language. According to Ian Cross, music might have been 'the most important thing we humans ever did.'[79] Moreover, if language sits alongside art as amongst the most distinctive features of the human species, this provides a further reason to see how, through art, the 'modern mind' evolved. From the musical animal emerges what scholar Jonathan Gottschall calls the 'storytelling animal.'[80]

Even the artification behaviours of play and mark-making amongst children can be seen as developing important mental skills like creativity and social bonding, as well as imagining 'other worlds' and 'other dimensions' beyond the present, immediate reality. All these behaviours can be understood as offering evolutionary advantages to individuals and the species, 'justifying' behaviour that might otherwise have been seen as 'non-utilitarian' and therefore problematic from an evolutionary perspective.

In the same vein, Currie believes that the 'costly' activity of beautifying early handaxes is explicable in terms of sexual selection.[81] The fine motor skills, attention, memory, and dedication required by the proficient artisan likely would have provided a 'fitness signal' that would have been attractive to prospective mates. This would have increased the chances of the skillset being genetically transmitted through reproduction. Indeed, it might have been assumed that those skills were also generalisable, beyond axe making. This should not necessarily be seen as a deliberate strategy on behalf of the axe maker, or a conscious reflection on behalf of the mate. It is more akin to the instinctive behaviours and judgements of the peacock and peahen. Similarly, the aesthetic judgements of human bodily form are largely instinctive and yet arguably have evolutionary explanations in terms of survival or reproductive fitness.[82]

Furthermore, given that beautification of handaxes was costly but without clear utilitarian value, such extravagant practices could have been a further signal of strength, wealth, energy abundance, and 'good genes'.[83] From this view it is the *making* or *artifying* of the well-crafted axe, rather than the axe itself, that would have been the 'fitness signal'. That said, in time such signals could have evolved into a *status symbol*, giving the possessor of the well-crafted axe an advantage in terms of sexual selection, irrespective of who made it.[84]

As the brains of ancestral humans enlarged and our minds developed, we began transcending the purely 'instinctive' life of other animals and were increasingly able to remember the past and imagine the future. It is often acknowledged that sitting around a fire at night, where the visual world available during daylight is gone, could have provided the fertile context for critical mental developments like abstract thought, language development, reflection on and learning from the events of the day, and storytelling. These developments were a two-edged sword, however, providing new skills for managing the world but bringing with them existential challenges because of more sophisticated mental apparatus. Specifically, the more developed consciousness could have induced increased anxiety about the vital uncertainties of life, including food supply, predators, or other tribes. In time, the human animal would have become conscious of its own mortality and had to adjust to the reality of living in the face of inevitable death.

For present purposes, the problem of existential anxiety is relevant because it can be seen as a driver for ritualistic and ceremonial behaviour. Such behaviour can be understood as a coping mechanism that sought to control or mitigate the range of discomforting emotions. It is plausible that here we see the roots of religious thought and practice, arising from the developed emotional capacities to fear the unknown and be anxious about death. Religious or spiritual perspectives may also have been fostered by the developing imaginative capacity to envision different worlds and dimensions. Both historically and today, we see that religiosity is so often entwined with cultural practices of art and artification, ritual and ceremony.

In an uncertain and fearful world, where so much would have been unexplained, ancestral humans would have spontaneously come together to engage in multi-modal ritualised behaviours of dance, song, chanting, self-adornment, environmental elaboration, and, in time, storytelling. Being in a group in times of anxiety and fear is better than being alone, offering reassurances and satisfactions that would have reinforced the practices with positive neurochemical consequences. Dissanayake notes that '[a]lthough particular ritual actions and cultural messages vary from group to group, all are built on the same psychobiological scaffold.'[85] She explains:

> Deep emotions (awe, wonder, fear, desire) and emotional bonding are produced less by esoteric knowledge than by engaging with others in stimulating shared activities. Rituals work because their artifications provide the excitement and drama that make their messages memorable and meaningful.[86]

As well as helping to deal with existential anxiety, ritualistic and ceremonial behaviour can also be understood from an evolutionary perspective as an efficient means of encouraging group cohesion in collective tasks and promoting social bonding. This was especially important in hunter-gatherer social systems without alternative (centralised, state-based, or hierarchical) mechanisms for encouraging communal action. The human species, like most animals, has significant vulnerabilities. We would have discovered that acting as a group offered a range of advantages, such as coordinating hunts, encouraging necessary but mundane work, and promoting bonding and trust within the tribe. Interestingly, Dissanayake reports that 'a number of archaeologists have noted an increase in indications of ritual (artification) at times of environmental stress, such as changing climate or competition with invaders over resources.'[87] For these reasons, '[s]ynchronized rituals may therefore have enabled some cultural groups to survive where others failed.'[88] This is not art for art's sake, then, but art (or artification) for life's sake.

In summary, art and artification can be understood as being adaptive for two main reasons: first, by alleviating existential anxieties and fears, and second, by instilling social emotions and bonding. It must also be acknowledged, more generally, that aesthetic practices tend to involve creative and imaginative behaviours that can induce awe, wonder, curiosity, or sheer pleasure which in various ways would have assisted in the relentless struggle for existence. Over countless millennia, as noted earlier, the aesthetic practices and sensibilities naturally evolved into what Dutton has called our 'art instinct'[89]. Similarly, Dissanayake describes this art instinct as a 'behavioural predisposition to make the ordinary extraordinary,'[90] a 'universal impulse to artify.'[91] These conclusions are perfectly consistent with, and indeed provide evidential support for, my underlying thesis regarding the Will to Art.

All the same, one can leave open the question regarding to what extent art is a biological instinct compared to simply being, as some argue, a culturally, non-adaptive 'spandrel'. In either case, we can see art and artification serving similar social and existential purposes and being constitutive of who we have become as an 'artful species'.[92] The closer one looks at contemporary society, the blurrier the boundaries between biology and culture become, as we realise our developed aesthetic capacities to shape and give form, not merely the world, but to ourselves. Nevertheless, the review and analysis above does present a strong case that our aesthetic natures have roots in biology, even if that nature is, now more than ever, being shaped and reshaped through culture.

Concluding remarks: The dual aspect nature of *homo aestheticus*

Throughout this collection of essays, I will use the notion of *homo aestheticus* to refer to a 'thin' theory of human nature which can be understood in two senses, one historical, the other of the future – a potentiality. In the historical view, as detailed in this essay, I have outlined a case that our biological inheritances, given to us through our evolutionary journey, have rendered us an artistic species, an aesthetic animal with aesthetic capacities and needs. I call this a 'thin' theory of human nature because what defines us as a species is our creative and aesthetic potentials and desires. This is only minimally substantive given that our nature is to create ourselves through our arts and aesthetic engagements. In other words, to argue that we are an artful species is to present a theory that enables rather than significantly constrains who or what we are, given that our nature is *to create who and what we are.*

However, the motivation to write these essays arose from a realisation that, today, our creative natures are being stifled by consumerist cultures and capitalist economics. We have all these (biologically inherited) aesthetic capacities and needs, which existing society is not meeting and indeed is actively repressing. That is, humanity today suffers from a chronic aesthetic deficit disorder, which I contend is both a contributing cause of contemporary crises of capitalism and also points toward their potential resolution. If our aesthetic natures are being repressed with dire social and ecological implications, this suggests that we might need to turn to the aesthetic realm to resolve them, and with urgency. As Joyce asserted: 'What we do with the arts, and what we consequently feel to be valuable, can be decisive in determining what we do with our means of production and our means of destruction.'[93]

The stifling of our creative natures gives rise to a second aspect of the notion of *homo aestheticus*, being an unfilled potential toward which, I argue, we ought to be striving. Capitalism has distorted our natures, beating us into the shape of *homo economicus* – a selfish, obedient, and consumptive species. Our challenge is to transcend this distorted nature that has been imposed upon us and reclaim our true nature as *homo aestheticus*. One way to do this, I contend, is to shift our individual and collective energies and attention away from superfluous material and energetic consumption and toward aesthetic and spiritual exploration. In short, a shift from 'having' to 'being' is required in our collective modes of existence.[94] In this great and necessary transition toward SMPLCTY – an idealised social order of *homo aestheticus* – art promises to be both the means and the end. We can begin this journey with a 'politics of the self', one that French philosopher Michel Foucault called an 'aesthetics of existence'. That is the subject of the next essay.

---

[1] To place humanity on the top of any hierarchy generally leads to the charge of anthropocentrism or speciesism, which is meant to imply an improper prioritising of human value over the value of other animals or lifeforms. For present purposes, all I

am suggesting is that the imaginative and creative capacities of the smartest chimp, pale in comparison to the abilities of an ordinary human child and is of a different order entirely than what the artistic genius is capable of, think Mozart, Shakespeare, Tolstoy, or Picasso. I do not believe that acknowledging this implies being anthropocentric in any pejorative sense.

[2] My greatest influence here is Robert Joyce, *The Esthetic Animal: Man, the Art-Created Art Creator* (New York: Exposition Press, 1975). See also, Ellen Dissanayake, *Homo Aestheticus: Where Art Comes from and Why* (Seattle: Washington Press, 1995); Dennis Dutton, *The Art Instinct: Beauty, Pleasure, and Human Evolution* (New York: Bloomsbury Press, 2010); Stephen Davies, *The Artful Species* (Oxford: Oxford University Press, 2014); Anjan Chatterjee, *The Aesthetic Brain: How We Evolved to Desire Beauty and Enjoy Art* (Oxford: Oxford University Press, 2015).

[3] See Joyce, *Esthetic Animal*, note 2, p. 5.

[4] See Davies, *The Artful Species*, note 2.

[5] See Joyce, *Esthetic Animal*, note 2.

[6] I borrow the phrase, without the metaphysical baggage, from Henri Bergson, *Creative Evolution* (New York: Dover, 1998).

[7] I have outlined my aesthetic view of existence in more detail elsewhere. See Samuel Alexander, 'Introduction: The Aesthetic Dimension' in this collection of essays. The full set will be available here: http://samuelalexander.info/s-m-p-l-c-t-y-ecological-civilisation-and-the-will-to-art/ (accessed 10 May 2023).

[8] Stephen Davies argues, regarding evidential uncertainty or interpretive uncertainty, that 'where a range of very different proposals about the evolutionary significance of some behavior are in competition, with none clearly established as superior to all the others, which is often the case where aesthetics and art are the topic, it will be more appropriate to reserve judgment than to opt for what we might like to be true.' Davies' position is fair and reasonable, but it is not conclusive, determinative, or even neutral. One could just as easily argue that, in conditions of uncertainty, one might justifiably explore a particular line of interpretation and see what it reveals or conceals. This isn't so much about what we might *like* to be true, as exploring hypothesises that *might* be true, we just don't know it at the level of knock-down evidential proof. If, as Davies argues, we should 'reserve judgement', we are at risk of paralysing ourselves on matters that are potentially of extreme significance, and one might sooner risk being wrong on some subject (and reap the potential benefits of being right) than assume that avoiding being wrong is always the best strategy. See Davies, *Artful Species*, note 2, p. 43.

[9] Joyce, *Esthetic Animal*, note 2, p. 6.

[10] I tell the story of cosmological unfolding in more detail elsewhere. See Samuel Alexander, 'Creative Evolution and the Will to Art' in this collection. See link in note 7.

[11] It is worth remembering that Beethoven (or pick your favourite genius) is directly descended from these microbes.

[12] For example, changing diets over recent millennia have led to increases in average human height, smaller jaws, and increased tolerance to lactose. In short, our biological constitutions continue to evolve.

[13] For a recent discussion of pre-agricultural civilisations, see David Graeber and David Wengrow, *Dawn of Everything*: *A New History of Everything* (London: Penguin, 2022).

[14] Sexual selection and competition manifests culturally today, especially in so-called consumer societies, where people (especially men) consume conspicuously to signal wealth as a strategy of status competition. In human societies, however, the nature of such status competition can change depending on cultural assumptions. For example, one can imagine a culture whereby driving a sports car and wearing expensive jewellery were consumption practices considered distasteful and unattractive to the opposite sex. This would not mean sexual selection was not at play, only that the relevant 'signals' had changed.
[15] Quoted in Davies, *Artful Species*, p. 12.
[16] See Ellen Dissanayake, 'Why Did Our Ancestors Artify' in Ekkehart Malotki and Ellen Dissanayake, *Early Rock Art of the American West: The Geometric Enigma* (Washington: Washington University Press), p. 200.
[17] See Dutton, *Art Instinct,* note 2, p. 7.
[18] Ibid, Ch 1.
[19] Ellen Dissanayake, 'The Concept of Artification' in Malotki and Dissanayake, *Early Rock Art*, note 16, p. 30.
[20] Ellen Dissanayake, 'Roots and Route of the Artification Hypothesis' (2017) *AVANT* 8(1): pp. 26-7. See also, Dissanayake, 'Artification', note 19, p. 30.
[21] Arthur Danto, *The Transfiguration of the Commonplace* (Cambridge, MA: Harvard University Press, 1981).
[22] See, e.g., John Carey, *What Good Are the Arts?* (London: Faber and Faber, 2005), p. 29.
[23] Morris Weitz, 'The Role of Theory in Aesthetics' *Journal of Aesthetics and Art Criticism* (1956) 15(1): pp. 27-35.
[24] Theodor Adorno, *Aesthetic Theory* (London: Continuum, 2002), p. 1.
[25] See Ludwig Wittgenstein, *Philosophical Investigations* (Oxford: Basil Blackwell, 1963).
[26] Dutton, *Art Instinct*, note 2, p. 25.
[27] Berys Gaut, '"Art" as a Cluster Concept' in Noel Carroll (ed), *Theories of Art Today* (Madison: University of Wisconsin Press, 2000), pp. 25-44.
[28] Ellen Dissanayake, 'Artification', note 19, pp. 23-4.
[29] Davies, *Artful Species*, note 2, pp. 28-9.
[30] Dissanayake, 'Artification', note 19, pp. 23-45; Dissanayake, 'Roots', note 20.
[31] Dissanayake, *Homo Aestheticus*, note 2, Ch. 3.
[32] Dissanayake, 'Roots', note 20, p. 26.
[33] See Dissanayake, 'Why Did Our Ancestors Artify', note 16, p. 197.
[34] Dissanayake, 'Roots', note 20.
[35] The human child would need to be born at around 18 months to conform with other primates. See Dissanayake, 'Why Did Our Ancestors Artify', note 16, p. 202.
[36] Ibid.
[37] Dissanayake, 'Roots', note 20, p. 19.
[38] Ibid. p. 26.
[39] Ibid, p. 27.
[40] Ibid.
[41] Dissanayake, 'Why Did Our Ancestors Artify', note 16, p. 202.
[42] Quoted in Dissanayake, 'Roots', note 20, p. 21.
[43] Ibid.
[44] Ibid. See also, Malotki and Dissanayake, *Early Rock Art*, note p. 11 and Ch. 3.

[45] Malotoki and Dissanayake, *Early Rock Art*, note 16, p. 73. They note that creating one cupule could take six hours over two days requiring ten hammerstones of hard quartzite. Some sites had hundreds or even thousands of cupules.
[46] Malotoki and Dissanayake, *Early Rock Art*, note 16, p. 8.
[47] Dissanayake, 'Roots', note 20, p. 22.
[48] Gregory Currie, 'The Master of the Masek Beds: Handaxes, Art, and the Minds of Early Humans' in Elisabeth Schellekens and Peter Goldie (eds.) *The Aesthetic Mind: Philosophy and Psychology* (Oxford: Oxford University Press, 2014), pp. 9-31.
[49] Ibid, pp. 9-10.
[50] Ibid, p. 10.
[51] Ibid, p. 15.
[52] For decades it was thought that Neanderthals were assumed to lack ritual and art, but recent discoveries have challenged that view. See Malotoki and Dissanayake, *Early Rock Art*, note 16, p. 31. Whether the practices discussed can be called art, they can be classified as artification or 'making special'.
[53] Note that some argue that there is evidence for symbolic drawing on caves as far back 78kya, in Blombos cave, Southern Cape, where pieces of ochre have been found with markings that are claimed to be symbolic. This claim, however, is disputed. See Davies, *Artful Species*, note 2, p. 3; see also Currie, 'The Master of the Masek Beds' note 47, pp. 18-19. On ochre, see also, Malotoki and Dissanayake, *Early Rock Art*, note 16, p. 31.
[54] See Malotoki and Dissanayake, *Early Rock Art*, note 16, p. 11.
[55] Currie, 'The Master of the Masek Beds', note 48, p. 17.
[56] Davies, *Artful Species*, note 2, p. 3.
[57] Jo Marchant, 'A Journey to the Oldest Cave Paintings in the World' *Smithsonian* (January 2016). Available here: https://www.smithsonianmag.com/history/journey-oldest-cave-paintings-world-180957685/ (accessed 10 January 2023).
[58] See Davies, *Artful Species*, note 2, p. 5.
[59] John Pfeiffer, *The Creative Explosion: An Inquiry into the Origins of Art and Religion* (Ithaca: Cornell University Press, 1982).
[60] Joyce, *Esthetic Animal*, note 2, p. 4.
[61] Ibid, pp. 18-20.
[62] Ibid, p. 18.
[63] See, e.g., Marshall Sahlins, *Stone Age Economics* (London: Routledge, 2017).
[64] Joyce, *Esthetic Animal*, note 2, p. 18.
[65] Ibid, p. 20.
[66] Joyce, *Esthetic Animal*, note 2, p. 27.
[67] Ibid, p. 21.
[68] Ibid.
[69] Ibid, p. 22.
[70] Ian Cross, 'Is Music the Most Important Thing We Ever Did? Music, Development, and Evolution' in Suk Won Yi (ed) *Music, Mind, and Science* (Seoul: Seoul University Press, 1999) pp. 10-39.
[71] Michael Spitzer, *The Musical Human: A History of Life on Earth* (London: Bloomsbury, 2022).
[72] Joyce, *Esthetic Animal*, note 2, p. 24.
[73] See Dutton, *The Art Instinct*, note 2.

[74] For a review of possibilities regarding the origins of music, see Anton Killin, 'The Origins of Music: Evidence, Theory, and Prospects' (2018) *Music & Science* 1: https://doi.org/10.1177/2059204317751971
[75] See Nicholas Bannan, 'Darwin, Music, and Evolution: New Insights from Family Correspondence on *The Descent of Man*' (2016) *Musicae Scientiae* 21(1): pp. 3-25.
[76] Spitzer, *The Musical Human*, note 71.
[77] John Blacking, *Music, Culture, Experience* (Chicago: University of Chicago Press, 1995).
[78] See, for example, Brian Levman, 'The Genesis of Music and Language' *Ethnomusicology* (1992) 62(2): pp. 147-170.
[79] Cross, 'Is Music the Most Important Thing', note 70.
[80] Jonathan Gottschall, *The Storytelling Animal: How Stories Make Us Human* (Oxford: Oxford University Press, 2013).
[81] Currie, 'The Master of the Masek Beds', note 48.
[82] Ibid.
[83] As Marek Hohn and Steven Mithen suggest: 'Just as a peacock's tail may reliability indicate its "success", so might the manufacture of a fine symmetrical handaxe have been a reliable indicator of a hominins' ability to secure food, find shelter, escape from predation and compete successfully within the social group. Such hominids would have been attractive mates...' Quoted in Currie, 'The Master of the Masek Beds', note 48, p. 21.
[84] Currie, 'The Master of the Masek Beds', note 48, p. 28-9
[85] See Dissanayake, 'Why Did Our Ancestors Artify', note 16, p. 219.
[86] Dissanayake, 'Roots', note 20, p. 24.
[87] Ibid, p. 216.
[88] Ibid, p. 213.
[89] Dutton, *Art Instinct,* note 2.
[90] Dissanayake, 'Roots', note 20, p. 23.
[91] Dissanayake, 'Artification', note 19, p. 45.
[92] Davies, *Artful Species*, note 2.
[93] Joyce, note 2, p. 3.
[94] On 'being' over 'having', see Erich Fromm, *To Have or to Be?* (New York: Continuum, 2007).

‘In our society art has become something which is related to objects, and not to individuals or to life. That art is something which is specialised or which is done by experts who are artists. But couldn’t everyone’s life become a work of art? Why should the lamp or the house be an art object, but not our life?’

– **Michel Foucault**

ESSAY EIGHT

GIVING BIRTH TO ONESELF: ETHICS AS AN 'AESTHETICS OF EXISTENCE'

In the previous essay I considered the role of art and aesthetic sensibility in human evolutionary history, exploring the ways in which such behaviours and dispositions shaped the artful species we have become. It was seen that there have been practices of 'artification' – that is, making the ordinary extraordinary – that date back millions of years, including the beautification of handaxes. Other aesthetic behaviours in prehistory include body adornment, ritual, and the collection of artefacts with no apparent utilitarian function. Nevertheless, it is the cave art and figurines of the Upper Palaeolithic Era, dating from around 35-40,000 years ago, which are typically held up as the 'origin of art', on account of these being the earliest examples of hominins producing symbolic or figurative imagery and artefacts.[1]

Sometimes referred to as the 'creative explosion',[2] this Upper Palaeolithic Era is often seen to signify a developmental leap in humankind, suggesting the emergence of a higher order of consciousness, the birth of the 'modern mind'.[3] Human beings had begun representing aspects of the world in aesthetic and abstract form, practices that were unique among the community of life and absent even from earlier hominin culture. These aesthetic representations of external reality are significant partly because they provide a stepping stone to broader, abstract conceptualisation. After painting a specific horse seen earlier in the day, it can be inferred that this led our distant ancestors to develop, over time, the abstract category of 'horses' as a general concept. This very distinction between concrete, physical entities in the 'real world' and the invisible classes of things in some abstract realm, is something that philosophers have been pondering ever since. As evolutionary theorist Robert Joyce suggested: 'Conceptual generalizations grew naturally out of the arts.'[4]

Many people would have seen pictures of the exquisite, prehistoric drawings of bulls and horses that appear on the walls of caves, such as those in the Lascaux cave in France. These drawings are astonishingly accurate and naturalistic depictions of the animals represented. As noted previously, when Picasso first saw early examples of cave art in Spain, he is reported to have declared: 'we have learned nothing!'[5] What is most striking about these drawings, however, is that sometimes, alongside the realistic depiction of animals, there are representations of human figures that are far from naturalistic or realistic.[6] Some of these figures have extremely exaggerated and distorted features or shapes, but this cannot have been due to lack of skill or artistic refinement. The artists were obviously more than capable of drawing humans naturalistically, as evidenced by the animal representations. So what was the significance of drawing the human form abstractly and with far greater creative licence? Sometimes the figures were faceless. Why?

In my view, the most plausible interpretation is that, even back in the Upper Palaeolithic Era, human beings had begun to see themselves not merely as something 'given' or 'predetermined' by nature, but in some sense an abstract and amorphous *idea*. Not only that, humanity was an idea capable of being aesthetically shaped and reshaped, by humans themselves. It is as if these ancient artists had recognised that they may not have been able to change the nature of the buffalo or the bull, but that they could explore the possibility of fashioning their *own* nature as an indeterminate and imaginative creature.

How were they to do that? Through their art – for through art they could become something new. At this stage in human development, purely biological evolution began to cede more ground to creative evolution, in which human beings were co-producers of their evolutionary path, creators not merely creatures. Indeed, perhaps it was at this moment in the human story – the creative explosion – when *homo sapiens*, as such, disappeared, 'like a face drawn in the sand at the edge of the sea',[7] never to reappear, leaving only *homo aestheticus* to walk the face of Earth as the art-created art creator. Henceforth our unique burden was to give birth to ourselves as aesthetic agents in an aesthetic universe.

♦ ♦ ♦

One of the philosophical problems I am trying to resolve at this stage in my project concerns the apparent conflict between biology and philosophy when it comes to understanding human beings. On the one hand, there is the view widely held amongst evolutionary biologists and psychologists that humans have a 'common nature' by virtue of our long, shared species' history. On the other hand, there is a philosophical view, widely held by post-Nietzscheans of various schools, that humans have no 'given' nature but are everyday tasked with creating it. In short, the first position holds that there is a common human nature; the second, anti-essentialist position holds that human nature, as such, does not exist. Can this conflict be resolved?

The anti-essentialist view arguably received its most extreme statement in the early work of Jean-Paul Sartre, who argued that human beings are 'radically free' and, as such, we will be what we make of ourselves and nothing else.[8] As the existentialist slogan states: our human existence precedes our essence. That extreme view, which largely dismisses the influence of both biological inheritances and other social or political structures, was later refined in the works of other so-called 'postmodernists' (and indeed in Sartre's later work).[9] These postmodernists variously accept that there are structures that shape human existence (social, political, economic, linguistic, and so forth) but nevertheless maintain that, due to the linguistic or social construction of reality, human beings are nevertheless free to shape and reshape their worlds through creative redescription and reinterpretation of self and society. Evolutionary psychologists, on the other hand, as well certain 'structuralist' philosophers, tend to argue that there are limits to self-creation given that our natures have, for millions of years, been shaped by evolutionary processes. Human nature is a product of that history.

I will attempt to offer a synthesis of these conflicting literatures, a possibility which was opened to me by a reading of evolutionary biology through the lens of art and aesthetics. Through this reading, I argue we can resolve the apparent conflict between philosophical notions of self-creation and biological arguments for a pre-existing human nature. When we see, as I maintained in the last essay, that human nature is fundamentally *aesthetic*, it becomes clear that there is no longer any problematic conflict between these perspectives but in fact a coherent harmony. Our inherited evolutionary nature is as an aesthetic animal, shaped by our artful and creative capacities and potentials. But this 'nature' should no longer be perceived as static or determinative, since the very nature of an artful species is to continuously reshape itself through its arts and aesthetic practices. Having offered that biological thesis in the last essay, I now explore the philosophical literature that arrives at similar conclusions albeit based on very different intellectual resources. In what follows I present a range of philosophical arguments that support the conception of human beings as 'self-creators', drawing primarily on Michel Foucault and Richard Rorty, both of whom build on the Nietzschean tradition.

We will soon discover, however, that this analysis draws us into the thorny terrain of ethics and morality. This is because grounding a moral code or ethical framework in human nature becomes problematic when one loses faith in a shared, stable, and rationalistic conception of human nature. In a postmodern age where the 'self' is considered fragmented and decentred, and where human nature is deemed a social construct, what becomes of traditional attempts to provide a moral code to guide human action? My purposes in this essay, therefore, are twofold: first, to explore the philosophical position that human beings must 'create themselves' rather than 'discover themselves', thus supplementing the analysis of last essay which defended an aesthetic conception of human nature; and second, to consider what becomes of ethics when the notion of a universal human nature grounded in reason is given up and ethics is necessarily 'aestheticised'. After reviewing Foucault's notion of ethics as an 'aesthetics of existence', I will conclude with a review and analysis of Rorty's vision of a 'poeticized culture', which explores how a post-metaphysical or aestheticised liberalism might be structured in order to accommodate a culture of self-creators. This will raise some key social and political questions that will be given more attention in later essays.

♦ ♦ ♦

Throughout the Western philosophical tradition, it has been asserted, or simply assumed, that beneath the various historical forms of human subjectivity there lies an ahistorical or transcendental 'self' or 'nature' that all human beings share. We human beings might look different from each other and find ourselves living in radically diverse cultures, giving the appearance of fundamental difference. But if we were to peel away all the contingencies of tradition and circumstance, the conventional philosophical view is that, at base, beneath all our various socialisations, we all share the same 'human nature'. Again, to be clear, this is a distinctly *philosophical* conception of human nature (derived from reason and reflection), not one derived from evolutionary science (an empirical inquiry). It is worth considering the importance of this philosophical conception, specifically in the domains of moral theory, asking why it remains so entrenched. After doing so I will consider the counter-position and its implications.

The dominant perspective just outlined is epitomised by the work of rationalistic philosophers such as Plato, Rene Descartes, and Immanuel Kant. Such philosophers argue that human beings are endowed in common with rational faculties, and that by correctly employing those faculties we can determine, on rational grounds, eternal truths about the world, including universal moral rules that ought to govern human life. We just need to use the tool of reason correctly, and these philosophers were kind enough to tell us how to do that. Their ambitions were to lead humanity out of the cave of illusion and ignorance, freeing us from erroneous thinking and showing us the True and the Good that lay hidden beneath appearances. In this light, ethics and morality have generally referred to the task of living in accordance with a body of objectively verifiable moral rules, of adhering to a moral code that is knowable through rational inquiry. Due to its rational basis, such a moral code would apply to all people in all places.

Of course, philosophers (and theologians) have always disagreed about which of the possible moral codes is the objectively true one. But there has been a widespread consensus that discovering such a code is the aim of moral thought and that living in accordance with such a code is the aim of moral behaviour. We can see this assumption underlying the work of almost all the great moral thinkers – from Plato, through Jesus, to Kant and Bentham, and beyond. Well into the twentieth century this assumption remained a largely unquestioned verity.

The logic beneath this assumption is understandable. If we are to live our lives according to the dictates of a moral code, even when it is not in our immediate self-interest to do so, then we should want the code to which we have subscribed to be somehow deserving of our obedience. Nobody would want to live according to moral rules if those rules were just the arbitrary assertions of some megalomaniac who simply wanted all humanity to abide by his or her personal standards of conduct. On the contrary, if anyone were to subscribe to a moral code, it would presumably always be on the condition that the code was an embodiment of some independent and verifiable moral truth, in the sense that the code reflected an objective and rational moral reality, not merely the idiosyncratic whim of some authoritarian personality.

Within this framework of understanding, the goal of moral philosophy is to base normative, value-laden conclusions upon secure, metaphysical foundations. These foundations would be external to the human mind, eternal, objective, universal, and unchanging, and which, for these reasons, transcend all personal or contextual perspectives. According to this view of moral philosophy, it is either right or wrong to act in this way or that, from which it would follow that the task of moral philosophers is to determine which acts are moral and which are not. Indeed, it could be said that using 'reason' to distinguish moral from immoral behaviour has been the defining goal of moral philosophers throughout history. This goal seems coherent, and in many ways it also seems quite commonsensical. It is understandable why human beings were drawn to reflect on questions of morality and attempt to develop answers to the questions: what is justice and why should we value it?

Needless to say, however, no consensus has been reached about which of the various moral codes proposed is, in fact, the objectively correct one. Christians, Kantians, Utilitarians, Marxists, and so on, are still debating each other over the truth of their respective moralities or conceptions of justice. Some might suggest that this lack of moral consensus must mean that there is no moral truth, as such; that morality has no rational foundation; or, perhaps, that human beings are fundamentally irrational and thus incapable of knowing moral truth when they see it. But this does not necessarily follow. In particular, a lack of moral consensus is not necessarily fatal to this universalist endeavour. After all, one might still believe that, *in the future*, human beings will finally uncover the moral reality that lies beneath the illusion of appearances and thus gain moral enlightenment. It would be a discovery that was assisted, one might suppose, by some philosopher who devised a means of proving, by way of rational demonstration, that a particular moral code is the one and only one that is *really* real; the one and only one that deserves our obedience. Should this day arrive, the narrative might go, then, at last, people could finally stop debating which morality was the correct one and instead dedicate their time and energy to actually trying to live morally.

It may be that such a day will indeed arrive. Some critical philosophers, however, such as Nietzsche, Foucault, and Rorty, among many others, have argued that the very search for universal moral truth, like the search for the Holy Grail, is a dubious one – if, by universal moral truth, one means a set of objectively verifiable moral rules, grounded in metaphysical reality, that apply to all people, in all places, at all times. These 'post-metaphysical' theorists have called into question, not simply the moral codes that philosophers have proposed hitherto, but, more fundamentally, the very goal of seeking objective, universalisable moral codes.

This scepticism arose, in various ways, out of a loss of faith in the correspondence theory of truth, which, in turn, led to a loss of faith in all forms of Moral Realism (i.e., the view that true moral statements reflect objective moral facts that are independent of human thought). The critical reasoning here is that since truth must be expressed in language, and since language is a human creation, so must truth, ultimately, be a human creation.[10] In other words, it is argued that there is no knowable moral or metaphysical reality which language should be seeking to reflect. From this perspective, human perception and understanding is always and necessarily mediated by language – 'there is nothing outside of the text', to borrow Jacque Derrida's phrase.[11] This means that knowledge, including moral knowledge, will always be a function of some conventional or 'socially constructed' linguistic framework or paradigm of understanding. It follows, therefore, that truth, knowledge, and meaning all lack the metaphysical foundations that philosophers throughout history had hoped to uncover for them. The metaphor of 'philosophy as the mirror of nature' thus loses its operational validity.[12]

Furthermore, since language is inherently unstable and always subject to various interpretive ambiguities, there will never be one and only one moral code that is true for all people, in all times and places. For even if we knew which moral code was the one and only one to obey – the Ten Commandments, for example, or Kant's 'categorical imperative', or Bentham's 'greatest happiness principle' – its context-dependent application would require interpretation, and interpretation is always a function of one or other 'interpretive community'.[13] People may, of course, have the *experience* of moral certainty; but the 'truth' of such moral certainty will never be rationally demonstrable to all people.

What, then, becomes of moral and ethical discourse and practice if the search for a universal moral code is given up? I will explore this question by turning primarily to the later works of Michel Foucault – the texts of his so-called 'ethical' turn.[14] It is in these texts where Foucault develops his notion of ethics as 'an aesthetics of existence', which he presents as an alternative mode of ethical practice that can be taken up in the absence of a knowable and universalisable morality. I will show that this idea of 'an aesthetics of existence' sits well with the vision presented in the last chapter of humanity as *homo aestheticus*, the artful species.

Foucault's strategy is to problematise the notion of 'selfhood' by arguing that the 'self', far from being as independent and autonomous as philosophers have typically supposed, is in fact inextricably shaped by external linguistic and contextual forces. It follows that *who we are* as individuals is not the determinate product of free decisions made by some autonomous agent, but instead the product of social and linguistic forces that are largely beyond our control. Foucault does not deny or exclude the possibility of human freedom, however, as some might infer from his early work. He does insist that our identities are socially constructed entities, and that we lack a transcendental or purely rational 'self'. Nevertheless, he carves out a limited degree of space within which our socially constructed identities can *act upon themselves* for the purpose of 'self-fashioning'. We may not get to choose the raw material of which our identities are constituted, but it nevertheless lies within our power to shape that raw material in various ways, just as the sculptor may make various things from a given lump of clay. And we must not think of shaping purely in terms of 'subtraction' of what the self has been shaped into. Self-fashioning can just as coherently be about 'adding' what is not yet there.

According to Foucault, this relationship of the self to the self is the terrain of ethics, and when engaging the age-old ethical question, 'How am I to live?,' Foucault suggests that we avoid the traditional search for a moral code and instead ask ourselves the further question, 'What type of person should I become?'. Using aesthetic metaphors to describe and develop this process of self-creation, Foucault summarises his ethical position with the pronouncement, 'Make life a work of art' – an intriguing, provocative, but ambiguous statement that we can now explore in more detail below.

Foucauldian ethics as an 'Aesthetics of Existence'

'Morality will gradually *perish* now',[15] asserted Nietzsche in 1887, with characteristic bluntness. '[T]his is the great spectacle in a hundred acts reserved for the next two centuries in Europe – the most terrible, most questionable, and perhaps also the most hopeful of all spectacles'.[16] The form of morality to which Nietzsche was referring, and to which he himself was instrumental in undermining, was the form, outlined above, of morality as obedience to a set of rules that are grounded in some knowable metaphysical reality. While previous philosophers had argued that human beings shared a common nature by virtue of being endowed with 'reason', Nietzsche claimed to have ended that particular myth and with it the myth of a morality knowable through an appeal to reason. Nietzsche predicted that as more people came to understand this – to experience this crisis of morality – morality itself would gradually 'perish'.

According to Foucault, Nietzsche's prediction has already come to pass: '[T]he idea of morality as obedience to a code of rules is now disappearing, has already disappeared. And to this absence of morality corresponds, must correspond, the search for an "aesthetics of existence".'[17] Foucault was extremely sceptical of the claim, made throughout the Western philosophical tradition, that beneath the various manifestations of human subjectivity which have arisen throughout history there lies an ahistorical or transcendental subject that all human beings share. 'I do indeed believe', he once stated, 'that there is no sovereign, founding subject, a universal form of the subject to be found everywhere'.[18]

Emerging from the Nietzschean counter-tradition, Michel Foucault helped expose the many problems with the universalist conception of the human subject and the idea of a universal moral code that flowed from it. Just as Nietzsche had announced the 'Death of God' to signify the loss of faith in a transcendental basis for morality, Foucault announced the 'Death of Man' to signify the loss of faith in a basis for morality that was somehow objectively grounded in 'reason' or 'human nature'.[19] He predicted a time, which perhaps has already come to pass, when the invented idea of an ahistorical or transcendental conception of humanity would be erased, 'like a face drawn in the sand at the edge of the sea.'[20] The argument I wish to advance is that Foucault's critique of the rationalist conception of 'human nature' is consistent with the argument of the last essay which concluded that humanity does share a nature of sorts – as the art-created art creator. Put otherwise, the idea of humanity as *homo aestheticus* is consistent with the Foucauldian conception of the fragmented and decentered self that is tasked with giving birth to itself.

If indeed there is no universal *subject* but only historically specific and contingent forms of *subjectivity*, what are the implications of this on how we understand the human situation? It is in response to this type of question or self-questioning that Foucault began developing his notion of ethics as an 'aesthetics of existence.'[21] Rather than trying to determine the moral code that would always and everywhere demand human obedience, Foucault's approach was to ask instead: What sort of person should I become? 'From the idea that the self is not given to us,' Foucault pronounced, 'I think that there is only one consequence: we have to create ourselves as a work of art.'[22]

This aesthetic metaphor might strike some people as strange or grandiose, for we are not normally accustomed to talking about life as a work of art. We might want to say that life is one thing, art is another, and that these distinct categories should not be conflated. But the distinction between art and life was precisely what Foucault was trying to question. In fact, it can be argued that Foucault was not actually using art as a metaphor here at all. That is, he was not proposing that we are related to our own lives *like* the way the artist is related to their raw materials; instead, he was suggesting that we are related to our lives *as* artists, whose raw material is life itself. He once lamented in an interview:

> [I]n our society art has become something which is related to objects, and not to individuals or to life. That art is something which is specialised or which is done by experts who are artists. But couldn't everyone's life become a work of art? Why should the lamp or the house be an art object, but not our life?[23]

Foucault's reasoning here is unusually clear and straightforward: if the nature of the self is not given to us in advance – that is, if there is no 'true self' to which we should be trying to interpret correctly or *discover* – then it follows, by default, that we must *create* ourselves. We are not, however, given a blank canvas to work with, so to speak. We do not get to create ourselves out of nothing, since our identities are by and large a *product* of linguistic, social, and institutional forces beyond our control or choosing. Nobody, for example, gets to choose the categories which structure their perception or interpretation of the world. Rather, we are all educated into – or subjected to – a form of life as we grow up. Through that process of socialisation we find ourselves embedded within elaborate and culturally-specific structures of power/knowledge that both enable and constrict our thoughts, feelings, and actions. This education and those power/knowledge structures shape who we are as individuals and they define the nature of our subjectivities.

Nevertheless, Foucault argued we can act upon ourselves – upon our socially constructed subjectivities – through processes that he variously called 'self-fashioning', 'care of the self', 'techniques of the self' and 'arts of the self'. Foucault defined these 'arts of existence' as 'those intentional and voluntary actions by which [people] not only set themselves rules for conduct, but also seek to transform themselves, to change themselves in their singular being, and to make their life into an *oeuvre* that carries certain aesthetic values and meets certain stylistic criteria.'[24]

Through these processes, in which the self engages the self, human beings have the potential to transform their subjectivities in much the same way a sculptor transforms a given lump of clay. The subject, Foucault insisted, 'is not a substance... [i]t is a form.'[25] What form that subject takes is, at least in part, up to us as individual agents, suggesting that the human condition is more akin to boundless and indeterminate poetic production than something that can be sharply defined and enclosed with philosophical precision. This is the creative challenge – one might say the aesthetic challenge – with which we are all tasked. We must, as Foucault proposed, 'create ourselves as a work of art.'[26]

To be clear, Foucault's argument was not that we should try to make ourselves as beautiful as possible. Instead, *creativity* rather than *beauty* was the primary aesthetic value that defined his aesthetics of existence. He was not calling on us to be 'dandies' in the tradition of Oscar Wilde or Charles Baudelaire (a tradition critically examined in an earlier essay).[27] Rather, he was calling on us to avoid being merely *products* of our socialisation; to avoid being merely *creatures* and to instead be *creators* also, by exercising our imaginations in response to the question: what sort of person should I become?

This explains, in essence, why Foucault's 'aesthetics of existence' is *aesthetic*. Life, he is suggesting, like art (or as art), is a fundamentally creative undertaking; a project that requires shaping, moulding, sculpting, and creating, in accordance with some (evolving) vision. But even if this aesthetic dimension of existence is accepted, on what basis could Foucault legitimately call his notion of an 'aesthetics of existence' an *ethics*? After all, if ethics concerns the question of 'how one ought to live', surely there is more to living ethically than merely being creative or stylistic? Undoubtedly there is, and Foucault never denied this. Occasionally Nietzsche seemed to conflate ethics and creativity, such as when he argued that what mattered when giving 'style' to one's life was not whether it was good or bad but simply whether it represented 'a single taste'.[28] Overall, however, I doubt whether that is a fair representation of Nietzsche's more refined position,[29] and in any case, a simplistic conflation of ethics and creativity certainly does not represent Foucault's position.

In developing his aesthetics of existence, Foucault drew upon the ancient Greeks, who regularly employed notions of moulding and sculpting when philosophising about the 'art of living,'[30] and Foucault's position must be understood in relation to that tradition. Indeed, with a nod to the Greeks, Foucault claimed that 'the problem of an ethics as a *form* to be given to one's conduct and to one's life has again been raised'.[31] It has been raised again, we might infer, due to the emergence of the postmodern condition in which human nature – the supposedly 'universal form' of the self – has been fragmented and is once again in need of being 'shaped' by self-engagement rather than merely 'discovered' by reason.

The ethical dimension of Foucault's aesthetics of existence deserves further attention, however, because it remains unclear whether this approach can legitimately be called an ethics. The first point here is to reiterate the important distinction Foucault draws between morality – which, from his perspective, concerns living in accordance with an objective and universal moral code – and ethics – which concerns the self's relationship with the self. Since the purpose of Foucault's post-structuralist critique of metaphysics was to cast doubt on the possibility of objective and universal forms of knowledge, including moral knowledge, it follows that his ethics would never aspire to be a new morality. Indeed, Foucault declared that it would be 'catastrophic'[32] if everyone submitted to a universal moral code. An inquiry into why he thought this would be so will illuminate the nature of his ethics as an aesthetics of existence.

Foucault thought that submission to a universal moral code would be 'catastrophic' because any code's purported or perceived universality would really be nothing more than a naturalised prejudice. The danger here is that the particular moral perspective that has been placed under a veil of universality might blind people to relationships of domination that ought to be questioned and, if possible, opposed and transcended. Think, for example, of the colonial Americans who for centuries assumed that black slaves were not moral agents deserving of respect but merely animals that should be put to work. From their perspective, it was not immoral to have slaves, since slaves were not objects of moral concern. This, of course, raises the question: Might we, today, have our own moral prejudices to which we are similarly blind?

The point here is that knowledge, including moral knowledge, is always a function of a particular, socially constructed conceptual framework – one that necessarily lacks metaphysical foundations, and which is therefore liable to shift or even collapse. It follows that 'ethical' activity requires questioning the moral assumptions of dominant paradigms for the purpose of exposing their contingency; exposing the possibility of things being otherwise. The goal of this ethical activity is not to replace an existing moral code with the *real* moral code, but instead to bring to consciousness the suffering, pain, domination, or oppression that existing moralities repress or deflect attention away from.

Notice that this 'bringing to consciousness' is a change in the self brought about by engaging the self. This is what ethics means for Foucault. Philosopher Edward McGushin, in his seminal work on Foucault's ethics, notes that Foucault, far from valorising narcissism, was suggesting that 'when one takes care of oneself, an essential dimension of the self that requires attention is the relationship one maintains with others'.[33] We can see similarities here between Foucault's aesthetics of existence and Derrida's ethics of deconstruction. As Derrida once explained: 'Deconstruction is not an enclosure in nothingness, but an openness to the other'.[34] This attempt to be 'open to the other' – not just to other people but also other perspectives – is also an essential aspect to Foucauldian ethics.

This is a process that has no end, because the underlying point is that *every* perspective has blind spots. Accordingly, ethical activity aims to constantly renew the self for the purposes of bringing those blind spots to one's attention, knowing, all the while, that a complete and undistorted perspective – the 'view from nowhere' – is always and necessarily inaccessible to us. 'I am an experimenter', Foucault once explained, 'in the sense that I write in order to change myself and in order not to think the same thing as before'.[35] The purpose of his work was to transform himself and thus his life, a process which he noted was 'rather close to the aesthetic experience'.[36] Why else, he asked, should a painter paint 'if he is not transformed by his own painting?'.[37] It is on this basis that Rorty (considered further below) highlighted the ethical importance of reading widely – especially novels – because by reading as many different types of 'narratives' as possible, we are less likely to become entrenched in any single narrative.[38]

An aesthetics of existence includes what Foucault called 'the practice of freedom'.[39] By this Foucault meant that transforming the self by the self is not an undertaking that is intended simply to benefit *others* but to benefit *oneself* too, by exposing the ways in which we are freer than we realise. Think, for example, of anorexics whose lives are destroyed by a warped understanding of 'beauty'; or the status seekers whose lives are wasted by defining 'success' in relation to the number of rich and famous people they can impress. By engaging the self by the self and questioning our own assumptions – assumptions, say, about the meaning of 'beauty', 'success', 'wealth', or whatever – then we may be able to free ourselves from assumptions that are locking us into lives of self-imposed servitude. While we may not suffer anorexia or chronic status anxiety, Foucault suggested that we will all have our own prejudices, and thus 'the practice of freedom' means constantly aiming to 'free thought from what it silently thinks'.[40] Again, this is not a process that has a destination. It is an ongoing, evolving process of creative self-renewal – a process of ethico-aesthetic engagement that Foucault called an 'aesthetics of existence'.

Like Nietzsche before him, Foucault did not want us to live our lives reading out a pre-written script given to us in advance. We need not be who society tells us that we are. No, Foucault and Nietzsche insisted that we owe it to ourselves to write our own story – to give birth to ourselves – by practising an aesthetics of existence. Nietzsche affirms our capacity for self-creation in stirring terms: 'One must still have chaos in oneself to be able to give birth to a dancing star. I say unto you: you still have chaos in yourselves.'[41] Nietzsche's call was to 'be the poet of your life,'[42] which philosopher Alexander Nehamas summarises as the view that 'life is literature'.[43] This perspective follows naturally from Nietzsche's literary model of existence. Here human beings find themselves related to the world and their own subjectivities in a way that is not dissimilar from the relation of the poet or novelist to their own texts – a task both of creation and interpretation.

Richard Rorty on 'poeticized culture'

In later essays I will explore in more detail the social and political implications of conceiving of human beings as aesthetic agents in an aesthetic universe. Presently, however, I will begin developing this aesthetic conception of humankind in terms relevant to society, not merely the self. The socio-political problem that arises is: how should we structure society if people are, in their own ways, self-creating. The concern is that if there is no human nature that lies beneath our diverse subjectivities, then there is nothing upon which to ground a sense of human solidarity. This risks giving rise to an anti-social elitism that cares little for community or social welfare beyond one's inner circle of initiates. This is how aestheticism is understood when the term is used in the pejorative sense – implying an indulgence of personal aesthetic value at the expense of moral and political concern. As I have said, the central project of this collection of essays is to propose and defend a new aestheticism, one that embraces the anti-foundationalist and anti-essentialist philosophical perspectives that underpin aestheticism, while showing that the celebration of beauty and aesthetic value is not just consistent with moral and political progress but, in many ways, necessary to it. That defence, however, will take the remaining essays to establish.

Throughout the history of philosophy – since Plato, at least – the problem of how to unify private interest and public good is resolved by attempting to show, based on a shared human nature, that acting in one's self-interest can be shown to be in society's interest too. Christianity deals with the matter by suggesting that a life of private fulfilment can be found in service to God, and that this personal devotion accords with the common good. In rationalistic philosophy we find various secularised forms of this general position. Socrates was fond of arguing that acting morally is good for one's soul, and conversely, that acting immorally is bad for one's soul. It follows that it is rational to be virtuous, since virtue is the only path to genuine happiness.

But what if people were to lose faith in these rationalistic or theological projects and conclude that there is no way of making self-creation always mesh smoothly with social justice? What if there are no demonstrable philosophical foundations that we can rely on to show that rational self-interest is necessarily consistent with the public good (and vice versa)? To grapple with this perennial issue, I will turn to the work of neo-pragmatist philosopher Richard Rorty, even if there are places when Rorty's political vision needs refining.

In what follows I provide an overview of Rorty's vision of a 'poeticized' or 'literary' culture. This vision is his attempt to explore what might become of a free and democratic society if its members give up hope of grounding their politics on rational or scientific foundations and instead were content with fostering solidarity through a shared vision based on metaphysically ungroundable assumptions. Rorty sees human beings, first and foremost, as language users, and through our use of language we are engaged in the process of playing with and deploying signs in ways that have personal, social, and political effects, and thus he invites us to 'view matters aesthetically'.[44]

Rorty maintained that there is no way to provide a metaphysical or foundationalist answer to someone who asks: why is cruelty wrong? Rather, we all subscribe, consciously or unconsciously, to what he calls a 'final vocabulary',[45] which he defines as a set of words we employ to justify ourselves and our actions, to formulate our 'long-term projects',[46] our 'highest hopes,'[47] and 'the story of our lives'.[48] Rorty calls such vocabularies 'final' because if people question them one has no non-circular argumentative recourse to fall back on: 'Those words are as far as one can go with language.'[49] I believe that a poeticized culture – itself a 'final vocabulary' that has no non-circular theoretical backup – is the most coherent formulation of an aestheticised society which consists of self-creating human beings who are situated in an aesthetic universe.

The best way to introduce Rorty's vision of a poeticized culture is to see how it flows from taking an anti-foundationalist stance with respect to epistemology and metaphysics, which leads into his anti-foundationalist or 'ironist' position on politics. Drawing from and synthesising a vast body of philosophical literature, Rorty spent decades offering a critique of the so-called 'correspondence theory of truth', which can be understood as Enlightenment's attempt to derive absolute or metaphysical truths from the correct application of reason. This is the view that the world 'out there' is cut up into bite sized chunks called 'facts' and that the goal of analytic philosophy is to discover sentences that correspond or truly reflect to the external world. He advanced an alternative view of philosophy, his anti-foundationalist position, through analyses of the notion of 'contingency', which were applied to language, selfhood, and conceptions of community.

With respect to language, Rorty recognised that only sentences or descriptions of the world can be true or false (truth propositions). He highlighted, however, how sentences are a part of language and that humans invented language. From this it follows that, fundamentally, our truth propositions are also human creations. Those propositions are dependent on the contingent linguistic frameworks that happen to be in place but could have been otherwise (i.e., they are historically contingent). The world is 'out there', in the sense of existing in space and time independently of human mental states, but the truth is not 'out there'.[50]

Throughout history philosophers and poets have invented all sorts of vocabularies for all sorts of reasons, and Rorty's pragmatist view of truth derives from his view that it's best to assess these vocabularies not in terms of whether they correspond with an independent, external reality but whether they 'work' for the purposes they were designed for. Rorty argued that scientists invent descriptions which are designed to help us achieve the goals of prediction and control, just as poets and political thinkers invent other descriptions for other purposes.[51] But there is no chance of ever seeing the world without *any* interpretive 'lens' – no chance, that is, of shedding our conceptual schemes entirely in order to perceive reality as it *really is*.[52] Rorty maintained, for example, that the French Revolution showed that 'the whole vocabulary of social relations, and the whole spectrum of social institutions, could be replaced almost overnight.'[53] Thus utopian politics sets about creating 'hitherto unknown forms of society.'[54]

This type of paradigm shift is not so much about discovery as creation. Occasionally brilliant thinkers emerge that induce revolutions in human thought and practice, but Rorty argued that this should not be considered a linear progression toward Truth or Reality, or as polishing the mirror of nature so that it better reflects the real world. Instead, as a pragmatist, he argued that such perspectival change is a contingent and creative redescription of reality that solves problems or achieves goals better than previous paradigms. Indeed, '[p]ost-Nietzschean philosophers ... write philosophy in order to exhibit the universality and necessity of the individual and contingent' and thereby try to 'to work out honorable terms on which philosophy might surrender to poetry.'[55] If there is objectivity in Rorty's worldview, it is redefined as intersubjective agreement not something that needs to be or can be rationally demonstrable to all people at all times.

With respect to selfhood, Rorty presents a similar anti-foundationalist view, perhaps better described as anti-essentialist. Like Nietzsche and Foucault, he highlighted the contingency of our subjectivities in order to highlight why it is implausible to think there is a universal 'human nature', grounded in reason, that persists across generations and cultures. Rather than trying to 'discover' our true selves or natures as a practice of authenticity, Rorty insisted that we are charged with 'creating' the self by describing ourselves in our own words, words which are not given to us in advance. What is more, we have a responsibility to ourselves to find our own words, invent our own self-descriptions, like the poet. Self-knowledge, therefore, becomes self-creation. Human nature, such that it is, is aestheticised.

Rorty's invitation was to broaden our conception of poetry to include more than just written or spoken verse. He proposed that we define it (as did the romantic poet Percy Bysshe Shelley) as 'the expression of the imagination'.[56] On that basis, to say 'be the poet of your life',[57] as Nietzsche implored, begins to make more sense. Blurring the distinction between art and life, it suggests that we should take hold of life, as the poet takes hold of language, and shape it into something new, something worthy. It is to imagine the best life we can and then set about creating such a life, through creative redescription of self and society.

Rorty maintained that to fail as a poet, in his broad sense, is to accept someone else's description of oneself. Success as a poet involves achieving what Harold Bloom calls 'giving birth to oneself.'[58] Although Rorty risked affirming Nietzsche's elitism by celebrating the 'strong poet' who is capable of spectacular originality (in contrast with the uncreative herd),

Rorty nevertheless came down on the side of egalitarianism, partly via the discipline of psychoanalysis: 'Freud's account of unconscious fantasy shows us how to see every human life as a poem.... [and capable of] generating a self-description.'[59] As Philip Rieff puts it, 'Freud democratized genius by giving everyone a creative unconscious.'[60]

Rorty acknowledged that the same point is made by Lionel Trilling, who said Freud 'showed us that poetry is indigenous to the very constitution of the mind; he saw the mind as being, in the greater part of its tendency, exactly a poetry-making faculty.'[61] Further support for this reading is found in Leo Bersani's claim that 'Psychoanalytic theory has made the notion of fantasy so richly problematic that we should no longer be able to take for granted the distinction between art and life.'[62] Given the contingent, anti-essentialist nature of the self, are we not each related to our own lives in a way comparable to how the artist is related to his or her own materials? Are we not each charged with the task of creating as an aesthetic project the meaning of our own lives? Rorty, like Foucault and Nietzsche before him, answered in the affirmative.

Rorty proceeded to explore the contingency of 'community', which developed the social and political implications of his analyses of language and selfhood. His main conclusion was that we should give up the hope of trying to unify the public and private, and instead treat 'the demands of self-creation and human solidarity as equally valid, yet forever incommensurable.'[63] For anti-foundationalists like Rorty, there is no way in which philosophy, or any other theoretical discipline, will ever resolve this socio-philosophical problem. 'The closest we will come to joining these two quests is to see the aim of a just and free society as letting its citizens be as privatistic, "irrationalist," and aestheticist as they please so long as they do it on their own time – causing no harm to others and using no resources needed by those less advantaged.'[64]

The project of balancing private and public does not imply a particular, determinate, set of institutions or practices, but it is a vision that can guide public discourse, even if there is no hope of that discourse ever coming to an end. The great American philosopher John Dewey once wrote: 'Every generation has to accomplish democracy over again for itself.' [65] His point was that, at each moment in history, citizens and nations inevitably face unique challenges and problems. Consequently, we should not assume the democratic institutions and practices inherited from the past will be adequate for the conditions of today. Our continuous political challenge, therefore, is to 'accomplish' democracy anew, every generation. This is especially so when politics is viewed aesthetically, as something to be created rather than discovered.

Rorty argued that '[w]e need a redescription of liberalism as the hope that culture as a whole can be "poeticized" rather than the Enlightenment hope that it can be "rationalized" or "scientized."'[66] He adds: 'To see one's language, one's conscience, one's morality, and one's highest hopes as contingent products, as literalizations of what once were accidentally produced metaphors, is to adopt a self-identity which suits one for citizenship in such an ideally liberal state.'[67] In advancing this social vision, Rorty sketched a figure which he called a 'liberal ironist', which is presented as the paradigmatic citizen in a poeticized culture.

This person, as a liberal, hopes for a society in which everyone is as free as everyone else to live the life they choose. This type of liberal also thinks that 'cruelty is the worst thing that we can do,'[68] a slogan Rorty borrowed from philosopher Judith Shklar. However, as an 'ironist' (in Rorty's sense), this citizen 'faces up to the contingency of his or her own most central beliefs and desires.'[69] For an ironist, 'there is no answer to the question "Why not be cruel?" – no noncircular theoretical back up for the belief that cruelty is horrible.'[70] This ironic stance flows necessarily from the earlier post-metaphysical arguments about the contingency of language and selfhood. We may *want* philosophical foundations, but the evolution of philosophy has shown that such a hope cannot be realised.

Instead of advancing solidarity by grounding theories of justice on rational or philosophical foundations, Rorty contended that justice is something to be achieved rather than demonstrated:

> It is to be achieved not by inquiry but by imagination, the imaginative ability to see strange people as fellow sufferers.... It is created by increasing our sensitivity to the particular details of the pain and humiliation of the other, unfamiliar sorts of people. Such increased sensitivity makes it more difficult to marginalize people different from ourselves...[71]

According to Rorty's vision, social solidarity is not something that can be demonstrated by 'theory' and is better achieved by aesthetic means – a topic to be explored more in the essays to follow. Through art and storytelling that has an emotional and affective impact on people, the goal of the liberal ironist is to expand what Wilfred Sellars called 'we-intentions' and 'we-consciousness'.[72] This is a process of coming to see other human beings, who live in different societies or inhabit different social circles, as 'one of us'. It can also imply the expansion of moral concern beyond humanity itself, to become inclusive of all sentient beings and even ecosystems. This type of moral progress is best achieved, Rorty argued, through 'detailed description of what unfamiliar people are like and of redescription of what we ourselves are like.'[73] And Rorty argued that novels and other artistic means can do this far better than books of moral philosophy. 'That is why the novel, the movie, and the TV program [for better or for worse] have, gradually but steadily, replaced the sermon and the treatise as the principal vehicles of moral change and progress.'[74] Indeed, he proposed that we should look to the novelist, the artist, the story-teller, and even the literary critic, for guidance on how to live, rather than to the moral philosopher or theologian,.

For all his insight as a philosopher, Rorty was at best a good political thinker. His primary failing, in my view, was that he did not seem to fully appreciate that the private/public distinction, upon which his poeticized culture relied, has been subjected to sustained critique almost as long as liberalism had been around. This is not fatal to his view, but it does complicate it. There is simply no way, based on Rorty's own anti-foundationalist and anti-essentialist philosophical outlook, to draw an analytically sharp line between private and public. For example, Rorty states we should be able to be as aestheticist as we like in our private lives, provided we don't harm others and don't take resources needed by others less advantaged. But what level of private wealth becomes unjust in a world where such extreme poverty exists amidst plenty? When does a person's right to free speech interfere unfairly with social needs? When human rights conflict, how should political society resolve such conflicts? Many such questions could be asked which cannot be answered with an appeal to reason. The private/public distinction is intrinsically fuzzy, unable to answer such conflicts through conceptual analysis.

Presumably Rorty knew this very well, but he did not seem to realise that it problematised his clean distinction between the private and public realms. In the private realm he believed we should be free to be as aestheticist or eccentric as we wish, provided we don't harm others. The public realm is where the goals of social solidary, welfare, and freedom were to be achieved.[75] The reason I say that this political naivety does not undermine his politics is because the only way to resolve or answer questions about the private-public distinction is through social and political discourse not conceptual analysis. That is certainly a political ethic to which Rorty subscribed. Accordingly, perhaps he merely focussed on philosophical exposition and left the political complexity of the issues he raised to political theorists and to public discourse.

I believe that we can and should subscribe to the private-public distinction inherent to his view of a poeticized culture – to recognise that there are parts of our lives where the state and society have no right to interfere with or regulate. At the same time, we should recognise that where that line resides is ambiguous and shifting, and that it is a key task of social and political discourse to draw that line. This is part of why I believe democratic politics is necessarily aesthetic, in the sense that politics requires citizens to creatively engage each other with the unstable and indeterminate tool of language. And it is why one could talk of an aesthetic state in ways that denote, not fascism, but rather a free and egalitarian social order of self-creators. I am not arguing that politics *should* be aestheticised; I am just acknowledging that politics *is* aesthetic. As Jacques Rancière states: 'Politics is aesthetic in principle.'[76]

When there is social and political discourse about matters of highest importance, we human beings are doing the best we can, even if the conversation will never end. When we are left resorting to physical force – which may at times be justified (only context can tell) – our democratic processes have broken down.

Conclusion: Transcending *homo economicus*

Foucault argued that, under modernity, human subjectivities have been fixed in an extremely effective and thoroughly 'naturalised' way. Our subjectivities, that is, may have become a 'second nature' from which it will require a massive labour to free ourselves. 'Maybe,' Foucault suggested, 'the task nowadays is not to *discover* what we are, but to *refuse* what we are.... We have to promote new forms of subjectivity through the refusal of this kind of individuality which has been imposed on us for several centuries'.[77]

The Greek and Roman Stoics were keen advocates of this form of self-cultivation and the inspiration for Foucault's 'aesthetics of existence'. As discussed, this approach to existence is to conceive of life as 'raw material' which individuals are responsible for sculpting. From this perspective, we are condemned to be artists of life, with the world as our shared canvas. This essay has proposed that giving birth to oneself requires nothing less than the passionate exercise of our creative imaginations, which, fortunately, is a capacity that has been instilled into our nature as *homo aestheticus* through our long evolutionary history. But the imagination does not exercise itself; it is a tool that needs an artisan.

Of course, Foucault insisted that we do not get to *choose* the raw material we work with, in the sense that the form one's life takes is inevitably shaped, at least in part, by the world around us and our circumstances at birth. To enlist Marx, we make our own history, but we do not make it as we please. We exist, that is, both as creatures and creators. But insofar as we retain some space for freedom within which we can make our own decisions, then we are responsible for creating our own lives in much the same way as the sculptor is responsible for the statue; the painter for the canvas; the poet, the poem.

Could it be that the 'Death of Man', to restate Foucault's phrase, was actually the first (and a necessary) phase in the demise of what has been called *homo economicus*? What forms of life, what modes of being, would or could materialise with the reclaiming of our indeterminate natures as *homo aestheticus*? These are large questions and in the following essays I grapple with them further. The aim, however, is not to legitimate 'what is already known'.[78] Rather, the aim, as Foucault would have advised, is to explore whether or to what extent it is possible to think differently, by 'free[ing] thought from what it silently thinks'.[79]

---

[1] See for example, John Pfeiffer, *The Creative Explosion: An Inquiry into the Origins of Art and Religion* (Ithaca: Cornell University Press, 1982).

[2] Ibid.

[3] Gregory Currie, 'The Master of the Masek Beds: Handaxes, Art, and the Minds of Early Humans' in Elisabeth Schellekens and Peter Goldie (eds.) *The Aesthetic Mind: Philosophy and Psychology* (Oxford: Oxford University Press, 2014), pp. 9-31.

[4] Robert Joyce, *The Esthetic Animal: Man, the Art-Created Art Creator* (New York: Exposition Press, 1975)

[5] Currie, 'The Master of the Masek Beds', note 3, p. 17.

[6] Joyce, *Esthetic Animal*, note 4, p. 38-9.

[7] Michel Foucault, *The Order of Things* (London: Routledge, 2002), p. 422.

[8] Jean-Paul Sartre, *Existentialism and Humanism* (London: Methuen and Co, 1970).

[9] Toward the end of his life Sartre would qualify his notions of radical freedom with the claim that: 'You can always make something out of what you have been made into.' See Jean-Paul Sartre, *Situations* (Paris: Gallimard, 1964), p. 101.

[10] Richard Rorty, *Contingency, Irony, and Solidarity* (Cambridge: Cambridge University Press, 1989), p. 5.

[11] Jacques Derrida, *Of Grammatology* (Baltimore: John Hopkins University Press, 1998), p. 158

[12] Richard Rorty, *Philosophy and the Mirror of Nature* (Princeton: Princeton University Press, 1979).

[13] See generally, Stanley Fish, *Doing What Comes Naturally: Change, Rhetoric, and the Practice of Theory on Literary and Legal Studies* (Durham: Duke University Press, 1989).

[14] See especially, Michael Foucault, *Ethics: Essential Works Vol. I*, edited by Paul Rabinow (London: Penguin, 2000).

[15] Friedrich Nietzsche, *On the Genealogy of Morals* (New York: Vintage Books, 1969), Essay III, 27.

[16] Ibid

[17] See Michel Foucault, 'An Aesthetics of Existence' in Lawrence Kritzman (ed.) *Michel Foucault: Politics, Philosophy, Culture: Interviews and Other Writings 1977-1984* (New York: Routledge, 1990), p. 49.
[18] Ibid, pp. 50-1.
[19] Foucault, *Order of Things*, note 7, p. 373.
[20] Ibid, p. 422.
[21] Foucault, 'An Aesthetics of Existence', note 17.
[22] Michael Foucault, 'On the Genealogy of Ethics' in Foucault, *Ethics*, note 14, p. 262.
[23] Ibid, p. 261.
[24] Michel Foucault, *The Uses of Pleasure: Vol. II of the History of Sexuality* (New York: Vintage, 1984), p. 10.
[25] Michel Foucault, 'The Ethics of Concern of the Self as a Practice of Freedom' in Foucault, *Ethics*, note 14, p. 290.
[26] Foucault, 'On the Genealogy of Ethics, note 22, p. 262.
[27] See Samuel Alexander, 'Rescuing Aestheticism from the Dandies: Critical Distinctions', in this collection of essays. The full set will be available here: http://samuelalexander.info/s-m-p-l-c-t-y-ecological-civilisation-and-the-will-to-art/ (accessed 10 May 2023).
[28] Nietzsche, *Genealogy*, note 15, p. 2.
[29] Alexander Nehamas, *Nietzsche: Life as Literature* (Cambridge, MA: Harvard University Press, 1985).
[30] See generally, Alexander Nehamas, *The Art of Living: Socratic Reflections from Plato to Foucault* (Berkeley: University of California Press, 2000.
[31] Michel Foucault, 'Concern for the Truth' in Lawrence Kritzman (ed.) *Michel Foucault: Politics, Philosophy, Culture: Interviews and Other Writings 1977-1984* (New York: Routledge, 1990), p. 263.
[32] Michel Foucault, 'Return of Morality' in Lawrence Kritzman (ed.) *Michel Foucault: Politics, Philosophy, Culture: Interviews and Other Writings 1977-1984* (New York: Routledge, 1990), pp. 253-4.
[33] Edward McGushin, *Foucault's Askesis: An Introduction to the Philosophical Life* (Evanston: Northwestern University Press, 2007), p. 115.
[34] Richard Kearney, *Dialogues with Contemporary Continental Thinkers* (Manchester: Manchester University Press, 1984) p. 124.
[35] Michel Foucault, *Power: The Essential Works of Foucault, 1954-1984*, edited by J. Faubion (New York: New Press, 2000) p. 240.
[36] Michel Foucault, 'The Minimal Self' in Lawrence Kritzman (ed.) *Michel Foucault: Politics, Philosophy, Culture: Interviews and Other Writings 1977-1984* (New York: Routledge, 1990), p. 14.
[37] Ibid.
[38] Rorty, *Contingency, Irony, and Solidarity*, note 10.
[39] Foucault, 'The Ethics of Concern', note 25.
[40] Michel Foucault, *The Uses of Pleasure: The History of Sexuality Vol II.* (New York: Random House, 1985) p. 9.
[41] Friedrich Nietzsche, *Thus Spoke Zarathustra*, in Walter Kaufmann (ed.), *The Portable Nietzsche* (London: Penguin, 1988), p. 129.
[42] Friedrich Nietzsche, *The Gay Science*, edited by Bernard Williams (Cambridge: Cambridge University Press, 2001), p. 170.

[43] Nehamas, *Nietzsche: Life as Literature,* note 29.
[44] Richard Rorty, 'The Priority of Democracy to Philosophy' in Richard Rorty, *Objectivity, Relativism, and Truth* (Cambridge: Cambridge University Press, 1991) p. 194.
[45] Rorty, *Contingency, Irony, and Solidarity*, note 10, p. 73
[46] Ibid.
[47] Ibid.
[48] Ibid.
[49] Ibid.
[50] Ibid, pp. 4-5.
[51] Ibid, p. 4.
[52] See Donald Davidson, *Inquiries into Truth and Interpretation* (Oxford: Oxford University Press, 1984), p. 185.
[53] Rorty, *Contingency, Irony, and Solidarity*, note 10, p. 3.
[54] Ibid.
[55] Ibid, p. 26.
[56] Percy Bysshe Shelley, *A Defense of Poetry* (Boston: Ginn and Co, 1890) p. 2.
[57] Fredrich Nietzsche, *The Gay Science*, trans. Walter Kaufmann (New York: Vintage Books, 1974). p. 240.
[58] Rorty, *Contingency, Irony, and Solidarity*, note 10, p. 29.
[59] Ibid, pp. 35-6.
[60] Ibid, p. 36.
[61] Ibid.
[62] Ibid.
[63] Ibid, p. xv.
[64] Ibid, p. xiv.
[65] John Dewey, *The Later Works: Volume 13*, ed. Jo Ann Boydston (Carbondale: Southern Illinois University Press, 1981-90), p. 299.
[66] Rorty, *Contingency, Irony, and Solidarity*, note 10, p. 53.
[67] Ibid, p. 61.
[68] Ibid, p. xv.
[69] Ibid.
[70] Ibid.
[71] Ibid, p. xvi.
[72] Ibid, p. 190.
[73] Ibid, p. xvi.
[74] Ibid.
[75] See, e.g. Jennifer Herdt, 'Cruelty, Liberalism, and the Quarantine of Irony' *Soundings: An Interdisciplinary Journal* (1992) 75(1): pp. 79-95; and Gregory Reece, 'Religious Faith and Intellectual Responsibility: Richard Rorty and the Public/Private Distinction' *American Journal of Theology and Philosophy* (2001) 22(3): pp. 206-220.
[76] Jacques Rancière, *Dis-Agreement* (London: University of Minnesota Press, 2006), p. 58.
[77] Michel Foucault, 'The subject and power', in H. Dreyfus and P. Rabinow (eds). *Michel Foucault: Beyond structuralism and hermeneutics* (Chicago: University of Chicago Press, 1982), p. 785 (emphasis added).
[78] Foucault, *The Uses of Pleasure*, above note 40, p. 9.
[79] Ibid.

‘If we are to solve the political problem in practice, [we must] follow the path of aesthetics, since it is through Beauty that we arrive at Freedom.’

– **Friedrich Schiller**

ESSAY NINE

THE POLITICS OF BEAUTY: SCHILLER ON FREEDOM AND AESTHETIC EDUCATION

The truth will set us free. This claim originates in religion but culminates in Enlightenment rationalism. The rationalist view assumes that humanity's primary 'lack' is cognitive; that when we acquire a certain knowledge or technological capability, we will be saved. Worry not about the absence of God, for science and reason will lead us to the promised land of liberty and abundance. If this is so, however, we should ask with Friedrich Schiller, who was an early critic of the Enlightenment: why is it that we remain barbarians?[1] Human beings have flown to the moon, mapped the genome, mechanised a great deal of hard labour, created computers and the internet, among a long list of other technological achievements that often seem miraculous. And yet, despite the wonders of science and technology, freedom is not a word that can easily describe the condition of humankind, neither historically nor today. This is clearly the case for the billions around the world who still live in material destitution. Their condition is all the more morally egregious given the unprecedented wealth and technological capacity of the modern world. But what freedom have those of us in the affluent world claimed for ourselves?

As twentieth-century critical theorist Herbert Marcuse would insist: 'a comfortable, smooth, reasonable, democratic unfreedom prevails in advanced industrial civilization, a token of technical progress.'[2] Poet Bertolt Brecht was even more scathing: 'What were bad harvests / To the need that ravages us in the midst of plenty?'[3] Today, we live in a world where consumerist cultures have become defined by the cruel emptiness of affluence, and where servitude to capital is disguised as the good life. Ever expanding economies are something to which we should, and must, aspire, consciously or unconsciously. Yet as our 'wealth' increases in proportion to the degradation of Earth's ecosystems, it seems that sometime this century – if we are clever enough to achieve our economic goals – our species might even become so rich we go extinct. What will pass through the minds of the corporate profiteers who, in accordance with economic reason, direct their workers to cut down the last trees, only to find themselves on an uninhabitable planet?

Having more or less solved the economic problem of how to produce enough for everyone on Earth to live well, this was supposed to be the historic moment when material needs were universally met; a time when we could design for ourselves a better, more humane social order, with more leisure, dignified work, and material security. But as a matter of historical record, when the consumerist rewards of advanced technological society did not satisfy or liberate, people and politics tended merely to intensify the pursuit of 'more' rather than reprioritise. Even the richest seem to need to get richer, on the assumption that with even more money and stuff, human life will finally be better. At last, we will be happy and free. Moreover, the material comforts and cultural entertainments provided by modern consumer capitalism seem to have sedated populations, such that resistance and rebellion are quashed or exchanged for 'nice things' (or merely the *promise* of nice things, eternally deferred). Even when we recognise or experience the spiritual malaise that defines the cultures of the so-called 'developed' world, how easy it is to merely go with the flow, reproducing the status quo out of habit or sheer apathy. We do not produce capitalism; capitalism produces us. Thus Empire marches on.

In this essay I'd like to consider these failures of modernity and the Enlightenment project in relation to Friedrich Schiller's ideas about freedom, aesthetic education, and the politics of beauty. Schiller argued that Europe in the late eighteenth century had fallen into the grasp of excessive reason, and because of this, the French Revolution was failing to fulfil its promises of liberty, equality, and fraternity. He believed that art and aesthetics were the best and perhaps the only means for resolving the social and political imbalances of Europe; the only means of creating harmonious human beings who would be ready and able to produce a harmonious society. It will be seen that his analyses in support of this provocative position were highly nuanced and strikingly original.

Schiller was a German playwright, poet, and philosopher, born in 1759. He is perhaps best known for being the author of the poem 'Ode to Joy', which Ludwig van Beethoven famously put to music in the final movement of his ninth symphony. Schiller would come to develop a close but complicated relationship with Johann Wolfgang von Goethe, with whom he collaborated at the Weimar Theatre, establishing it as the leading theatre in Germany. Although Schiller has arguably been most influential through his poems and plays, it is his aesthetic and philosophical writings which are the focus of this essay. Most notably, I will focus on the ideas presented in his *Letters on the Aesthetic Education of Man*,[4] published in 1795 (hereafter '*Aesthetic Letters*'). This text is aptly described by philosopher Frederick Beiser as 'an apology for beauty, a defence of the aesthetic dimensions of life.'[5] Schiller was no naive aesthete, however, but rather a bold and insightful thinker whose aesthetic writings deserve more attention than they receive.

The *Aesthetic Letters* were written as correspondence with his patron, Friedrich Christian. The original versions were destroyed in a fire, but Schiller partially rewrote them, with revisions and additions. No doubt this strange writing process over several years partly explains why, at times, the arguments he presented seem fragmented, obscure, and perhaps reflecting an evolution and refinement of his views over time. In what follows I reexamine this neglected work and explore a reconstructive reading of Schiller's aesthetic theory. I will assess the contemporary relevance of his theses on the importance and role of aesthetic education, including the neglected role that emotions play in ethics and politics. Herbert Read, widely considered the twentieth century's most compelling advocate for the role of art in education, noted it was 'one of curiosities of history'[6] that the idea that art should be the basis of education has been given scant attention – Schiller being a rare exception.

The purpose of reviewing Schiller's rather complex theory is not to conduct an intellectual history but rather to evaluate whether his position illuminates contemporary problems. I will invite readers to consider the extent to which aesthetic education – that is, a deeper cultural engagement with art and the aesthetic dimensions of life – points to an appropriate and coherent response to the crises of our time. To place my conclusion up front: I have come to believe that aesthetic education is our last best hope, and Schiller can help articulate this thesis.

A critique of the culture and politics of Enlightenment rationalism

Any understanding of the *Aesthetics Letters* must begin by acknowledging its social and political context. Written soon after the French Revolution, the early letters in the collection are infused with a mood of lost hope and failed promises, even passionate disappointment, regarding both the revolution in particular and the Enlightenment project more broadly. Schiller viewed the revolution as a societal transformation with vast potential, whereby people 'had awoken from their long lethargy'[7] and through 'an impressive majority... [were] demanding the restitution of their inalienable rights.'[8] There seemed to be a '*physical* possibility of setting Law upon the throne, of honouring Man at last as an end in himself and making true freedom the basis of political association.'[9]

Within a few years, however, it had become clear that this promising political rupture had been contaminated by the violence of the Reign of Terror (circa 1793-4). Contemplating the unfolding of European society, Schiller declared that the 'rotten foundations are yielding',[10] and suggested that 'the *moral* possibility is wanting, and the favourable moment finds an apathetic generation.'[11] The so-called Age of Reason had promised so much, with scientific and intellectual advances suggesting that enlightened society would be able to realise, at last, the dream of ensuring freedom and justice for all. Why then, Schiller asked, 'is it that we still remain barbarians?'[12]

It is a critique that still resonates today, perhaps more so than ever, which suggests that Schiller's call to respond through aesthetic education might be worth considering too. At base, his view was that, as a consequence of the Enlightenment project having gone astray, European society had developed in ways that over-emphasised the role of reason and science and marginalised the place of sensibility and the creative imagination. Whereas Francisco Goya's famous etching of 1799 warned through its title that 'The Sleep of Reason Produces Monsters', Schiller turned that concern on its head, suggesting that reason, excessively applied, is itself a form of sleep, which can breed its own monsters and monstrosities. This is clearly a critique steeped in, as it shaped, the romantic tradition, upon which Schiller was to be a great influence both in Germany and England.[13]

At the same time, Schiller cannot be dismissed as a mere romantic in any pejorative sense. The violence of reason which he was reacting against was, in his eyes, a betrayal of the modernist project, not something inherent to it. He would likely have concurred with philosopher Bruno Latour who claimed, two centuries later, that 'we have never been modern.'[14] This position encompasses a critique of reason with reason itself, even if, as we will see, Schiller believed 'the way to the head must lie through the heart.'[15] Contrast this with Immanuel Kant who had announced the sole authority of reason with respect to moral and political duty. Schiller framed this domineering rule of reason as the 'barbarian'[16] in whom 'principles destroy his feeling,'[17] adding that '[t]he intellectual enlightenment of which the refined ranks of society, not without some justification, pride themselves, reveals on the whole an influence upon the disposition so little ennobling that it rather furnishes maxims to confirm depravity.'[18] He saw the governing classes exemplifying manners of 'affected proprietary'[19] in a culture defined by a 'materialistic moral philosophy':[20]

> Selfishness has established its system in the very bosom of our exquisitely refined society, and we experience all the contagions and all the calamities of community without the accompaniment of a communal spirit.[21]

In the self-interested pursuit of material wealth through industrial development, scientific advance, and technological progress, Schiller saw humankind being reduced to cogs in a machine. Among other factors, this was due to an ever-sharpening division of labour: '[B]y confining our activity to a single sphere we have handed ourselves over to a master who is not infrequently inclined to end up suppressing the rest of our capacities.'[22] Those remaining aptitudes of the human character get neglected, for only those skills which bring 'profit'[23] are valued in a market society focussed on acquisitiveness, economic growth, and imperialist expansions of power and territory.

These insights no doubt paved the way for a critique of industrialisation that received sharper and more sustained expression half a century later in the works of Marx and Engels. The cruel and undignified social consequences of industrialisation were also to be highlighted powerfully through literature, most prominently in the novels of Charles Dickens. Without romanticising the life of medieval peasants, living in the dense and polluted centres of early industrial cities was typically a horrid and undignified existence, with so-called economic progress emptying life of its richness, depth, diversity, and meaning.

Schiller saw that most people, both historically and of his own time, were given little or no opportunity to fulfil their innate potentials, which he found dehumanising. Think of the pin makers in Adam Smith's *Wealth of Nations*,[24] who divided up pin making construction into various tasks to increase efficiency; or the factory or office workers today who spend their working lives pushing the same button or shuffling papers in relentless, uncreative monotony.[25] As Schiller stated:

> Eternally chained to only one single little fragment of the whole, Man himself grew to be only a fragment; with the monotonous noise of the wheel he drives everlastingly in his ears, he never develops the harmony of his being, and instead of imprinting humanity upon his nature he becomes merely the imprint of his occupation, his science.[26]

Due to this dehumanising process, Schiller lamented that 'we see not merely individual persons but whole classes of human beings developing only part of their capacities, while the rest of them, like a stunted plant, shew only a feeble vestige of their nature.'[27] The consequence was that 'gradually individual concrete life is extinguished, in order that the abstract life of the whole may prolong its sorry existence.'[28] In Schiller's view, the market economy, driven by insatiable materialist desires and avarice, had turned his fellow citizens into mere machines of production and consumption, deadening the creative spirit and the sensuous love of life: 'So far from setting us free, culture only develops a new want with every power that it bestows on us.... and the maxim of passive obedience passes for the supreme wisdom of life.'[29]

This critique anticipated, by half a century, Marx and Engel's writings on alienation. In the twentieth century these ideas were developed further by critical theorists of the Frankfurt school, who bore down upon consumer culture, surveillance capitalism, instrumental reason, and technocracy, with unrestrained ruthlessness[30] – influenced, to be sure, by our philosopher-poet under examination.[31] Indeed, if Schiller were alive today, he would be the first to highlight that we have gained new freedoms, but also developed new and insidious forms of servitude in a one-dimensional society:

> Terrified of the freedom which always declares its hostility to their first attempts, men will in one place throw themselves into the arms of a comfortable servitude, and in another, driven to despair by a pedantic tutelage, they will break out into wild libertinism of the natural State. Usurpation will plead the weakness of human nature, insurrection its dignity, until at length the great sovereign of all human affairs, blind Force, steps in to decide the sham conflict of principles like a common prize-fight.[32]

Schiller criticised the so-called 'lower classes',[33] wherein 'we find crude, lawless impulses'[34] and which are 'hastening with ungovernable fury to their brutal satisfaction.'[35] But he reserved far more of his venom for the 'civilized classes',[36] who 'present to us the still more repugnant spectacle of indolence, and a depravity of character which is all the more shocking since culture itself is the source of it.'[37] Like 'fugitives from a burning city everyone seeks only to rescue his own miserable property from the devastation.'[38] These are the polemical words of a poet, of course, not the dry, measured assessments of a social or political scientist. But the accusations beneath the rhetoric are not easily dismissed, then or now.

In these conditions, Schiller resigned himself to the conviction that the French Revolution could scarcely have ended in any other way but failure, tightly related to the misapplication of its theoretical foundations.[39] 'We know that the sensibility of the mind depends for its degree upon the liveliness, and for its extent upon the richness, of the imagination. But the predominance of the analytical faculty must necessarily deprive the fancy of its strength and its fire, and a restricted sphere of objects must diminish its wealth.'[40] He continued his critique by arguing that:

> The greater part of humanity is too much harassed and fatigued by the struggle with want, to rally itself for a new and sterner struggle with error. Content if they themselves escape the hard labour of thought, men

> gladly resign to others the guardianship of their ideas, and if it happens that higher needs are stirred in them, they embrace with eager faith the formulas which state and priesthood hold in readiness for such an occasion.[41]

In sum, Schiller saw European society made up of people who were not yet capable of being good citizens in a free Republic. People were not ready for the freedom that they had received, and yet political society can be no better than the people who constitute it. When this expanded (though still imperfect) freedom was granted through the revolution, it should have come as no surprise, in Schiller's view, that the barbaric excesses of the Reign of Terror would follow. This was because the spirit of the time was 'fluctuating between perverseness and brutality... and it is only the equilibrium of evil that still occasionally sets bounds to it.'[42] Nevertheless, there is an implicit optimism in Schiller's project. By writing the *Aesthetic Letters*, he implied that though the battle he was witnessing had been lost, the war for liberty, equality, and fraternity must be won – even if, he noted, with some prescience, it was a task for 'more than a single century.'[43]

This was the defining social and political context which provides the backdrop to Schiller's *Aesthetic Letters*, and the motivation for writing them. Not only was he convinced that this diagnosis accurately described his own society, he insisted that 'it resembles any people at all that is in the process of civilization, since all without distinction must fall away from Nature through over-subtlety of intellect before they can return to her through Reason.'[44] Despite always remaining a champion of reason, he was also, as we have seen, one of its severest critics, and in a decisive and original move which will be examined in more detail below, he argued that 'the way to the head must lie through the heart.'[45] This is not, however, an anti-intellectual point. He was proposing that our intellects might be engaged most effectively if our emotions are engaged first. More directly, he argued that such emotional or even spiritual engagement is best achieved through art and beauty – through the works of poets, painters, musicians, and storytellers. Moreover, he believed that moral, ethical, and political reasoning *must* engage the heart to be effective, for reason and rationality will fail to motivate or transform behaviour without an emotional engagement.

The striking conclusion Schiller drew was that political freedom had been granted to a citizenry that was not yet mature or awakened enough to deal with it properly. Lacking what he called a 'totality'[46] or 'wholeness'[47] of character, human nature was out of balance, in a society out of balance. This was not an argument for constraining that freedom, of course, it was merely a diagnosis of social and political realities. But it also provided insight into what might be the proper response to this reality. How might people become better suited to thrive with the expanded freedoms they had achieved through political struggle? How might people become 'capable and worthy of exchanging the State of need for the State of freedom?'[48] Is more reason and technology needed to solve the problems caused by reason and technology? Schiller answered in the negative, turning instead to explore the potential of aesthetic education.

Here Schiller acknowledged a circular problem with respect to the State: 'All improvement in the political sphere is to proceed from the ennobling of character – but how, under the influence of a barbarous constitution, can the character become ennobled?'[49] He had no faith in the possibility of change originating in or through the apparatus of the state. In any case, he noted, 'we must continue to regard every attempt at reform as inopportune, and every hope based upon it as chimerical, until the division of the inner Man has been done away with.'[50] Consequently, Schiller was prompted to seek out some other instrument. In the Ninth Letter, he was ready to announce to his readers what that instrument had to be: the Fine Arts. Schiller felt humanity's best hopes for individual and social flourishing lay in beauty, which was his general term for aesthetic value more broadly. Aesthetic value includes the pleasurable experience of beauty. But it might also include other forms of aesthetic experience, such as a heightened sense of *meaning* in life that can arise from creative activity or from the contemplation of art or nature, even if this is not always pleasurable.

Schiller acknowledged that readers would be right to doubt his project. Should he not be able to make better use of his own liberty than focus attention on the arena of Fine Arts? 'Is it not at least untimely to be looking around for a code of laws for the aesthetic world, when the affairs of the moral world provide an interest so much more urgent ...?'[51] Schiller hoped to convince his readers that 'this subject is far less alien to the need of the age than to its taste, that we must indeed, if we are to solve the political problem in practice, follow the path of aesthetics, since it is through Beauty that we arrive at Freedom.'[52] Not only has this thesis struck many readers as strange, the very possibility of a connection between freedom and aesthetics, both personally and politically, is in need of (and will receive) explanation.

Schiller saw in his society that art was being marginalised: '*Utility* is the great idol of the age, to which all powers must do service and all talents swear allegiance. In these clumsy scales the spiritual service of Art has no weight; deprived of all encouragement, she flees from the noisy mart of our century.'[53] He added: 'The very spirit of philosophical enquiry seizes one province after another from the imagination, and the frontiers of Art are contracted as the boundaries of science are enlarged.'[54]

In a direct affront to the Age of Reason, Schiller summarised his approach by stating that 'the development of man's capacity for feeling is, therefore, the more urgent need of our age.'[55] Thus he exhorted his fellow artists to surround people with 'great and noble forms of genius, and encompass them about with the symbols of perfection, until semblance conquer reality, and art triumph over nature.'[56] In essence, he was proposing that the arts and a renewed aesthetic education were required to bring forth a refined aesthetic sensibility and expanded outlook. Only through this cultural process could human beings resolve the dissonance and imbalance in their natures and become the 'noble souls'[57] that are needed for political society to function harmoniously. A noble soul is 'not content to be itself free; it must also set free everything around it.'[58] In the celebrated line quoted above, Schiller declared that 'it is through Beauty that we arrive at Freedom.'

This process involved passing through what Schiller called 'the aesthetic condition',[59] whereupon our dual nature as sensuous-rational beings could, at last, find harmonious resolution. In other words, beauty could help us realise our highest potentials as free and creative beings. In this ideal condition, humans would not only *behave* as good citizens, they would *want* to do so, which is essentially what Schiller means by a 'noble soul' or a 'beautiful soul'. It is an ideal, Schiller admits, that may never be achieved. But he presents it as a goal towards which we can move and to which we can make some progress through aesthetic education. It is 'the direction [that] is at once the destination, and the way is completed from the moment it is trodden.'[60]

Schiller's 'sensuo-rational' theory of human nature

Having outlined Schiller's critique of modernity and stated his view that true progress depended on aesthetic education, I will address the complex arguments with which he supported this thesis. Schiller was steeped in Kantian philosophy and often claimed merely to build upon it (consistently) rather than amend it (through revision). Most commentators, however, contend that there are various places in which Schiller misrepresents Kant, or even contradicts him, in order to make room for his own ideas. This is not the place to rehash that technical debate, so in the following review I will try to let Schiller speak for himself rather than in conversation with Kant.

I will, however, attempt to re-present Schiller's views as far as possible without getting too caught up in his sometimes archaic sounding language of the eighteenth century. If this results in something of a 'reconstructive' presentation of Schiller rather than a pure, scholarly or historic review, then that is a charge I am happy to accept. My motivations are not to discover what Schiller 'really thought' but instead to assess how his strikingly original ideas might be of value for us today. It will be seen that beauty relates to freedom both as an *end* and as a *means*, a subtle point that will become clear in due course. After reviewing Schiller's theory of the sense, form, and play drives, I will draw on some contemporary scholarship to unpack Schiller's notion of beauty and aesthetic freedom. In later essays I will develop some of these ideas and apply them to contemporary social and political issues.[61]

Fundamentally, Schiller saw personal, social, and political problems arising from a fundamental tension in human nature – a tension between passion and reason, or sensuality and form. Schiller maintained that only through resolving or reconciling this tension could we fulfil our natures and achieve freedom. On the one hand, Schiller recognised that we clearly have a 'sensuous' aspect to our characters. The bodily organs give us sensory apparatus with which we experience and perceive the material or external world. Through what he calls the 'sensuous drive' (or 'sense drive' or 'material drive'),[62] we are drawn to a wide range of pleasures and we instinctively avoid pains; we experience a range of emotions, passions, feelings, and desires, and we use our imaginations to dream and create. We are drawn, that is, to what Schiller simply calls 'life',[63] and he argued that this drive calls us towards diversity of experience and 'demands that there is change',[64] making us naturally inclined to explore sensuous existence and 'make all [our] potentialities fully manifest.'[65] Since all human beings have different tastes, desires, and skills, this sense drive leads to a wide variety of human capacities and potentials, a human diversity which Schiller, as a true liberal, valued as something to be celebrated.[66]

On the other hand, Schiller highlighted that we humans also have a 'rational' side to our natures. Through the application of reason, we conceptualise and try to theoretically understand the world through reflection and analysis; we try to impose some 'form' on the chaos and flux of the world and to engage in discourse and deliberation; we set goals and pursue them according to a plan. Schiller called this aspect of our nature the 'form drive' (or the 'rational drive').[67] This refers to the human disposition to develop principles, rules, and categories, and to highlight patterns and regularities that bring order and uniformity to the world. As he explained, the form drive 'is intent on giving [us] the freedom to bring harmony into the diversity of [our] manifestations, and to affirm [our] person among all [our] changes of condition.'[68]

Both the sense drive and the form drive exist within us as 'motive force[s] in the sensible world'[69] that are oriented toward the 'realization of their object.'[70] The goal of the sense drive is a diversity of sensuous experience. The form drive seeks uniformity, regularity, and rational understanding, which, among other things, is important for orderly social coexistence in a society of diverse individuals. Schiller saw both these drives as important and valuable aspects of our natures, but he recognised the tension between them. He argued that if either of them dominates, we will be 'at odds'[71] with ourselves, and if governments let one or the other dominate, society as a whole will be out of balance. This antagonistic yet mutually dependent relationship between reason and sensuality thus manifests at both the personal and political levels.

Schiller proposed that in order to overcome this kind of tension in our natures we need to develop what he calls 'wholeness of character'[72], which he believed was an achievable synthesis, or at least a critical and necessary goal to work toward. The basic idea here is to point to an 'ideal'[73] form of the human being where both drives are in balance, neither dominating the other, but rather acting in harmony and coordination.

Schiller's language of 'drives' might sound a bit antiquated, but his fundamental characterisation of the tension within humanity's sensuo-rational nature is a plausible way to explain and understand the type of creature we are. It is almost commonsensical, and scholar Susan Bentley has done work re-presenting Schiller's theory to show how it fits with contemporary evolutionary biology and the social sciences.[74] Though overly binary and incomplete as an analytical tool, this Schillerian lens has the potential to be revealing. Furthermore, it is a lens that does not contradict the conception of human beings as *homo aestheticus* described in previous essays. Schiller's analysis, I propose, is merely the next layer for understanding our complex human condition, and one that can illuminate the nature of contemporary problems and point toward ways of resolving them.

We could even see Schiller's theory of the drives as being a precursor to Freud, who, in *Civilisation and its Discontents*,[75] explained how neuroses and pathologies emerge in human society when our animal instincts (sex drives and aggression) are rationally repressed in order to make social order possible. One difference is that Freud did not think that such tension could ever be resolved, suggesting that the benefits of civilisation required a repression of instincts but that such repression would inevitably lead to psychological problems. Schiller, on the other hand, held out the possibility of finding some way to reconcile this tension and bring human nature into harmony, both internally and in social relations. That said, Schiller was openly of the view that complete harmonisation of the drives was an 'ideal' that could never be fully achieved. Rather, harmony was a goal towards which we should attempt to move. In the end, then, perhaps Schiller and Freud were not so far apart on this point.

Even if perfect reconciliation is not possible, we might still accept that finding ways to *better* balance those competing drives is a coherent way to live a full and free life. Indeed, there are many philosophical and spiritual traditions, dating from the ancients up to the present, which maintain that the proper balancing of reason and the passions is the key to human flourishing. This implies an approach that enjoys the pleasures and diversity of sensuous experience without, in anti-social ways, acting purely out of animal instinct. And it would be an approach to life that utilises the sophistication of our rational intellects and helps us coexist with other people, without repressing our sensuous natures by focussing too much of our energy and attention to logic, reason, and order. It is about balance.

We see here that each drive needs to limit itself so as not to dominate the other. At the same time each drive is needed to support the other, since each can help the other achieve its distinct objectives. By developing this type of coordination and harmony between the drives, Schiller argued we can achieve 'wholeness of character' and only then do we become free and fully human. In doing so we would come to represent the 'archetype of a human being'[76] which we all carry within ourselves and which is our 'life's task'[77] to achieve.

This balancing task is not merely of individual significance but also represents a political challenge. Just as the individual must ensure neither drive dominates, so too would an ideal state need to balance and reconcile these competing, yet co-dependent, aspects of existence. As already discussed, however, Schiller saw his society as badly out of balance, grossly excessive in its use of reason to govern life, at the cost of humanity's creative and sensuous experience. Among other things, through the extreme specialisation emerging out of the division of labour, he highlighted how the nature of society diminished the inherent creative capacities and potentialities of each human being, reducing individual workers to a fragment of what they could be. They are 'imprisoned within the unvarying confines of [their] own calling'[78] and 'incapable of extending [themselves] to appreciate other ways of seeing and knowing.'[79] This lack of balance, harmony, and wholeness in life therefore interferes with human freedom and inhibits the full realisation of our whole natures or characters.

Social and political matters will be considered more closely in later essays, but for now I simply note that Schiller's view has clear socio-political implications. Just as a state or society can *interfere and repress* the creative potentialities in each human being, so too could a well-formed social order *support* people achieving 'wholeness of character'. As noted above, however, Schiller did give precedence to the individual and social over the political, in the sense that he did not see the state creating the conditions for individual wholeness of character. Rather, individuals must achieve wholeness of character in order to create well-ordered political rules and functioning institutions. Put otherwise, cultural change will need to usher in political change, more than the other way around, even though the relationship between culture and political economy is dialectical, with each shaping, as it is shaped by, the other. As English author J.G. Ballard noted: 'Many of the great cultural shifts that prepare the way for political change are largely aesthetic.'[80]

The 'play drive' awakens

Having outlined Schiller's conception of human beings, I return to his central but still mysterious thesis that beauty is the only path to freedom. Even if it were accepted that freedom consists in balancing the drives, it remains unclear where beauty fits in his theory. To understand Schiller's reasoning, we need to consider one of his most original and complex (and sometimes confusing) notions: what he calls the 'play drive'.[81]

In the *Aesthetic Letters*, Schiller explained the emergence or 'awaken[ing]'[82] of the play drive as part of the development of human nature in history. He believed that prior to the emergence of political society – that is, in the hypothetical 'state of nature' so widely discussed in Schiller's time – human life was shaped solely by the sense drive. Put otherwise, the earliest hominin species that emerged millions of years ago, lived purely in accordance with animal instinct, given that the intellectual apparatus capable of rationality and reflection had yet to develop. As the modern mind developed its capacity to reason, the form drive was established, and the defining dual nature of our species arose for the first time.

Nevertheless, Schiller maintained that the rational side of our nature soon discerned that the form drive was in tension with the sense drive; that reason and passion sometimes pull us in different directions. The form drive, however, being based in reason, seeks the complete fulfilment of our human nature where both drives are in balance: 'Reason must make this demand because it is reason.'[83] Accordingly, Schiller claimed that as rational beings we reflect on our need to limit our own rationality in order to harmonise the drives. This gives rise to the 'play drive', the nature of which is to bring the sense and form drives into a balanced, reciprocal relationship.[84] Given that the play drive emerges out of reason, it is a specifically a human drive, one not shared with other (pre-rational) animals.

Misunderstandings of Schiller arise when 'play' is taken to imply something childish or trivial. Of course, he is not suggesting that, in response to the Reign of Terror, one should joke around and make light of things. While he is not using play in any conventional way, the sense in which he does employ the term is not always obvious or clear. In her analysis of 'play' in Schiller's work, Susan Bentley offers an etymological reading of play and notes that the term is derived from words that mean 'to engage oneself'[85] (which, incidentally, resonates with Foucault's conception of ethics as 'the self engaging the self'). There is an element of wildness about the concept, something without bounds, unknowable, indeterminate, fertile, and creative. As Bentley suggests, 'Schiller's goal of ensuring human freedom required a play that opened up our potentials as human beings.'[86]

At a fundamental level, then, the play drive invites us into a space of experimental self-creation, raising open questions about how best to balance the two fundamental drives (sense and form). Play should be broadly interpreted with these serious overtones implied. In an earlier essay in this collection, *homo aestheticus* was presented as a theory of human nature that was not determinative of our being but expansive and malleable. So too can we see Schiller's theory of human nature as grounded in the aesthetic dimensions of life, inclined toward self-fashioning through play; through the playful exploration of who one might yet become, by practising techniques of the self that seek to balance the sense and form drives.

Importantly, the play drive is *not* a third 'fundamental drive'. Schiller makes clear that the category of fundamental drives is exhausted by the sense and the form drives. Instead, the play drive emerges *from* the reasoning processes of the form drive, in order to reconcile the tension between our competing drives and make human nature complete. Schiller explained:

> Such a reciprocal relation between the two drives is, admittedly, but a task enjoined upon us by reason, a problem which man is only capable of solving completely in the perfect consummation of his existence. It is, in the most precise sense of the word, *the idea of his human nature*, hence something infinite, to which in the course of time he can approximate ever more closely, but without ever being able to reach it.[87]

Just as the two fundamental drives have 'objects' towards which they strive (sensuality and form), so too does the play drive have an object. At this point in the analysis Schiller advises that the object of the play drive is beauty. He states that beauty is 'the object common to both [sense and form] drives'[88] too, since beauty is what is sought when the other two drives exist in a harmonious, reciprocal relationship. At this stage one might fairly ask: why beauty? The meaning and significance of this central aspect of Schiller's aesthetic theory will become clearer as we come to understand how he defines beauty.

Beauty as an *end* or *object* can be understood, in part, as implying harmonisation or balance. Since reason demands harmonisation of the primary drives, and since the play drive functions to enact that harmonisation, Schiller argued that reason's demand is that there be beauty:

> Reason... makes the following demand: ... let there be a play drive, since only the union of reality with form, contingency with necessity, passivity with freedom, makes the concept of human nature complete... Consequently, as soon as reason utters the pronouncement: let humanity exist, it has by that very pronouncement also promulgated the law: let there be beauty.[89]

Let's pause for a moment to examine Schiller's notion of beauty more closely, which he defined at one point as 'living form'[90] and which he argued has the capacity to engage us in play. When contemplating an object or a person, Schiller suggested that, on the one hand, we appreciate the sensuous or material side of what we are considering – which could be described as the 'content' of our life experience. On the other hand, however, we also appreciate the 'form' that is given to this sensuous or material content. For example, when contemplating a painting, we might notice its bright colours or the house that is depicted (the painting's *content*), but we might also notice the *form* given to the painting by its unique brush strokes or the way the elements of the painting are ordered or placed in space, their relations between each other. Similarly, with a piece of music, we will hear the content of the notes but also the form or order in which the notes are played. Schiller advised that '[t]he highest degree of beauty is, therefore, to be sought in the most perfect possible union and equilibrium of reality and form.'[91] Taken together – perceived *holistically* – the form and content of something reflects its 'aesthetic style', such that objects will have varying degrees of beauty depending on how closely they approximate the ideal of beauty.[92]

Schiller's notion of 'living form' therefore invites us to judge the beauty of something according to whether or to what extent its content sits in harmonious relationship to its form. If either content or form is out of balance or dominates, then, to that extent, the beauty of the object under consideration is diminished. A painting might use spectacular colours but be poorly executed or arranged, just as a piano sonata might have an enticing melody but be played too fast or harshly. An object in experience moves closer to the ideal of beauty the better it manifests a harmonious balancing of 'life' and 'form' – hence, Schiller's definition of beauty as 'living form.'

The structure of this aesthetic analysis obviously mirrors the dual aspects of 'life' and 'form' in Schiller's conception of human nature – which is no accident. The same harmonisation between form and content in a work of art is required when considering how to realise the dual aspects of our human nature. We have seen that the object of the play drive is beauty, which is achieved by reconciling the conflict between the sense and the form drives. Indeed, when the sense and form drives have been harmonised or held in proper balance, where neither drive dominates, they also seek beauty as their object, by way of the play drive. Beauty awakens the play drive, just as the play drive seeks beauty. As Bentley explains, play 'engenders a state of harmonious balance, a contemplative position that opens the individual up to internal possibility and chance.'[93] Bentley adds that, according to Schiller, 'humans have a basic design: the play drive structure gives humans the capacity to be flexible, primed for possibility. The template given in nature and carried by each individual; the fulfilment is the destiny of each person to accomplish.'[94]

Now that Schiller's definition of beauty as 'living form' is outlined – the harmonious balancing of life and form – we have taken a step closer to understanding his thesis that only through beauty can we arrive at freedom. If, as we have seen, humans cannot be free or complete in their nature if one of the primary drives dominates, then the connection between beauty and freedom becomes apparent. A drug-abuser is not free if the sense drive dominates, just as the waiter living in Sartrean 'bad faith' is not free if he dictates for himself rules to live by which are excessively rational and constraining. Human beings will not be free, nor will our natures be complete, until our drives are harmoniously balanced in 'living form', which we have seen is Schiller's definition of beauty. And it is through the play drive that this reconciliation is achieved, for beauty is its object. In a well-known line from the *Aesthetic Letters*, Schiller highlighted the fundamental importance of the play drive by asserting that: 'man only plays when he is in the fullest sense of the word a human being, and *he is only fully a human being when he plays*.'[95]

The role of beauty

Beauty is the object of the play drive insofar as it consists in achieving harmonisation between the fundamental drives. But how does the play drive actually achieve that goal and what is the role of beauty in this process, not as an *end*, but as a *means*? Moreover, if freedom is about governing oneself rather than being governed, and beauty or aesthetic value is about the affect we feel when perceiving an object's 'living form', how do these issues – freedom and beauty – relate to each other? Schiller, one has to admit, is not as clear as he could have been on these issues, which has led to a range of conflicting scholarly analysis. The interpretation presented below is indebted to a recent analysis by Samantha Matherne and Nick Riggle, whose astute reading of Schiller informs the following account.[96]

According to Matherne and Riggle, Schiller 'endorses a conception of aesthetic value [or beauty] as that which has the capacity to put us in a state of "play."'[97] To be in a state of play is to have 'volitional openness with respect to the ways one has constituted or ruled oneself.'[98] As outlined above, Schiller's ideal person is one who has balanced the sense and form drives by way of the play drive, and this involves escaping or transcending those demands and maintaining a healthy capacity to play. In other words, beauty or aesthetic value can induce a state of play, and through that state human beings can temper the authority of the drives and achieve the harmonisation that is required for freedom and 'wholeness of character.'[99] On this account, 'engagement with aesthetic value, both as appreciators and creators, is necessary for a fully autonomous life.'[100]

This position requires some explaining. In one sense, a human being might be free if they govern their sensuo-rational existence according to their own rules – we could call this 'human freedom'. But Schiller believes that at times the rules one has cultivated for oneself might become counterproductive or oppressive, even if they seem to be freely chosen. For example, we might begin to live habitually, without reflection, or too cautiously, oblivious to the fact that our lives have become routine and perhaps no longer serving our highest ideals or goals. Our commitments can calcify. We might begin to live in bad faith – in fear of our own freedom to live otherwise – but be oblivious to our self-imposed constraints.

At such times Schiller contended that we need a state of 'aesthetic freedom'[101] in order to achieve a volitional openness that allows us to transcend our ordinary existence and our normal sense of self. In other words, we should maintain a healthy capacity to play in order to achieve the aesthetic freedom or volitional openness that is required to keep an eye on the authenticity of our human freedom. Schiller believed that beauty is the *means* of inducing or activating the necessary state of play or volitional openness. Readers might notice a certain similarity here with Schopenhauer's understanding of aesthetic experience – a state of being in which we are, if only temporarily, able to transcend our egoistic desires, transcend what Schopenhauer called 'the Will'. I surmise that most people, at some point, will have been induced into a profound aesthetic experience where one 'loses oneself' in music, a novel, or a film. This can produce a quasi-manic mood, slightly insane and unstable, but in a way that is somehow liberating, as if freed from one's conventional thoughts and instincts. Although the differences between Schiller and Schopenhauer are profound, they seemed to share a sense that through aesthetic experience we are, to some extent, able to transcend the ego. Schopenhauer focussed on how this aesthetic state could alleviate suffering. Schiller, by contrast, focussed on how it could unshackle us from ourselves and open pathways to becoming someone new through play.

Schiller offered some insight into the 'mood' of aesthetic experience when he wrote: 'This lofty equanimity and freedom of the spirit, combined with power and vigor, is the mood in which a genuine work of art should release us, and there is no more certain touchstone of true aesthetic excellence.'[102] In the aesthetic mood, the grip of our practical and affective dispositions is loosened, as Matherne and Riggle explain: 'Instead of our will being constrained by certain patterns of action, choice, deliberation, or emotion, we are volitionally open.'[103]

At this point it is worth noting that Schiller distinguished between two different categories of beauty, namely, 'melting beauty'[104] and 'energising beauty'.[105] These two categories correspond to particular human needs, depending on how, in any particular individual, the sense and the form drives are balanced or imbalanced. Melting beauty is beneficial to the overly rational person, who needs to be released from excessive reason and ushered into a more relaxed state; to be brought back to one's 'senses'. Energising beauty is for the overly sensuous person, whose emotions are out of balance and who needs to be brought back into equilibrium through exposure to form and the perspective of reason. Although Schiller doesn't provide examples, we can no doubt imagine that different forms of art (say, a soothing sonata compared to a tragic but inspiring film) might respond to our needs at different times, depending on our moods and dispositions, even if his dualistic distinction is rather too simplistic.[106]

At this stage one might think Schiller is about to argue that beauty will offer us some rational insight or perhaps make us more inclined to fulfil our moral duties. However, he maintained that the aesthetic condition, induced by the experience of beauty, 'produces no particular result whatsoever, neither for the understanding or the will. It accomplishes no particular purpose, neither intellectual nor moral; it discovers no individual truth, helps us to perform no individual duty.'[107] Instead, as Matherne and Riggle explain, aesthetic experience frees us from the strong constraints typically imposed on us via our sense and form drives: 'Aesthetic experience thus releases us from the constraint of what we might call our "normal sense of self" – our normal dispositions to prefer modes of feeling, sensing, imagining, acting, or thinking'.[108] This leaves us volitionally open to prefer other modes. We may not, in fact, choose different modes of living and being, or rethink conventional dispositions or commitments. But in the aesthetic condition – in a state of play – we have the capacity to do so.

Furthermore, should our sensuous experience of the world expand as a result of engaging with beauty, our rational understanding of the world might have to adjust too. Conversely, should our rational frameworks or categories be shaken up by some aesthetic experience, that might lead to an expanded sensuous experience of the world. In this way, play induces the reciprocal relationship between the sense and the form drives and seeks the harmonisation thereof.

It's clear that aesthetic value, or beauty, consists in the capacity of some object or person to induce a state of play. Through the aesthetic freedom which play confers upon us, we are better able to move toward a harmonisation of our drives and the completion of our being, with beauty or 'living form' being the ideal end state. Human freedom, therefore, is achieved through the capacity for play, which is induced by aesthetic value, or beauty. Once again, beauty is presented both as a means and an end, for it is through beauty that beauty is achieved. Not only that, given that harmonisation of human nature is achieved through beauty, Schiller reasoned that art and aesthetic education are the paths to human realisation:

> By means of aesthetic culture... the personal worth of man, or his dignity, inasmuch as this can depend solely on himself, *remains completely indeterminate*; and nothing more is achieved by it than that he is henceforth enabled by the grace of nature to make of himself what he will – that the freedom to be what he ought to be is completely restored to him.
>
> But precisely thereby something infinite is achieved. For as soon as we recall that it was precisely of this freedom that he was deprived by the one-sided constraint of nature in the field of sensation and by the exclusive authority of reason in the realm of thought, then we are bound to consider the power that is restored to him in the aesthetic mode as the highest of all bounties, as the gift of humanity itself.[109]

On these grounds Schiller maintained, '[i]t is, then, not merely poetic license but philosophical truth when we call beauty our second creatress... [for it] offers us the possibility of being human.'[110] Becoming fully human in Schiller's sense, however, is not an event but an ongoing process. That is, a healthy capacity for play is needed not simply to bring our drives *into* harmonisation but also to *maintain* that state of balance. Thus, engaging with aesthetic value must not merely be a pastime but become a way of life – an art of living, an aesthetic condition.

Matherne and Riggle contend that Schiller is committed to 'a more robust conception of a healthy capacity to play, according to which it involves developing an aesthetic sensibility, a style, which disposes us to seek and create beauty, in a way that reflects who we are.'[111] It follows that 'aesthetic value, play, and aesthetic freedom are not just our entry point into becoming human beings; they are the cornerstone to wholeness of character and integral parts of a fully flourishing, full free, and beautiful human life.'[112] Only by exercising and cultivating our aesthetic sensibilities and creative capacities – that is, only through aesthetic education and engagement – can a culture produce the aesthetic value which is needed to achieve human freedom. And thus, to end this section where we began much earlier, it is only 'through Beauty that we arrive at Freedom.'[113]

The politics of beauty

What is particularly distinctive about Schiller's aesthetic theory is that it isn't simply concerned or directed toward individual freedom. It is explicitly a political project that seeks to establish, and which relies upon, human beings developing a *social character* – a character that recognises, respects, and supports the realisation of freedom in all people. Schiller argued that through aesthetic education and engagement we can become sensitive not merely to 'the claims of humanity... *from within*'[114] but also to the claims 'of humanity *from without.*'[115] This vision culminates in Schiller's notion of an 'aesthetic state',[116] which will be sketched very briefly below and developed in later essays. In what follows I will return to the work of Matherne and Riggle, whose political analysis of Schiller's theory of aesthetic education is as astute as their understanding of its application to individual freedom.[117]

This political basis of Schiller's theory is introduced when, in Letter Five, he argued that the social character required for political freedom must emerge through 'a heart that is truly sociable.'[118] To understand this social ethos we must turn to his theory of the drives again. Schiller's way of describing a lack of social character is when a person lets one of the drives dominate in social relations. We might find ourselves governed by 'compulsion'[119] from either the sensible or rational sides of our natures. For example, by treating people merely as objects of desire we act under the 'compulsion of nature'[120] which he described as an 'egotism of the senses',[121] since action is directed by what *I* want and *I* need. Similarly, by rationally interacting with someone as a means to an end, or even out of (Kantian) moral duty, we act under the 'compulsion of reason.'[122] This is egotism of a different sort – *my* reason, *my* duties, *my* goals.

By contrast, Schiller maintained that a person of social character relates to others in a spirit he variously calls 'compassion', 'sympathy', 'kindness', 'affection' and 'love.'[123] This is not merely respecting other people by virtue of our *common* humanity. Consistent with his own precepts, Schiller insisted that social character also implies a respect for what is *unique* or *individual* in other people. He argued that while the sense drive can move us to coordinate with others and the form drive can give rise to principles or rules that manage social life, it is beauty alone that gives us social character. This is because engaging with aesthetic value is the only path to bringing 'harmony' within the individual in a way that is necessary to transcend our egotism and self-centredness. 'Taste alone brings harmony into society, because it fosters harmony in the individual',[124] adding that 'only the aesthetic mode of communication unites society, because it relates to that which is common to all.'[125]

Again, this position needs some explanation. Schiller's argument seems to be that when our drives are in balance in response to aesthetic value, we can find ourselves in a state of aesthetic freedom or volitional openness. In this state we look upon the world with 'disinterest', in the specific sense that we are not compelled by either of our primary drives and thus free from the 'fetters of ends and purposes'[126] that arise from our 'needs'[127] and 'attachment[s]'.[128] Liberated from our own self-interested desires and goals, we are able to engage with other people on their own terms. And when, in this disinterested state, we see the humanity within other people, we also see within them (and within ourselves) the 'ideal' of humanity – an ideal which is beautiful. Emotions are aroused in and through this aesthetic experience, and moral and political claims can then influence social character in a way that is diminished if morality and politics are perceived through pure reason. The emotional claim provides a practical reason.

Philosopher Josef Chytry explains that this process might begin through the aesthetic appreciation of natural objects: 'if individuals learn to regard natural objects for their sakes, they will in turn recognise other individuals for their sakes.'[129] He adds that '[i]n broadening the realm of empathy by extending sensibility to cover the uniqueness of things in nature, aesthetic awareness contributes to a more universal framework for the cultivation of awareness of the freedom of other human beings.'[130] I would suggest that this approach might bear fruit both socially and ecologically, given that through this process human beings could learn to become less instrumentalist in their evaluation of others or of nature, such that the value of others or nature arises not because of their usefulness (as a means) but in recognition of their intrinsic worth (as ends in themselves).

Having explained how, by engaging in aesthetic value, we come to see other people as beautiful, Schiller then argued that we will 'concede freedom'[131] and 'independence'[132] to the beautiful individuals we encounter. 'Beauty, or rather taste, regards all things as *ends in themselves* and will not permit one to serve the purpose of another or to be under its control. Everyone is a free citizen and has the same rights...'[133] It hardly needs pointing out that Schiller's conception of 'beauty' here does not imply that we should only concede freedom to those who are cosmetically attractive in the sense of 'good looking in appearance'. Rather, in a disinterested state we see that all people, as ends in themselves, have innate capacities and potentialities of a 'noble soul'. Thus each and all are deserving of the respect and dignity which only freedom can confer. People are beautiful people because they have the capacity for beauty – again, in Schiller's sense of 'living form'.

On this reasoning Schiller formulated his aesthetically derived law: 'to give freedom by means of freedom.'[134] Through this law we determine ourselves when we exercise our aesthetic freedom in play, as Matherne and Riggle explain: 'We "give freedom" by aesthetically recognizing the independence, freedom, and status of [another]... as an end in itself.... And we do this "by means of freedom" in the sense that we do not feel compelled in this recognition, but rather it is one we freely give in the volitional openness of play.'[135]

Importantly, Matherne and Riggle highlight the egalitarian consequences of Schiller's theory – an egalitarianism derived aesthetically rather than from pure reason. As we see other people exercising their aesthetic freedom and giving a unique 'living form' to their lives through their capacity for play, we come to see others as free and equal, such that the 'ideal of equality [is] fulfilled.'[136] Schiller insisted that this induces 'a complete revolution in [one's] way of feeling',[137] as our 'hearts'[138] become attuned towards other people in ways that social character requires.[139] Harmony in society, therefore, depends on harmony in the individual, and harmony within the individual involves both reconciling the primary drives within, as well as becoming attuned to the humanity within all people. Both aspects of internal harmony flow from engaging with aesthetic value. This is how Schiller arrives at the political framing of his thesis that only through beauty can we arrive at freedom.

Here we can return to Schiller's earlier critique of the French Revolution and his explanation for its degeneration into the Reign of Terror. He argued that the 'moment found an apathetic generation', with society governed by selfishness and crude, lawless impulses. Human capacities were being diminished by a division of labour that, through excessive reason, reduced each person to a fragment of their potential. In short, the social character on which political society depended to flourish and endure was lacking. Only by engaging with aesthetic value could humanity develop that social character, and only by *remaining engaged* with it can that social character endure. Schiller recognised that there are dangers of an unbridled aestheticism, but he interpreted these risks as resulting not from *too much* beauty but from an *insufficient* experience of beauty – dangerous only to those whose natures have not yet been brought into harmony through aesthetic education. Aesthetic education, therefore, is also political training. The paradox is that the dangers of aestheticism are best resolved by and through beauty.

The aesthetic state: preliminary comments

To close this essay I will turn briefly to Schiller's conception of the 'aesthetic state', anticipating the social and political analyses of forthcoming essays. I make no pretence here to present a developed theory of the state, nor did Schiller provide one in the *Aesthetic Letters* or elsewhere. He made comments to the effect that he would develop this concept, but this ambition never came to fruition, and ultimately, he said remarkably little about forming state apparatus or institutions. Nevertheless, the *Aesthetic Letters* should be read for what they are: a political document. As he noted in the Second Letter, 'the most perfect'[140] of all works of art is the 'construction of true political freedom.'[141]

In the most extensive study of the concept of an 'aesthetic state', Josef Chytry offers a preliminary definition of the term as 'a social and political community that accords primacy, although not exclusiveness, to the aesthetic dimension in human consciousness and activity.'[142] This implies that an aesthetic education will permeate the minds and bodies of the individuals who do political decision making. I interpret this claim broadly, applying to all political agents, from those acting at the grassroots level all the way up to those running the institutions of government. The personal is political, and so the aesthetic state has implications for society at large, not merely an enclosed political class. Political institutions themselves ought to be 'graded according to the degree to which they enhance the development of human nature as a harmonious blending of the sensuous and the rational.'[143] And 'no state is to be regarded as supportive of human harmony and the totality of the individual if it hinders or fails to support the cultivation of the play dimension in the human being.'[144] This, of course, is vague, but it is suggestive of a value system based on what I've called the politics of beauty, deserving of further inquiry.

Nevertheless, consistent with Schiller's reservations about politics leading the way, any aesthetic state would presumably need to be preceded by an extended period of self-cultivation of individuals, supported by a robust aesthetic culture and education. If our natures swing toward imbalance, the aesthetic life will restore us to a sensuo-rational harmonic whole. Chytry goes on to write: 'For Schiller, all authentic political change begins through the poet. He alone knows the individual as a sensuous-rational being and can fashion his or her ideal image through the artwork. Since all immediate political ventures for improving humans are vain in theory and injurious in practice, the only genuine revolution will be one in which the individual becomes truly human through "a total revolution in his entire sensibilities."'[145] I am reminded here of the oft-quoted line from Percy Bysshe Shelley's *Defense of Poetry* (1840): 'Poets are the unacknowledged legislators of the world.'[146] This provocative statement is an invitation to broaden our conception of poetry to include more than just written or spoken verse, and define it as 'the expression of the imagination'.[147] On those terms, one might get a clearer sense of the relationship of poetry to politics, in so far as the latter is inevitably shaped by the ways in which political actors across society express their imaginations (for better or for worse). Change the imaginative landscape and new political frontiers present themselves.

Returning to Schiller, Chytry argues that 'by promoting empathy and awareness of others, aesthetic sensibility gives rise to the development of a society and state in which the individual becomes, as it were, the state'[148] In Schiller's words: 'If the inner man is at one with himself, he will also retain his uniqueness in the highest universalisation of his conduct, and the state will be merely the expounder of his beautiful instinct, the clearer form of his inner legislation.'[149] Philosopher Philip Kain elaborates on this position: 'The individual will become the state because the individual will no longer be a fragment, restricted in his capacities and outlooks, incapable of dealing with the general, universal, and varied concerns of the whole.'[150] He adds that: '[t[here will be agreement between the individual and the state because the state will be determined by the individual. The state will reflect the individual.'[151] In short, duty and inclination will be in harmony.

These comments no doubt raise more questions than they provide answers, and such a cursory statement risks coming across vague, at best, and idealistic, at worst. In a forthcoming essay in this collection, I intend to focus in more detail on the nature of an aesthetic state and how aesthetic citizens might conceive of themselves, and conduct themselves, in relation to such an entity. In the previous essay, I began anticipating some of these issues when discussing Richard Rorty's notion of a 'poeticized culture'. There I considered some challenges regarding how politics is to be managed in a post-metaphysical age where Reason is unable to provide philosophical foundations to political ideologies or theories of state. But before I can delve further into these complex issues, there is more groundwork to lay. After all, Schiller believed, as do I, that an aesthetic state is likely to be the *outcome* of an aestheticised culture and citizenry, not the *driving force* in that great transformation. In short, the aesthetic revolution must precede the paradigm shift in politics, just as a horse must drag the cart.

---

[1] Friedrich Schiller, *Letters on the Aesthetic Education of Man*, in Friedrich Shiller, *Essays*, eds. Walter Hinderer and Daniel Dahlstrom (New York: Continuum, 2005), pp. 86-178.

[2] Herbert Marcuse, *One Dimensional Man: Studies in the Ideology of Advanced Industrial Society* (London: Routledge, 2002), p.4.

[3] Bertolt Brecht, 'On Judging' in Bertolt Brecht, *Poems 1913-1956* (London: Methuen, 1987) p. 308.

[4] Friedrich Schiller, *Letters on the Aesthetic Education of Man*, ed. Reginald Snell (New York: Dover, 2004). I reference two different translations of Schiller's *Aesthetic Letters* (this note and note 1), from which I cite as necessary depending on the suitability of the translation.

[5] Friedrich Beiser, *Schiller as Philosopher: A Re-Examination* (Oxford: Clarendon Press, 2005), p. 123.

[6] Herbert Read, *Education Through Art* (New York: Pantheon Books, 1948), p. 1.

[7] Schiller, *Aesthetic Letters*, note 4, p. 34.

[8] Ibid.

[9] Ibid, p. 35.

[10] Ibid.

[11] Ibid.

[12] Ibid, p. 49.

[13] See Irving Babbitt, 'Schiller and Romanticism' (1922) *Modern Language Notes* 37(5): pp. 257-268.

[14] Bruno Latour, *We Have Never Been Modern* (Cambridge, Harvard University Press, 1993).

[15] Schiller, *Aesthetic Letters*, note 4, p. 50.

[16] Ibid, p 34.

[17] Ibid.

[18] Ibid, p. 36.
[19] Ibid.
[20] Ibid.
[21] Ibid.
[22] Ibid, p. 39.
[23] Ibid, p. 41.
[24] Adam Smith, *The Wealth of Nations* (Books 1-V) (Copenhagen: Titan Read, 2020).
[25] See David Graeber, *Bullshit Jobs: A Theory* (London: Penguin, 2019).
[26] Schiller, *Aesthetic Letters*, note 4, p. 40.
[27] Ibid, p. 38.
[28] Ibid, p. 41.
[29] Ibid, pp. 36-7.
[30] Herbert Marcuse, *One Dimensional Man: Studies in the Ideology of Advanced Industrial Society* (London: Routledge, 2002).
[31] Marcuse, for example, has a chapter that addresses Schiller in Herbert Marcuse, *Eros and Civilisation* (London: Sphere Books, 1969), Ch. 9.
[32] Schiller, *Aesthetic Letters*, note 4, p. 47.
[33] Ibid, p. 35.
[34] Ibid.
[35] Ibid.
[36] Ibid.
[37] Ibid.
[38] Ibid, p. 36.
[39] Ibid, p. 42.
[40] Ibid.
[41] Ibid, p 49.
[42] Ibid, p. 37.
[43] Ibid, p. 47.
[44] Ibid, 37.
[45] Ibid, p 50.
[46] Ibid, p. 34. Italics removed.
[47] Schiller, *Aesthetic Letters*, note 1, p. 95. Italics removed.
[48] Schiller, *Aesthetic Letters*, note 4, p. 34.
[49] Ibid, p. 50.
[50] Ibid, p. 46.
[51] Ibid, p. 25 (translation amended, replacing 'unseasonable' with 'untimely' and 'keener' with 'urgent').
[52] Ibid, p. 27.
[53] Ibid, p. 26.
[54] Ibid.
[55] Schiller, *Aesthetic Letters*, note 1, p. 107.
[56] Ibid, p. 111.
[57] Ibid, p. 155, fn 1.
[58] Ibid.
[59] Schiller, *Aesthetic Letters*, note 4, p. 110, p. 113.
[60] Schiller, *Aesthetic Letters*, note 1, p. 110.

[61] In the forthcoming analysis of Schiller's theses in the *Aesthetic Letters*, I am especially indebted to the following two articles. Samantha Matherne and Nick Riggle, 'Schiller on Freedom and Aesthetic Value: Part I' (2020) *British Journal of Aesthetics* 60(4): pp. 375-402; and Samantha Matherne and Nick Riggle, 'Schiller on Freedom and Aesthetic Value: Part II' (2021) *British Journal of Aesthetics* 61(1): pp. 17-40.
[62] Schiller, *Aesthetic Letters*, note 1, p. 118, p. 126, p. 128.
[63] Ibid, p. 128.
[64] Ibid, p. 118.
[65] Ibid.
[66] Ibid, p. 94.
[67] Ibid, p. 126, p. 143,
[68] Ibid, p. 119.
[69] Ibid, p. 106.
[70] Ibid, p. 118.
[71] Ibid, p. 95.
[72] Ibid. Emphasis removed.
[73] Ibid, p. 92.
[74] Susan Bentley, 'Friedrich Schiller's Play: A Theory of Human Nature in the Context of the Eighteenth-Century Study of Life' (2009) *Electronic Theses and Dissertations*. Paper 101. https://doi.org/10.18297/etd/101, Epilogue.
[75] Sigmund Freud, *Civilization and its Discontents* (London: Penguin, 2004).
[76] Schiller, *Aesthetic Letters*, note 1, p. 93.
[77] Ibid.
[78] Ibid, p. 102.
[79] Ibid.
[80] See Samuel Alexander, *Art Against Empire: Toward an Aesthetics of Degrowth* (Melbourne, Simplicity Institute, 2017), p. 1.
[81] Schiller, *Aesthetic Letters*, note 1, p. 128.
[82] Ibid, p. 119.
[83] Ibid, p.128.
[84] For a comprehensive discussion of Schillerian play, see Bentley, 'Friedrich Schiller's Play', above note 74.
[85] Ibid, p. 35, fn 5.
[86] Ibid, p. 37.
[87] Schiller, *Aesthetic Letters*, note 1, p. 125.
[88] Ibid, p. 129.
[89] Ibid, p. 128.
[90] Ibid.
[91] Ibid, 132.
[92] See Matherne and Riggle, 'Schiller on Freedom and Aesthetic Value: Part I', note 61, p. 389.
[93] Bentley, 'Friedrich Schiller's Play', above note 74, p. 39.
[94] Ibid, p. 40.
[95] Schiller, *Aesthetic Letters*, note 1, p. 131.
[96] See Matherne and Riggle, 'Schiller on Freedom and Aesthetic Value: Part I', note 61; and Matherne and Riggle, 'Schiller on Freedom and Aesthetic Value: Part II', note 61.
[97] See Matherne and Riggle, 'Schiller on Freedom and Aesthetic Value: Part I', note 61, p. 377.

[98] Ibid.
[99] Schiller, *Aesthetic Letters*, note 1, p. 95. Emphasis removed.
[100] See Matherne and Riggle, 'Schiller on Freedom and Aesthetic Value: Part I', note 61, p. 378.
[101] Schiller, *Aesthetic Letters*, note 1, p. 147.
[102] Ibid, p. 149.
[103] See Matherne and Riggle, 'Schiller on Freedom and Aesthetic Value: Part I', note 61, p. 391.
[104] Schiller, *Aesthetic Letters*, note 1, p. 133.
[105] Ibid.
[106] Notably, each of these forms of beauty can be dangerous or regressive if they do not correspond to the needs of the individual – e.g., if an overly rational person is exposed to energising beauty and the overly sensuous person is exposed to melting beauty.
[107] Schiller, *Aesthetic Letters*, note 1, p. 147.
[108] See Matherne and Riggle, 'Schiller on Freedom and Aesthetic Value: Part I', note 61, pp. 391-2.
[109] Schiller, *Aesthetic Letters*, note 1, p. 147.
[110] Ibid, p. 148.
[111] See Matherne and Riggle, 'Schiller on Freedom and Aesthetic Value: Part I', note 61, p. 401.
[112] Ibid.
[113] Schiller, *Aesthetic Letters*, note 3, p. 27.
[114] Schiller, *Aesthetic Letters*, note 1, p. 124, fn 3.
[115] Ibid.
[116] Ibid, p. 147.
[117] See Matherne and Riggle, 'Schiller on Freedom and Aesthetic Value: Part II', note 61.
[118] Schiller, *Aesthetic Letters*, note 1, p. 97.
[119] Ibid, p. 127. Emphasis removed.
[120] Ibid. Emphasis removed.
[121] Ibid, p. 123, fn 3.
[122] Ibid, p. 127. Emphasis removed.
[123] Ibid, pp. 123-4, p. 127, pp. 175-6.
[124] Ibid, p. 176.
[125] Ibid, p. 177.
[126] Ibid, p. 173.
[127] Ibid, p. 166.
[128] Ibid.
[129] Josef Chytry, *The Aesthetic State: A Quest in Modern German Thought* (Berkeley: University of California Press, 1989) p. 85.
[130] Ibid, p. 102.
[131] Schiller, *Aesthetic Letters*, note 1, p. 175.
[132] Ibid, p. 163.
[133] As quoted in Matherne and Riggle, 'Schiller on Freedom and Aesthetic Value: Part II', note 61, p. 23 (from Schiller's *Kallias Letters*).

[134] I am here following Matherne and Riggle's modified translation. See Matherne and Riggle, 'Schiller on Freedom and Aesthetic Value: Part II', note 61, p. 23.
[135] Ibid, p. 24.
[136] Schiller, *Aesthetic Letters*, note 1, p. 178.
[137] Ibid, p. 171.
[138] Ibid, p. 175.
[139] Note that this solidarity here is an aesthetic achievement not something based on independent philosophical foundations. See Richard Rorty on 'solidarity' in Richard Rorty, *Contingency, Irony, and Solidarity* (Cambridge: Cambridge University Press, 1989).
[140] Schiller, *Aesthetic Letters*, note 1, p. 88.
[141] Ibid.
[142] Chytry, *The Aesthetic State*, note 129, p. xii.
[143] Ibid, p. 78.
[144] Ibid, p. 102.
[145] Ibid, p. 95.
[146] Percy Bysshe Shelly, *A Defense of Poetry* (Boston: Ginn and Co., 1891), p. 46.
[147] Ibid, p. 2.
[148] Chytry, *The Aesthetic State*, note 129, p. 85.
[149] As quoted in Chytry, *The Aesthetic State*, note 129, p. 85.
[150] Philip Kain, 'Labor, the State, and Aesthetic Theory in the Writings of Schiller' (1981) *Interpretation* 9: p. 273.
[151] Ibid.

BOOK TWO

THE POLITICAL ECONOMY OF ART

‘Modern man lives under the illusion that he knows what he wants, while he actually wants what he is *supposed* to want... [He] is deeply afraid of taking the risk and the responsibility of giving himself his own aims.’

– **Erich Fromm**

BAD FAITH AND THE FEAR OF FREEDOM: CAN ART SHAKE US AWAKE?

In Book One of this collection of essays ('The Will to Art') I presented two different yet mutually supportive ways of understanding humanity as *homo aestheticus*, the artful species.[1] The discussion of human evolution showed why our historical practices of art and artification, along with the emergence of our aesthetic sensibilities, are fundamentally constitutive of how evolution has shaped us into creative, aesthetic animals. To the extent that humans share a nature, I argued that it is best understood as the art-created art creator – a being whose nature it is to transform itself and the world through art, aesthetic experience, and creative activity. I call this a 'thin' or 'minimalist' theory of human nature because the characteristics which our species share are fundamentally aesthetic. They do not fix or determine what type of creature we *must be* but rather show how and why we are *malleable and indeterminate* all the way down.

In short, our essence as a creature of evolution is to create our own essence, even as one must accept that we are also creatures shaped by the vagaries of history and context. As existentialist philosopher Jean-Paul Sartre put it: we can always make something new out of what we have been made into.[2] Our species is not so much a blank canvas as a surface that has been painted and repainted throughout history, waiting to be reworked endlessly through deliberative, creative expression and action. Our nature as *homo aestheticus* is open-ended because there will never come a time when all the possible pictures of our species have been drawn. We can always become something new.

My philosophical analysis of self-creation presented a parallel case for why our natures are not given to us in advance. By engaging Michel Foucault, I set out to explain why the 'self' is not a substance but a form, from which it follows that we must each give shape to the content of our lives and subjectivities. That is, we must create ourselves as an aesthetic project through 'techniques of the self' and aspire to poeticize our existence, to write our own stories rather than merely act out a pre-written script. By placing this conception of the self in cosmological context, this collection of essays is presenting a narrative about how the creative evolution of human aesthetic sensibility is fundamentally about the search for meaning and beauty. This is the telos of existence, the implicit goal of the cosmos. Through our aesthetic activity and contemplation, the universe is able to experience itself as an aesthetic phenomenon, the manifestation of the Will to Art coming to fruition.[3] To paraphrase Immanuel Kant, beauty indicates that human beings have a place in the universe,[4] at least potentially.

Nevertheless, in this essay I wish to acknowledge a significant problem regarding this conceptualisation of human beings as *homo aestheticus*. It is a difficulty that is evident as soon as one turns from theory to the world as it is: if we are an artful species, one that is creative and self-constituting, why is it that the world is so full of oppression, servitude, anxiety, and ugliness? If we are evolutionarily shaped to be aesthetic agents in an aesthetic universe, why do we see so many people in the 'advanced' affluent cultures seemingly content to distract themselves with the trinkets and baubles offered by consumer capitalism? If we are free to create ourselves according to our own conception of the good life, why do so many people anxiously march like lemmings into the machine only to be chewed up and spat out in some homogenised form, the commodified maker and consumer of commodities, one-dimensional man in a one-dimensional market society?[5]

My explanation for this grim, uncreative reality is that our aesthetic natures have become deadened by the oppressive logic of economic reason – dying, but not dead. Too often we choose merely to obey the logic of acquisitive society, as if it were the only way. Our malleable selves are indeed being shaped, but not by ourselves as sculptors of personal existence, but by global capitalist society that needs obedient producers and consumers, not self-governing people who want to create themselves, as artists of life, forging their own paths into the future. After all, you cannot sell an infinite array of things to artists and artisans who are content with their aesthetic practices and basic material needs. This is why, throughout history, and in small subcultures today, artists and artisans often live relatively austere, non-consumerist lives of voluntary simplicity, in order to practise their arts and crafts. Capitalism has largely succeeded in beating this creative ethic out of humanity in order to maximise profits.

In what follows I will illuminate aspects of this problematic by drawing on Sartre's notion of 'bad faith', as well as the idea of 'fear of freedom' developed by German psychoanalyst Erich Fromm. I believe that these existential critiques can help explain the dire state of human freedom and creativity today, while also showing why the problems to which they point are within our power to resolve. In the second half of the essay, I explore how the failure to grasp one's own freedom can have deleterious effects on mental health, which on a cultural scale can produce a society that seems sick or even insane. This raises the question of what sanity might look like in an insane society. The discussion of these complex issues will lay the foundation for the next essay, which returns to consider the role of aesthetic education in advancing the cause of human self-creation in a world that so often interferes with the realisation of this innate potential.

Sartre on 'bad faith'

There are many political and structural challenges that can 'lock' people into the machinic systems of growth capitalism and consumer culture. These include purchasing land and housing, working long hours, financial insecurity, excessive advertising, and so forth.[6] It would be foolish to deny that these types of structural challenges exist or that they constrain the forms of life that are available for pursuing, depending on social context and circumstance. We must acknowledge, that is, what the existentialists sometimes called 'facticity' – those external pressures that shape our lives without our consent or choosing.

But while we may have little immediate agency over the nature of those structures and external pressures, and as representative democracy seems to be nose-diving into an ever-deepening crisis of legitimacy, it becomes ever more necessary to carve out spaces at the personal and household levels where *spheres of agency* remain. Moreover, we must grasp hold of those spheres while they still exist. If we are indeed an artful and creative species, it is these spheres of agency that we must reclaim first and foremost, for they are there for the taking, waiting to be embodied by bold practitioners of self-creation.

Nevertheless, it is precisely in these remaining spheres of agency where it seems so many people today are acting in what Sartre called 'bad faith'.[7] In what is perhaps his most well-known pronouncement, he declared that human beings are 'condemned to be free'.[8] The imposing language of 'condemnation' is deliberate, intending to imply a heaviness and seriousness to our most important life decisions, which can often leave the individual in a condition of anguish, not knowing what to do but knowing that the decision is important. Sartre's notion of bad faith was introduced to denote a psychological or existential condition of inauthenticity.

A person living in bad faith yields to the external pressures of society, and adopts dominant values unthinkingly, thereby denying one's own freedom to determine one's fate, one's values, and one's life project. Thus, bad faith is akin to a form of self-deception. It involves pretending that we are not free to choose when in fact we are always and already choosing, even in overwhelming circumstances. In contrast with bad faith, Sartre's notion of 'radical freedom' is intended to remind us that there are *always* choices to be made, no matter the circumstances. Even with a gun in one's mouth, one is still free to resist, to stay silent and still, or to smile at one's executioner.

Human existence is inherently burdened with the responsibility of choice. We are never *entirely* at the mercy of circumstances. The residue of freedom, which will differ for every individual in their unique life circumstances, is what I am calling our spheres of agency. To act in bad faith is to embrace a self-imposed delusion that these spheres of agency do not exist; that we don't have choices, when we do. In a famous example to illustrate this notion, Sartre discussed a waiter who excessively embodies his social role, whose movements and conversations are contrived and overdetermined, who seems overly eager to please, whose laugh is affected. This exaggerated or inauthentic behaviour suggests that he is play-acting as a waiter, choosing self-imposed rules of conduct that seem to be required by his role, but which are, in fact, voluntarily chosen to avoid the anguish of having to choose for himself how to live and to act. One might imagine that this waiter has dreams of being a musician or an activist, but instead of pursuing that life project he tells himself a narrative that there is no time, no money, no energy, and that he wouldn't succeed anyway. His life is disenchanted, apparently determined by circumstances.

Sartre suggested that this waiter is living in bad faith, consciously deceiving himself by freely choosing to deny his inescapable freedom. By pretending to be bound by external circumstances, the anguish of freedom is deferred, even if deferring the responsibility to choose is itself a choice. Circumstances matter, of course, but no circumstances dictate a single response. We are forced to choose. Most importantly, we are free to choose differently than the decisions made in the past. The self, as we saw in previous essays, is not a constant, static, or determinate substance. It is a form. One of the central themes of existentialism is the anguish and dread that can arise as we acknowledge the responsibility we each have to make difficult decisions throughout life. To uncritically defer to circumstances – to one's parents, to a religious code, to a moral system, to public opinion, to habit, and so forth – is to negate the self and deny accountability, as if there were no choices to be made.

Just as there are no objective truths about life's meaning or purpose waiting for us 'out there' in moral or metaphysical reality, it is no good 'looking inward' to seek answers from your 'authentic self', for there is no self that precedes the decisions we make in our lives. There is nothing to observe. So how do we become who we really are? By taking hold of our freedom and acting, one way or another. The unsettling challenge is that we are free to reappraise our situation at every moment; free to give birth to ourselves anew everyday. This defining aspect of the human condition is as terrifying as it is exhilarating. To deny oneself this creative task, to avoid it, is to live in bad faith.

Fear of freedom

The question, then, is this: why might a person live in bad faith? Part of the answer, as noted above, is that living in bad faith can be a strategy for deferring the anguish of having to choose how to live (even though living in bad faith is itself a choice). Perhaps an even more powerful way to express this phenomenon is to say, with Erich Fromm, that many people live as they do out of a 'fear of freedom'.[9] Can freedom become a burden too heavy for humanity to bear, something from which we might try to escape? This is, admittedly, a perplexing, even paradoxical, proposition, given that many people throughout history have sooner died in the struggle against oppression than live without freedom. And yet, Fromm's diagnosis – arguably as applicable to our time as his own – was that, in fact, many people, and indeed entire cultures, were escaping their own freedom. They were doing so to avoid the burden of responsibility and accountability that comes with such liberty.

Fromm argued that this fear of freedom was manifesting in three main ways. First, he was witnessing a voluntary surrender of power to authoritarian states – notably, his book *Fear of Freedom* was published in 1942.[10] This was obviously an era of German and Italian fascism, but Fromm maintained that the emergence of these fascist states was not primarily a result of a mad dictator, the cunning and trickery of a few megalomaniacs, or cultural inexperience in democracy. Rather, he saw that millions of Europeans were as willing to surrender their freedom as the previous generations were to fight for it.

Far from suggesting this was an isolated problem for Germans and Italians, Fromm asserted that this surrender was observable within every modern state. Fromm quoted American philosopher John Dewey, who formulated this concern forcefully in the following words: 'The serious threat to our democracy,' Dewey suggested, 'is not the existence of foreign totalitarian states. It is the existence within our own personal attitudes and within our own institutions of conditions which have given a victory to external authority, discipline, uniformity and dependence upon The Leader in foreign countries. The battlefield is also accordingly here – within ourselves and our institutions.'[11] Fromm worried that, just as there was an innate human urge for freedom, there may also be an instinctive wish for submission. This submissive disposition could take the form of deferring to external forces (such as a state or an economic system), internal forces (such as a moral code of conscience), or anonymous forces (such as public opinion).[12] In all such cases, the individual escapes freedom and finds a form of security through submitting to some authority that prescribes how one ought to think and act.

The second manifestation of the fear of freedom, according to Fromm, is the observable urge to destroy. Without getting into the intricacies of his psychoanalytical theory, Fromm maintained that when a human being gained 'freedom from' an oppressive authority in the past (e.g., a state or a church) but failed to find meaningful 'freedom to' engage in self-directed creative activity, the individual can try to resolve the burden of their freedom by desperately destroying the world or themselves. He explained:

> Any observer of personal relations in our social scene cannot fail to be impressed with the amount of destructiveness to be found everywhere. For the most part it is not conscious as such but is rationalized in various ways. As a matter of fact, there is virtually nothing that is not used as a rationalization for destructiveness. Love, duty, conscience, patriotism have been and are used as disguises to destroy others or oneself.[13]

Fromm argues that such destructiveness can emerge either from anxiety or from what he calls the thwarting of life. Regarding anxiety, the reasoning is that when a person's vital interests (material or emotional) are threatened, this induces a state of anxiety, from which destructive tendencies often follow out of a sense of powerlessness. Destruction can be an anxious grasping for power and security. Regarding the thwarting of life, Fromm argues that 'the isolated and powerless individual is blocked in realising his sensuous, emotional and intellectual potentialities,'[14] such that 'the amount of destructiveness to be found in individuals is proportionate to the amount to which expansiveness of life is curtailed.'[15] In other words: '*Destructiveness is the outcome of unlived life*.'[16] The flawed assumption of this strategy is that by destroying others or the world, the individual will be less threatened by the external world. The result, however, is that destructive individuals usually end up destroying themselves in the process.

The final strategy for escaping freedom, and one deserving of special emphasis, is the tendency for individuals to evade their freedom by uncritically adopting the personality offered to them by cultural patterns. Fromm calls this mechanism 'automaton conformity':[17]

> The discrepancy between 'I' and the world disappears and with it the conscious fear of aloneness and powerlessness. This mechanism can be compared with the protective colouring some animals assume. They look so similar to their surrounds that they are hardly distinguishable from them. The person who gives up his individual self and becomes an automaton, identical with millions of other automatons around him, need not feel alone and anxious anymore. But the price he pays, however, is high; it is the loss of his self.[18]

Fromm developed this line of thinking as follows:

> ... the truth [is] that modern man lives under the illusion that he knows what he wants, while he actually wants what he is *supposed* to want. In order to accept this it is necessary to realize that to know what one really wants is not comparatively easy, as most people think, but one of the most difficult problems any human being has to solve. It is a task we frantically try to avoid by accepting ready-made goals as through they were our own. Modern man is ready to take great risks when he tries to achieve the aims which are supposed to be 'his' but he is deeply afraid of taking the risk and the responsibility of giving himself his own aims.[19]

So why do we sometimes act in bad faith? In summary, Fromm argued that we fear our freedom. We are sometimes inclined to prefer submission to an authority rather than the agony of choice and responsibility; we sometimes tend toward destruction as a self-defeating strategy for managing our sense of isolation and powerlessness. And we often seek the anonymity of conformity in the hope of dissolving into a faceless crowd where decisions are made for us. For all these reasons, and more, our inherent creative capacities and potentials as *homo aestheticus* too often lie dormant and repressed. The result can be a society that looks insane. This is another topic on which Fromm showed profound insight. Let us turn to this now.

Delusions of sanity: deconstructing madness in an insane world[20]

In his 1955 book, *The Sane Society*,[21] Fromm suggested that nothing is more common than the assumption that we, people living in the advanced industrial economies, are eminently sane. The fact that so many individuals will suffer from more or less severe forms of mental illness does not seem to shake our conviction with respect to the overall state of our mental health. According to Fromm, we are inclined to see incidents of mental illness as strictly individual and isolated disturbances, while acknowledging – with some discomfort, perhaps – that so many of these incidents should occur in a culture that is supposedly sane.[22]

Fromm haunts our self-image even today, unsettling these assumptions of sanity: 'Can we be so sure that we are not deceiving ourselves? Many an inmate of an insane asylum is convinced that everybody else is crazy, except himself.'[23] This line of inquiry is especially disconcerting in a world where, to use Fromm's somewhat antiquated language, inmates evidently have taken over the asylum and seem intent on running it into the ground. The existential threat of climate breakdown is only one of the ominous indicators of this reckless death drive, but it alone has the potential to lay waste to our species as well as most others. In an age now widely described as the Anthropocene, the conventionally held distinction between sanity and insanity is at risk of collapsing.

The distinction, therefore, is ripe for deconstruction. At least since Michel Foucault's *Madness and Civilization* (1961),[24] it has been understood that the idea of (in)sanity is, in some respects, an evolving, socially constructed category. Not only does the medical validity of mental health diagnoses and treatments shift with the times, but what has been judged 'sane' in one era has the potential to blur into what is not in another – and without announcement. This can disguise the fact that social practices or patterns of thought that may once have been considered healthy may now be properly diagnosed as unhealthy. And while this can apply to individual cases, there is no reason to think it should not also apply more broadly to a society at large. That is, a society might go insane without being aware of its own degeneration.

Surely we would know if our society was insane? Not necessarily. One does not need to be a conspiracy theorist to recognise, with Foucault, that power shapes knowledge. If profits and economic growth are the benchmarks of success in a society, it cannot be profitable to expose a society as insane. Even members of an insane society may sooner choose wilful blindness than look too deeply into the subconscious of their own culture. Thus an accurate diagnosis can be easily obscured or ignored if it does not accord with dominant interests. But merely *assuming* something or someone is sane does not make it so. We should always reserve the right to think for ourselves about these matters, to be brave enough to stare into the abyss – and be prepared for the abyss to stare back – no matter what we find.

It feels important to delve into these critical provocations: are the societies of globalised capitalism sane? If they are not – and I find myself pointing towards this thesis – another question follows: what might sanity look like in an insane world? After all, as the Indian guru Jiddu Krishnamurti is often credited with saying: 'It is no measure of health to be well adjusted to a profoundly sick society.'[25] This makes it all the harder to diagnose the state of a society's sanity, given that it is never clear whether it is the people who are sick or the society. We should at least leave open the possibility, as investigative journalist Johann Hari suggests in *Lost Connections*,[26] that some mental health conditions might be perfectly normal responses to a particular state of society, not resolvable simply with a rebalancing of chemicals in the brain through pharmaceuticals. Indeed, to paraphrase Martin Luther King Jnr, there are some things in our world to which we should be proud to be maladjusted.

Accordingly, in this final part of the essay I would like to reflect, at a 'macro' level, on the sanity or insanity of the dominant culture and political economy in contemporary capitalist societies, asking how the world 'out there' can impact the inner dimension of our lives. Following Fromm's lead, I will inquire not so much into individual pathology, but into what he calls 'collective neuroses' or 'the pathology of normalcy'. Of course, collective neuroses are not easily observed, for they are, by nature, the background fabric of existence and so easily missed. Be warned, then: we might be like the fish that do not know they swim in water. The purpose of this analysis is to lay the foundation for forthcoming essays which will argue that art and aesthetic education are the best means of shaking humanity out of its fear of freedom. Such an education, I will argue, also has potential to resolve or at least mitigate some of the mental health issues which can flow from living in bad faith in a sick society.

Is our society insane?

It is the cultural relativity of sanity that Fromm calls into question in *The Sane Society*. 'The fact that millions of people share the same vices,' he wrote, 'does not make these vices virtues, the fact that they share so many errors does not make the errors to be truths, and the fact that millions of people share the same forms of mental pathology does not make these people sane.'[27] He felt that society needed certain objective conditions to be sane, including environmental sustainability. If too many of humankind's most basic needs were not being met despite unprecedented wealth, he felt it would be proper to declare a society sick, even if the behaviour producing the sickness was widespread and validated by its own internal cultural logic. This invites critical reflection on what is deemed 'normal' behaviour today, just in case we are participating in practices that, from an external or objective perspective, would be diagnosed as patently insane. After all, if our society were sick, surely we'd want to know.

Let us, in good psychiatric fashion, look at the facts. The climate emergency has already been mentioned, pointing to humanity's fatal addiction to fossil fuels. We know their combustion is killing the planet, but we can't seem to resist the short-sighted convenience. The Intergovernmental Panel on Climate Change was established in 1988 to advise on the science of climate change, yet here we are, more than thirty years later, and carbon emissions continue to rise (excepting only the years of financial crisis or pandemic). As of 2022, approximately thirty-seven gigatons of carbon dioxide are emitted into the atmosphere each year from energy production, in full knowledge of their impacts. Driven by a fetish for economic growth, we continue using these fossil fuels to supply around 84 per cent of global primary energy demand, voting in politicians who celebrate coal and enthusiastically cut the ribbons of new fossil fuel power stations. It is a tragedy disguised as a grim joke.

Scientists warn that current trajectories of climate heating are not compatible with civilisation as we know it, with potentially billions of lives at risk in coming decades, both human and non-human. You know something is wrong when the Arctic is burning, and in recent years this is precisely what has happened. And yet nothing is more 'normal' than hopping into a fossil-fuelled car or consuming products that have been shipped around the world to satisfy the carboniferous desires of affluent society. I mention these features of industrial civilisation not to sit in judgement: we are, so to speak, in the soup together. But let us not divert our gaze just because it is embarrassing and uncomfortable to look in the mirror.

The same fossil fuels underpin our destructive systems of industrial agriculture. Humanity is deforesting the planet and destroying topsoil to feed a population that is growing by over 200,000 people every day. The United Nations project that we will reach almost ten billion people by mid-century. This human dominance of the planet under global capitalism is devastating wildlife populations and biodiversity, with the World Wildlife Fund recently reporting that populations of vertebrate species have declined by 68 per cent since 1970. It is no exaggeration to say that we are living through the sixth mass extinction, driven by human economic activity that is not just normal but encouraged, rewarded, and widely admired.

The flow of materials and resources through the global economy is now in excess of 100 billion tonnes per year, and that's expected to double in coming decades despite deluded hopes for 'green growth'. And how easily are we blinded to our incrementally destructive practices. It is seen as perfectly normal to purchase and discard single-use plastics that end up polluting our rivers and oceans for hundreds or thousands of years. We direct our growing and increasingly toxic waste streams away from cities and into the natural environment to be dealt with by future generations or poorer communities. Human trash has been found in Antarctica, in the deepest parts of the ocean, and 'space junk' is now a concern for orbiting spacecraft and satellites. Nowhere and nothing is sacred. In 2017, more than 15,000 scientists signed the second 'Warning to Humanity' – the first was published in 1992 – advising that misery and catastrophe await if fundamental shifts in our civilisation are not urgently taken. And still, as if suffering a collective neurosis, Empire marches on like a snake eating its own tail, pursuing growth for growth's sake – the ideology of a cancer cell.

Added to this is the fact that humanity lives in the terrifying shadow of its own nuclear arsenals, representing a unique technological capacity for mutually assured destruction. Whether the furnace of climate change or a nuclear winter lies ahead, it is too early to say. Alternative pathways are getting harder to imagine. In the twentieth century, ordinary people marched off to war after war, resulting in the death of more than 100 million. One dares not imagine what the next global military clash might bring, as we nervously watch superpowers butt heads. The geopolitical arena remains a nuclear tinderbox of fiercely competing interests. What's next?

Of course, ecological and geopolitical tragedies cannot be isolated from the humanitarian crises of poverty and inequality. In 2017, Oxfam released a study concluding that the richest eight men now own more than the poorest half of humanity. Dwell on that for a moment if you have the courage. We can debate research methodologies or 'theories of justice', but the point is now undeniable: the distribution of wealth in our world is harrowingly unjust, with small islands of unfathomable plenty surrounded by vast oceans of humiliating poverty. There is nothing 'natural' about this concentration of wealth. It is a result of choices that we humans make about how to structure our economies. Things could be different, but we've been duped into thinking this is 'just the way the world is' and that the trickle-down effect will sort things out. The moral egregiousness of poverty is all the more disturbing given that the human capacity to eliminate hunger has never been greater. The global development agenda is failing. It is a sign of idiocy to keep doing the same thing over and over and expecting a different result.

This is not happy reading, I know, but things get even worse. A spiritual malaise seems to be spreading throughout advanced capitalist societies, as if the material rewards of consumerism have failed to fulfil their promise of a happy and meaningful existence. Scholars publish books about it, with suggestive titles like Robert Lane's *The Loss of Happiness in Market Democracies*; David Myers' *The American Paradox: Spiritual Hunger in an Age of Plenty*; and Clive Hamilton and Richard Denniss' *Affluenza: When Too Much Is Never Enough*. For whom, then, do we destroy the planet? Is a greater abundance of 'nice things' what we are lacking in the overdeveloped world? Or is there, as historian and philosopher

Lewis Mumford once opined, an inner dimension to our crises that must be resolved before the outer crises can be effectively met?[28]

In the face of all this it is easy to feel chronically disenchanted with life, to feel disconnected from people, place, and purpose. We humans of late capitalism have all felt, and perhaps currently feel, this disconnection. How easy it is to live by regurgitating the prewritten script of advanced industrial society: cogs in a vast machine, easily replaced. Perhaps we see our disenchantment reflected in the eyes of those tired, alienated commuters, a class into which it is so easy to fall simply by virtue of being subjects of the capitalist order. We all know that there is more to life than *this*. We find ourselves living in an age where the old dogmas of growth, material affluence and technology are increasingly exposed as false idols. Like a fleet of ships that has been unmoored in a storm, our species is drifting in dangerous seas without a clear sense of direction.

Where are the new sources of meaning and guidance that all societies need to fight off the ennui? Émile Durkheim, the nineteenth-century pioneer of sociology, used the term 'anomie' to refer to a condition in which a culture's traditional norms have broken down without new norms arising that can give sense to a changing world. Perhaps this is the term that best explains our existential condition today. We are coming to realise that we have lost our way, as the factors that are supposed to represent 'progress' according to dominant cultural myths are increasingly experienced as breakdown.

One could go on, but it would be perverse to do so. 'Doom porn' is not my business or purpose. My point is simply to present a summary case for diagnosing our society as insane – not as rhetorical strategy, but in the pursuit of literal truth. If an individual knowingly destroyed the conditions of his or her own existence, we'd question their sanity. If a mother only fed her children if she could make a profit, we'd doubt the soundness of her mind. If a father took all the household wealth and left the rest of the family in destitution while building bombs in the basement that could destroy the neighbourhood, we'd call him psychopathic. And yet these are characteristics of our society as a whole. Fromm would not permit us to diagnose ourselves and our society as sane just because the actions that produce the features outlined above are considered 'normal'. There is a pathology to our normalcy, and this pathology is no less pathological just because it is shared by millions upon millions of people.

♦ ♦ ♦

The issue at the heart of this exploration concerns the mental health effects that might naturally and justifiably arise when otherwise sane people find themselves living in an insane world. The paradox that threatens to emerge has already been variously noted. In *Welcome to the Monkey House* (1968), Kurt Vonnegut Jnr wrote, 'a sane person in an insane society must appear insane'. Thomas Stephen Szasz contended that 'Insanity is the only sane reaction to an insane society.' And the British psychiatrist R.D. Laing concluded that insanity was 'a perfectly rational adjustment to an insane world'. I think I recall Dr Spock saying something similar.

But perhaps Fromm's words offer the most incisive diagnosis for our time:

> A person who has not been completely alienated, who has remained sensitive and able to feel, who has not lost the sense of dignity, who is not yet 'for sale', who can still suffer over the suffering of others, who has not acquired fully the 'having' mode of existence – briefly, a person who has remained a person and not become a thing – cannot help feeling lonely, powerless, isolated in present-day society. He cannot help doubting himself and his own convictions, if not his sanity. He cannot help suffering, even though he can experience moments of joy and clarity that are absent in the life of his 'normal' contemporaries. Not rarely will he suffer from neurosis that results from the situation of a sane man living in an insane society, rather than that of the more conventional neurosis of a sick man trying to adapt himself to a sick society.[29]

Indeed, how can we not get depressed when reading the newspapers today or watching political leaders go about their business with such confident incompetence? How can we not grieve the wildlife and natural habitat being destroyed each moment? What parent can look to the future and not feel a foreboding dread at what world their children and grandchildren will inherit? At the same time, and because of that dread, it is hard to maintain the emotional resources to care for strangers or 'join a movement' when stress, agitation, worry, and busyness clutter our mental lives. This can make society seem like a harsh place, lacking in generosity of spirit or compassion.

As I see it, cultural disenchantment is capitalism's most significant achievement. Its function is to ensure that we, the people, often lack the energy to mobilise in resistance or renewal. The austerity politics of neoliberalism is syphoning ever more of us into the 'precariat' – the growing class of workers who live anxiously with the financial insecurity that flows from the casualisation of the workforce. The COVID-19 pandemic has expanded its ranks and cast even more into unemployment. All this can curdle the imagination and tempt one to despair.

I am reminded of a 2003 poem by Australian poet Michael Leunig that speaks to our current condition:

They took him on a stretcher
To the Home for the Appalled
Where he lay down in a corner
And he bawled and bawled and bawled.
'There's nothing wrong with me,' he wailed,
When asked about his bawling,
'It's the world that needs attention;
It's so utterly appalling.'

Whether such dark moods arise from watching white supremacists march or listening to climate deniers speaking in parliament or given platforms in mass media, a nausea sets in, a sickness not so much of the mind but of the soul. To be mentally and spiritually disturbed in the face of today's overlapping cultural, economic, and ecological crises is, I maintain, a sign that one's faculties are intact, that one's heart has not fully closed up. This is an existential diagnosis, not a medical or psychiatric one. It would be wrong to make peace with this madness. The world we live in should not be treated as normal, and it should not be a sign of good health to become 'well adjusted' to a society that is casually practising ecocide, celebrating narcissism, institutionalising racism, and assessing the value of all things according to the cold logic of profit maximisation.

We must not assume that behaviour that makes an individual 'functional' within a sick society is sufficient evidence of sanity. In such a society, it is okay not to feel okay, to cry and feel grief, to feel dread and alienation. In our tears, let us find solidarity, for we are not alone. Remember this when you wake up prematurely in the morning with an anxiety without object, or as you stare at the ceiling late at night as you try to fall asleep. You are not losing your mind. It is precisely because you have a grip on reality that reality seems so out of whack.

Shaken awake: Disrupting the self through aesthetic education

This essay began by highlighting how human creativity is being voluntarily though insidiously suppressed by people who are, to varying extents, living in bad faith and with fear of freedom. The second half of the analysis offered a broader critique of the features of contemporary society that can, with good cause, be categorised as insane. I showed that being maladjusted to an insane society is paradoxically a sign of mental health, of sanity. My primary purpose, however, has been diagnostic rather than prescriptive: my assessment is that failing to take hold of our freedom – within those spheres of agency waiting for us to embody – is antithetical to our natures as creative beings. To live in bad faith and with fear of freedom is not the whole cause of the insanity of our societies but it is a contributing cause, perhaps a leading one. The good news, however, is that we are free to choose otherwise. If we are to resolve some of the many features of our insane society that are inhibiting our creative potentials and deadening our aesthetic sensibilities, then we need to be brave enough to reclaim our spheres of agency – brave enough to be aesthetic agents in an aesthetic universe.

Having offered this diagnosis, I now point to a prescription, which was anticipated in the previous essay on Friedrich Schiller and which will be developed in the next essay. In essence, the prescription offered is that we should look to reignite our innate need for freedom and the love of life through aesthetic education and engagement. To the extent that we are living in bad faith and with fear of freedom – and we *all* will be to some extent – then I believe we need to find ways to disrupt our 'normal sense of self'. My argument is that art and aesthetics may be the best means of shaking us awake. We need to awaken or reawaken a state of 'play', being the condition of aesthetic freedom in which our normal sense of self can be disrupted; when our normal sense of self is liberated from its own self-imposed rules and regulations.

I put this forward as the best antidote to living in bad faith and fear of freedom. It is a promising coincidence that this aesthetic ignition of our need for freedom may also offer a form of 'art therapy', a welcome and perhaps necessary existential salve as we find ourselves living in an insane society. My intention, at this stage, is not to argue for the particulars of an alternative form of life, but to find ways for more people to discover that there *are* different forms of life. As Henry Thoreau insisted, there are 'as many ways as there are radii from one center.'[30] If people can arrive at this conclusion, their freedom will have expanded.

---

[1] See Samuel Alexander 'Homo Aestheticus, the Artful Species: An Evolutionary Perspective' and Samuel Alexander, 'Giving Birth to Oneself: Ethics as an "Aesthetics of Existence"', in this collection of essays. The full set is being published here:

---

http://samuelalexander.info/s-m-p-l-c-t-y-ecological-civilisation-and-the-will-to-art/ (accessed 10 May 2023).

[2] Jean-Paul Sartre, *Situations* (Paris: Gallimard, 1964), p. 101.

[3] See Samuel Alexander, 'Creative Evolution and the Will to Art' in this collection of essays. See link in note 1.

[4] Kant's phrase is: 'Beautiful things indicate that man fits into the world', as quoted in Wolfgang Welsch, 'Schiller Revisited: "Beauty is freedom in Appearance" – Aesthetics as a Challenge to the Modern Way of Thinking' *Contemporary Aesthetics* (2014) 12: fn 1.

[5] Herbert Marcuse, *One Dimensional Man: Studies in the Ideology of Advanced Industrial Society* (London: Routledge, 2002).

[6] See, e.g., Christer Sanne, 'Willing Consumers – or Lock-In? Policies for Sustainable Consumption' *Ecological Economics* (2002) 42(1-2): pp. 273-287.

[7] Sartre on bad fait

[8] Jean-Paul Sartre, *Existentialism and Humanism* (London: Methuen and Co, 1970), p. 34.

[9] Erich Fromm, *The Fear of Freedom* (Oxon: Routledge, 2001).

[10] Ibid, p. 3.

[11] Ibid.

[12] Ibid, p. 4.

[13] Ibid, p. 154.

[14] Ibid, p. 156.

[15] Ibid, p. 157.

[16] Ibid, p. 158 (emphasis in original).

[17] Ibid.

[18] Ibid, p. 159.

[19] Ibid, p. 218.

[20] This section draws on my essay, 'Delusions of Sanity: Deconstructing Madness in an Insane World' (2021) *Griffith Review* 72: pp. 238-247.

[21] Erich Fromm, *The Sane Society* (London: Routledge, 2002).

[22] Fromm, *The Sane Society*, note 21, p. 3.

[23] Ibid.

[24] Michel Foucault, *Madness and Civilization: A History of Insanity in the Age of Reason* (London: Routledge, 2006).

[25] See The Foundation Staff, 'Regarding the Quote' *Krishnamurti Foundation Trust*. Available at: https://kfoundation.org/it-is-no-measure-of-health-to-be-well-adjusted-to-a-profoundly-sick-society/ (accessed 18 February 2023).

[26] Johann Hari, *Lost Connections* (London: Bloomsbury, 2019).

[27] Fromm, *The Sane Society*, note 21, p. 15.

[28] Lewis Mumford, *The Condition of Man* (London: Mariner Books. 1973).

[29] Erich Fromm, *The Art of Being* (New York: Open Road, 2013), p. 136.

[30] Henry Thoreau, *Walden*, in Carl Bode (ed.) *The Portable Thoreau* (New York: Penguin, 1982), p. 266.

'The development of man's capacity for feeling is... the more urgent need of our age.'

– **Friedrich Schiller**

BANISH THE POETS! THE POWER AND POLITICS OF AESTHETIC EDUCATION

One of the most famous and controversial elements in Plato's *Republic* concerns his policy proposal to banish the poets from his ideal city-state.[1] It was not a blanket dismissal, however. He didn't banish *all* poets, just those whom he considered the wrong kind of poet. Admittedly, this included the greatest names in Greek literature, such as Homer, Aeschylus, Sophocles, Euripides, and Aristophanes. In Plato's view, these poets told lies about the gods, sometimes depicted villains that were happy and virtuous people in misery, and they would seduce audiences and actors through imitation or 'mimesis' to embody improper characters. These features and more besides were criticised on the grounds that they might have a lasting negative effect on the state of one's soul. Plato argued that what we imitate or are exposed to, we become, without necessarily being aware that we are being changed. Poetic mimesis, even when we recognise it as such, might interfere insidiously with the proper functioning of the rational mind (the epistemological critique) and one's emotional balance (the moral critique). So even philosophers and virtuous people were at risk of intellectual deception and ethical corruption through exposure to degenerate forms of poetry. Accordingly, such undesirable poets should be banished from the city-state and their works should not be available to young ears, or indeed culture at large, owing to their corrupting influence on the soul.[2]

On the other hand, Plato maintained that the *right* type of poets – those who tell edifying stories that celebrate virtues like temperance, courage, and sobriety – were critical to establishing a good, well-ordered society. They were a necessary means of promoting proper values, communicating rational beliefs persuasively, and encouraging sound dispositions, all of which were necessary for the achievement of political harmony and social prosperity. Plato recognised the great power, not just of poetry, but of the arts more generally. These aesthetic modes of communication and expression were prominent means of cultural transmission – a means of shaping social norms and traditions. So the role of art in culture, then as now, should be taken very seriously for what it is: education.

Whether or not some poets are banished from society might seem to be of trifling significance for the contemporary reader, given that not many people seem to read poetry today. The stereotype of the poet as the misanthropic, self-indulgent bohemian, or nature-loving romantic, might even tempt the modern reader to sympathise with Plato's decree – good riddance! But in the Athens of ancient Greece, poetry did not lie at the margins of culture but at its centre, with an influence more akin to mass media in the twenty-first century in terms of cultural influence and impact. When we appreciate this point, the political regulation of poetry acquires a contemporary relevance and poses problems that still demand attention. Plato recognised how poetry, music, and the arts more broadly shaped culture. Being no democrat, he did not hesitate to advocate for the use of state power to regulate artistic creation and performance according to his vision of the common good.

Most people of liberal sensibility are likely to object to Plato's authoritarian solution to the problem of how to create a good culture and an ideal Republic. We would defend the liberty of artists to create as they wish, as a corollary of the inalienable right of free expression. Even if we felt confident in our own aesthetic judgement of what was socially beneficial, we would be unlikely to feel comfortable imposing our views on everyone else. Individual choice and taste in aesthetic matters are to be valued, and the avant-garde should have the freedom to advance in its own unforeseeable ways, as the call of genius (or madness) dictates. Allowing the state to decide what art is permitted seems like a terrible idea, socially, politically, and aesthetically.

At its extreme, Plato's reasoning could even produce dictators like Stalin, who also recognised the power of the arts, calling writers and poets 'engineers of the human soul'.[3] This insight into art's power motivated Stalin and his secret police to round up those artists whom the Communist Party did not like and either execute them or send them off to the gulags for a most unpoetic life of hard labour. The very threat of execution would also have created a 'chilling effect' on the creation of new art, becoming a self-regulating policy to some extent. In one of the more disturbing lines ever expressed by a human being, Stalin is reported to have said: 'Ideas are more powerful than guns. We would not let our enemies have guns, why should we let them have ideas?'[4] And thus, the arts, always brimming with new ideas and perspectives, were purged of so-called dissidents. Anyone who thinks that art lacks political or social effects needs to explain why authoritarian governments have always seen art as dangerous and in need of severe – albeit selective – repression.

Leaving aside Stalin's murderous tendencies, I surmise that most people living in liberal democratic societies today would shudder at the idea of any government department being judge and censor of cultural production; of state officials being tasked with determining what art is edifying and permissible and what art must be prohibited. Nevertheless, if we recognise the cultural significance of the arts – if Athenian poetry is transposed into a cultural force as significant as mass media – we ought to be concerned by the same issues that disturbed Plato. Specifically, that bad culture can corrupt, just as good culture can edify and nourish. Even if we would deny governments the role of being arbiters of aesthetic value, that does not relieve us of the responsibility of considering what forces shape culture and whether there are things we can do to improve our world by shaping a better culture. This might include the role of art and aesthetic practices in that process.[5]

As an alternative to Plato's aesthetic authoritarianism, is our only option the policy of letting the 'free market' determine the shape of our cultures? Hopefully not. Reflecting on the vapidity of reality TV, social media, and pop music today – what the Frankfurt school would have called products of the 'culture industry'[6] – we might have concerns about where market capitalism has taken contemporary culture and what it is doing to us as citizens. One might suggest that the good poets have already been banished from contemporary society, albeit through the insidious workings of the market rather than by the dictates of the state. The bad poets – those soul-numbing 'artists' who merely distract or entertain us with formulaic gruel – have come to dominate cultural life. After all, turn on the television, scroll through social media, and read the news: where is the good art to be found? The art that energises and inspires? The art that makes existing injustices intolerable and the path to a more humane world clear and inviting? Too often the primary evidence is absence. We suffer, as I have suggested, from an aesthetic deficit disorder. People everywhere seem hungry for soul-nourishing art and self-determined creative activity, but we find ourselves living in conditions of aesthetic and spiritual famine. Perhaps, as Dostoyevsky once declared, we have arrived at a time when only 'beauty can save the world.'[7]

This brief engagement with Plato's view on the arts was intended to re-introduce the theme of aesthetic education in society, which is the focus of this essay.[8] In what follows I will consider three obstacles to societal transformation that are inhibiting the transition to a just and sustainable society, in response to which I highlight, in each case, the critical role of aesthetic education. First, I will offer a broad critique of the existing educational paradigm under capitalism, which I call 'education for economic growth' or 'economic for profit', following philosopher Martha Nussbaum.[9] This paradigm is designed to maximise profits and economic growth and its social function is to shape citizens into obedient worker-consumers. An alternative education is needed. Building upon my previous analysis of Friedrich Schiller's aesthetic theory, I will propose that the *process* of bringing about an alternative education serendipitously overlaps directly with the *goals* of such education. That is, aesthetic education, engagement, and value are both the means and the ends of this strategy of emancipation and cultural enrichment.

Second, I will consider the so-called 'information deficit model' of change, which assumes human beings are fundamentally rational, evidence-based thinkers. On that basis, the theory maintains that the primary means of societal progress is more evidence and better arguments.[10] I believe that this is at best a partial and often misleading theory of change that marginalises the role of the arts and aesthetic education in social and political transformation. We human beings are as much influenced by our hearts as by our heads, as even the arch-rationalist Plato recognised. This suggests that the arts and aesthetic interventions in culture are highly significant shapers of the world, for better or for worse. Perhaps it is not better evidence that we are lacking today, but better art. Perhaps what is needed, more than anything, is a new aesthetic education, one that emerges from the grassroots and thereby avoids the dictates of state and market. Indeed, I have come to believe that aesthetic education is the most promising means of expanding the social imagination. Accordingly, it is an essential ingredient to cultural change – more powerful, perhaps, than the rational provision of better evidence and stronger arguments.

The third issue to consider, closely related to the first two, concerns what could be diagnosed as an imaginative sterility in contemporary culture, one that seems to have left so many citizens unable to envision forms of life beyond consumer capitalism. Political and cultural theorist Mark Fisher called this enclosing of the imagination 'capitalism realism',[11] often defined as the view that it is easier to imagine the end of the world than the end of capitalism. This is both a condition of imaginative sterility and an affective enclosure related to our felt needs. After all, the world does not seem to be on the cusp of a revolution whereby humanity claims its dignity as a free and self-determining species. Social movements for resistance and renewal exist, but they seem highly marginal and underdeveloped, perhaps because different, better, more liberated worlds can barely be imagined.

The same forces that have shaped our needs, desires, sensibilities, and rationalities, have shaped – that is, enclosed – our imaginations. The result is a growing and intensifying homogenisation of consciousness and again, the prescription to be explored in this essay will be a renewed aesthetic education. The purpose of this education would be to break through the crust of conventional thinking about possible futures and shatter the ruts in which we find ourselves, opening the horizons of possibility and allowing us to create something new. But in order to create something new, first we need the aesthetic capacities to *imagine* it in our minds and *feel* it in our hearts. Only later do we need to *reason* and *act* our way to its fruition.

Education for profit

I begin by framing the problems under discussion in terms of education. This will also clarify the role an alternative mode of education must play in any resolution of these problems. Today it seems we have been educated into a species that is most accurately described as *homo economicus*. Given that economic growth is the most important benchmark for measuring societal progress under the global capitalist order, it follows that the purpose of education should be to create obedient, docile worker-consumers who are most likely to contribute to that ultimate value. Critical thinking or imagination might be relevant to the economic elites in positions of authority, where the skills and capacities for independent thought can maximise profit through astute innovation of processes, products, and marketing. But for most workers, the primary expectation is simply to obey and efficiently undertake their tasks in the factory, office, or farm, without question. In these typical circumstances, it is best that the imagination is numbed in order to facilitate the efficient achievement of menial but profit-maximising tasks. Curiosity, creativity, and the love of wisdom are not often seen as 'profitable' and, as such, should not be encouraged, and indeed, should be actively suppressed. One simply ought to do what one is told.

Of course, growth-obsessed cultures do not *only* desire growth, but it is the nature of the capitalist paradigm to treat growth as something of a 'false target' to aim for. That is, it is assumed that if a society aims for growth, the other things that are desired – health, security, education, and so forth – will be most effectively advanced. Within the capitalist growth paradigm, what is of paramount important is to educate people so they can 'get jobs' and contribute to profit-maximisation as workers and consumers. This 'jobs and growth' mantra is so powerful and deeply entrenched that in capitalist societies today, politicians can sometimes see an advantage in denigrating the humanities allegedly on the grounds that they aren't needed for economic growth. The humanities might be desirable perhaps, but something of a luxury, even superfluous, in these tough economic times.[12]

The risk of course – with effects we are already seeing – is that 'education for economic growth' or 'education for profit'[13] will produce generations of worker-consumers that are quite useful productive machines but not always very good at being free and community-orientated citizens; not well-versed in the art of critical thinking, or being imaginative, open-minded, compassionate, or sensitive to the sufferings of others or planet. This is not so much a moral critique as an economic one, given that people, when beaten into the shape of *homo economicus*, are usually just trying to survive in a hostile economic environment, and are not *inherently* greedy, selfish, or subservient.

Nevertheless, such an education can give rise to citizenries composed of people who engage or rather manipulate each other in terms of economic self-interest in the marketplace. Adopting a business model approach to social engagement, fellow citizens are treated as a means to an end, rather than an end in themselves. These market actors will know nothing or too little of what it is like to interact with people in due recognition of their mysterious complexity, depth, and beauty. Instead, subjects of capitalism are educated to deal with others in terms of advancing their own exchange value in the market.

But surely something noble or essential in the human spirit is lost when we are reduced to antagonistic atoms in a totalising marketplace. As philosopher and social reformer Rabindranath Tagore wrote: 'while making use of [material possessions], man has to be careful to protect himself from [their] tyranny. If he is weak enough to grow smaller to fit himself to his covering, then it becomes a process of gradual suicide by shrinkage of the soul.'[14] In other words, education purely for profit is a grossly impoverished conception of education, a subterranean assault upon the integrity of any citizenry, and it is not clear whether democratic society can survive such as assault.

The external forces of this assault arise from the cultural, economic, and political contexts of our lives, which provide inhospitable soil for self-creation, rendering us cogs in a machine, managed by the exigencies of instrumental reason. But even within spheres of potential agency and freedom, there are internal forces within us, whereby people often *choose* to live in bad faith and in fear of freedom. Such inauthentic living strategies deflate creative resistance and turn us into conforming, subservient beings that go with the flow of the status quo, created but not creative. Modernity has given with one hand and taken back with the other. Yes, many of the citizens in the affluent regions of the world find themselves with unprecedented wealth and technological capacity. Nevertheless, so many are also disenchanted with life, disconnected from people, nature, and indeed themselves. Our natures are out of balance.

Martha Nussbaum calls this the 'silent crisis'[15]. It is silent because it is hard to hear the crisis coming, even though its effects are everywhere. An economic or political crisis is generally obvious. Politicians and corporate leaders can leap into coordinated action to try to resolve it. But an educational crisis can be – and is – in many ways invisible, silent, operating more like a cancer than an earthquake. The point of this critique of education for profit is not to disparage the often critical, necessary, and important education for things like engineering, computing, maths, science, and so forth. There are obviously material foundations that must be established for any good society to emerge and sustain itself. But a far broader education, beyond the realm of economic contribution, is needed not just for good citizenship but for the fostering of meaningful lives. Indeed, educators for profit might even fear (not merely tolerate) education for genuine citizenship, since the latter might lead to the realisation that profit is not the ultimate value it is currently held out to be. An education for citizenship, which I'll soon argue needs to include a robust aesthetic education, is likely to be dangerous to the established order, and this is why, no doubt, it is currently repressed.

Maverick priest and political radical, Ivan Illich, wrote extensively on such issues in the 1970s, making a case for the 'deschooling' of society.[16] He argued that the industrialisation of centralised, compulsory schooling had resulted in mere anti-intellectual learning for certificates, fostering ignorance with little true education. He saw a 'hidden curriculum' in Westernised education that served to indoctrinate the youth into accepting industrial society without question, churning out obedient consumers with little capacity for critical thinking. His proposal was to develop alternative modes of education that would assist in the unlearning of capitalist culture.

Despite the existence of a critical counterculture, education for profit remains the dominant model and this has aesthetic effects. Earlier, I recounted the story about the world-famous violinist who unassumingly performed on his three-and-a-half-million-dollar violin in a Washington train station. What was striking was how few people stopped to listen or admire the aesthetic spectacle, at most a few young children (from whom we might have something to learn). The disturbing lesson is that the world might be full of more beauty than we know, which we just miss while rushing through our lives, conditioned to focus our attention on other things. What were people rushing by to do? Get home to watch television? Even if people were rushing to get to work in order to pay the rent, we should condemn an economic structure that has left us too busy to absorb such beauty, especially when it is freely on offer. But this indictment is also grounds for hope. If the world is more beautiful than we appreciate, perhaps there are ways of restructuring our consciousness to be more receptive to these aesthetic rewards, and even to become creators of aesthetic value ourselves.

Can we overcome our current condition as *homo economicus* – obedient, self-interested producers and consumers – and become something new? Or rather, looking back through history, can we reclaim our creative and sensuous natures and potentials as *homo aestheticus*? Perhaps it is less about looking backwards than it is about looking forward. If we come to realise that our aesthetic natures have yet to be fulfilled, we can look forward to, and fight for, a *homo aestheticus* 'to come'. Culture has certainly created deep ruts whereby we are seduced into conforming and obeying. It is so easy to go with the flow. But, as outlined in the earlier essay on Schiller, we need to find ways to disrupt our 'normal' or 'conventional' senses of self and claim our freedoms, both individually and politically. We need change, but how might change come about?

The 'information deficit' theory of change

Currently there is little evidence within advanced, industrialised nations that people within the dominant culture think or feel that there is any need to transcend consumer culture or the capitalist forms of political economy that drive and are driven by it. The highly developed state of global capitalism in the twenty-first century corresponds to a very low revolutionary potential.[17] This is the given reality and there is little use in denying it; little use in fabricating a false hope merely to ease our sense of foreboding and dread. The Marxian idea that the working classes would develop a revolutionary consciousness as the contradictions of capitalism intensified has not transpired in the advanced capitalist nations, and does not seem to be threatening to emerge. While capitalism is evidently in the process of catabolic collapse, the resistance to this unfolding reality has yet to emerge, at least beyond the margins.

At the same time, as capitalism continues to develop its means of exploitation, pushing into every new frontier, what becomes clear is that the true benefits of this mode of production are being distributed to fewer and fewer people, even if material rewards are growing for some sectors of the global population. What this suggests is that the class of people who have a *genuine material interest* in system change is growing. This demographic extends well beyond the confines of the traditional proletariat and expands into ever larger portions of consumer society – as well, of course, into the populations exploited by consumer society. So a mass base for transformative change certainly exists and is growing – both globally and specifically in the 'affluent West'. Yet the *revolutionary consciousness* seems to be weak or even absent. Indeed, the classes capable of societal transformation are so integrated into consumer society that it would be fair to say that there is not merely a lack of revolutionary consciousness, but an even more stabilising anti-revolutionary or counter-revolutionary sensibility.[18]

To state this problem in aesthetic terms: within mainstream culture there does not seem to be any *felt need* to act for deep and urgent change, and without that sensibility it is not clear how deep and deliberate change could ever eventuate. A radicalised consciousness seems to be a precondition for a voluntary transformation of the social order, thus its absence should be a subject of critical concern. One way to assess this problem of inaction in the face of civilisational deterioration is to consider the process of human decision making. Why don't people mobilise en masse to stop the brutal degradation of Earth and the immiseration of humankind? How do we make our life decisions? Let us consider these questions.

The Enlightenment conception of human decision-making is, notoriously, a highly rationalistic one, assuming that our species shares a common nature by virtue of our rational faculties. The essential idea is that scientific progress and technological advancement are slowly lifting human beings out of the domains of historical ignorance, primitiveness, and superstition, and by applying the scientific method we will continue this linear progression. We will develop an ever-broader range of knowledge and technologies which can better control and predict the workings of nature, thereby advancing human ends more effectively. The faith is that human beings are, by nature, rational – or capable of rational deliberation and reflection – and that increasingly we will shape how we act in the world according to the best scientific evidence we have at our disposal.

I am hardly the first to contend that human beings are far less rationalistic than this picture assumes (see the works of Nietzsche, Freud, Derrida, and so forth). To take the ecological crisis as a case in point: arguably there was enough evidence in the 1970s or earlier to justify a fundamental transformation of our destructive modes of economic activity.[19] If not historically, then certainly today. Climate breakdown, deforestation, biodiversity loss, the extinction of species, pollution, topsoil erosion, etc – at what point, one might ask, will there be 'enough' evidence to provoke change? The premise of this essay is that perhaps it isn't 'better evidence' that is lacking. There is not an information deficit but an aesthetic deficit – a lack of art, imagination, creativity, and nourishing sensuous experience. We suffer a confusion of desire so deep that it cannot be resolved rationally but must be confronted, first and foremost, at the mythopoetic level. This is less about our minds being in need of refinement and enrichment than our emotions and sensibilities. We might *know* what needs to change, but for change to actually transpire people en masse need to *feel* the demand for freedom and justice in their bodies. We need to develop the aesthetic sensibility to react physically to injustice in the same way we react to a foul and intolerable stench.

Granted, there are numerous vested interests at play which influence how citizenries respond to the issues they face (e.g., mass media and the megacorporation prefer a passive, obedient population). But the fact is that cultures around the world broadly *know* about the dire ecological crises that are unfolding. Yet, people continue to vote for politicians that are essentially maintaining not subverting business-as-usual. Little change seems to be coming from the personal or household domains either, even though marginalised countercultures are everywhere bubbling under the surface. Who, then, seriously thinks that yet another scientific report on the declining state of the environment is going to be the catalyst for transformative change? It is important that evidence-based thinkers answer this question based on the evidence.

If humanity's social and environmental problems were just a result of 'information deficit' or 'knowledge deficit', then perhaps a purely rationalistic approach to societal change would be justifiable. That is, the primary task would be simply to conduct the scientific research and publish the findings, and trust that human beings, as rational agents, will read and understand the evidence, change how they live, and vote for an appropriate political and economic response. It could be argued that this has been the defining faith of the environmental movement to date, and perhaps points to its deepest failing.

This line of reasoning is not, in the slightest, to denigrate the necessary and important work of environmental and social scientists. We know that science has social impacts. Think, for example, of the significant decline of smoking in response to the overwhelming scientific evidence that it is carcinogenic. The point, however, is to suggest that relying on 'the evidence' alone to do the hard work of societal transformation is naive. Yes, it is critical to apply the scientific method rigorously to better understand the world; to pose and test hypotheses; to develop and apply appropriate technologies; to create cultures that think critically about the world; and to endeavour to be evidence-based decision makers at all levels of life. But it is just as important to recognise that it is not just *what* is communicated that matters, but also *how* it is communicated. It could be that the environmental movement (broadly speaking) has trusted too much in the provision of evidence, neglecting the critical task of presenting the evidence in socially digestible forms.

As Herbert Marcuse contended, the 'strong emphasis on the political potential of the arts which is a feature of this radicalism is first of all expressive of the need for an effective *communication* of the indictment of the established reality and of the goals of liberation.'[20] Put otherwise, radicals need to find forms of communication which break with the oppressive rule that the established language and images have over mind and body. Through diverse acts of creation, the counterculture must give rise to a new language and universe of images that point to new ways to live and paths for their realisation.

This is an aesthetic challenge because it highlights the importance of giving *form* to *content*. Social movements today (environmental and otherwise) should be exploring ways of being more creative and engaging in the presentation of their own scientific and ethical foundations, in order to do those foundations justice. After all, it is not enough merely to be correct in one's diagnoses and prescriptions; one must also find a way to expand the sympathetic audience beyond those people who are already converted, and that points to a communications challenge. For better or for worse, emotive imagery and language might well be more persuasive than sober reasoning (a lesson the political Right has historically tended to exploit more effectively than the Left).

Another way to put this is that social movements should be trying harder to appeal not merely to the head, but also – or especially – to the heart. A persuasive case for societal change must not only be made *intellectually* or *rationally* but also *affectively* or *emotionally*. As Schiller argued: 'the development of man's capacity for feeling is... the more urgent need of our age.'[21] It might be said that we are not short of good ideas, as such, but we have yet to make good ideas seem powerful. No doubt there will be and are people who, when exposed to new evidence, reconsider their current thinking and adjust their worldviews and actions to better reflect the facts. This is the rationalistic ideal and probably the self-image we all have of ourselves. But most people would also probably accept that in many cases human beings fail to live up to this self-image, especially in this age increasingly called 'post-truth'. When confronted with evidence that challenges a cherished worldview (e.g., the growth paradigm), people can simply look away; assume the evidence is flawed; attack the authors rather than the evidence; blindly trust that markets or some new technology will solve the problem; go searching for evidence that validates (however dubiously) their current position or lifestyle; or undertake any number of other evasive strategies.

This speaks to the limitations of reason and rationality as transformative and progressive forces. After all, can we sit down and reason with corporations or governments who only know the rationality of capital expansion? As Marcuse wrote:

> Can you reason with the Pentagon on any other thing than the relative effectiveness of killing machines – and their price? The Secretary of State can reason with the Secretary of the Treasury, and the latter with another Secretary and his advisors, and they all can reason with Members of the Board of the great corporations. This is incestuous reasoning; they are all in agreement about the basic issue: the strengthening of the established power structure. Reasoning 'from without' the power structure is naïve.[22]

It is in these non-rational contexts where the artist becomes a necessary agent of change, having the potential to provoke social change via different mechanisms of persuasion, making emotional, psychological, or even spiritual impacts on an audience at those times when science, logic, and argument have failed. The artist can conjure up new modes of perception, providing a feast of sensuous experience that anticipates, often explosively, a different way of living and being in the world, reshaping in some mysterious way not just the thoughts of individuals, but also their needs, hopes, and drives. Indeed, Marcuse pointed out that art can communicate truths 'not communicable in any other language.'[23]

Beyond the work of art narrowly defined lies the potential of aesthetic interventions in culture and politics more broadly. The 'culture jamming' movement, for example, seeks to incite cultural and political change not through argument, evidence, and logic, but through provocative and jarring images that disrupt and unsettle our sense of normality. The purpose is to expose the violence often hidden in our habits of thought and practice, opening our minds to alternative ways of living and being. Cultural theorist David Cox defines the practice of culture jamming as 'a vibrant counter-attack on the empire of signs',[24] and this counter-attack need not just be the production of images, but can include other acts or activities that function to disrupt people's ordinary experience and open new doorways of perception and understanding. Some refer to this as 'artivism'.[25]

It is worth noting that the Canadian journal *Adbusters*, which is the global hub of the otherwise decentralised culture-jamming movement, was the institution that conceived of the Occupy Movement. In recent decades this is the closest thing we have ever seen to a global uprising, but *Adbusters* did not create the discontent at the heart of the Occupy Movement. It merely gave imaginative form to content – created an ingenious 'branding' of that discontent – in ways that were able to mobilise and organise it for political and economic purposes. It fought the 'Society of the Spectacle'[26] on its own terms, and met with some success. Perhaps culture jamming is an oppositional aesthetic practice that has yet to fulfil its potential. As a slogan of the 1968 uprising in France stated: bring imagination to power! That is what is needed, but it is difficult to achieve when the imagination itself is under attack – and losing.

A failure of imagination

'Capitalist realism' is a term popularised by the cultural and political theorist Mark Fisher in a provocative and unsettling book by that name.[27] The term implies that, ever since the fall of Soviet Communism in 1989, capitalism has been the only game in town; the only *realistic* system of production and distribution to structure globalised human society. Everything else is sheer utopianism in the pejorative sense – naïve dreaming of what can never be.

Capitalist realism points to a failure of imagination, suggesting that it is now easier to imagine the end of the world than the end of capitalism.[28] The diagnosis has almost become a cliché. As one looks around the world today, the case for capitalist realism is, admittedly, disturbingly persuasive – as Fisher himself was the first to admit, even as he resisted it. It can tempt one to despair, for it often seems that there is in fact no realistic alternative to what we know today. The material wealth that capitalism has created far exceeds what Marx would have considered necessary for the construction of a socialist society. But it is precisely the emergence of consumer society that now serves to support and sustain capitalist relations of production, discrediting, rightly or wrongly, the vision and desirability of socialism, even as the hedonic rewards of consumerism seem to be eternally deferred.

To say that capitalist realism is real is to acknowledge the *zeitgeist* of the twenty-first century, one shared not only by neoliberal conservatives but also by most on the green-left who, despite a 'progressive' self-image, remain insidiously entrenched in capitalism's growth paradigm. In Fisher's words, there is 'a widespread sense that not only is capitalism the only viable political and economic system, but also that it is now impossible even to *imagine* a coherent alternative to it'.[29] He describes this consciousness as a 'pervasive atmosphere' that conditions 'not only the production of culture but also the regulation of work and education, and acting as a kind of invisible barrier constraining thought and action'.[30]

But here is the disturbing paradox of capitalist realism: just as the dominant cultural imagination has contracted into a singularity of vision – there is no alternative to capitalism! The very system to which there is apparently no alternative shows itself to be in the process of self-destructing, like a cancer cell growing itself to death, killing its host. At the hour when modern humanity has arrived at a self-aggrandising pinnacle of triumph – a global market economy promising riches for all – the skies have been darkened by the terrible spectres of ecological degradation and social decline and polarisation. The climate emergency is only one of these storm clouds, but this alone has the potential to radically disrupt civilisation as we know it. In other words, capitalist realism is unrealistic, non-viable, a dead end – literally. The system is full of internal contradictions that the system cannot resolve, most notably the myth that through market mechanisms we can purchase and consume our way to sustainability.

At the same time, vast oceans of debilitating poverty surround small oceans of unfathomable plenty, exposing the violent betrayal of the capitalist growth agenda, euphemistically (or just deceptively) known in public discourse as 'sustainable development'. This is a race leading towards an abyss, both enabled and entrenched by a sterility of imagination called capitalist realism. Fortunately – if that is the right word – capitalist realism 'can only be threatened if it is shown to be in some way inconsistent or untenable; if, that is to say, capitalism's ostensible "realism" turns out to be nothing of the sort'.[31]

The grand narrative of progress via economic growth has been widely internalised in consumer cultures. The working class – once the locus of the revolutionary sentiment – has found little need or desire to replace the 'economic base' of capitalism, even if little wealth has been trickling down. Even when ecological and social justice concerns are given attention by politicians or mass media, the social imaginary is so limited that resolutions to such problems are conceived of within the paradigm of growth, technology, and affluence, rarely if ever beyond it. People may shake their heads in concern when they hear of the latest warnings from climate scientists, or shake their heads in outrage when they learn that a small handful of men now own more than the poorest half of humanity. But when reflecting on what an alternative mode of existence might look like, the dominant culture shrugs its shoulders, unable to imagine anything other than green consumerism in a technocratic world. This is obviously a non-confronting response to the crises we face because it does not question the growth paradigm, overpopulation, or consumerist conceptions of the good life.

It is all very well for scholars to present a range of devastating critiques of the existing order of neoliberal capitalism, but if people are unable to envision what a just, sustainable, and liberated world would actually look like, then the necessary task of mobilising communities for collective action will face insurmountable barriers. People will continue to seek meaning and advancement in the only ways the dominant culture permits: through consumption. Indeed, people may consume as means of objecting to the dehumanising ways they have been treated under capitalism, not realising they are in fact being counter-productive.

Thinking and acting 'beyond capitalism' is not easy in a one-dimensional world that is increasingly homogenised, commodified, and standardised. Yet, breaking through the cracks of capitalism to *think* otherwise and *be* otherwise is more essential now than ever. In the words of poet and novelist Herman Hesse: 'Nothing is harder, yet nothing is more necessary, than to speak of certain things whose existence is neither demonstrable nor probable. The very fact that serious and conscientious people treat them as existing things brings them a step closer to existence and to the possibility of being born.'[32]

Aesthetic education: 'art therapy' on a mass scale

I have highlighted three obstacles in the path of progressive transformation of society, offering essentially the same solution to each of them: aesthetic education. The first obstacle was the problem of 'education for profit', through which human beings are increasingly shaped into obedient, docile workers whose creative capacities and potentials are suppressed in order to maximise economic growth. The second issue I considered was the information deficit model of change, a theory I criticised for holding the naively optimistic assumption that human beings usually make decisions based on the best evidence and strongest arguments. Third, I suggested that contemporary culture is in the grip of what Fisher called 'capitalist realism', referring to an enclosure of the imagination, whereby better futures beyond capitalism can barely be envisioned and thus not fought for.

In response to all these problems, I proposed that what is needed most fundamentally is a renewed aesthetic education. Today humanity suffers less from a lack of knowledge or technological capability than from a *confusion of desire*. Too often meaning and happiness is pursued through consumption, status, and power, and when that approach does not satisfy personal, social, and spiritual needs, the same approach is reapplied hoping for a different outcome. By reimagining the good life beyond consumer culture, an aesthetic education would rewire our tastes and desires and shift our modes of thinking by first shifting how we feel. In contrast to an education for profit, an aesthetic education would recognise the fundamental importance of supporting our creative and imaginative natures and capacities. It would immerse us more deeply in the arts, allowing us to revel in the sensuous and soulful pleasures of great art, and to absorb the infinite wisdom that lies scattered throughout art history.

But recall that I have defined art, inspired by William Morris, as the pleasurable and meaningful expression of creative labour. On that basis an aesthetic education would also train and empower us to be artists ourselves, in the broad sense, which includes being an artisan who makes useful and beautiful things. Thereby we would drive the Great Transition onwards, together, building the new world from within the shell of the old. As I will detail further in later essays, the more we infuse art into the everyday rituals and practices of our lives, the less inclined we will be to seek meaning in ecologically destructive and socially corrosive consumption. The more we let our senses be enchanted by nature's sublimity, the less inclined we will be to destroy the community of life or the magnificent life-support system called Earth.

In other words, I am proposing that only by passing through a new aesthetic condition, induced by aesthetic experience and creative activity, can humanity hope to respond adequately or appropriately to our current predicament. That response is going to involve a shift away from ever-expanding materialistic goals and turning to the realm of the spirit to satisfy our hunger for infinity. As noted from the beginning, the two guiding premises that underlie these essays are first, that material sufficiency is all that is *needed* for human beings to live rich, meaningful, and artful lives; and second, that material sufficiency is all that is *possible*, over the long term, on a finite planet in an age of environmental limits. Through aesthetic education, we would not merely discover this to be true, we would feel it to be good, beautiful, and meaningful.

Thus I have been motivated in this project by the belief that an aesthetic education provides a key both to driving the transition and shaping the new society – an ecological civilisation of artisan-artists. Aesthetic education could drive the transition as more people exercised their imaginations to intervene in culture and politics to better expose the violence that often lies hidden in cultural values and dominant institutions. This creative unveiling of existing injustices would help demystify capitalism, exposing it as a choice not a natural or inevitable order. Upon that realisation, pathways beyond capitalism would become clearer to more people, providing social movements with the emotional and spiritual energy needed to fight what often seems to be a never-ending defeat.

Sometimes that energy can emerge from powerful art that wears its politics on its sleeve – a novel that indicts or a film that inspires. But our inner fire can also be stoked from the spine-tingling beauty of a sorrowful piano sonata or a poem about the smell of an old growth forest. As philosopher of enchantment, Jane Bennett, argues: 'to some small but irreducible extent, one must be enamoured with existence and occasionally even enchanted in the face of it in order to be capable of donating some of one's scarce mortal resources to the service of others.'[33] Therein lies some of the transgressive power of beauty – a category too often dismissed as being apolitical. Art can enchant in ways that provide the necessary propulsion to activity. After all, moral, ethical, and political reasoning *must* engage the heart to be effective, given that reason and rationality will fail to motivate or transform behaviour without an emotional engagement.[34] Eighteenth-century Scottish philosopher David Hume put it this way: 'Reason is, and ought only to be, slave to the passions.'[35] This, in a sentence, speaks to the importance of educating the passions, and I am holding up the aesthetic as the best tool for that task. At the very least, aesthetic experience can induce a state of 'play' which allows us to break free from habitual modes of thought and reason differently.

Art can also inform the nature of the new society, not merely the transition thereto. I have used the term SMPLCTY to refer to an *orientating vision* of an ecological civilisation, one in which individuals and communities thrive in humble conditions of material sufficiency but cultural richness, meaningfully engaged in pleasurable and creative labour in collaboration with others. According to this vision, life itself would become an aesthetic project, a never-ending process of creative activity, sensuous experience, aesthetic engagement, and spiritual exploration. Such a society would be structured with the aim of sustainably providing opportunities for all people to find meaning and pleasure through creative labour and aesthetic experience. This signifies an anarcho-socialist form of life in which human beings minimise material and energetic demands for reasons of social and ecological justice, while creatively exploring the good life in non-materialistic sources of meaning and happiness, especially through art and aesthetic experience. This vision is supported by an interpretation of the universe as embodying a primordial energy called the Will to Art, which seeks to experience itself through the aesthetic flourishing that would be cultivated in such an ecological civilisation.

In contrast to the information deficit model of change, a focus on aesthetic education would also better appreciate that we are not as rationalistic as we might like to suppose. That is to say, an *effective* politics of change will need to be an *affective* politics. This is not to dismiss the importance of reason, logic, and evidence, but it does suggest that any appeal to those rationalistic aspects of our nature might need to be preceded by an aesthetic approach that first appeals to the emotional and sensuous sides of our nature. As Schiller wrote, 'the way to the head must lie through the heart,'[36] such that 'the development of [humanity's] capacity for feeling is... the more urgent need of our age.'[37] He was offering the profound and subtle insight that through beauty – through the works of poets, painters, musicians, and storytellers – we are best able to engage the intellect *having first affected the emotions*. In this way aesthetic education can be seen as the foundations for a theory of change.

Finally, I drew on Mark Fisher's work to examine how social transformation is being suppressed by a contracting of the cultural and political imagination. On that basis I argued that a bold and creative aesthetic education might be required to expand the imagination to envision the pluriverse of post-capitalist futures waiting for us to realise through collective and creative action. The same aesthetic education would also immerse us in meaningful and pleasurable art, both as creators and spectators. This would expose us throughout the day to beauty that stimulates and consoles us, in ways that again provides emotional and spiritual energy for acts of resistance and renewal.

In short, I am proposing, as a political strategy, 'art therapy' on a mass scale. And if governments will not support such a strategy for fear of what an aesthetic education might produce, then it follows that that we must induce this aesthetic revolution ourselves, at the grassroots level. Under capitalism, the poets have been banished. We must welcome them back, and become poets ourselves, for they are needed more than ever. Indeed, if we define poetry as the expression of the imagination, then it is no overstatement to declare, with Percy Bysshe Shelley, that 'poets are the unacknowledged legislators of the world.'[38]

---

[1] Plato, *The Republic* (London: Penguin, 1955), especially Books II, III, and X.

[2] For a more detailed analysis of these themes, to which I am indebted, see MF Burnyeat, 'Art and Mimesis in Plato's "Republic"' (1998) *London Review of Books* 20(10). Available at: https://www.lrb.co.uk/the-paper/v20/n10/m.f.-burnyeat/art-and-mimesis-in-plato-s-republic (accessed 2 February 2023).

[3] See Liu Yunshan, 'An Examination of the "Engineer of Human Souls" Metaphor' in Liu Yunshan *Trends in Chinese Education* (London: Routledge, 2016).

[4] Although this quote is often attributed to Stalin, I was unable to track down a source.

[5] See e.g., Martha Nussbaum, *Not for Profit: Why Democracy Needs the Humanities* (Princeton: Princeton University Press, 2016). See also, Martha Nussbaum, *Love's Knowledge: Essays on Philosophy and Literature* (Oxford: Oxford University Press, 1992, revised ed.).

[6] See generally, Theodor Adorno, *The Culture Industry: Selected Essays on Mass Culture* (London: Routledge, 2001).

[7] Fyodor Dostoyevsky, *The Idiot* (New York: Bantam, 1981), p. 370.
[8] For a leading text on aesthetic education, see Herbert Read, *Education Through Art* (New York: Pantheon Books, 1948).
[9] Nussbaum, *Not for Profit*, note 5.
[10] For a review and critical discussion of the literature, see Paul McDivitt, 'The Information Deficit Model is Dead. Now What? Evaluating New Strategies for Communicating Anthropocentric Climate Change in the Context of Contemporary American Politics, Economy, and Culture' (Thesis, Master of Arts, University of Colorado, 2011).
[11] Mark Fisher, *Capitalist Realism: Is There No Alternative?* (Winchester: Zero Books, 2009).
[12] See Nussbaum, *Not for Profit*, note 5.
[13] Ibid, p. 10
[14] Cited in Nussbaum, *Not for Profit*, note 5, p. 1.
[15] Ibid, p. 1.
[16] Ivan Illich, *Deschooling Society* (London: Marion Boyars, 1995).
[17] See Herbert Marcuse, *One Dimensional Man: Studies in the Ideology of Advanced Industrial Society* (London: Routledge, 2002).
[18] Herbert Marcuse, *Counter-Revolution and Revolt* (Boston: Beacon Press, 1972).
[19] See, e.g., Donella Meadows et al, *Limits to Growth* (New York: Singlet, 1972).
[20] Marcuse, *Counter-Revolution and Revolt*, note 18, p. 79.
[21] Friedrich Schiller, *Letters on the Aesthetic Education of Man*, in Friedrich Shiller, *Essays*, eds. Walter Hinderer and Daniel Dahlstrom (New York: Continuum, 2005), p. 107.
[22] Marcuse, *Counter-Revolution and Revolt*, note 18, pp. 132-3.
[23] Herbert Marcuse, *The Aesthetic Dimension: Toward a Critique of Marxist Aesthetics* (London: MacMillan Education, 1979), p 10.
[24] David Cox, *Sign Wars: The Culture Jammers Strike Back* (Melbourne: University of Melbourne Custom Book Centre, 2010).
[25] John Jordan, 'Artivism: Injecting Imagination into Degrowth' in *Degrowth in Movements*. Available at: https://degrowth.info/blog/artivism-injecting-imagination-into-degrowth (accessed 10 January 2023).
[26] Guy Debord, *Society of the Spectacle* (London: Rebel Press, 2006).
[27] See Fisher, *Capitalism Realism*, note 11.
[28] Ibid, p. 1.
[29] Fisher, *Capitalist Realism*, note 11, p. 2.
[30] Ibid, p. 16.
[31] Ibid.
[32] Herman Hesse, *The Glass Bead Game* (London: Penguin, 1972), p. 14.
[33]Jane Bennett, *The Enchantment of Modern Life: Attachments, Crossings, Ethics* (Princeton: Princeton University Press, 2001). p. 4. I discuss Bennett further in a forthcoming essay in this collection.
[34] Ibid.
[35] David Hume, *A Treatise on Human Nature* (1739), Bk III, Part III, Sect. III.
[36] Friedrich Schiller, *Letters on the Aesthetic Education of Man*, ed. Reginald Snell (New York: Dover, 2004), p. 50.
[37] See note 21.
[38] Percy Bysshe Shelley, *A Defense of Poetry* (Boston: Ginn and Co., 1890) p. 2.

‘Politics is aesthetic in principle.’

– **Jacques Rancière**

ESSAY TWELEVE

MAKING ART WHILE THE WORLD WEEPS: POLITICAL REFLECTIONS ON AESTHETICS

Today the world is trembling with a disturbing number of global crises, ranging from the geopolitical to the financial, through to the cultural and spiritual, and extending out to the ecological. It is easy to conclude, therefore, that political practice demands an urgent and radical engagement with the unsustainable structures, goals, and values of global industrial society. This civilisation has no future – a statement that is both normative and descriptive.[1] It is normative in the sense that this civilisation *ought* to have no future, owing to its ecological contradictions and social injustices. The claim is descriptive in the sense that this civilisation *does* have no future, for the same reasons. Fortunately, there is still indeterminacy concerning when and how global industrial society becomes an historical phenomenon – there are many ends of the world. It follows that we must not sit on our hands and simply watch the ship of civilisation drift over the cliff. There are things to do!

But *what* is to be done? This is surely one of the central questions for those who are animated by what Charles Eisenstein calls 'the more beautiful world our hearts know is possible';[2] a central question for those of us with the fire of ecological democracy burning in our eyes. In this collection of essays I have been exploring the human condition through the lens of aesthetics, and have arrived at a point where I am increasingly confronted by questions of political and social import. What is the relationship between, on the one hand, the social, ecological, and political imperatives for a new civilisational trajectory, and, on the other, the aesthetic dimensions of human experience? Beyond direct political engagement – such as voting, protesting, or practising civil disobedience – might societal change also require, perhaps first and foremost, an engagement and transformation of our aesthetic sensibilities, capacities, and practices? Those questions are the guiding lines of inquiry to be explored in this essay, which I will develop by offering political reflections on aesthetics that prove indistinguishable from aesthetic reflections on politics. This relatively short analysis is designed as a primer for the longer engagement with the politics of art in the next essay.

As outlined in the introduction, aesthetics can be understood as a domain of inquiry pertaining both to *art* and the *senses*, with these two aspects often overlapping. Central considerations include not merely the meaning and function of art and the role of the artist in society, but also broader considerations pertaining to taste, beauty, judgement, perception, imagination, creativity, emotion, and sensuous or bodily experience. To now I have defended the thesis that the aesthetic dimensions of life, far from being fringe or marginal, are in fact definitory of what it means to be alive.[3] We – *homo aestheticus* – can be coherently understood as an artful species in an aesthetic universe. Our individual existence, our societies, and indeed the cosmos itself, are aesthetic to the primordial core, such that time itself can be seen as an unfolding of creative evolution.

Nevertheless, it would not be unreasonable for readers to approach my aesthetic inquiries with a degree of scepticism. After all, in an age where ecocide, financial crisis, war, and creeping fascism loom ominously on the horizon like dark clouds gathering for a perfect storm, a turn to aesthetics certainly needs justification. We find ourselves in a situation which clearly demands a radical political engagement in order to dissipate and transcend the various tragedies already taking form. How, then, could one justifiably look to poetry, literature, music, or the imagination in a world immiserated by violence, oppression, and unspeakable suffering? Wouldn't a turn to aesthetics be what Marxists sometimes call a 'pessimistic retreat'?[4]

As critical theorist Herbert Marcuse noted when he began his own meditation on aesthetics: 'It would be senseless to deny the element of despair inherent in this concern: the retreat into a world of fiction where existing conditions are changed only in the imagination.'[5] At first, aesthetic concerns might seem like a petty indulgence or trivial distraction, reserved for the comfortable few who do not have to worry about the problems of the real world. Art, one might contend, is not a serious subject for the activist or theorist of political economy. Philosopher Emmanuel Levinas went further when he stated that 'there is something wicked and egoist and cowardly in artistic enjoyment. There are times when one can be ashamed of it, as of feasting during a plague.'[6] In the same critical spirit, philosopher and novelist Simone de Beauvoir once dismissed art as 'a position of withdrawal, a way of fleeing the truth of the present.'[7] These critiques imply that one should not make or enjoy art while the world weeps. There are more important things to do.

Even if one were not persuaded that that art is positively wicked or egotistical, an objection might still arise that condemns art for being *useless*, in the sense of it not being able to change the world. Artists must not merely interpret or represent the world; the point is to change it! Did anyone lay down their guns after seeing Picasso's evocative critique of fascism in *Guernica*? The poet W.H. Auden would reflect with some despondency that 'poetry makes nothing happen,' lamenting that 'all the verse I wrote, all the positions I took in the thirties, did not save a single Jew.'[8] In a manuscript he worked on in 1939 we read:

> Artists and politicians would get along better at a time of crisis like the present, if the latter would only realize that the political history of the world would have been the same if not a poem had been written, nor a picture painted, nor a bar of music composed.[9]

I have been attempting to deconstruct such simplistic dismissals of aesthetics by examining the blurry distinction between art, life, and politics. Continuing that project, my purpose in this essay (and the next one) is to show that there is in fact an inherent aesthetic dimension to politics, just as there is a political or even revolutionary potential inherent to certain forms of art or aesthetic practice. In doing so, the analysis is shaped by the emerging 'aesthetic turn'[10] in political theory, and by various political interpretations of art and aesthetics. My approach is to mix and develop these substantive bodies of thought in the hope that this alchemy produces a deeper understanding of the nexus that conjoins (as it attempts to separate) art, life, and politics.

To be clear, my premise is not that we *should* or *should not* infuse politics with aesthetic considerations, but rather, as Jacques Rancière states, that 'politics is aesthetic in principle.'[11] Terry Eagleton makes a similar point when acknowledging that the aesthetic is 'politics in non-political disguise.'[12] The insight here is that politics has various aesthetic dimensions which should not be ignored. Most fundamentally, politics is shaped and even underpinned by social narratives about what is possible, proper, and important. These narratives, often supported by imagery, icons, public gestures, and soundbites, are critical not only in how citizens *think* about political life but, perhaps more importantly, how they *feel* about it – and thus how they act and vote. Usually operating beneath the level of consciousness, social narratives, myths, and stories both reveal and conceal possible forms of life, colouring them with value-laden judgements about their worth. Thus, political society is both enabled and constrained by the aesthetic soil in which it is rooted. Change the soil, and different things can grow, and in different ways.

Consequently, an *effective* politics must be an *affective* politics, engaging the heart as much as the head (a distinction always threatening to collapse). This implies that political messaging that conveys societal hopes, dreams, fears, and promises, must be communicated effectively, for even the best policies, programs, or social movements will fail if they are unable to successfully appeal to the public imagination. Good ideas need to be powerful ideas – or else they will be condemned to being good but ineffective. Political argumentation, therefore, is not merely about providing 'reasons' or winning the political debate through the non-coercive force of 'better arguments'. Rather, political success is partly about creating imaginative and emotional space that allows people to believe that 'other ways' of doing things are possible. This involves the aesthetic challenge of opening up alternative political spaces and contexts where new visions of self and society can be received in aesthetically engaging and digestible ways.[13]

Poet-philosopher Friedrich Schiller argued, 'the way to the head must lie through the heart.'[14] This is not in any way an anti-intellectual or anti-scientific position. Schiller offered the profound and subtle insight that through the works of artists and aesthetic experience, the intellect can be engaged most effectively *having first affected or shifted the emotions*. Note that this is a politically neutral insight. Aesthetics is a tool that can be employed to advance either progressive or regressive agendas, just as fire can be useful or harmful depending on how it is used. Accordingly, it is no objection to a political vision that it is, at base, aesthetic. The critical issues to be addressed are *how* politics is aesthetic, to what *ends*, and for *whose benefit*.

When the public imagination expands or contracts, political space for radical innovation and progress can be created or enclosed. A utopian vision, for example, can be understood as an imaginative and sensuous extension of our socio-political concepts, understandings, and pathways. Such visions can be progressive or transgressive if they energise a citizenry for political participation. They can be regressive or conservative, however, if they merely mislead, distract, or sedate a population with unrealisable fantasies (or with realisable cruelties). Furthermore, in a world where public consciousness is shaped to varying degrees by media and marketing, it becomes clear that a 'politics of attention' is always and everywhere at play.[15] Some issues are brought to the surface of public discourse, not necessarily because they are the most pressing; while other matters, often the most pressing, can be pushed to the margins, usually because they are not politically useful or expedient.

This is one example of what Rancière calls a 'distribution of the sensible',[16] a framework for understanding how political decisions, actions, and narratives determine what presents itself to sense experience. In other words, politics shapes what can be seen, felt, and spoken about – and by whom. At the same time, in a dialectical fashion, what can be seen, felt, and spoken about shapes politics. This is to say, the aesthetic sensibilities of a citizenry provide the contours within which realisable political action takes place.

Of course, the inherent aesthetic dimensions of politics complicate the very valid concern over how aestheticising politics gives rise to the spectre of fascism. One way to understand fascism is precisely in aesthetic terms – a totalitarian government entrenching and expanding power and authority by using the mechanisms of mythology, narrative, and propaganda to glorify a nation-state and to scapegoat enemies. Such scapegoating can deflect attention away from internal societal difficulties and thereby operate as a counter-revolutionary force. By these means the aesthetic can be a tool for igniting national passion, fervour, and obedience, exemplified by the spectacle of Nazi films like *Triumph of the Will*. As scholar Desmond Manderson writes, 'the emotive paraphernalia of fascism – propaganda films, marching troops, flags, insignia, and the rest – clearly recognised the potential that aesthetics held to marshal collective experience as a powerful social force.'[17]

Linked to these issues is concern over how the application of aesthetic criteria to politics can produce callous and inhumane results. Mussolini's son-in-law compared the bombs exploding among fleeing Ethiopians in 1936 to flowers bursting into bloom. Mussolini himself once boasted that:

> when the masses are like wax in my hands, or when I mingle with them and almost crushed by them, I feel myself to be a part of them. All the same there persists in me a certain feeling of aversion, like that which the modeler feels for the clay he is molding. Does not the sculptor sometimes smash his block of marble into fragments because he cannot shape it into the vision he has conceived?[18]

Another notorious example is the response given by the poet Laurent Tailhade to a deadly anarchist bomb thrown into the French Chamber of Deputies in 1893: 'What do the victims matter if the gesture is beautiful?' As philosopher Martin Jay writes: 'The aestheticization of politics in these cases repels not merely because of the grotesque impropriety of applying criteria of beauty to the deaths of human beings, but also because of the chilling way in which nonaesthetic criteria are deliberately and provocatively excluded from consideration.'[19]

Walter Benjamin, writing in a time of rising fascism in Europe, sounded a warning that remains relevant today: 'All efforts to aestheticize politics culminate in one point. That one point is war.'[20] While this warning needs to be taken seriously, I challenge Benjamin's claims that '[t]he logical result of Fascism is the introduction of aesthetics into political life.'[21] My position is that aesthetics is *always and already* a part of political life, and Fascism is just a particularly objectionable form of this inevitable intermingling. It follows that one cannot merely advocate for aesthetic education, in general, as a means of societal progress. After all, as Paul de Man once wrote, under fascist ideology, aesthetic education 'succeeds all too well, to the point of hiding the violence that makes it possible.'[22]

If fascism is an obscene and disturbing example of *aestheticising politics*, Soviet communism was an example of the *politicisation of aesthetics*.[23] This means more than merely appropriating art and culture as vehicles for ideological communication and propaganda. It can refer to the ways in which Stalin and the Communist Party provided the political filter through which art had to proceed. Any artists that produced work that criticised or resisted Party rule or undermined the socialist imaginary, were at high risk of being murdered or sent to the gulags.

Conversely, Socialist Realism – the 'official style' of the Soviet Union from 1922-1988 – became one of few 'legitimate' forms of art. What this style required was a promotion of communist values and the expression of ideas and visions that celebrated the proletariat. It was believed that such instrumental art could assist in the cultural education of citizens to be ideal Soviets. During the Soviet Congress of 1934, four guidelines were laid out for Socialist Realism. The work must be: 1. Proletarian: art relevant to the workers and understandable to them; 2. Typical: scenes of everyday life of the people; 3. Realistic: in the representational sense; and 4. Partisan: supportive of the aims of the State and the Party. This naturally resulted in art that would depict scenes celebrating the revolution or workers happily labouring in the field or factory in post-revolutionary society. The truth or otherwise of these images or scenes was not the point. Politicising art in this way reduces or abolishes art's critical function, becoming merely a handmaiden to politics.

I argued earlier, however, that politics is inherently and inescapably aesthetic, and thus aesthetics is something that shapes *every society*, including those with a liberal democratic self-image. In advanced capitalist societies today, where mass media have been concentrated in the hands of a few (often private hands), the potential to manipulate public consciousness with the subtle or not so subtle art of propaganda is perhaps historically unrivalled. This is a power shaped by aesthetics. Indeed, the aestheticisation of politics under capitalism creates and condones what Marxist theorist Guy Debord called the 'Society of the Spectacle.'[24] That is, the programming of mass media risks creating – or perhaps has already created – a passive, obedient citizenry that is willing to embrace its own servitude so long as it is distracted and entertained. This has helped entrench the 'one-dimensional society' and the 'culture industry' of which the Frankfurt school warned in the twentieth century. These concepts of critical theory were developed to highlight the smooth, comfortable, democratic 'unfreedom' present in advanced industrial societies. Looking toward the United States, especially, the Frankfurt school suggested that this paragon of capitalism was being shaped by its own forces of fascism, albeit in cultural disguise.[25] Benjamin would bitterly observe that 'self-alienation has reached such a degree that [humankind] can experience its own destruction as an aesthetic pleasure of the first order.'[26]

In this context the affective dimensions of political authority and submission should also be acknowledged. The eighteenth-century theorist of conservatism, Edmund Burke, wrote of the 'delight' that citizens can take in their own subordination.[27] His terminology of 'proud submission' and 'dignified obedience' points to the role affect can play in maintaining and naturalising the existing order of things.[28] Burke's conservative instincts also identified a worrying aesthetic energy that radicals and revolutionaries were displaying as they watched the French Revolution unfold. We can go further back, to antiquity, and recall that it was Plato who defended the policy of governments telling a 'noble lie' to the masses in order to maintain the social order through fabricated stories about natural hierarchies.[29]

But if politics, like power itself, is *inherently* aesthetic, highlighting those dimensions is not an invitation to fascism but a warning against it. Michel Foucault said of power that it is not necessarily evil, but it is always dangerous – because power is everywhere.[30] And because it is everywhere, we always have something to do: 'my position leads not to apathy,' Foucault said, 'but to a hyper- and pessimistic activism.'[31] One could say the same thing concerning the role of aesthetics in politics. It is pointless regretting the fact that politics is aesthetic in principle, any more than we should regret gravity, because this is simply a feature of the ways things are. And so acknowledging the aesthetic dimensions of politics certainly should not be assumed to be a prologue to tyranny. As Martin Jay argues, '[t]he wholesale critique of "the aesthetic ideology"... can thus be itself deemed ideological if it fails to register the divergent implications of the application of the aesthetic to politics.'[32]

Accordingly, it makes little sense to talk of the 'modern aestheticisation of politics' since, again, politics is and has always been aesthetic in principle, even as one can accept that it takes on new and often worrying forms in technocratic society of the twenty-first century. A fascist aestheticisation of politics is always worryingly possible – a spectre to be on guard against. But if politics is inherently aesthetic then the question is: what will be done with this critically important tool? What is not possible is a politics entirely devoid of aesthetic dimensions. The perennial challenge, therefore, is to ensure that the tools of aesthetics are used out in the open, rather than insidiously sharpened and employed by oligarchs and elites in the dark corridors of political and financial power. If such risks are not respected, we might, as George Orwell warned in *1984*, casually usher in a future whose image is a boot stamping on the human face – forever.

There are alternative futures, however, based on human emancipation and ecological viability. My overarching argument in this collection of essays is that any hope for deep revision in the established politico-economic order depends on acknowledging, appreciating, and operating within the aesthetic dimension. It is one thing to establish firm scientific, ethical, and philosophical foundations for an alternative form of societal organisation. But if there is no *felt need* in society for such a political transformation then this can be understood in part as an aesthetic obstacle that demands an aesthetic intervention or series of interventions. J.G. Ballard once wrote: 'Many of the great cultural shifts that prepare the way for political change are largely aesthetic.'[33]

A major prerequisite to societal transformation, as Marcuse recognised, is 'the fact that the need for radical change must be rooted in the subjectivity of individuals themselves, in their intelligence and their passions, their drives, and their goals.'[34] Specifically with respect to the 'advanced capitalist societies', currently these felt needs are, for the most part, absent, confused, or severely underdeveloped. It follows that the ongoing neglect of the aesthetic realm is a mistake that political movements for human emancipation and sustainability cannot afford to make. The critical role of art and culture is not merely to assist with transgressive political communication or social education. It also plays a role prosecuting the existing order, of holding politics to account, not merely ushering in the new. More deeply still, art is tasked with *undoing* the alienation of the corporeal sensorium, the felt needs of the body, and to restore the instinctual power of the human bodily senses for the sake of the preservation and flourishing of humanity and the planet.[35] Having laid the groundwork for an aesthetic analysis of politics, I will delve more deeply into these matters in the next essay, through an exploration of Marcuse's aesthetic writings on the relationships between art, politics, and revolt.

---

[1] Rupert Read and Samuel Alexander, *This Civilisation is Finished: Conversations on the End of Empire – And What Lies Beyond* (Melbourne: Simplicity Institute, 2019).

[2] Charles Eisenstein, *The More Beautiful World Our Hearts Know is Possible* (Berkeley: North Atlantic Books, 2013).

[3] See Samuel Alexander, 'Introduction: The Aesthetic Dimension' and 'Creative Evolution and the "Will to Art', in this collection of essays. The full set will be published

here: http://samuelalexander.info/s-m-p-l-c-t-y-ecological-civilisation-and-the-will-to-art/ (accessed 10 May 2023).
[4] See Pauline Johnson, *Marxist Aesthetics: The Foundations Without Everyday Life for an Emancipated Consciousness* (Abingdon: Routledge, 2011) p. 3.
[5] Herbert Marcuse, *The Aesthetic Dimension: Toward a Critique of Marxist Aesthetics* (London: MacMillan Education, 1979), p. 1.
[6] Emmanuel Levinas, 'Reality and its Shadow' in Sean Hand (ed.) *The Levinas Reader* (Oxford: Basil Blackwell, 1989), p. 142.
[7] Simone de Beauvoir, *The Ethics of Ambiguity* (New York: Open Road, 2015), p. 81.
[8] Quoted in Artur Danto, 'The Philosophical Disenfranchisement of Art' ((1985) *Grand Street* 4(3): p. 172.
[9] Ibid.
[10] See generally, Nikolas Kompridis (ed.) *The Aesthetic Turn in Political Thought* (New York: Bloomsbury, 2014).
[11] Jacques Rancière, *Dis-Agreement* (London: University of Minnesota Press, 2006), p. 58.
[12] Terry Eagleton, *Culture and the Death of God* (New Haven: Yale University Press, 2015), p. 123.
[13] See, e.g., Ernesto Laclau, *The Rhetorical Foundations of Society* (London: Verso, 2014).
[14] Friedrich Schiller, *Letters on the Aesthetic Education of Man*, in Friedrich Shiller, *Essays*, eds. Walter Hinderer and Daniel Dahlstrom (New York: Continuum, 2005), pp. 86-178.
[15] See generally, Peter Doran, *The Political Economy of Attention, Mindfulness and Consumerism: Reclaiming the Mindful Commons* (London: Routledge, 2017); see also, Bryan Jones and Frank Baumgartner, *The Politics of Attention: How Government Prioritizes Problems* (Chicago: University of Chicago, 2005, new edition).
[16] Jacques Rancière, *The Politics of Aesthetics* (New York: Continuum, 2006), p. 12.
[17] Desmond Manderson, 'Here and Now: From "Aestheticizing Politics" to "Politicizing Art"' (2016) *NoFo* 13: p. 3.
[18] I draw these examples from Martin Jay, '"The Aesthetic Ideology" as Ideology: Or, What Does it Mean to Aestheticize Politics?' (1992) *Cultural Critique* 21: pp. 42-5.
[19] Ibid, p. 44.
[20] Walter Benjamin, *The Work of Art in the Age of Mechanical Reproduction* (London: Penguin, 2008), p. 36 (emphasis removed).
[21] Ibid.
[22] Paul de Man, *The Rhetoric of Romanticism* (New York: Columbia University Press, 1984) p. 289.
[23] Ibid.
[24] Guy Debord, *Society of the Spectacle* (London: Rebel Press, 2006).
[25] Herbert Marcuse, *One Dimensional Man: Studies in the Ideology of Advanced Industrial Society* (London: Routledge, 2002); Theodor Adorno, *The Culture Industry: Selected Essays on Mass Culture* (London: Routledge, 2001).
[26] Benjamin, *The Work of Art*, note 20, p. 38.
[27] For a discussion, see Jason Frank, 'Delightful Horror', in Jason Frank, *The Democratic Sublime: On Aesthetics and Popular Assembly* (Oxford: Oxford University Press, 2021), Ch. 4.
[28] Ibid.

[29] Similarly, in the ethical domain. A case can (and will) be made that art and aesthetics have the potential to expand and refine the moral imagination, but this spiritual tool has the potential, at least, to cut both ways: the aesthetic perspective always raises the risk that someone misapplies the discipline and attempts to make the suffering of others an object of aesthetic pleasure or focusses on aesthetic pleasure in ways that marginalise or ignore the suffering of others.
[30] Michael Foucault, 'On the Genealogy of Ethics: Overview of a Work in Progress' in Michael Foucault, *Ethics: Subjectivity and Truth* (London: Penguin, 2000), p. 256.
[31] Ibid.
[32] Martin Jay, '"The Aesthetic Ideology" as Ideology: Or, What Does it Mean to Aestheticize Politics?' (1992) *Cultural Critique* 21: p. 56.
[33] See Samuel Alexander, *Art Against Empire: Toward an Aesthetics of Degrowth* (Melbourne, Simplicity Institute, 2017), p. 1.
[34] Marcuse, *Aesthetic Dimension*, note 4, pp. 3-4.
[35] Susan Buck-Morss, 'Aesthetics and Anaesthetics: Walter Benjamin's Artwork Essay Reconsidered' (1992) *October* (62): p. 5.

‘Art cannot change the world, but it can contribute to changing the consciousness and drives of the men and women who could change the world.’

‘The struggle for an expansion of the world of beauty, nonviolence, and serenity is a political struggle.’

– **Herbert Marcuse**

ART AGAINST EMPIRE: MARCUSE ON THE AESTHETICS OF REVOLT

In this essay I explore Herbert Marcuse's aesthetic writings, epitomised by his final book, *The Aesthetic Dimension: A Critique of Marxist Aesthetics* (1979).[1] In that book, and in his other aesthetic writings,[2] Marcuse questioned the 'orthodox' Marxist position on aesthetics, which can be summarised crudely as the view that art (as a cultural superstructure) is a reflection of the productive relations in society (the material base). From this perspective, works of art will tend to entrench or advance the interests and worldview of the dominant class in society, consciously or unconsciously. When the material conditions shift, so too will the aesthetic or cultural superstructure, sometimes anticipating but usually lagging the change in productive relations. Thus the role of art and aesthetics in driving social and political change is minimised, almost to a vanishing point.

This view, however, is unable to explain why art from previous societies (e.g., ancient Greece) can remain so relevant and stimulating today, despite the drastically different productive relations in society. Marcuse's explanation, contra orthodox Marxism, is that art can achieve a degree of autonomy from the material conditions of society, such that art can illuminate not merely the injustices and potentials of a particular class, in a particular society, but can speak to aspects of the human condition that seem perennial. It also implies that art need not merely reflect a society's mode of production but can transgress, indict, and surpass that material base. This means that existence and the world can be aesthetically engaged in ways that transcend a specific class society and shine through its specific social conditions. If this opening theoretical move by Marcuse is valid, as I believe it is, the base-superstructure model of art and aesthetics is called into question, inviting a deeper critique.

According to the orthodox Marxist perspective, to the extent art has a political function, the only truly progressive or revolutionary examples are those which express the material interests, and advance the class consciousness, of the proletariat. This theory of art was taken to its logical extreme in the Soviet Union and came to be known as 'Socialist Realism'. Bourgeois art is rendered merely 'decadent' in contrast. This base-superstructure schema, which is presented here more rigidly than Marx and Engels ever did,[3] has nevertheless had implications on how aesthetics is perceived as a social or political force. In particular, Marcuse maintained that by privileging the role of the 'material base' as the true or fundamental reality, this devalued the political function of individual consciousness, subjectivity, inwardness, emotion, sensuality, and imagination. To the extent that consciousness matters in this stylised Marxian framework, it is dissolved into *class* consciousness, and thus the individual remains invisible and insignificant.

By marginalising culture and individual sensibility, major drivers of revolution are minimised, and Marxism for too long has neglected the radical potential of aesthetics to induce transformative shifts in subjectivity. As Marcuse argued, 'the need for radical change must be rooted in the subjectivity of individuals themselves, in their intelligence and their passions, their drives and their goals.'[4] This political function of inward experience is devalued to the extent that 'inwardness' is dismissed as bourgeois decadence or merely escapism. The inner reality of an individual, though not a 'force of production', as such, is nevertheless decisive as a social force. Our emotions and sensibilities *constitute* our lived reality. Accordingly, something has gone astray if this inner reality is relegated to some secondary or marginal place in the social order or in social change.

Marcuse claimed that, even in bourgeois society, the affirmation of inwardness allows people to step outside market relations and exchange values, opening up space for different dimensions of being. This process itself can function to delegitimise capitalist values, by shifting focus from one's identity merely as worker or consumer to someone who embodies imagination, passion, conscience, and the capacity to create and self-govern. If this implies a certain withdrawal and retreat from market realities, it retains oppositional force provided escaping is not the last position; provided opposition does not *culminate* in withdrawal.

The critical function of art – that is, its contribution to the struggle for liberation – lies in its 'aesthetic form', which Marcuse defined as:

> the result of the transformation of a given content (actual or historical, personal or social fact) into a self-contained whole: a poem, play, novel, etc. The work is thus 'taken out' of the constant process of reality and assumes a significance and truth of its own. The aesthetic transformation is achieved through a reshaping of language, perception, and understanding so that they reveal the essence of reality in its appearance: the repressed potentialities of man and nature. The work of art thus represents reality while accusing it.[5]

We see, then, that Marcuse ascribed to art a political function. Extending Marx, he sought to show that the nature of art, by virtue of its aesthetic form, is not merely a reflection of the material base. This does not deny that the 'content' of art is always and necessarily drawn from existing society and influenced by productive relations. Art is autonomous insofar as it can transcend the constraints of the established reality, enabling the artist both to protest that reality and offer insight into an alternative one – the beautiful image of liberation. Art can thereby bring to the surface feelings, visions, and even other forms of 'reason' that are otherwise denied or unheard. The alienated character of existing society is exposed by the non-alienated or independent character of art. As art theorist Peter Burger states: 'The citizen who, in everyday life, has been reduced to a partial function (*mean-ends activity*) can be discovered in art as a "human being."'[6]

Through this process, art is able to give rise to a perceived reality that is suppressed and distorted in actual experience, exploding normal modes of communication, perception, and behaviour. Paradoxically, these new truths and insights of art, though fictional, can be more 'real' than the mystified realities of the existing society and its social institutions and norms. When art is able to transcend the established order, the perceived 'objectivity' of that reality is shattered, and this creates space for the rebirth of a rebellious sensibility. When successful, art can *define* what is real, and in this rupture, 'the fictitious world of art appears as true reality.'[7] What capitalism conceals, art can reveal.

Herein lies the potential revolutionary character of art. Marcuse recognised that art can be called 'revolutionary' in several senses. An artist can revolutionise their field through a highly original development of technique or style, signalling the avant-garde. However, Marcuse is primarily interested in the way art could be revolutionary in a different, political sense, even as the former could lead to the latter. Art is revolutionary in Marcuse's sense when it can present or re-present reality in an aesthetically transfigured way through which the unfreedom of the oppressed is highlighted and exposed, and visions of liberation are clarified or presented in energising ways. In this way, aesthetic interventions in culture can break through the mystified and petrified social conditions that entrench that unfreedom and open the horizon for radical change.[8] Indeed, the autonomy of art, Marcuse insisted, contains the categorical imperative: 'things must change.'[9]

Of course, art is not always transgressive, progressive, or critical. 'Great art has never had any problem coexisting with the horrors of reality,'[10] Marcuse admitted. It can be affirmative of the existing social order in ways that normalise, glorify, or absolve it. Marcuse noted that the militant bourgeois literature of the eighteenth century represented a struggle of the ascending class with the nobility, essentially over matters concerning bourgeois morality, not productive relations. With rare exceptions, this was not a critical literature seeking to advance the consciousness of the working class. Rather, it was content to envisage freedom merely in the imagination or within subsections of a population, displacing universal liberation to the realm of the daydream, and representing escapist illusionism or mere decoration in an otherwise miserable reality. The social order is not threatened but rather affirmed. As political theorist Charles Reitz noted, Marcuse was perfectly aware of 'the paradoxical circumstances in which the aesthetic treatment of social realities could actually lead to an *anesthetic* "tranquilization" of perception and thought.'[11] Furthermore, art that was once transgressive and oppositional can, over time, become assimilated: 'All indictments are easily absorbed by the system they indict... Picasso's *Guernica* is a cherished museum piece.'[12]

Still, there can be a role for art that criticises the existing reality without providing a way forward in Marxian terms. In the nineteenth century, the poet Baudelaire was hardly a prophet for the working class, but as Walter Benjamin observed, he 'was a secret agent, an agent of the secret discontent of his class with its own rule. One who confronts Baudelaire with this class gets more out of him than one who rejects him as uninteresting from a proletarian standpoint.'[13] The self-indictment of art can help invalidate reality through subterranean rebellion, even if it does not always point to a new society.

There is also a question here about whether art is being assigned a role which is better suited to theory. If social critique relies on conceptual analysis, this may not suit the medium of literature, poetry, music, etc. However, Marcuse argued that because people are constituted by an unfree society, their 'repressed and distorted potentialities can be represented only in an *estranging* form... and only as estrangement does art fulfill its *cognitive* function: it communicates truths not communicable any other way.'[14]

Any realisation of free and classless society presupposes 'a radical transformation of the drives and needs of the individual.'[15] This hopeful vision raises the prospect of the 'end of art', since in a free society one might imagine the traditional function of art would become obsolete. Images of beauty and freedom would cease to have a critical role to play to the extent that beauty and freedom are no longer denied by society and have become aspects of reality. The emergence of such free and beautiful social relations, however, are incompatible with capitalist society, or even with a socialist society that tries to compete with capitalism on the former's terms.[16]

Even in a radically transformed society, this would not signal the end of art, since Marcuse recognised that there are limits to freedom and fulfilment by virtue of the human condition. Human beings will remain embedded in nature as tragically suffering creatures. Thus, art will forever retain a transhistorical role and significance. The vision of establishing social conditions for the development of the life-enhancing faculties of humanity is an ideal that ought to be pursued but will never be finally achieved. Art must appeal to a consciousness that is able to participate in the furtherance of this species' defining project.

Marcuse's next questions was: who is assumed to be the *subject* of this revolutionary consciousness? According to orthodox Marxist aesthetics, the subject is the proletarian, who has no interest in preserving the existing society. As outlined elsewhere in these essays,[17] this radical consciousness does not (yet?) exist in advanced capitalist societies, for it seems that the proletariat has been more or less fully integrated in the existing order in ways that Marx never anticipated. Furthermore, under capitalism, the exploited populations extend far beyond the conventional proletariat and comprise a large proportion of the so-called middle class. This includes white collar workers, government bureaucrats, and those in the service and information sectors.

The result, according to fellow critical theorist Theodor Adorno, is for art to take an extreme form – as uncompromising estrangement and radical autonomy.[18] While Marcuse acknowledged that this can make art appear elitist or decadent, removed from the class struggle, he nevertheless maintained that such estranged art remains authentic by opposing society through its very estrangement. But still, he added, 'the subject to which authentic art appeals is socially anonymous; it does not coincide with the potential subject of revolutionary practice.'[19]

The point here is that the consciousness needed to change society and emancipate people from the rule of capital does not yet exist. In a celebrated passage Marcuse declared: 'Art cannot change the world, but it can contribute to changing the consciousness and drives of the men and women who could change the world.'[20] But if revolutionary art is supposed to speak the language of the people, who are 'the people'? The contradiction here, as Marcuse and others in the Frankfurt School contended, is that there does not seem to be a large mass of people ready to receive the radical vision of the counterculture. There is at most a militant minority.

The vexed problem that follows is that it is not clear why art should speak the language of the people if that language is not yet the language of liberation.[21] For example, little is to be achieved if a culture thinks that the existential malaise caused by consumerism can only be solved by more consumption; or if the ecological problems caused by capitalist growth and extraction can only be solved by more of the same. Until some form of transformation of consciousness occurs, artists cannot simply speak the language of the people. Instead, Marcuse argued, artists 'must rather first create this [oppositional] place, and this is a process which may require them to stand against the people, which may prevent them from speaking their language.'[22] This is the sense in which 'elitism' in aesthetic practice today can retain a radical content. 'To work for the radicalization of consciousness means to make explicit and conscious the material and ideological discrepancy between the writer [or artist more broadly] and "the people" rather than obscure and camouflage it. Revolutionary art may well become the "Enemy of the People."'[23]

Marcuse's work is premised, nonetheless, on the need for political struggle and that such struggle depends on a radical change in consciousness. This refers not merely to a shift in political outlook but a deeper transformation of human needs and drives that are emancipated from the dictates of the existing order. The transformative potential of art presupposes that the people administered by capitalism are able to 'unlearn the language, concepts, and images of this administration, that they experience the dimension of qualitative change, that they reclaim their subjectivity, their inwardness.'[24] This is no limp celebration of escapism, but rather a recognition that the subversion of experience and the creation of new universes are birthed from within, and only later achieved outwardly. A new consciousness will not emerge unaided – nor will a new society.

The aesthetic method

The question becomes: *how* can art transfigure consciousness in a way that leads to post-capitalist political praxis? I propose that there are several modes of aesthetic operation, including but not limited to: (i) aesthetic indictment; (ii) aesthetic imagination (both visionary and moral); (iii) an aesthetic revision of 'needs'; and (iv) aesthetic enchantment. This is my categorisation, not Marcuse's, but by and large it can be placed over his aesthetic theory without being forced. I will now briefly consider these four modes in turn.

Aesthetic indictment

An aesthetics of indictment relates to the capacity of art to expose how the established reality oppresses sectors of society, or does violence against things one cares about, in ways that are not always obvious or have even been embraced by the oppressed. By redescribing 'normality', the status quo can come to seem abnormal, unacceptable, even obscene, giving voice to undercurrents of cultural disillusionment. What had been subconscious or unconscious is raised to the surface of experience, reshaping and transfiguring what is perceived and how it is perceived.

There can be an intellectual or cognitive component to this redescription, but most importantly it is felt in the body. What had been tolerable becomes viscerally intolerable. Something must be *done*. Thus, a new subjectivity of rebellion – or affect *for* rebellion – can emerge through aesthetic intervention, born of outrage. The complacent consciousness can be shaken awake, and ordinary categories or frames for interpreting miserable reality can be interrupted and disrupted. In a 'one-dimensional society', art can invite us to question reality and reassert the plurality of possible worlds. To the extent that we have become puppets manipulated by the forces of capital and technology, art threatens to cut the strings and liberate us through the very act of exposing our condition as puppets. Marcuse made the point as follows:

> Experience is intensified to breaking point... The intensification of perception can go as far as to distort things so that the unspeakable is spoken, the otherwise invisible becomes visible, and the unbearable explodes. Thus the aesthetic transformation turns into indictment – but also into a celebration of that which resists injustice and terror, and of that which can still be saved.[25]

In this way, through an encounter with art – being powerfully challenged by aesthetic indictment and the celebration of revolt – we can find that, in some way, human consciousness gets restructured. A different moral sensibility can emerge that grounds new ways of seeing, feeling, and acting. When a new generation grows up adopting and normalising these redescriptions, we find that the world has changed. This is perhaps why Percy Bysshe Shelley was prepared to declare that 'poets are the unacknowledged legislators of the world',[26] suggesting that aesthetic revolutions often precede revolutions in political economy, sometimes in subtle ways. As quoted in an earlier essay, J.G. Ballard once stated that 'many of the great cultural shifts that prepare the way for political change are largely aesthetic.'

Aesthetic imagination (visionary)

Beyond the negation of indictment, art is also the promise of liberation and can point to new forms of prosperity. Art and aesthetic interventions in culture can offer or invent alternative mythologies of existence, expanding the imagination in ways that make new ways of living and being comprehensible, plausible, and attractive. These visions or creations are only appearances – they cannot be *realised* in the domain of art alone. But they do threaten to develop social and political significance when they move from the imagination into the body, guiding action, providing hope, opening new intellectual and emotional possibilities, and thereby shattering the oppressive conformism of the present. This significance presumably can be felt both in the artist and the audience, both creator and spectator, especially insofar as aesthetic engagement is itself an act of creation (e.g., through interpretation).

Aesthetically creating new mythopoetic foundations of a society underpins everything else that follows – including politics and economics. This is because myth and narrative are what structure and rework the popular imagination, including the consciousness of the agents of change. Politics and economics always operate in the service of story, so what that story is obviously matters a great deal. But a culture's 'story' is never stable, nor are the values, meanings, and possibilities implicit in any given story. Fiction and the imagination can open up new realities, just as, through art, old worlds can be made new. The artist does not escape reality, then, but augments and expands reality.

In an age when it can sometimes seem as if there is no alternative to the carbon-intensive, consumer way of life, being exposed to new ways of living and being through art has the potential to expand and radicalise the imagination. In this way, 'the world of a work of art is "unreal" in the ordinary sense of the word: it is a fictitious reality. But it is "unreal" not because it is less, but because it is also more as well as qualitatively "other" than the established reality. As a fictitious world, as illusion, it contains more truth than does everyday reality.'[27]

At such times, more hopeful and liberated futures can flicker in and out of existence, demanding that we *choose* a future where once we had thought there was no alternative to the status quo. In these moments, when we are able to break through the crust of conventional thinking and feeling, we see that the world, as it is, is not how it has to be. One might think of utopian novels like William Morris' *News from Nowhere* (1890; to be discussed in later essay)[28] or, more recently, *The Ministry for the Future* (2020) by Kim Stanley Robinson. These authors give imaginative content to futures that were otherwise barely thinkable, reshaping the contours of what is possible by describing other worlds in engaging and creative ways. This type of work has two primary functions: first, a cognitive one, by expanding the imagination regarding possible worlds; second, an affective one, by shifting our emotional states on account of the cognitive shift that has taken place (or, conversely, by shifting emotional states that *enable* a cognitive shift to occur). It is that emotional shift which can ultimately lead to shifts in behaviour, producing acts of resistance and renewal that try to change the world, and sometimes succeed in doing so.

Marcuse offered a cautionary note, however, regarding how 'directly' art should present its message. He resisted the notion of 'instrumentalist' art whose purpose it is to advance a political cause, and would sooner see radical potential in art that is less direct, doing its work in a more subterranean way. 'The more immediately political the work of art is, the more it reduces the power of estrangement and the radical, transcendent goals of change.'[29] When exercised well, the aesthetic imagination can change us as it changes reality, requiring a new set of relationships to be established between self, other, and world. Imagining a different future, therefore, is a necessary step in its realisation, even if it is only a first step.

Faced with aesthetic statements of how life can be different – if only, at first, in the fictional world of art – the structures and narratives that define the contours of the human situation can suddenly seem less compelling. The world's perceived objectivity can be shattered. The 'real' starts getting redefined. New, less violent or oppressive future pathways are cut into the landscape of the human journey. Initially this takes place only in the realm of the imagination, but that is a necessity, for 'what other faculty other than the imagination could invoke the sensuous presence of that which is *not* (yet?)?'[30] Marx and Engels, and most of the key figures of the Frankfurt School, were always cautious (often dismissive) about envisioning what the 'new society' might look like. But if ever that position were justified historically, it seems unjustified today. Action needs to be *motivated* by visions of an alternative, and ought to be guided by a map, even if that map must be constantly revised.

This offers some insight into why art has transformative or revolutionary potential and always threatens to perform a political function, albeit usually indirectly. One of the most important roles of the artist in society is not merely to make beautiful objects, images, stories, or songs, but to expand conditions of possibility by breaking through the petrified social reality and unshackling the human imagination. Far from representing an escape from reality, art and the artist can in fact expose the falseness and contingency of the established order, leaving the truth of alternative realities more accessible. As philosopher and novelist Mark Burch says: 'When all appeals to reason have failed, tell a new story.'[31]

But Marcuse insisted that the promises of art must not be made too easily:

> If art were to promise that at the end good would triumph over evil, such a promise would be refuted by the historical truth. In reality it is evil

> which triumphs, and there are only islands of good where one can find refuge for a brief time.'[32]

In any case, '[a]rt cannot redeem its promise, and reality offers no promises, only chances.'[33] As noted earlier, art itself cannot change the world, it can only change the minds and sensibilities of *people* who must then act in the world to change it. Marcuse claimed that the 'indictment and the promise preserved in art lose their unreal or utopian character to the degree to which they inform the strategy of oppositional movements...'[34] The hope which art represents must not remain 'ideal' – again, this is art's hidden categorical imperative. It must not point to a world of *mere* fiction or fantasy, but articulate through aesthetic form the *concrete possibilities* that call for realisation.

Beyond the visions of liberation and happiness, the aesthetic imagination can also offer *dystopian* futures. These extrapolate the present into the future to highlight the gravity of what is at stake if current trajectories are not changed. Whereas the positive futures seek to motivate out of hope, the dystopian future is designed to motivate out of fear – fear of losing what one loves and holds most dear. At the extreme lie novels like George Orwell's, *1984*, or Cormac McCarthy's, *The Road* – breathtakingly grim pictures of possible human futures, designed to shake us awake. Whether optimistic or pessimistic, imagining alternative future pathways is designed to break us away from the complacency of routine ways of seeing, feeling, and acting, establishing the conditions for alternative modes of consciousness.

Aesthetic imagination (moral)

Most of what I've just described could apply to the 'visionary imagination' – art that helps expand our perspectives on the future, or shift our perspectives on the present, in ways that influence our sensibilities and shape our action. But we could also speak of the aesthetic expansion of the 'moral imagination' (which, at times, can overlap with the visionary imagination). From this perspective, the moral imagination can refer to what philosopher Wilfred Sellars called 'we-intentions' or 'we-consciousness.'[35] Expanding the realm of sympathy, care, and concern is a marker of moral progress, as we come to include more people in the category of 'us'.

How might the moral imagination expand? Neo-pragmatist philosopher Richard Rorty has made a compelling case that art – the novel, in particular – is a far more effective means of provoking an expanded moral or ethical sensibility, and reshaping social relations in the world, than logic, science, or books of moral philosophy.[36] Indeed, Rorty argued that paradigm shifts in human culture, science, and political economy rarely occur because a society has been rationally convinced, based on the evidence, of a new framework of understanding. Instead, such revolutions are usually a result of a new 'sentimental education,'[37] that is, a result of creative interventions in the dominant story whereby many significant aspects of the old mode of understanding have been *redescribed* in new and emotionally engaging ways.

Rorty suggested that the emotions we have toward others depend on 'the liveliness of our imagination', rather than on 'facts' that are 'discoverable independently of sentiment.'[38] He provided the example of Harriet Beecher Stove's novel *Uncle Tom's Cabin* (1852), a book that redescribed slave society in the United States in ways that expanded the moral compass of many white readers, as they came to see slaves as people, just like them, rather than creatures for whom moral concern was not required. Readers came to feel sympathy with slaves, and feel shame about the existing conditions, in ways that they previously did not. Social relations were somehow demystified, social conditioning was undermined, and aspects of the world were seen in a new light as ethical attention shifted focus. Through the 'true illusions' of art, reality was delegitimised.

Philosopher Martha Nussbaum makes a similar point when she defends the humanities and the liberal arts ability to refine character and foster compassion, noting that 'the ability to imagine the experience of another – a capacity almost all human beings possess in some form – needs to be greatly enhanced and refined if we are to have any hope of sustaining decent institutions across the many divisions that any modern society contains.'[39] By exposing ourselves to new and unusual stories, about people different to 'us', we minimise the chances of being confined to a single, myopic perspective on the world and increase the chances of expanding our sympathies. This does not diminish the role of reasoning in ethical progress, but acknowledges that our emotions and sentiments play an essential role in rational argument.[40] After all, we only reason about things we care about, and thus sentimental education – through art – provides the foundation for moral debate and ethical progress.

Marcuse gave a disturbing example that testifies to the truth of art, highlighting its power to enchant and soften the sharp edges of humanity – if we let it. He told the story of how Lenin resolved not to listen to Beethoven's sonatas, which he admired so deeply, because he feared they would enforce a humanitarian spirit on him which he felt obliged to reject. 'All too often,' Lenin admitted, 'I cannot listen to music. It would work on one's nerves. One would rather babble nonsense, and caress the heads of people who live in dirty hell and who nevertheless can create such beauty. But today one should not caress anyone's heads – one's hand would be bitten off. One must beat heads, beat unmercifully – although ideally we are against all violence.'[41] Totalitarian governments acknowledge the power of art through the ferocity of their censorship. If art did not threaten the power structures of political society, presumably novelists, poets, and playwrights would be free to write whatever they wanted, no matter how critical.

Aesthetic revision of 'needs'

Capitalism does not merely produce things. It conditions the subjectivities and sensibilities of human beings. In affluent societies today, the system goes beyond the provision of material needs and constructs the rationalities, desires, and sense experience of people. As noted in a previous essay, Jacques Rancière uses the rather infelicitous phrase 'the distribution of the sensible'[42] to politicise this aesthetic reality, exploring how the structures of political economy not only distribute material wealth and power amongst a population, but also sensuous and aesthetic experience. A new political economy, therefore, would not only redistribute wealth and power, but change what people are able to feel or not feel, and in what ways. Rancière invites us to consider how political decisions, actions, and narratives determine what presents itself to sense experience; that is, how politics shapes what can be seen, felt, and spoken about – and by whom. Marcuse's aesthetic theory sheds light on how art can contribute to changing or destabilising the existing distribution of the sensible.

As material wealth expanded over recent centuries, one might have thought that wealth would have become less important and desired; that affluent societies, in particular, would have recognised the diminishing marginal utility of money, and redirected social energies toward non-materialistic pursuits. But somehow, the diminishing returns have been not just disguised but inverted. Growth in consumption seems more important than ever, as if we have been conditioned against the desire for freedom. In the relentless pursuit of 'more' – a goal that it was assumed would liberate us – we have bound ourselves to a conception of progress that perpetuates our servitude while at the same time making ecological devastation a way of life.

Why is this so? And by what means? In affluent societies, people have become objects of administration, even as we are offered the prefabricated 'freedoms' of consumer choice. And through this administration – the operation of which is sometimes transparent, often insidious – we reproduce the commodities that are needed for profitable enterprise. But we also reproduce the values and practices that turn the cogs of the industrial machine. The technological capacity to shape public consciousness has never been more powerful, facilitated by the internet and social media. If we were ever to wonder why most social media platforms are 'free' (i.e., of no financial cost to the user), it would become clear that it is because they are not selling a product but creating one. The product is us – a docile, distracted, and subservient population.

The 'needs' that have been engineered into us have a stabilising, conservative force: the counterrevolution of capitalism has become embedded in the structure of our instincts and 'second nature'. Marcuse argued that this 'militates against any change that would disrupt and perhaps even abolish the dependence of man on a market ever more densely filled with merchandise – abolish his existence as a consumer consuming himself in buying and selling.'[43] But exploitation does not become less exploitative just because wage slaves are 'compensated' with superfluous comforts they have been educated to need. Still, this reality has turned the mass of the population into a conservative, even counter-revolutionary, force. Quantitative progress in an economy's growth militates against the qualitative changes that are needed regarding what the economy is *for*. Leisure is provided merely to regenerate workers so they can get back to work.

We have arrived at a stage in history where we cannot transcend the existing system without transcending ourselves. That is, we must liberate ourselves from the exploitative apparatus of this society but first we must free ourselves from what we have been made into. As explained in a previous essay, the aesthetic condition of 'play', as theorised by Friedrich Schiller, is precisely the state in which we are most likely to be able to question our 'normal sense' of self.[44] This presents us with a vicious circle however, as Marcuse recognised: 'the rupture with the self-propelling conservative continuum of needs must *precede* the revolution which is to usher in a new society, but such a rupture itself can only be envisaged in a revolution...'[45]

No radical change is possible without the emergence of a new sensibility, a new universe of desires and aspirations – and thus new agents of society's radical reconstruction. This qualitative change must occur in the infrastructure of our very being, itself a dimension of the infrastructure of society at large.[46] Marcuse wrote that 'the new direction, the new institutions and relations of production, must express the ascent of needs and satisfactions very different from and even antagonistic to those prevalent in the exploitative societies.'[47] The roots of capitalism lie within us, which is the system's greatest achievement but also its greatest weakness. After all, we have seen both in our biological inheritance as *homo aestheticus* and our philosophical condition as 'self-fashioners' that we have the capacity to make something new from what we've been made into.[48]

Marcuse claimed, however, that:

> capitalism cannot satisfy the needs which it creates. The rising standard of living itself expresses this dynamic: it enforced the constant creation of needs that could be satisfied in the market; it is now fostering *transcending* needs which cannot be satisfied without abolishing the capitalist mode of production.[49]

Thus capitalism will ultimately be its own gravedigger, because it gives birth to the class of gravediggers. By liberating ourselves from ourselves, we are freer to rediscover the life-enhancing forces and sensuous aesthetic qualities that are largely absent in a life often wasted in unending competitive performance and materialistic pursuits. Without this transformation of our inner realities, the consumer mentality and its mutilated experience would merely be reproduced in the new society. Think of the closing passages in Orwell's *Animal Farm* (1945), where the animals look through the window to see their pig leaders argue with the human farmers: 'The creatures outside looked from pig to man, and from man to pig, and from pig to man again but already it was impossible to say which was which.'[50] All revolutions are at risk of merely reproducing what the revolution was meant to leave behind.

What this suggests is that the transition to a radically new type of society will not involve the broader satisfaction of existing needs, but a rupture with the needs and desires that currently define advanced capitalism. That is, there must be a *qualitative* leap not a limitless *quantitative* achievement. 'The revolution involves a radical transformation of the needs and aspirations themselves, cultural as well as material; of consciousness and sensibility; of work process as well as leisure.'[51] The emancipation of the senses, therefore, has a negative and positive function. The new sensibility will come to see the contemporary world of aggressive acquisition, competition, and (dis)possession as distasteful, repelling the violence, cruelty, and brutality those things rely upon. The new sensibility will also crave new forms of aesthetic experience in community, nature, art, creative productive activity, and leisure. 'The emancipation of the senses,' Marcuse insisted, 'would make freedom what it is not yet: a *sensuous need...*'.[52] Art can express and revitalise the longing for the realisation of human creative potential that has been deadened or lies dormant under capitalism. If the purpose of art, for Schopenhauer, was to abolish desire, it was, for Marcuse, the primary means of re-educating desire.

This does not deny the primary demand of any justifiable economy: the universal provision of basic material needs. It only points to the truism that defining our needs purely or primarily in material terms is a gross failure of imagination. It also diminishes the inherent creative capacities of our species to explore and flourish in the non-material realm of existence, especially through art and aesthetic experience. Not only does art and aesthetics provide a non-materialist source of flourishing, but these forms of experience can also help bring such a poeticized society into existence. Art, that is, can expose the falsity or artificiality of many 'needs' of the existing society – 'needs' through which a form of voluntary servitude is achieved – and give rise to 'new needs' consistent with liberation. Indeed, art could create, precisely, the *need* for freedom itself, recapturing aesthetic needs as forces of subversion and political praxis. 'Permanent aesthetic subversion,' Marcuse declared: 'this is the way of art'.[53] He added that:

> The autonomy of art reflects the unfreedom of the individuals in the unfree society. If people were free, then art would be the form and expression of their freedom. Art remains marked by unfreedom; in contradicting it, art achieves its autonomy.[54]

It would seem that one of the roles of the artist is to help people see or feel more clearly the violence too often hidden in our cultural practices and economic and political institutions. Moreover, the artist can show that there are forms of flourishing and liberation, based on new needs and a new sensibility, that lie beyond consumer culture. These forms of flourishing would not be founded upon affluence, growth, competition, and technology, but upon the visions and values of sufficiency, moderation, permaculture, community, cooperation, and self-governance. The words of poet Gary Snyder speak to this approach with eloquent insight: 'it would be best to consider this an ongoing "revolution by consciousness" which will be won not by guns but by seizing the key images, myths, archetypes, eschatologies, and ecstasies so that life won't seem worth living unless one is on the transforming energy's side'.[55] This speaks directly to the power and necessity of art and aesthetics. As Marcuse stated: 'Art represents the ultimate goal of all revolutions: the freedom and happiness of the individual,'[56] even if this must ultimately be achieved through collective action.

Aesthetic enchantment and the power of beauty

According to Marcuse, 'Marxist aesthetics has sharply rejected the idea of the Beautiful, the central category of "bourgeois" aesthetics. It seems difficult indeed to associate this concept with revolutionary art; it seems irresponsible, snobbish to speak of the Beautiful in the face of the necessities of the political struggle.'[57] Indeed, the aesthetic experience of beauty is arguably, at best, 'neutral', since it can only be judged by effects and consequences. Beauty risks being mere distraction or sedation, perhaps even functioning to repress the imagination or disguise truths that ought to be revealed.

Nevertheless, this orthodox Marxist critique of beauty arguably gets things back the front, and risks damaging the revolutionary cause in an attempt to advance it. One should not reject eating on account of it not being a direct engagement in politics, and perhaps the same goes for engagement with beauty and aesthetic value, which may be forms of nourishment almost as vital as food. But what are the sources of this radical potential?

In developing an answer to that question, and in defence of beauty, I will now draw on Jane Bennett's book, *The Enchantment of Modern Life* (2001),[58] which rejects modernity's dominant narrative of disenchantment and seeks to tell an alter-tale. Such an alter-tale would be one that recognises that the world still has the capacity to enchant in ways that has ethical (and, one can argue, political) significance. Bennett's novel approach is to seek out 'enchantments' in a modern world that deceptively imagines itself free of this ancient value. I will extend Bennett's philosophy by focussing on the capacity for art (and nature) to enchant our lives in ways that serves ethical and political objectives. The goal, in part, is to rescue beauty's political relevance by highlighting its power to enchant. This can be understood as a development of Marcuse's view on the energising and even intoxicating effects of art.

At this point the notion of 'enchantment' needs further explanation. Max Weber argued that modernity was increasingly disenchanted and stamped with 'the imprint of meaning-lessness.'[59] Even today the prevailing view is that modern life – with its cars, concrete, over-crowdedness, pollution, and noise – cannot be experienced as enchanted. Indeed, in our post-Enlightenment age, any appeal to this notion requires not just definition but justification, since it normally belongs to past ages of superstition. While Bennett admits that there are plenty of aspects of contemporary life that fit the disenchantment story, her thesis is that 'there is enough evidence of everyday enchantment to warrant the telling of an alter-tale.'[60]

At base, Bennett employs the term enchantment to signify a particular affective or aesthetic state – a *mood* of enchantment. She argues that this mood is a necessary precondition to ethical practice and political engagement, in that it can create the emotional capacity for wonder, compassion, engagement, and generosity. To be enchanted, she explains, 'is to be struck and shaken by the extraordinary that lives amid the familiar and the everyday... [it is] the uncanny feeling of being disrupted or torn out of one's default sensory-psychic-intellectual disposition.'[61]

It is this surprising emotional disturbance that Bennett believes has ethical potential. To be enchanted – if only for a moment – is to see life as worth living and to see the world as a place that has the latent capacity to be transformed in more humane and ecologically sane ways. More importantly, it provides the *propulsion* to act and engage, functioning as an antidote to apathy, resignation, and perhaps even despair. Thus the enchantments of art can have a politicising effect, via its affective impact. As we have seen, Marcuse made a similar point about how social and political change depends on reshaping needs and sensibilities through aesthetic interventions in culture.

Bennett's premise is that disenchantment with and in life poses an ethical and political problem. Marcuse would have agreed. Transformative action is not set in motion merely by an intellectual appreciation of crisis, immiseration, and exploitation. One can know of these horrors and yet not act... out of disenchantment. For disenchantment's primary consequence is passive resignation to the status quo, which is capitalism's greatest achievement and its greatest tragedy. To act, to resist, to revolt – these necessary orientations and interventions arguably depend on a state or mood of enchantment, the absence of which seems to be haunting politics today.

It should be clear, then, that assessing the ethical and political potential of aesthetic enchantment implies no theoretical degeneration into New Age mumbo-jumbo or any cruel aestheticism. To be enchanted by 'the wonder of minor experiences'[62] helps transform the affective register of politics, by altering 'the emotions, aesthetic judgements, and dispositional moods that shape political wills, programs, affiliations, ideological commitments, and policy preference.'[63] This invites us to explore the political relevance of mood(s) and the capacity of art to shape our moods through aesthetic experience.

Enchantment, in this sense, can expand the contours of what seems possible and it can provoke a revaluation of what is valued. Bennett maintains that everyday moments of enchantment can build an ethics of generosity, care, and engagement, stimulating the vital energy needed to resist injustice and participate in practices of solidarity, compassion, experimentation, and renewal. To be disenchanted is to feel one lives in a world in which meaning and purpose are absent, and in which a better world is unimaginable and so not worth fighting for. Thus disenchantment is a political and ethical problem, even as enchantment remains elusive and its experience temporary. But temporary though they are, moments of enchantment can outlive their immediate experience, changing us forever even when the moment has passed.

Through art and aesthetic experience, it is still possible to experience enchantment, despite the ugliness and violence of the world. My point in engaging Bennett's theory is to highlight how this affective state is crucial to motivating the ethical and political sensibilities and behaviours needed to transform the world and its dangerous trajectories. This challenges the narrative of disenchantment, which serves only to immobilise or deflate collective action. Again, this is based on a recognition that an *effective* politics must be an *affective* politics, one that changes (or challenges) not only how we think about the world, but also the way we feel, perceive, judge, create, and thus, exist in the world. The lens of disenchantment is only one lens through which to see the contemporary world, and a dangerous one at that, with regressive social, political, and economic implications. There are alternatives, even as one must accept that the disenchanted worldview holds certain necessary truths. This is not a utopian or romantic diagnosis, although it retains a touch of what Terry Eagleton calls 'hope without optimism.'[64]

Thus Bennett rather cheekily invites enchantment, normally an anti-modern notion, back on to the agenda. She is not seeking to reinstate fairies, magic, or superstition, but to give licence to doubt about the claims of capitalism to be the rational, and thus, *natural* expression of modernity. Might there not be other ways to theorise and experience modernity? According to Bennett, to experience the world as merely the mechanical workings of lifeless matter, commodified and traded in a marketplace, is to see the world as disenchanted, and her concern is that the tendency of modernity to disenchant our lives has destructive social and ethical consequences. It can tempt us 'moderns' to quietly live a life of resignation, apathy, individualism, and acquisitiveness, leaving people without the necessary 'affective propulsions'[65] required to create purpose in their lives and struggle for a more humane world. A disenchanted culture is one suffering the strange ache of malaise, the cause of which is difficult to identify, like a knot of anxiety that cannot be easily untied.

To actively seek out and appreciate moments of enchantment in art, on the other hand, has ethical and political potential. It can give people the energy – the impulse to care and engage – in a world that is desperately in need of ethical and political revaluation and provocation. What Bennett highlights is how the *feelings* one has participates in and shapes the *thoughts* one has, and vice versa. And what people feel and think obviously affects how they act, both personally and politically. She wagers that 'to some small but irreducible extent, one must be enamoured with existence and occasionally even enchanted in the face of it in order to be capable of donating some of one's scarce mortal resources to the service of others.'[66]

In this way the interconnections between affect, thought, ethics, and politics become apparent, even if those interconnections always and everywhere remain mysterious and shifting. Indeed, Bennett begins her treatise by noting that 'a discomforting affect is often what initiates a story, a claim, a thesis.'[67] Or, in the words of political theorist John Holloway: 'The starting point of theoretical reflection is opposition, negativity, struggle... an inarticulate mumble of discontent.'[68]

This points to what might be called the affective or even aesthetic dimension of ethics and politics, too often marginalised by the pose of pure reason. One cannot, even in principle, master all things in life by calculation – neither physically nor economically. This critical doubt opens theoretical space beyond calculation where moments of enchantment might be able to rewire the circuitry of the dominant imaginary and lay the foundations for alternatives to arise. Meditating in this territory – this blurry nexus between affect, ethics, and politics – can be enlightening but also discomforting. Enchantments can disturb, and disturbances can enchant, from which one might inquire: might such affective and intellectual provocations have the potential to awaken more people from the dogmatic slumber into which our age has fallen? Put otherwise, can an aesthetically enchanted or disturbed *affect* lead to a genuinely progressive and enchanting *effect*? This is the question art poses. As Marcuse wrote: 'In the last analysis, the struggle for an expansion of the world of beauty, nonviolence, and serenity is a political struggle.'[69] We could say the same of enchantment: it can energise a political struggle, and a more enchanted world might also be the result.

Conclusion

Marcuse did not predict a revolution or even anticipate it. Rather, he elaborated on what he called 'the conditions of its possibility.'[70] We have seen that it was in art where he placed much of his faith. Over a century earlier, French economic and political theorist Henri de Saint-Simon made a similar point, albeit in more poetic language. He declared that, in bringing forth the new society, it would be the artists who:

> will lead the way in that great undertaking; they will proclaim the future of mankind... they will inspire society with enthusiasm for the increase of its well-being by laying before it a tempting picture of a new prosperity; by making it feel that all members of society will soon share in enjoyments which, up to now, have been the prerogative of a very small class; they will hymn the benefits of civilization and they will employ all other resources of fine arts, eloquence, poetry, painting, and music, to attain their goals; in short, they will develop the poetic aspects of the new system.[71]

Aesthetic interventions in culture and politics are always occurring – with both progressive and regressive effects – but we are still waiting for the groundswell of creative activity that makes a radically new and liberated society irresistible. We are waiting for the arrival of some mysterious monolith, as in Stanley Kubrick's film *2001: A Space Odyssey,* that provokes a quantum leap in consciousness, something that tears through the veil of ordinary experience and opens new spaces to think and be, forcing us to adapt to a new horizon, to broader contours of being. That is to say, we are still waiting for a new 'aesthetic education' that teaches us how to live in harmony with nature; a new aesthetic education that re-enchants our lives in ways that make the status quo utterly unacceptable and the joys of defiant activism seem impossible to pass up. But now, at least, the challenge has been laid down – both to artists, in particular, and to artists-of-life more broadly. This may or may not emerge in the sudden 'mass revolt' envisioned by earlier theorists of revolution. It is possible that artists must prepare themselves to wage a long, piecemeal cultural and educational undertaking, which, of course, may end up being a 'never-ending defeat.'

If it turns out, however, that art, science, and politics cannot provoke the transformations needed to avoid the looming apocalypse, then the role of the artist will only become more important. Creative imaginations will be tasked with interpreting civilisational descent in terms that give meaning to the inevitability of suffering; give sense to the pain we will feel (perhaps are already feeling) as global capitalism dies its inevitable death. At that stage, the therapeutic or even spiritual role of art will take precedence over its political function. As Terry Eagleton notes, the 'imagination can be a revolutionary force, but it also holds out some spiritual solace for revolutions that have gone astray.'[72]

As I noted at the beginning of this collection of essays, the term 'apocalypse' has a dual meaning, not simply referring to the 'end of the world' but also signifying 'a great unveiling or disclosure' of knowledge. It will be the artist, not the scientist, who will contribute most to the human understanding of such a disclosure when, or if, it arrives. Rather than wallow helplessly as civilisation descends into barbarism, we must hope that our artists, novelists, musicians, poets, and filmmakers, are up to the task of weaving narratives of human and ecological suffering into a meaningful web of solidarity and compassion. Thereby, the artists 'to come' might be able to give birth to a new golden age of Grecian tragedy that offers both an education and cleansing of the emotions and passions in these turbulent times.

Perhaps that is the new dawn that lies beyond this dark hour.

---

[1] Herbert Marcuse, *The Aesthetic Dimension: Toward a Critique of Marxist Aesthetics* (London: MacMillan Education, 1979).

[2] Beyond *The Aesthetic Dimension*, note 1, Marcuse addresses aesthetics, at various points, in many of his writings. See especially, Herbert Marcuse, *Eros and Civilization* (London: Sphere Press, 1969); Herbert Marcuse, *An Essay on Liberation* (London: Allen Lane, 1969); Herbert Marcuse, *Counter-Revolution and Revolt* (Boston: Beacon Press, 1972). For an extremely valuable collection of Marcuse's aesthetic writings, see Douglas Kellner (ed.), *Art and Liberation (Collected Papers of Herbert Marcuse, Vol. IV)* (London: Routledge, 2007). For a review of Marcuse's aesthetics, see Malcom Miles, *Herbert Marcuse: An Aesthetics of Liberation* (London: Pluto Press, 2012).

[3] See generally, Lee Baxandall and Stefan Morawski (eds.), *Karl Marx and Frederick Engels on Art and Literature* (Nottingham: Critical, Cultural and Communications Press, 2006).

[4] Marcuse, *Aesthetic Dimension*, note 1, pp. 3-4.

[5] Ibid, p. 8.

[6] Peter Burger, *Theory of the Avant-Garde* (Minneapolis: University of Minnesota Press, 2004) pp. 48-9.

[7] Marcuse, *Aesthetic Dimension*, note 1, p. 9.

[8] Ibid, p. xi.

[9] Ibid, p. 13.

[10] See Herbert Marcuse, 'Society as a Work of Art' in Kellner (ed.), *Art and Liberation*, note 2, p. 127.

[11] Charles Reitz, *Art, Alienation, and the Humanities: A Critical Engagement with Herbert Marcuse* (Albany: State University of New York Press, 2000), pp. 85-6.

[12] Herbert Marcuse, 'Some Remarks on Aragon: Art and Politics in the Totalitarian Era' in Douglas Kellner (ed.) *Technology, War, and Fascism (Collected Papers of Herbert Marcuse, Vol. I)* (London: Routledge, 1998), p. 201.

[13] Quoted in Marcuse, *Aesthetic Dimension*, note 1, p. 20.

[14] Marcuse, *Aesthetic Dimension*, note 1, p. 10.

[15] Ibid, p. 17.

[16] Ibid, p. 28.

[17] See Samuel Alexander, 'Banish the Poets! The Power and Politics of Aesthetic Education' in this collection of essays. The full set will be available here: http://samuelalexander.info/s-m-p-l-c-t-y-ecological-civilisation-and-the-will-to-art/ (accessed 10 May 2023).
[18] Marcuse, *Aesthetic Dimension*, note 1, p. 31.
[19] Ibid, p. 32.
[20] Ibid.
[21] Ibid, pp. 33-4.
[22] Ibid, p. 34.
[23] Ibid, p. 35.
[24] Ibid, p. 37.
[25] Ibid, p, 45.
[26] Percy Bysshe Shelly, *A Defense of Poetry* (Boston: Ginn and Co., 1891), p. 46.
[27] Marcuse, *Aesthetic Dimension*, note 1, p. 54.
[28] See forthcoming essay in this collection: Samuel Alexander, 'Democratising the Poet: William Morris and the Art of Everyday Life'. See link in note 17.
[29] Marcuse, *Aesthetic Dimension*, note 1, p. xiii.
[30] Marcuse, *Counterrevolution,* note 2, p. 96.
[31] Mark Burch, *Euterra Rising: The Last Utopia* (Winnipeg: Mark Burch, 2016).
[32] Marcuse, *Aesthetic Dimension*, note 1, p. 47.
[33] Ibid, p. 48.
[34] Ibid, p. 28.
[35] See Richard Rorty*, Contingency, Irony, and Solidarity* (Cambridge: Cambridge University Press, 1989), p. 190.
[36] Ibid, p. xvi.
[37] Richard Rorty, *Truth and Progress: Philosophical Papers (Vol. III)* (Cambridge: Cambridge University Press, 1998), p. 176.
[38] Richard Rorty, *Philosophy and the Mirror of Nature* (Princeton: Princeton University Press, 1979), p. 191.
[39] Martha Nussbaum, *Not for Profit: Why Democracy Needs the Humanities* (Princeton: Princeton University Press, 2016), p. 10. See also, Martha Nussbaum, *Love's Knowledge: Essays on Philosophy and Literature* (Oxford: Oxford University Press, 1992, revised ed.).
[40] See Nussbaum, *Love's Knowledge,* note 39.
[41] Quoted in Marcuse, *Aesthetic Dimension*, note 1, p. 57.
[42] Jacques Rancière, *The Politics of Aesthetics* (New York: Continuum, 2006), p. 12.
[43] Marcuse, *Essay on Liberation*, note 2, p. 11.
[44] See Samuel Alexander, 'The Politics of Beauty: Schiller on Freedom and Aesthetic Education' in this collection of essays. See link in note 17.
[45] Marcuse, *Essay on Liberation*, note 2, p. 18.
[46] Ibid, p. 4.
[47] Ibid.
[48] See my essays in this collection: Samuel Alexander, 'Homo Aestheticus, the Artful Species: An Evolutionary Perspective' and Samuel Alexander, 'Giving Birth to Oneself: Ethics as an "Aesthetics of Existence". See link in note 17.
[49] Marcuse, *Counterrevolution*, note 2, p. 16. (In this quote I have changed 'on the market' to 'in the market' which I presume corrects an error.)

[50] George Orwell, *Animal Farm* (London: Penguin, 2021).
[51] Marcuse, *Counterrevolution*, note 2, pp. 16-7.
[52] Ibid, p. 71 (my emphasis).
[53] Ibid, p. 107.
[54] Marcuse, *Aesthetic Dimension*, note 1, p. 73.
[55] Gary Synder, 1970. 'Four Changes' *Modern America Poetry*. Available at: https://bioneers.org/four-changes-by-gary-snyder/ (accessed 10 January 2023).
[56] Marcuse, *Aesthetic Dimension*, note 1, p. 69.
[57] Ibid, p. 62
[58] Jane Bennett, *The Enchantment of Modern Life: Attachments, Crossings, Ethics* (Princeton: Princeton University Press, 2001). In this section I draw from work published in Samuel Alexander and Brendon Gleeson, *Urban Awakenings: Disturbance and Enchantment in the Industrial City* (Singapore: Palgrave, 2019).
[59] Max Weber, 'Science as a Vocation' in Max Weber, *From Max Weber: Essays in Sociology* (New York: Oxford University Press, 1946), p. 140.
[60] Bennett, *Enchantment*, note 58, p. 4.
[61] Ibid, p. 4-5.
[62] Ibid, p. 3.
[63] Jane Bennett, *Thoreau's Nature: Ethics, Politics, and the Wild* (Lanham: Rowman & Littlefield, 2002) p. xxii.
[64] Terry Eagleton, *Hope without Optimism* (New Haven: Yale University Press, 2017).
[65] Bennett, *Enchantment*, note 58, p. 3.
[66] Ibid, p. 4.
[67] Ibid, p. 3.
[68] John Holloway, *Change the World Without Taking Power* (London: Pluto Press, 2010, second ed.) p. 1.
[69] Herbert Marcuse, 'Ecology and Revolution' in Douglas Kellner (ed.), *The New Left and the 1960s (Collected Papers of Herbert Marcuse, Vol. III)* (London, Routledge, 2005), p. 175.
[70] See Douglas Kellner (ed.) *Philosophy, Psychoanalysis, and Emancipation (Collected Papers of Herbert Marcuse, Vol V)*, p. 241.
[71] Cited in Miles, *Herbert Marcuse*, note 2, p. 20.
[72] Terry Eagleton, *Culture and the Death of God* (New Haven: Yale University Press, 2015), p. 103.

‘Vladimir: Say you are, even if it’s not true.
Estragon: What am I to say?
Vladimir: Say, “I am happy.”
Estragon: I am happy.
Vladimir: So am I.
Estragon: So am I.
Vladimir: We are happy.
Estragon: We are happy.’

– **Samuel Beckett, ‘*Waiting for Godot*’**

ESSAY FOURTEEN

ANSWERING ESTRAGON: ART, GODOT, AND UTOPIA

In the epigraph for this essay, taken from Samuel Beckett's play *Waiting for Godot*, we hear the two tramps, Vladimir and Estragon, who are sitting by the roadside, state that they are both happy. After realising that their existential circumstances persist despite their declarations, Estragon says to his companion: 'What do we do now, now that we are happy?' Vladimir responds: 'Wait for Godot.'[1]

It becomes apparent that neither of the tramps is quite sure who Mr Godot is, why they are waiting for him, or even if they are waiting at the correct time or location. The play ends without resolution, leaving the audience none the wiser. When Beckett himself was asked who or what Godot was, he replied: 'If I knew, I would have said so in the play.'[2] Both acts finish with one of the tramps, tired of waiting for a man who never arrives, saying to the other: 'Well, shall we go?', to which the other responds: 'Yes, let's go.'[3] Neither of them move, and the curtain closes.

In this play, as in all his work, Beckett is expressing his bleak view that the human situation is objectively meaningless and without any discernible purpose. We have all been thrown into an empty and indifferent universe, in which we suffer, suffer some more, and then die. The best we can hope for, like a tramp chewing on an old carrot, is that we get used to the muck as we go along. We keep waiting for the meaning of life to announce itself, to arrive – whether in the form of God, Godot, the Revolution, consumer satisfaction, fame, or whatever. But Godot does not objectively exist 'out there', so we feel that it is necessary to invent him. Life is what happens while waiting for Godot.

When – or if – our Godot arrives, Vladimir assures us, 'We'll be saved.'[4] But he never arrives. And so we wait, suffering, without understanding why. Life is absurd. At some point, the curtain closes and, without metaphysical comfort or understanding, our existence expires. Worms slowly consume our decaying bodies. The end. Absolutely. Life's mystery is never resolved and there is no moment of redemption that offers us consolation for our transcendental loneliness. We're just endlessly dead.

The lines about happiness in *Waiting for Godot* always struck me as central to Beckett's profoundly pessimistic worldview. They are especially unsettling to people who are interested in the political question of what societal structures might best advance human flourishing – or at least reduce unnecessary suffering – in a just and sustainable way. Beckett makes the disconcerting point that the question of life's meaning would remain unanswered, even when or if a person or society were fortunate enough to attain happiness. What do we do now, Estragon would ask, now that we are happy? Attaining happiness might even induce a profound existential crisis, for we would confront the question of life's meaning (or lack thereof) directly. We'd stare into the abyss, as Nietzsche said, only to find the abyss staring back.[5] Is happiness all there is? Is it the ultimate value for which we ought to be striving? Mightn't we discover that life is tragic and absurd, even in a 'happy' utopia?

In *Civilization and its Discontents,*[6] Sigmund Freud made a compelling case that happiness itself is an unrealistic goal for our species. Human nature, he argued, is driven by various sexual and aggressive drives that we must restrain in order to live according to the norms of civilised society. But repressing our primal and anti-social urges to maintain social order forces us to 'bottle things up inside', as the saying goes, leaving our psyches merely fluctuating between hysterical misery and ordinary unhappiness. For Freud, like Beckett, the search for transcendental meaning is a lost cause – religion is an illusion – and happiness is simply not part of the 'plan of creation' for human beings. Are we thus condemned both to meaninglessness and unhappiness?

Consider this utopian thought experiment: Suppose the industrial growth economy solves the 'economic problem' of poverty and manages to provide material affluence for all. Assume also – if you can imagine the impossible – that this globalisation of consumer lifestyles is achieved without fatally degrading planetary ecosystems. Due to the automation of production, everyone in this society now has an abundance of stuff as well as an abundance of free time. Furthermore, constitutionally protected civil liberties afford everyone an equal opportunity to shape their own life. For the sake of argument, I invite readers to imagine that this utopian society is structured according to their favourite vision of political economy (e.g., capitalism, socialism, anarchism, etc). In this world of universal affluence and leisure, what would we do with our lives? In what condition would we find our species?

All at once it becomes clear that the permanent problem of human existence – the question of life's meaning – would remain entirely unanswered, despite the affluence and the leisure. Indeed, as implied above, the problem of what to *do* with our freedom might well become more acute than ever. With the traditional purpose of life resolved (the economic struggle for existence), there might even be a risk of society-wide nervous breakdown, the onset of a profound cultural malaise.[7] Faced with the burden of our own freedom, we might become more unhappy than ever, choosing instead a shallow, cosmetic existence, full of 'entertainments', simply to contain our anxieties and distract us from our empty condition. The following lines of verse come to mind:

Don't mourn for me, friends, don't weep for me never
I'm going to do nothing for ever and ever.[8]

It is possible, I suppose, that in this affluent society human beings might pass their time eating nice food, enjoying exotic vacations, talking about cosmetic house renovations, sleeping in the sun, watching sport, making love, and drinking fine wine. This sounds like a good life, or at least good enough, full of earthly pleasures and entertainments. Whether they are happy or not, many of the world's most affluent people spend their days like this, even if the vast majority of the human population still suffer in material destitution. But I wish to suggest that for most people in this utopian society, one day a 'why' would arise, and the existential problem of life's meaning would come to saturate consciousness. Like a stone in one's boot, these lingering questions could not be ignored; they would follow us around everywhere we went. An acute state of affluenza might set in as we came to realise our pre-packaged, consumptive lifestyles were akin to 'doing nothing for ever and ever.'

One dark night of the soul we might face the source of our simmering discontent: is consumer affluence all there is to life? Is it the proper goal of our earthly struggles? Should the pursuit of economic growth without limit define and structure our political economies? In the affluent utopia I have sketched, at some point our lives would become tinged with an unsettling existential doubt about these questions. We would begin to wonder whether we had been foolishly climbing a ladder that had been placed against the wrong wall. Staring at our diamond-studded Rolex, we might enter a state of hallucination and find the watch posing unsettling questions: Is this it? Is this the peak of civilisation? Has superfluous consumption and entertainment lifted us to the heights of human achievement and capacity?

From an existential or spiritual perspective, I contend that we would come to see that material comfort was no longer 'enough'. It never was enough and never will be. Despite what consumer advertisements imply, human beings are not creatures that could ever be truly satisfied with 'nice things', merely. At most they provide cosmetic, pleasing distractions, or ego-boosting status signals, in an otherwise difficult and often tragic existence. Material abundance is preferable to material destitution, of course, but ultimately the superfluities of consumer lifestyles are spiritually beside the point, representing a failure of imagination, a mistaken idea of wealth and freedom. Consciously or unconsciously, most of us, it seems, seek meaning in ways that market commodities simply cannot offer, even if our actions often betray this insight. In a utopian society of universal affluence, whenever we look at our Rolexes we'd be reminded of the passing of time, the approaching spectre of death, and thereby confront the question: What shall we do now, now that we are happy?

Utilitarian philosophers would have no answer for Estragon, given that happiness within that paradigm is considered *fundamental*, and thus the question isn't even coherent. The most a utilitarian could say is that the tramps should aim for *more* happiness, since happiness is the fundamental good; the ultimate value; the benchmark of success in life. We should just continue marching along the hedonic treadmill and shouldn't ask why or to what end. At some stage, however, happiness, in the sense of a comfortable life of leisure, material abundance, and sensuous pleasure, will not satisfy the inquiring mind – the spiritual seeker. If we found ourselves living in Huxley's *Brave New World* (1932), soon enough we would start doubting – like the protagonist, John – whether a happy life induced by the drug 'soma' was a satisfactory way to live. Eventually we would want to live *deeper*, and that leaves open the possibility of passing up a comfortable and happy life and choosing a meaningful life, even if that entails increased suffering. Choosing meaning over happiness doesn't make sense within a utilitarian framework that posits happiness as the ultimate value. The best a utilitarian could do is fudge their central value, conceding that meaning is the highest good but insisting, by definitional fiat, that we must call this happiness. But that's another way of saying that utilitarian philosophy, at base, gets things wrong.

A similar challenge could be made to 'rights-based' philosophers of justice who ground their political theories, not in happiness, but in freedom. What would we do with our lives if we managed to attain freedom, Estragon might have asked? Beckett suggests that we would be free only to endure the horrors of 'this bitch of a world.'[9] In *Waiting for Godot*, even the wealthy, slave-owning character, Pozzo, who occasionally makes an appearance, certainly didn't seem content with his wealth, status, and power. He was suffering the human predicament just as the tramps were, only in different material and social circumstances. Beckett suggests that, fundamentally, Pozzo and tramps were experiencing the same old shit – an absurd existence – by virtue of sharing the same human condition. We see this today in the twisted faces of those 'lucky' celebrities, whom we would be wise not to envy. They, too, are still waiting for Godot. Affluence and fame seem to be inadequate, misconceived life goals. Emptiness remains, even or especially in a nice car surrounded by a crowd of adoring fans and enthusiastic photographers.

If the dominant theories of justice in our time seek to maximise either happiness or freedom, it would seem that they have failed to ground political society on an accurate appreciation of the human situation. Those philosophers are quite right, of course, to value happiness and freedom – even if, at times, these values conflict due to their incommensurable natures. It would be a strange creature who declined or rejected freedom and happiness if they were on offer. But if we were to achieve those goals, my point is that we would still face the uncertain question of life's meaning. We would still be left waiting for Godot, who would never arrive, biding time until we were relieved of our existential predicament by death. This would be the case even if we were sitting poolside with a bittersweet cocktail.

Admittedly, human existence might be given a sense of purpose as we *struggle* for happiness and freedom, and some people achieve a genuine sense of purpose by struggling to advance the condition of others. Albert Camus, for example, in closing his essay on the myth of Sisyphus, suggested that the struggle itself is enough to fill our hearts: 'One must imagine Sisyphus happy.'[10] But Beckett's unrelenting pessimism is highlighted when he implies that, having attained happiness or freedom, we might discover that our struggles had been in vain, that life remains meaningless, even if everyone were happy and free. Our struggles would have been merely a distraction from the inescapable tragedy that is human existence, which, in the haunting words of Danish philosopher Soren Kierkegaard, is merely a 'sickness unto death.'[11] Refusing to make any 'leap of faith' into either religion or rationalistic metaphysics, Beckett arguably took pessimism to its logical extreme – rivalling the 'great pessimist' Arthur Schopenhauer (1788-1860). Both writers articulated the harshness of the human predicament in the most powerful and compelling ways, without any hope of consolation or redemption.

This reasoning suggests that what is needed is a politics of meaning, and I believe this insight draws us necessarily into the realm of art and aesthetic experience. In a world without God, and where neither human reason nor material affluence can provide answers to life's mysteries, it seems to me that art and aesthetics are the best tools we have for negotiating the problems of human existence; the best tools for creating meaning and managing absurdity by engaging absurdity; the best tools for sublimating our primal desires and converting those psychological tensions into personally or socially useful, stimulating, or at least benign, creative activity. What is art if not the creative engagement with questions of meaning? What is beauty if not the definitive, albeit temporary, source of existential consolation?

Despite engaging in utopian speculation about an affluent society, it should be clear that my purposes in this essay have been entirely practical and pragmatic, related to the here and now. These ruminations on happiness, freedom, and meaning can be taken as philosophical touchstones, an invitation to explore ways of negotiating Beckett's unmitigated existential pessimism. Rather than wait in futility for Godot, even if one were to attain happiness and freedom, I am proposing that 'make art' and 'contemplate art' are the best and fullest responses that human beings have to Estragon's (hypothetical) question: what do we do now, now that we are happy?

I arrive at these conclusions by conceiving of human beings not as mere consumers, but as artists, with an innate urge to engage in creative and aesthetic activity, driven by the Will to Art.[12] As we struggle toward an ideal society, I believe we will universally become what we already are – artists – broadly defined to include not merely practitioners of the 'fine arts' but also those who exercise and explore their creative imaginations and aesthetic capacities in daily living. Through our art and aesthetic experience, we might grapple with the eternal mysteries of our strange existence, exploring our creative potentials, and revelling in the profound aesthetic pleasures of sharing our art and experiencing the art of our fellow human beings. The inherent and delightful ambiguities in art also serve a social purpose, as we come to engage each other in social discourse as we struggle meaningfully to understand and digest great art and our relation to it. I believe art can assist with managing an absurd universe like *nothing else can*. If there is any truth to this, then we might consider, as a social project, the goal of universalising and maximising opportunities for aesthetic engagement with our absurd existence, so that humanity might attain a degree of spiritual peace – or, with a nod to Freud, at least convert our neuroses and misery into ordinary unhappiness.

Of course, we are not living in a world where affluence has been universalised. The point of my thought experiment, however, was to highlight why consumerism – the dominant notion of the good life today – is a misconceived vision of prosperity, one unable to assist with living in an absurd universe. Do not art and aesthetic experience provide more coherent ultimate values? What if these aesthetic values came to orientate and guide our lives, our economies, our education, and our politics? This obviously wouldn't mean material provision was unimportant. It would only mean that material provision and economic growth were not considered as ends in themselves but rather a means to aesthetic ends. When material pursuits and the urge to accumulate receive too much of our life energies, we discover – as affluent society today is discovering – that 'superfluous wealth can buy superfluities only',[13] as Henry Thoreau once wrote. There is an emptiness to affluence that simply cannot satisfy the human craving for meaning. The developed consciousness of *homo aestheticus* demands meaning, and this is both a blessing and a curse. It is the source of life's profound richness but also the cause of our unique struggles. It would be easier to be a cat.

If opportunities for art and aesthetic experience are the highest good for a species such as ours, then it follows that we should structure our social, economic, and political institutions, and shape our own lives, to support that vision. This essay is a further step in my attempt to explore and encourage that approach to life and society. This should not be interpreted as an elitist position that holds up the 'artistic genius' as being of more worth than the rest of us who are less able to capture the social imagination with our creative activity. And it doesn't look to art at the expense of justice but rather to serve social (and ecological) justice. Against the grain of most 'aestheticist' philosophy, I counterpose an egalitarian and communitarian celebration of 'human as artist'. This contrasts, for example, with the aristocratic celebration of the *Übermensch* in Nietzsche's philosophy – although, to be fair, one can offer a creative reading of Nietzsche in which a communitarian ethic seems more consistent with his worldview than the admittedly elitist sounding passages in his oeuvre which dismiss 'the herd'. In any case, my goal, to be developed further in due course, is to 'democratise the poet', by highlighting the ways in which there is genius and poetry in us all, a lesson powerfully advanced by the likes of Friedrich Schiller, Ralph Waldo Emerson, Henry Thoreau, and William Morris.

I have outlined the problematic vision of an affluent utopia and engaged the questions to which it gave rise. From here I will invite readers to work backwards from this derivation of ultimate value to explore how humans might respond to the problem of existence today, and what implications this might have on questions of political economy. My speculative question – what do we do now, now that we are free and happy? – was designed to shed light on the human condition in ways that can guide action here and now, in a world which perhaps seems closer to dystopia than utopia. Political economy today, global capitalism, is designed to maximise growth, the planet be damned. If there is a vision implicit to this economic system, it is that the rich get richer and the poorest eventually catch up. Not only is this ecocidal, but my point has been that if we ever achieved that goal, we'd discover we'd been chasing a false target. A politics of meaning, in contrast, would ensure that everyone had 'enough' to explore their aesthetic potentials as artist and art-lover. This vision is inconsistent with any economy focussed on economic growth as a good in itself and any culture that searches for meaning in consumer goods and services.

Of course, 'make art' was also the answer Samuel Beckett gave through the course of actually living his life, even if this lies in direct contrast with the answer he gives in his writing, which was: 'wait for Godot'. Why Beckett said one thing and did another is a question that admits no easy or clear answer. Perhaps the tramps' injunction to 'wait for Godot' wasn't Beckett's positive answer or advice but rather his view on how human beings, living in bad faith or in fear of freedom, actually spend their days. Beckett couldn't escape the fact, however, that writing itself is a form of revolt and an expression of care – a rejection of the belief that 'nothing matters' or that 'everything is meaningless'. As the narrator utters at the end of Beckett's novel *The Unnameable:* 'I can't go on, I'll go on.'[14]

If people were to reflect on the analysis above and come to agree that 'making and contemplating art' is a promising means of managing existential challenges, then it would follow that material affluence and hi-tech industrial society are not needed to ensure these ultimate aesthetic values are attained. The major premises of this collection of essays are, first, that material sufficiency is all that is *needed* for a good life of artistic activity and aesthetic contemplation; and, secondly, that sufficiency is all that is *possible* for an ecologically viable existence on a finite planet. If we need art to help us manage absurdity, and that lifestyles of artistic creation and contemplation need not cost the Earth, there is a sense in which I can be understood to be offering 'hope without optimism'.[15] I have not established the case herein, but I invite readers to consider the possibility that, just maybe, art can save us from capitalism, and that '[b]eauty will save the world.'[16]

Here the implications of my analysis become apparent, for it provides grounds for a radical critique of existing society. If industrial growth economies are trying to provide material affluence for all as a path to the good life, then our global mode of political economy is structured in ways that are neither necessary for satisfying our deepest needs (autonomous creative activity and aesthetic experience) nor sustainable (since globalising affluence is demonstrably unsustainable). In short, industrial civilisation is suppressing the creative nature of our species by grossly overvaluing material affluence while at the same time undermining the environmental foundations for universal artistic opportunity. We can, and must, do better, and I'm suggesting that aesthetic interventions in the world are amongst the best ways to achieve an ecological civilisation of artists and art lovers. In creating this new form of aestheticised society, art is both the means and the end.

The vision of political economy I am working toward is one that I will call the *aesthetic state*. This implies that societal structures would be collaboratively designed so as to maximise opportunities for self-governing human beings to practise and contemplate art, as well as immerse themselves in nature's beauty, while minimising material and energy demands of the economy on a finite planet. This will involve considering what implications this aesthetic worldview might have on questions of distributive justice, sustainability, and the good life. Specifically, in order to answer the economic question, 'How much is enough?', one has to answer the normative question: 'Enough for what?'. I am presenting 'art' as an answer to that normative question, and upon that premise I am proposing that a humble, non-consumerist life of voluntary simplicity provides 'enough' material wealth to live a full and artful life of infinite diversity, sensuous pleasure, and imaginative possibility. Throughout this collection of essays, art has been defined broadly as the pleasurable and meaningful expression of creative labour. This conception of art has been defended as the fundamental value and ultimate end point for an aesthetic species, such as ours, in an aesthetic universe, such as this.

On that basis, my goal is to examine the role and importance of art and the artist in *non-utopian* societies such as our own, for within today's capitalist dispensation, artful living upon 'sufficient' material foundations seems to be the exception rather than the rule. I diagnose this as an aesthetic deficit disorder, a discordant condition that I believe can only be harmonised through art. This is related to matters of *taste* – and it is to such matters that I now turn more directly. After all, to paraphrase the poet Samuel Taylor Coleridge: we must create the taste by which we will be judged.

---

1 Samuel Beckett, *Waiting for Godot* (London: Faber and Faber, 1965) p. 60.

2 See Nasrullah Mambrol, 'Analysis of Samuel Beckett's *Waiting for Godot*' *Literary Theory and Criticism*. Available at: https://literariness.org/2020/07/27/analysis-of-samuel-becketts-waiting-for-godot/ (accessed 20 April 2023).

3 See Beckett, note 1, p. 94.

4 Ibid.

---

[5] Friedrich Nietzsche, *Beyond Good Evil: Prelude to a Philosophy of the Future* (Oxford: Oxford University Press, 1998) p. 68.
[6] Sigmund Freud, *Civilization and its Discontents* (London: Penguin, 2004).
[7] John Maynard Keynes, 'Economic Possibilities for our Grandchildren' in John Maynard Keynes, *Essays in Persuasion* (New York: Palgrave MacMillan, 2010) pp.321-332.
[8] Quoted in Keynes, 'Economic Possibilities', note 8, p. 327. Keynes references these lines as 'the traditional epitaph written for herself by the old charwoman.'
[9] See Beckett, *Godot*, note 1, p. 38.
[10] Albert Camus, *The Myth of Sisyphus* (London: Penguin, 2000), p. 111.
[11] Soren Kierkegaard, *The Sickness unto Death* (London: Penguin, 1989).
[12] See Samuel Alexander, 'Creative Evolution and the Will to Art' in this collection of essays. The full set will be available here: http://samuelalexander.info/s-m-p-l-c-t-y-ecological-civilisation-and-the-will-to-art/ (accessed 10 May 2023).
[13] Henry Thoreau, *Walden*, in Carl Bode (ed.) *The Portable Thoreau* (New York: Penguin, 1982), p. 568.
[14] Samuel Beckett, *The Unnameable* in Samuel Beckett, *Three Novels* (New York: Grove Press, 1955).
[15] Terry Eagleton, *Hope without Optimism* (New Haven: Yale University Press, 2017).
[16] Fyodor Dostoyevsky, *The Idiot* (New York: Bantam, 1981), p. 370.

‘Getting and spending, we lay waste our powers.’

– **William Wordsworth**

INDUSTRIAL AESTHETICS: A CRITIQUE OF TASTE

Every individual and every society are enactments of stories we tell ourselves about the nature and purpose of our existence and of the world we live in.[1] We might conceive of ourselves as children of God or speaking apes; dead matter or enchanted spirits; revolutionaries or conservatives; entrepreneurs or bureaucrats, producers or consumers – perhaps all of these things or none of them. But in the end, all of us give a narrative structure to our lives, or at least we adopt the default narratives of the dominant culture, usually unconsciously. The myths and stories we tell ourselves situate us in space and time, shape our perceptions of the present and guide us as we move into the future, influencing our interpretations of what is possible, proper, and important. As those individual narratives are woven together, the social fabric of a civilisation takes form.

One important function of story and myth is how they can shape what a person or culture finds beautiful or ugly. That is, social narratives influence our tastes. Moreover, our tastes influence what we desire, and our desires obviously shape how we act, both personally and politically. These sensuous dispositions are often taught to us through aesthetic education, including the ways in which a society 'distributes' opportunities for different forms of sense experience. On that basis, I propose that humanity will need a new aesthetic education, and a new 'distribution of the sensible,'[2] if we are to move beyond the industrial societies of late capitalism and toward an ecological civilisation that is constituted by radically different conceptions of beauty.

The myth of progress

Put simply, the grand narrative of industrial civilisation is a story of progress within which societies advance by way of continuous economic growth, rising affluence, and technological innovation. The very vocabulary of 'development' implies that some societies have reached maturity – the rich nations of advanced capitalism. The further implication is that the rest of the world is lacking the same degree of civilisation, and therefore needs more growth, more industrialisation, and more capitalism in order to civilise, just as healthy children must grow to maturity in order to fulfil their potential. This is a coherent metaphor until one realises that a child that never stops growing has a fatal disease. So convinced are the developed nations of their linear story of progress that over the last three centuries they have been imposing this narrative on the rest of the world, seeking to establish a 'fully developed' world, created in their own image of growth without limit.

Can humanity survive this growth model of progress? Although industrial development across the globe has brought with it many benefits, the dominant story of progress is not without its anomalies – anomalies so deep, one might argue, that today they are threatening the coherency of the paradigm itself. For many decades, environmental scientists have been demonstrating that the global growth economy is destroying the ecological foundations of life. From a social justice perspective, the critique has been that the system has produced socially corrosive inequalities of wealth and left billions in conditions of humiliating poverty, despite unprecedented capacity to eliminate hunger. These realities are often ignored or marginalised, but even when they are acknowledged, the dominant political and economic response is simply to reassert 'sustained growth' as the only solution. Very few people seem to recognise that growth may now be causing the very problems that it is supposed to be solving. As novelist and essayist Edward Abbey once wrote: growth for the sake of growth is the ideology of a cancer cell.

What is most troubling of all, perhaps, is that even those individuals who have achieved the so-called 'consumerist ideal' – the house, the car, the gadgets, the clothes, the travel, and so forth – all too often find themselves discontented despite their material abundance. In recent decades this finding has been established consistently and independently by a litany of sociological and psychological studies.[3] Industrial civilisation's defining goal appears to be misconceived. There seems to be an emptiness to affluence that is never acknowledged in glossy advertisements, let alone discussed in schools or around the dinner table. It is perhaps the dominant culture's final, unspeakable taboo. Few people dare to ask themselves, 'How much is enough?' Fewer still dare to meditate on the real question: 'Enough for *what*?'

Needless to say, within mainstream discourse these criticisms are rarely considered fundamental flaws in the basic story of industrial development. Instead, they are treated as matters of detail in need of refinement, a little tweaking around the edges – nothing that technology, market mechanisms, and more economic growth cannot manage or resolve. So dominant and uncompromising is this narrative that its contingency and historicity are easily missed, as if there were no other stories to tell, no other paths of progress. This 'myth of progress' has reified into an ideology, sometimes even shaping the consciousness of those it oppresses, marginalises, and alienates.[4]

Moving from the civilisational level to that of individual subjectivity, the narrative of industrial development is merely regurgitated in a personalised form. In the stories we tell ourselves, we create ourselves, and our world. The dominant 'story of self' in consumer cultures today is one that treats material advancement as the clearest indicator of social success and the best means of acquiring self-esteem, social status, happiness, and respect. Anthropologists and sociologists have done considerable work studying and analysing the ways in which people communicate through their consumption; how they convey social messages and tell stories about who they are through the symbolic content of commodities.[5] Commodities are purchased not just for their functionality or use-value but also or primarily for what they signify about the people who possess them. By accumulating a certain body of commodities, individuals in consumer societies thereby shape their identities through consumption, defining themselves not by what they do but by what they own. This provides a basis to update Rene Descartes' famous dictum in consumerist-existential terms: 'I shop, therefore I am.'

The industrial aesthetics of consumption

While this process of self-creation through the symbolic content of consumption can be considered an aesthetic process, it should be acknowledged that individuals do not simply shape, but are also shaped by, the dominant consumerist aesthetic to which they are exposed. Members of advanced capitalist societies (and increasingly all people around the globe) are bombarded, literally thousands of times every day, with advertisements, images, and other more subtle cultural and institutional messages insisting that 'more is better'. These cultural messages are devised by sophisticated marketers, highly skilled at manipulating people by preying on our deepest insecurities or emotional needs. It is no exaggeration to state that the implicit (sometimes explicit) message in every advertisement is: 'Your life is unsatisfactory as it is, but with this commodity you can attain happiness, beauty, meaning, love, respect, etc.' The rich and famous are glorified and celebrated at every turn, serving only to entrench the assumption that money means fame, success, happiness, and social admiration. A cult of youthfulness distorts cultural conceptions of beauty, just as last season's fashion can be discarded by those who have been socially engineered to perceive it as 'of bad taste'. There is barely a social space or even a private space today where one can find sanctuary from the onslaught of the consumerist aesthetic. We internalise the world 'out there' even as we produce and reproduce it. What we are exposed to, and what we give our attention to, we become.

The consumerist-industrial aesthetic is compromised further (or compromises us further) as people in highly developed societies today find themselves ever more disconnected from nature. This is not to defend or idealise some mythical pre-industrial 'wild' but only to acknowledge that 'nature deficit disorder'[6] is a real condition, threatening to become an epidemic, albeit largely undiagnosed. The nature deficit can be understood as part of the broader aesthetic deficit disorder I have been diagnosing throughout these essays. As creatures of Earth who spent our entire evolutionary history living outdoors, in the most intimate connection with the ecosystems upon which we rely, it should come as no surprise that we suffer existentially as we find ourselves disconnected from this rich source of material and spiritual nourishment. Biophysically we are essentially the same creature who lived in caves tens of thousands of years ago. Culturally, our highly artificial and technologised existence today could hardly be further from the conditions of our evolutionary upbringing. This dislocation should be expected to have, and is having, negative health and psycho-spiritual effects.

In the same vein, cultural theorists have diagnosed and investigated a strange existential condition they label 'affluenza'[7] – a spiritual malaise that seems to afflict many people in consumerist societies. Both the causes and symptoms are numerous and varied. In urban and suburban contexts, the natural environment has been progressively covered with concrete or tarseal. Skies are scarred with wires, power lines, and the contrails of aircraft. Lives are lived mostly indoors under artificial lights, in front of computers or machines, disconnected from the changing seasons. The music of birdsong is becoming rarer as urban trees are cleared for apartments or a new freeway, while warnings of a 'silent spring' continue to be ignored. The long, typically monotonous working day often begins and ends with a slow commute to or from work, in loud, heavy traffic, past the ubiquitous advertising billboards which demand attention. Returning home one can be so tired that there is no life-energy to do anything but sit in front of the television or computer, in nice clothes, eating highly processed takeaway food and relying on the sedations of alcohol or drugs to fight off the ennui. This is a polemical statement, of course, painting with too broad a brush. But the picture is accurate enough. Consumer culture seems to have failed to fulfil its promise of a meaningful and satisfying life, even as it destroys the planet. Is it any wonder that cultural analyst Theodore Roszak looked into the eyes of modern consumers and saw only faces 'twisted with despair'?[8]

The point is that consumerism is not just a relationship to material culture. It can also be understood as a mode of existence, an aesthetic state of being-in-the-world, one that seems to be generally coloured with a mood of disenchantment, disconnection, and disillusionment. The real genius of consumerism, however, seems to be in how it seduces people into believing that, no matter how affluent they might become, the main things lacking from their lives are money and possessions. Thus the 'iron cage' of consumerism succeeds because it fails, ensuring that the vicious circle of consumption continues.[9] The spiritual malaise only deepens, for as the Parisian graffiti of 1968 stated: 'those who lack imagination cannot imagine what is lacking'.

The aesthetic education of taste

To better understand the industrial-consumerist aesthetic and its implications on consumption practices, these issues could be explored through the lens of 'taste'. In the twentieth century, French philosopher Pierre Bourdieu, in his seminal text, *Distinction: A Social Critique of the Judgement of Taste* (1979),[10] took aesthetics beyond philosophy and into sociology, by demonstrating empirically that taste is closely related to class. What forms of clothing, music, literature, interior décor, leisure, etc, a person or household consumes is obviously a matter of taste, but in his research Bourdieu discovered that children are taught their tastes from an early age, and what they are taught is shaped along class lines.

This aesthetic education becomes internalised, making taste seem natural or objective, yet this ends up serving an ideological function by entrenching certain cultures of consumption that demarcate class. At some intuitive level, it seems this has long been understood. At least since Thorstein Veblen's work in *The Theory of the Leisure Class* (1899), there has been discussion of practices of 'conspicuous consumption' that show off high levels of wealth for the purpose of socially emphasising high status.[11] Bourdieu argued that the acceptance of dominant forms of taste is a form of 'symbolic violence',[12] because individuals in lower classes do not always have the economic or cultural means of accessing 'highbrow' cultures of consumption. Thus they are dominated by taste, forever trying to conform to the reigning aesthetic for fear of being socially ostracised by appearing crude, vulgar, or tasteless. The essential message here remains valid even if the Marxist framing is dropped. Irrespective of the class implications, it seems clear that 'taste' is often a matter of aesthetic education, and accordingly deserves social and political analysis.

Anthropologist Mary Douglas offered further insight into how cultural tastes shape expectations about consumption, arguing that what is considered appropriate or necessary consumption is always culturally dependent. People do not merely consume to meet biophysical needs but also to meet social needs. In fact, Douglas argued that 'an individual's main object in consumption is to create the social universe and to find in it a creditable place'.[13] This means that what are considered acceptable or appropriate practices of consumption in one society or social setting may be very different in an alternative social setting. The corollary is that even the notion of poverty can be understood as something that is culturally specific, not merely a universal biophysical threshold. A particular level of consumption that is considered wealthy or prestigious in one society might be so low in another society as to be shameful; a particular object that is admired as tasteful or refined in one culture might be considered tasteless or uncouth in another. This can function to lock people into practices of consumption higher than they may feel necessary, not because they truly desire a certain level or manner of consumption but because they naturally desire social legitimation and acceptance, knowing that there are cultural expectations in this regard. Transcending consumerism therefore must include overcoming aesthetic obstacles regarding taste.

One particularly pernicious aesthetic phenomenon in relation to consumption is the apparent need for uniformity in consumption practices, a phenomenon known by consumer researchers today as 'the Diderot effect'.[14] Someone once gave Dennis Diderot (the French Enlightenment thinker) a beautiful, new scarlet robe, and without thinking he discarded his old one.[15] But the next morning as he sat down to write he noticed that his old desk no longer did his robe justice. So he upgraded his desk. Then he realised that his chair, tapestries and bookshelves looked dated against his new acquisitions, and slowly his entire material surroundings were upgraded. Sociologist Juliet Schor describes this taste for uniformity in the following way:

> The purchase of a new home is the impetus for replacing old furniture; a new jacket makes little sense without the right skirt to match; an upgrade in china can't really be enjoyed without a corresponding upgrade in glassware. This need for unity and conformity in our lifestyle choices is part of what keeps the consumer escalator moving ever upward. And 'escalator' is the operative metaphor: when the acquisition of each item on a wish list adds another item, and more, to our 'must-have' list, the pressure to upgrade our stock of stuff is relentlessly unidirectional, always ascending.[16]

This highlights the insidious effect that taste can have on our consumption practices, and how the growth economy more broadly is driven by (just as it produces) the seemingly insatiable desires of the modern consumer. Note, however, that Diderot eventually found himself sitting in the stylish formality of his new surroundings regretting the work of this 'impervious scarlet robe [that] forced everything else to conform with its own elegant tone'.[17] Diderot had been master of his old robe but became slave of the new one. 'Opulence has its obstacles,'[18] he concluded – a lesson consumer societies might have much to learn from today.

A politics of taste

The analysis above attempted to offer some insight into various aesthetic dimensions of life in advanced industrial societies. I have suggested that transcending consumerism and the growth economy will depend on first overcoming various aesthetic obstacles, practices, and tastes. These obstacles include the stories and myths we tell about ourselves and societies, and the ways we shape our identities and communicate through consumption. Other such obstacles include the disaffection and alienation that evidently is widely experienced in consumer societies, even by those who have achieved the consumerist ideal. In that light, I outlined some of the ways that dominant conceptions of taste and social legitimation, especially regarding material living standards, can entrench materialistic conceptions of the good life.

Given that humans are largely 'socially constructed' beings, it should come as no surprise that our modes of subjectivity in advanced, industrial societies have been shaped by the dominant social and institutional forces that celebrate consumerism as a way of life. This marginalises consumption as a subject of ethical concern. Far from challenging us to explore lifestyles of reduced consumption in response to the ecological and social justice imperatives of our time, dominant forms of culture, economics, and politics call on us to consume as much as possible 'for the good of the economy'. Given that these cultural narratives have been widely internalised, often unconsciously, it follows that ethical activity today may require us to engage the self by the self for the purpose of *refusing who we are* – insofar as we are uncritical consumers – and creating new, post-consumerist forms of subjectivity. Few people, it seems, have a taste for sufficiency, a taste for degrowth, which I maintain is a leading aesthetic obstacle in the way of any transition to a just and sustainable society. There is an elegance and beauty to the clothesline, the bicycle, and the water tank, that the clothes dryer, the automobile, and the desalination plant decidedly lack. When such an aesthetics of sufficiency is more widely embraced in a culture, it will be clear that we are on the path to an ecological civilisation.

In summary, the self-creation of new forms of subjectivity is a necessary first step in any transition to a new society. In previous essays, I argued (drawing on Friedrich Schiller) that art and aesthetics are promising means for disrupting our 'normal sense of self', inducing a sense of play that liberates us from habit and conformity and provides the conditions for giving birth to someone new.[19] Until there is a culture that embraces voluntary simplicity, the social underpinnings for an ecological civilisation will be absent. After all, consumerist cultures that seek and expect ever-rising material living standards will not *desire* a politics or macroeconomics of degrowth, and politicians will never campaign for degrowth if it is clear there is no social mandate for it. Accordingly, the emergence of a culture of voluntary simplicity seems to be a prerequisite to any degrowth transition, and the first step in this cultural shift involves transforming our subjectivities beyond the consumerist default setting. Among other things, this will involve taking seriously the questions, 'how much is enough?' and 'enough for what?', and reshaping our relationships to material culture in line with the aesthetic values of balance and harmony. Through a new aesthetic education, we can resist capitalism and usher in an ecological civilisation by learning to find different things beautiful and different things ugly. Revolt is a matter of taste.

Nevertheless, a re-fashioning of the self in line with voluntary simplicity will not be enough on its own to produce an ecological civilisation, owing to the fact that consumption practices take place within structural constraints. Within consumer capitalism it can be very difficult, at times even impossible, to consume in ways that accord with one's conception of justice and sustainability, because structural constraints can lock us into high consumption, high carbon modes of life. For these reasons a personal aesthetics of existence is a necessary though not sufficient response to existing crises. A systemic perspective is also required, which is why this analysis must be expanded further into social, economic, and political domains.[20] Current crises are ultimately systemic crises that require a systemic response – not merely a cultural response – even if that systemic response begins with the aesthetic self-transformation of our given subjectivities. To paraphrase Samuel Taylor Coleridge: *we must create the taste by which we will be judged.*

In the next essay I turn to consider the growth paradigm of consumer capitalism from an energetic perspective. The alternative model of degrowth or 'voluntary simplification' will also be examined, critically engaging the work of anthropologist and historian Joseph Tainter.[21] As to be expected by now, I will focus on this alternative paradigm through the lens of aesthetics, exploring to what extent art and aesthetics can help facilitate an overcoming of the dominant paradigm. The goal is to help open future pathways of prosperous descent, whereby many existing social, ecological, and political challenges can be resolved through planned contraction of energy and resources demands in the overdeveloped regions of the world. This will only be possible, however, after first developing a *taste* for the lifestyles of voluntary simplicity that degrowth implies.[22]

I will argue that this living strategy remains valid even if it turns out that a degrowth economy is never created and the collapse of civilisation ends up dictating humanity's future. This is because resilience – the capacity to withstand societal shocks and crises – will be increased if a household or community is mentally and socially prepared for simpler lifestyles of radically reduced consumption, whether voluntarily chosen or externally imposed. As historian and futurist John Michael Greer quips: collapse now and avoid the rush![23]

---

[1] Daniel Quinn, *Ishmael: A Novel* (New York: Bantam, 2017); Thomas Berry, *The Great Work: Our Way into the Future* (New York: Bell Tower, 1999).

[2] Jacques Rancière, *The Politics of Aesthetics* (New York: Continuum, 2006), p. 12. As discussed in previous essays, Rancière's notion of the 'distribution of the sensible' refers to the way in which political decisions, actions, and narratives determine what presents itself to sense experience. In other words, politics shapes what can be seen, felt, and spoken about – and by whom.

[3] See generally, Robert Lane, *The Loss of Happiness in Market Democracies* (New Haven: Yale University Press, 2000); Tim Kasser, *The High Price of Materialism* (Cambridge, MA: MIT Press, 2004); Robert Frank, *Luxury Fever: Why Money Fails to Satisfy in an Era of Excess* (New York: The Free Press, 2009).

[4] See generally, Wolfgang Sachs (ed) *The Development Dictionary: A Guide to Knowledge as Power* (New York: St Martin's Press, 1992).

[5] See, e.g., Juliet Schor, *The Overspent American: Upscaling, Downshifting, and the New Consumer* (New York: Basic Books, 1998); Daniel Miller, *Stuff* (Cambridge: Polity, 2010).

[6] Richard Louv, *The Nature Principle: Human Restoration and the End of Nature-Deficit Disorder* (New York: Algonquin, 2011).

[7] Clive Hamilton and Richard Denniss, *Affluenza: When Too Much is Never Enough* (Crows Nest: Allen & Unwin, 2005).

[8] Theodore Roszak, *Where the Wasteland Ends: Politics and Transcendence in Postindustrial Society* (New York: Doubleday Press, 1972), p. xxviii.

[9] Tim Jackson, *Prosperity Without Growth: Economics for a Finite Planet* (London: Earthscan, 2009), Ch 4.

---

[10] Pierre Bourdieu, Distinction*: A Social Critique of the Judgement of Taste* (London: Routledge, 1984).
[11] Thorstein Veblen, *Theory of the Leisure Class* (Oxford: Oxford University Press, 2009[1899]).
[12] Bourdieu, *Distinction*, note 9, p. 358.
[13] Mary Douglas, 'Relative Poverty – Relative Communication' in Tim Jackson (ed) *The Earthscan Reader in Sustainable Consumption* (London: Earthscan, 2006), p. 243.
[14] See Schor, *Overspent*, note 4, p. 145.
[15] Denis Diderot, 'Regrets on Parting with my Old Dressing Gown', available at: https://www.marxists.org/reference/archive/diderot/1769/regrets.htm (accessed 10 March 2023).
[16] Schor, *Overspent*, note 4, p. 145.
[17] Diderot, 'Regrets', note 14.
[18] Ibid.
[19] See Samuel Alexander, 'The Politics of Beauty: Schiller on Freedom and Aesthetic Education', in this collection of essays. The full set will be available here: http://samuelalexander.info/s-m-p-l-c-t-y-ecological-civilisation-and-the-will-to-art/ (accessed 10 May 2023).
[20] The systemic nature of growthism and consumerism has been the focus of much of my academic work. Most of my writing is freely available here: www.samuelalexander.info (accessed 15 June 2023).
[21] See especially, Joseph Tainter, *The Collapse of Complex Societies* (Cambridge: Cambridge University Press, 1988).
[22] Samuel Alexander, *Sufficiency Economy: Enough, for Everyone, Forever* (Melbourne: Simplicity Institute, 2015).
[23] John Michael Greer, 'Collapse Now and Avoid the Rush' *Resilience* (6 June 2012).

ARTFUL DESCENT: A COSMODICY OF SMPLCTY

Are we, the creatures and creators of industrial civilisation, destined to face the same fate as people in previous civilisations, having collectively risen to such great heights only to fall? Barely three centuries old, industrialisation has induced what some scientists and theorists are now calling 'the Anthropocene' – a geological blink-of-the-eye during which human impact on Earth has been so severe that it constitutes a new epoch. This is a time where biodiversity and wildlife populations are in catastrophic decline, and where carbon emissions are destabilising climate systems with tragic consequences that are already unfolding and promising to intensify. It challenges the imagination, I admit, to envision a time when our present civilisation is being studied as Rome is studied today, as an object of history – a dead civilisation. But is this the future we face? Or is there a door hidden in the wall through which we might be able to negotiate alternative pathways and escape what seems to be our impending fate? The Four Horsemen of the Apocalypse may not wait long to let us answer. The dreadful clatter of hooves is already audible to those who have the courage to pay attention.

Contemporary discussion about 'sustainability transitions' seems to operate under the assumption that change itself is progress – or at least that a movement toward 'better' is good enough. But in order to transition in the *right direction*, what is needed is an accurate assessment of where we are, in its full and ghastly reality. As a guide to action, some understanding of where we would like to end up is also required, even if the destination seems distant, shifting, and perhaps unattainable. We should dare to imagine better worlds and more humane and nourishing social arrangements, provided these 'fictions' are used to inform action rather than induce passive escapism. Imagineers are easily dismissed as utopian dreamers or escapists who lack a sense of political reality. But just as vision without politics is naive, politics without vision is dangerous. We must dream before we shape our politics, or else we will never awaken from the existing nightmare of pragmatism without principle.

The aesthetic form of life

Let me begin this essay by outlining the defining characteristics of the aesthetic form of life which I believe is a viable and desirable pathway beyond industrial civilisation. As I have noted before, this is neither a utopian statement nor a prediction. Rather, it is an *orienting vision* designed to guide prefigurative action in the here and now. I am employing the term SMPLCTY to refer to an idealised 'end state' of an ecological civilisation. In developing this vision, my two guiding premises have been, first, that material sufficiency is all that is *needed* for human beings to live rich, meaningful, and artful lives; and second, that material sufficiency is all that is *possible*, over the long term, on a finite planet in an age of environmental limits.

To live simply is to embrace an economics of sufficiency and moderation, finding harmony and balance in life by walking the middle way between too little and too much. This living strategy seeks to maximise opportunities for meaningful co-existence through artful and creative living, while minimising material and energy demands for reasons of justice, sustainability, and wellbeing. The archetypal member of this envisioned civilisation is someone I characterise as a poet-farmer (discussed further in the next essay). This is an aesthetic citizen who identifies as a creative and artistic being (broadly conceived to include not just artists but also artisans), and who embraces voluntary simplicity while contributing to material provision, community governance, and cultural richness.

By removing the 'i' from the conventional spelling of simplicity, the neologism SMPLCTY is intended to evoke a 'less is more' philosophy – or rather, a philosophy of 'just enough is plenty'. This defines the ethos of sufficiency underpinning my vision of ecological civilisation. The removal of the 'i' is also meant to imply the achievement of a diminished egoism (or increased communitarianism) compared to the possessive individualism that has come to define globalised industrial capitalism. This transcendence of crude individualism could also be understood as a deeper communion with the creative impulse or art-force underpinning our shared aesthetic reality.[1] Paradoxically, this diminished egoism, induced in part by 'losing oneself' in aesthetic experience, promises to increase opportunities for individual self-creation. As the Marxian dictum states: the free development of each is the condition for the free development of all. As I conceive of it, the central goal of political theory is to determine which institutional arrangements and governance structures would allow this to happen to the greatest extent.

In what follows, SMPLCTY will be presented as the desirable outcome of a process of 'voluntary simplification' or 'artful descent'.[2] In the broadest terms, the goal of this ecological civilisation is to provide enough, for everyone, forever. I believe this is a necessary vision to embrace if humanity (as a whole) and affluent societies (in particular) are to move toward an equitable form of life that not only avoids ecosystemic collapse but also ensures the flourishing of all life on Earth within environmental limits. This creative process – what I have elsewhere called an 'aesthetics of degrowth'[3] – involves consciously transferring ever more time and attention to non-materialistic sources of meaning and happiness, both individually and socially. These practices would reflect a post-consumerist conception of the good life, where fulfillment in life is achieved through such things as self-directed creative labour, social and political engagement, enjoyment of nature, artistic activity, and aesthetic immersion and contemplation.

This vision is founded upon a conception of humanity which holds that our species, *homo aestheticus*, can live its fullest existence, and with infinite diversity, while living simply on modest material foundations.[4] Thus, with the support of appropriate social and political institutions,[5] and based on an ethic of enlightened self-interest, it will be recognised that moderation and even austerity in our material lives does not condemn us to hardship or deprivation. Instead, a way of life that is 'outwardly simple and inwardly rich'[6] illuminates the most direct path to sustainable wellbeing into the deep future, provided profound cultural changes are supplemented and supported by correlative structural changes in political economy. In ways I have explained throughout these essays, art, creative activity, and aesthetic experience can do most of the heavy lifting in justifying existence as an aesthetic phenomenon.[7]

Through this shift in emphasis from the material (or external) dimensions of life to the spiritual (or internal) dimensions, the goal is to achieve maximum flourishing for the community of life, while minimising energy and resource demands in due respect of biophysical limits.[8] As psychoanalyst and philosopher Erich Fromm put it, this implies a shift from 'having' to 'being'[9] – an insight into the human condition which is ancient but ever new.[10] SMPLCTY is, by definition, an 'ideal' state that can never be fully or permanently achieved, due to the inherent tendency of civilisations to become more complex as new and unforeseen societal problems arise. But as outlined below, civilisations based on growth and ever deepening socio-technical complexification eventually grow themselves into a condition of deterioration and collapse.[11] Accordingly, I believe that voluntary simplification is the *only* means of avoiding this process of complexity-to-collapse – a process that has brought about the demise of all prior civilisations in history, and which is in the process of bringing down industrial civilisation.

My argument is that art and aesthetic experience are promising and available means of 'living more with less' – of flourishing in simplicity. Industrial civilisation has developed in ways where the human search for meaning is undertaken in ways that are often violent, unsustainable, unjust, and perhaps worst of all, largely unsuccessful. My thesis is that voluntary simplification presents a meaningful alternative to collapse, grounded in an aesthetics of existence. On that basis, opportunities for low-impact aesthetic practice and experience ought to be expanded as our material and energy demands contract for reasons of justice, sustainability, and wellbeing. I maintain that this is the door hidden in the wall, through which we have an opportunity, however slim, to escape the Four Horsemen.

Below I draw on the work of historian and anthropologist Joseph Tainter to understand the dynamics of complexification, before explaining why I believe, contra Tainter, voluntary simplification presents itself as the singular coherent response. By offering a sympathetic critique of Tainter's work, seemingly minor disagreements and refinements are shown to have major implications. I conclude the essay by offering a few more words on the nature of SMPLCTY as an orienting vision, including a brief re-examination of 'The Law of Progressive Simplification' as proposed by historian Arnold Toynbee in his *Study of History* (1934-61).

The collapse of complex societies

In his influential work, *The Collapse of Complex Societies* (1988), Joseph Tainter presented an original theory about the rise and demise of civilisations throughout history.[12] Tainter's theory is based on the observation that societies become more 'complex' as they solve the problems they face, and that such complexification necessitates increased energy use. For a society to sustain itself, therefore, it must secure the energy needed to solve the range of societal problems that emerge. Since problems continually arise, there is persistent pressure for growth in complexity, and thus growth in the energy supplies needed to support that complexity.

Both historically and today, such 'problems' might include securing enough food for a growing population, adjusting to demographic, climatic, or other environmental changes, dealing with aggression within or between states, organising society and developing institutions, managing public health, and so on. At a meta level, all societies must also solve, or try to solve, the first-order problem of life's meaning, even if this problem is usually confronted indirectly through the range of second-order challenges that life presents. Solving such societal problems, large or small, generally requires what Tainter calls 'complexification'. This might include creating new social roles, new social, political, or economic institutions, new technologies, new infrastructure, increasing production or information flows, etc. Indeed, the challenges any society might face are, for practical purposes, 'endless in number and infinite in variety',[13] and responding to societal problems generally requires energy and other resources. Tainter describes this development in human organisation and behaviour as a process of socio-political complexification.

The most original aspect of Tainter's theory is that he maintains that complexity has diminishing marginal returns. Given that we naturally solve the most important problems first, the early benefits of complexity offer significant benefits. Over time, however, Tainter argues that the benefits of complexity diminish in relation to the material, energetic, and social costs. (For example, the invention of the phone was a major leap forward in human communications, whereas the shift from iPhone 12 to iPhone 13 was much less significant). Upon these dynamics, there comes a point when societies may no longer be able to secure sufficient energy or other key resources to solve the range of problems faced. Accordingly, without corresponding advances in resource-use efficiency, such societies may be unable to maintain arrangements corresponding to their peaks of complexity.

Put more directly, large-scale societies can collapse (i.e., undergo rapid involuntary reduction in socio-political complexity) when the costs of sustaining their complexity become energetically unaffordable. In Tainter's words: 'A society or other institution can be destroyed by the cost of sustaining itself.'[14] As outlined below, this is the essential dynamic that Tainter argues 'can explain collapse as no other theory has been able to do.'[15] Not only is Tainter's theory of historical interest, it can offer insight into the evolving nature and dynamics of globalised industrial civilisation, today and in the future.[16]

Energy and civilisation

It is not necessary to resort to energy determinism or crude reductionism to insist on the fundamental role energy has played, and continues to play, in shaping the rise (and demise) of complex, large-scale societies.[17] Energy is not just another resource or commodity: it is the key that unlocks access to all other resources and commodities, thereby giving shape to the physical boundaries within which human societies must take form. In other words, a society's energetic foundations delimit the socio-economic forms that it may take. This is simply to concede that a particular form of society cannot emerge without sufficient energy supplies, in the appropriate forms, to support it. Furthermore, a society must be able to meet its *ongoing* energy demands if its specific socio-economic form is to persist. If it cannot, the society will transform or be transformed, voluntarily or otherwise.

To understand the dynamics of social complexity, it can be helpful to begin by focusing on prehistoric times, prior to the uptake of agriculture, when human life was about as 'simple' (in Tainter's sense) as can be. During these times, the main biophysical problem human beings faced was securing an adequate food supply, and this was solved, often relatively easily, by hunting wild animals and gathering wild plants. Notably, anthropologists have concluded that prehistoric hunter-gatherers were the most leisured societies to have ever existed,[18] which confirms that food supply was generally secure and easily obtained. It seems that once essential biophysical needs were adequately met, hunter-gatherers stopped labouring and took rest or leisure rather than work longer hours to create a material surplus or more advanced technologies for which they did not seem to desire.[19]

This form of life was sustained by a minimal and largely static supply of energy – essentially just food, passive solar energy, and eventually fire. This tightly constrained energy supply placed strict bounds on the types of society that could arise, for the reason that more 'complex' social organisations and behaviours require greater supplies of energy. In other words, hunter-gatherer societies had no food surplus (i.e., energy surplus) to feed any non-food specialists – such as soldiers, bureaucrats, technologists, aristocrats, and so forth – so there was very little differentiation in social roles. Accordingly, for hundreds of thousands of years, early hunter-gatherer societies did not develop any significant degree of social complexity. (Note, an absence of social complexity in Tainter's sense does not imply any 'simplicity' or 'primitiveness' in cultural or spiritual depth.)

Human societies began to change, however, around 10,000 years ago as a consequence of the agricultural revolution. The greater productivity of agriculture for the first time gave human societies a significant boost in their food (i.e., energy) supply, and this set in motion the development of social complexity that continues to this day. Being so much more productive per acre than foraging, agriculture meant that not everyone had to spend their time securing food supply, and this gave rise to an array of non-food specialists, including those noted above and many more. Furthermore, the sedentary nature of agricultural societies made it practical to begin producing and accumulating new material artefacts (e.g., houses, furniture, collections of heavy tools and weapons, etc.), all of which would have been too cumbersome for nomadic peoples to justify creating, or too energy intensive.

Eventually wind energy (boats, windmills, etc.) and hydro energy (waterwheels) further enhanced humankind's energy surplus, paving the way for further increases in social complexity. The greatest energy revolution, however, was initiated early in the eighteenth century in Europe, when human beings first began harnessing on a large scale the extraordinary potential of fossil fuels. Over recent centuries, coal, gas, and oil have provided the vast energy foundations required to establish and maintain a form of life as complex as globalised industrial civilisation. While it is believed that hunter-gatherers had no more than a dozen distinct social personalities, modern European censuses recognise as many as 20,000 unique occupational roles, and industrial societies may contain more than 1,000,000 different kinds of social personalities.[20] If nothing else, this is evidence of unprecedented social complexity.

At this stage it is important to note that social complexity does not always follow an energy surplus, but often precedes a surplus. In fact, Tainter argues that complexity *typically* precedes an energy surplus. While he accepts that historically there were a few isolated 'revolutions' in energy supply that certainly made further complexity possible, he argues that normally complexity arises when new problems present themselves. In solving those problems, societies are forced to find a way to produce more energy, if that is possible. This contrasts with the isolated situations (following an energy revolution) when societies voluntarily become more complex due to an availability of surplus energy. As Tainter puts it, 'Complexity often compels the production of energy, rather than following its abundance.'[21] This is significant because it means that increasing complexity often is not voluntary, in that it is typically a response to the emergence of unwanted problems, rather than being a creative luxury chosen in response to the availability of surplus energy. This is a point to which I will return as the case for and against voluntary simplification is assessed.

Energy descent futures

Below I outline the role of energy in large-scale societies through the lens of Tainter's theory of socio-political complexification and collapse, focusing on what *energy descent futures* could mean for the current growth-orientated and globalised industrial civilisation. The prospect of energy descent – defended elsewhere[22] – is based on a view that post-carbon sources of energy (e.g., wind turbines and solar panels) will be unable to fully replace the magnitude and nature of energy services currently supported by fossil fuels. As fossil fuel availability declines – either voluntarily due to climate change mitigation or involuntary due to increasing resource scarcity – humanity will find itself with declining energy supply. This is certainly not an argument against renewable energy. It is an argument that the necessary and desirable transition to 100% renewable energy implies having less energy than is available in affluent, carbon-based societies today. The requirement to embrace energy descent in high energy societies is especially compelling in time frames relevant to meeting shrinking carbon budgets (requiring swift and deep decarbonisation) and if distributive equity is taken into account.

Given the close connection between energy and economic activity,[23] the existing form of (industrial) civilisation will be unsupportable in an energy descent future. Furthermore, maintaining current energy supply while facing rising societal costs (e.g., climate breakdown) functions similarly to energy descent. This is because solving new problems draws scarce energy away from what would otherwise have been invested in solving old problems (such as maintaining existing societal institutions and infrastructure). Deterioration or collapse of civilisation follows. Our choice is either to try to maintain this industrial-growthist form of civilisation – which is impossible because it is unsustainable – or build a new form of civilisation. The former is the dominant position today, advocated by governments, businesses, and cultures with consumerist aspirations; the latter is the pathway I will be recommending.

Complexification of society involves a balancing of costs and benefits. That is, when a society solves a problem by becoming more complex it will receive the benefits of solving the problem, but it will also incur the costs of doing so. These costs will include, most importantly, energy and resources, but also costs like time, labour, and annoyance. This balancing exercise takes place every time a society considers responding to a problem by creating a new institution, adding new bureaucrats, developing some new technology, or establishing new social or physical infrastructures, etc. Societies pursue complexity – that is, develop new practices or technologies that attempt to solve the problems they face – when it seems that the benefits of doing so will outweigh the costs. Critically, there must also be the energy and resources available to actually subsidise the problem-solving activity, or at least the potential to acquire more energy and resources, if current supplies are already exhausted in simply maintaining existing complexity.

As noted above, Tainter's central thesis is that while increasing social complexity initially provides a significant net benefit to a society, eventually the benefits derived from complexity diminish and the relative costs begin to increase. He explains that the diminishing returns on complexity arise from the fact that 'humans always tend to pick the lowest hanging fruit first, going on to higher branches only when those lower no longer hold fruit. In problem-solving systems, inexpensive solutions are adopted before more complex and expensive ones.'[24] Over time, the energy and resource costs of problem-solving tend to increase and the relative benefits decrease, which is another way of saying that the marginal return on complexity starts to decline.

Eventually, Tainter argues, the costs of solving a problem will actually be higher than the benefits gained. At this point further problems will not or cannot be solved – or only at the expense of not solving other problems – and societies become vulnerable to deterioration or even rapid collapse. Another way of expressing this is to say that there comes a point in the evolution of societies when all the energy available to that society is exhausted by simply maintaining the existing level of complexity. When further problems arise, as history tells us they inevitably will do, the lack of an energy surplus means that new problems cannot be solved and thus societies become liable to collapse.

This highlights the point explained above about how complexity is not always, and not even normally, a voluntary response to surplus energy, but instead is usually required for a society to sustain itself as new problems emerge. Societies can be destroyed, however, when the costs of sustaining their complexity become unaffordable in terms of resources in general and energy resources especially. This is the essential dynamic that Tainter argues 'can explain collapse as no other theory has been able to do.'[25]

Implications on sustainability discourse

One of the most challenging aspects of Tainter's theory is how it reframes – even revolutionises – how we understand sustainability. Tainter argues that sustainability is about problem solving and that problem solving increases social complexity. However, he also argues that social complexity requires energy and resources, and this implies that solving problems, including ecological problems, can actually require *increases* in energy and resource consumption, not reductions. He explains his position by presenting a critique of voluntary simplification:

> *Voluntarily reduce resource consumption.* This strategy is constrained by the fact that societies increase in complexity to solve problems. Resource production must grow to fund the increased complexity. To

> implement voluntary conservation long term would require that a society be either uniquely lucky in not encountering problems, or that it not address the problems that confront it.[26]

Indeed, Tainter maintains that sustainability is 'not a passive consequence of having fewer human beings who consume more limited resources',[27] as many argue it is. In fact, he suggests that voluntary simplification – that is, the pursuit of forms of social organisation that remain viable with reduced resource use – may no longer be an option for industrial civilisation. Instead, Tainter's primary conception of sustainability involves subsidising ever-increasing complexity with more energy and resources in order to solve ongoing problems.[28] I say 'primary conception' because there are subtleties in Tainter's position that leave open theoretical space (explored below) for alternative conclusions and pathways.

In order to defend SMPLCTY as a viable and desirable form of life, I need to critically examine Tainter's contention that voluntary simplification is not a viable path to sustainability. Given the plausibility of future energy descent, I argue that voluntary simplification is by far the best strategy to implement, even if this conflicts directly with the dominant strategies today which focus on promoting economic growth, material affluence, and advanced technological solutions. Part of the theoretical tension between my position and Tainter's critique of voluntary simplification turns on differing notions of 'sustainability'. Whereas in Tainter's sense sustainability infers *sustaining existing forms of socio-political organisation*, I extend this to *changing the forms of organisation* through voluntary simplification, insofar as that is required for humanity to operate within the carrying capacity of the planet.

Furthermore, even if attempting to sustain existing forms of organising through ever-increasing complexity continues to be humanity's dominant approach to solving societal problems, I maintain the alternative path of voluntary simplification remains the most effective means of building 'resilience' (i.e., the ability of an individual or community to withstand societal or ecological shocks). Such an approach could even lay the foundations for societies to develop the 'antifragile' characteristic of living systems that *strengthen* in response to stress. This is significant because it justifies the practice and promotion of voluntary simplification, irrespective of the likelihood of it ever being broadly accepted. That is, if industrial civilisation's increasing socio-political complexity is coming to an end one way or another due to energy descent, then it would be better to accept this energetic trajectory and prepare for it, rather than wait for it to arrive through crisis and collapse. The aim is not to achieve some passive socio-ecological stasis, but to move toward a way of life that achieves some form of dynamic equilibrium within ecologically sustainable limits.

While I accept that problem solving generally implies an increase in social complexity of the nature Tainter describes, the position I present below is that there comes a point when such complexity itself becomes a problem, at which point voluntary simplification, not further complexity, is the most appropriate response.[29] Not only does industrial civilisation seem to be at such a point today, or well beyond it, I hope to show, albeit in a preliminary way, that voluntary simplification presents a viable and desirable option for responding to today's converging social, economic and ecological problems. This goes against Tainter's primary conception of sustainability, while accepting much of his background theoretical framework.

Given that Tainter seems to accept, as we will see, that his own conception of sustainability will eventually lead to collapse, I believe he is wrong to be so dismissive of voluntary simplification as a strategy for potentially avoiding collapse. It is, I argue, our only alternative to collapse, and if that is so, voluntary simplification ought to be given our most rigorous attention and commitment, even if the chances of success do not seem high. Tainter seems flippant about our best hope, and given what is at stake, his dismissal of voluntary simplification should be given close critical attention.

Tainter's critique of voluntary simplification

Tainter maintains that the argument for sustainability based on voluntarily consuming less and reducing social complexity follows logically from what he considers a flawed assumption – the assumption that surplus resources and energy *precede* and *facilitate* innovations that increase complexity. 'Complexity, in this view, is a voluntary matter. Human societies became more complex by choice rather than necessity. By this reasoning, we should be able to choose to forgo complexity and the resource consumption that it entails.'[30] Tainter rejects that reasoning. In his view, complexity is generally forced upon societies as they respond to new problems, not voluntarily embraced due to an energy surplus, and this leads Tainter to reject voluntary simplification as a path to sustainability:

> Contrary to what is typically advocated as the route to sustainability, *it is usually not possible for a society to reduce its consumption of resources voluntarily over the long term.* To the contrary, as problems great and small inevitably arise, addressing these problems requires complexity and resource consumption to increase.[31]

Elsewhere, Tainter arrives at the same conclusion: 'Sustainability is an active condition of problem solving, not a passive consequence of consuming less.'[32] More directly still, he insists that 'sustainability may require greater consumption of resources rather than less. One must be able to afford sustainability.'[33] He concludes an essay with the following statement, epitomising his environmental stance: 'Developing new energy is therefore the most fundamental thing we can do to become sustainable.'[34]

His essential argument, therefore, is that if we have enough energy to solve the problems we face, civilisation will not deteriorate or collapse. The flip side of that argument, of course, is that if we cannot secure the necessary energy, our future looks much bleaker. That is, we will be destined to repeat the growth cycle of all previous civilisations that have developed and collapsed according to the same logic of diminishing returns on complexity. According to Tainter, the tendency of all societies to become more complex over time, coupled with the diminishing marginal returns on complexity, means that eventually all societies get locked into a process of mandatory growth in complexity that eventually becomes unsupportable. This theory of social complexity implies that all societies have an inbuilt tendency to collapse.

Despite Tainter's approach to sustainability being coherently and rigorously argued (if one accepts his assumptions), his position directly contradicts those who advocate reducing overall energy and resource consumption, which is the strategy I am defending. For reasons already outlined, Tainter rejects that strategy as flawed in theory, and naïve in practice, perhaps even impossible. Given that Tainter is equally dismissive of the other approaches to sustainability (e.g., population reduction, internalising externalities, technological advancements, etc.), one can understand why he resigns himself to the fact that 'the study of social complexity does not yield optimistic results.'[35]

There is something deeply tragic about Tainter's view, because it suggests that civilisation, by its very nature, gets locked into a process of mandatory growth in complexity that eventually becomes unsupportable. Furthermore, history provides a disturbingly consistent empirical basis for this tragic view,[36] leading Tainter to conclude that 'all solutions to the problem of complexity are temporary.'[37] This seemingly innocuous statement is actually profoundly dark, for it implies that ultimately and inevitably social complexity will outgrow its available energy supply. Despite this situation, or rather, because of it, Tainter argues that '"success" consists substantially of staying in the game,'[38] and he believes that sustainability in this sense depends on developing new energy sources to subsidise ongoing problem-solving activity.

Voluntary simplification as an alternative to collapse

I have explained why Tainter believes voluntary simplification is not a readily available civilisational pathway for sustainability. He asserts that such a strategy would 'require that a society be either uniquely lucky in not encountering problems, or that it not address the problems that confront it.'[39] I hope to show, however, that on this critical point he is in error. Furthermore, I will argue that given the tendency of societies to become more complex than they can afford to be, sustainability – in the sense of being sustained into the deep future – requires that societies embrace voluntary simplification when the costs of complexity exceed the benefits. If they do not, they collapse.

Another way of expressing this argument is to say that as the benefits of social complexity diminish and become outweighed by the costs, the benefits of voluntary simplification increase. To be clear, I do not argue that voluntary simplification is *likely* to be embraced as a response to existing crises; my argument is that it is the *only* alternative to collapse, and thus it is a strategy we should do our very best to adopt, no matter our prospects of success. Indeed, given the devastating consequences of any collapse scenario, voluntary simplification becomes a moral imperative.

Building upon the analysis so far, voluntary simplification can be defined more precisely as *choosing a form of life in which the overall consumption of energy and resources is progressively reduced and eventually stabilised at a level that is sufficient for a good life and which lies within the planet's sustainable carrying capacity*. Furthermore, *because social complexity requires energy and resources, voluntarily reducing energy and resource consumption would generally imply a reduction in social complexity*. This definition of voluntary simplification raises many questions, which I will now endeavour to answer.

Most importantly, the definition must be situated in the context of Tainter's theory of social complexity, for in that context the notion of voluntarily reducing energy and resources seems like an incoherent strategy to achieve sustainability. This demands an immediate explanation, because if one were to accept that solving problems generally requires energy and resources – and I do accept that – it would seem to follow that voluntary simplification means *choosing to solve fewer problems*. I will now try to explain that the apparent incoherency here disappears when we take a closer look at what Tainter means when he uses the term 'problem', which is a central concept in his theory. It seems that Tainter oversimplifies here what is a complex term, and that misunderstanding or misuse locks him into the tragic worldview outlined above. I believe that clearing up this misunderstanding provides the key to escaping Tainter's tragic worldview.

We have seen that societies increase their social complexity when they solve the problems with which they are presented. However, Tainter employs the term 'problem' as if it were self-defining and unambiguous. He assumes that a society just knows what is and what is not a problem, which of course is not an unreasonable assumption. On closer inspection, however, a 'problem' in Tainter's sense is actually a radically indeterminate notion, requiring various value judgements in order to give it content. There are at least three causes of this indeterminacy.

First, indeterminacy can arise over the very question of what constitutes a problem. For example, if a nation perceives a problem of national security, it may wage war on a threateningly powerful neighbouring state, rather than risk being attacked by surprise. Solving the 'problem' of security, therefore, might require (a) creating an army; and (b) if the war were successful, defending a larger territory, perhaps requiring a larger army. This solution to the problem of security is a classic example of how increasing social complexity can require increased energy and resources.

However, the 'problem' here is by no means something independent of human values or perspectives. That is, the problem is not just imposed on the society for it to deal with as best it can. There are *choices* involved about what problems to focus on. For example, rather than seeing the problem as being one of 'security', a different society might have seen a problem of 'economic growth', and rather than waging war, this alternative society might have tried to solve its problem by seeing if it could create a relationship of mutual benefit with its neighbours, perhaps through trade. Even through this simple example (which could be endlessly multiplied) it can be seen that the 'problems' that exist for any given society are often a value-laden function of their perspective or goals, not objective or externally imposed challenges that arise independently.

A second cause of indeterminacy lies in the fact that there is rarely only one means of *solving* a particular problem. In the example above, the problem of security could have been solved by waging war, building a defensive wall, trying to negotiate a treaty, some mixture of these strategies, or through some other strategy entirely. Likewise, the problem of 'economic growth' could have been solved by creating new trade relationships, developing new technologies, marketing goods more effectively, or perhaps realising that growth was not actually so important (or was even harmful). Just as different worldviews might produce or dissolve certain problems, different worldviews also provide different ways of dealing with the problems that do exist (or are perceived to exist). Significantly, this means that shifts in perspective, values, or desires can affect the level of energy or resources that are needed to deal with societal problems.

Finally, indeterminacy can also arise over the question of 'whose' problems have to be solved, for society is not a harmonious entity with a single set of goals and desires. This raises distributive questions of real importance. All societies have a limited pool of energy and resources, and the nature of any society is shaped significantly by how those limited resources are distributed and to what ends those resources are directed. Accordingly, when a society invests energy and resources to solve certain 'problems', we are entitled to ask questions about whose interests are being served by addressing those particular issues as opposed to others. It may be, after all, that some people in a society do not see such and such a problem as being a legitimate concern, or perhaps they see other issues that are not being addressed as being more urgent.

Tainter, it should be noted, is not wholly unaware of this issue. He writes: 'In a hierarchical institution [or society], the benefits of complexity often accrue at the top, while the costs are paid primarily by those at the bottom.'[40] But he does not seem to appreciate that this is evidence of indeterminacy over what constitutes a problem; nor does he seem to appreciate how all these causes of indeterminacy impact on his theory. Even in a context of energy descent, for example, it could be that many civilisational problems (including environmental problems) could be solved if existing concentrations of wealth were redistributed toward solving those problems, rather than merely satisfying the indulgences of a small global elite. Less positively, in circumstances of civilisation deterioration or collapse, the most likely outcome of socio-economic stress is that poverty is forced on the poorest social classes while the elite continue to reap the benefits of the complexity that remains.

My point in exposing these three indeterminacies is to show that societal problems are not objective phenomena that exist independently of humankind and which we must simply deal with the best we can. Rather, problems are often the product of a particular worldview or value-system, in the sense that they only exist as problems because society (or a particular subset of society) desires a certain state of affairs. This analysis could be applied to all aspects of industrial civilisation, including: the way energy is produced and used; the way we transport ourselves; the way we organise ourselves and our economies; the way we attend to our health or educational needs; the way we house and clothe ourselves; the way we entertain ourselves; and so on. Rather than solving the problem of water security by creating expensive and energy intensive desalination plants, for example, people could simply use less water; rather than addressing obesity with expensive diet pills or liposuction, people could choose to eat better and do more exercise; rather than buying a clothes dryer, people could dry their clothes on a string outside.

This is not always the case, of course. Some very serious problems – climate change, for example – will obviously not disappear merely because human beings decide to think differently about the world. But many perceived problems and perceived solutions are in fact dependent on the way human beings view the world, or dependent on whose particular perspective is adopted. What this means is that if the world came to be looked at through a different lens of understanding, a society might well find that it was faced with different problems, and perhaps different solutions would present themselves to existing problems. Again, this is significant because it means that changing perspectives or values can affect the level of energy or resources that are needed for a society to deal with its problems.

The implications of this analysis are profound. Most importantly, it opens up space within Tainter's theory for voluntary reductions in energy and resources. The key point is this: *the energy intensity of industrial civilisation is primarily a function of the values that produce or shape the perception of its problems*. Those values also produce and shape the perception of what constitutes a solution to perceived problems. Change those values, however, and many of the energy intensive problems that industrial civilisation currently feels the need to solve may well disappear. Although in places Tainter seems to acknowledge this,[41] he does not appear to grasp its implications for his own conception of sustainability. If energy intensive problems can be solved or rather dissolved by changing one's values or perspective, this will reduce the overall energy requirements for 'problem solving', thus creating an option for voluntary simplification.

When this is understood, the apparent incoherency of voluntary simplification disappears (i.e., the perceived implication that it would require choosing 'to solve fewer problems'). Simplification might instead involve solving different problems, or perhaps solving the same problems in different, less energy-intensive ways. Tainter does not seem to appreciate this, or at least its significance, for otherwise he would not dismiss simplification so readily. He argues that voluntarily reducing consumption would require that a society be either uniquely lucky in not encountering problems, or that it not address the problems that confront it.[42] But the analysis above shows that there is a third option: rethinking both what constitutes a problem and what constitutes an appropriate response. It may be that many problems that industrial civilisation currently invests in are not actually problems that need to be solved, or not in such energy intensive ways. For example, we could 'solve' the 'problem' of transport with more bikes and fewer cars, suggesting that sustainability is not always about *maintaining* a certain way of life but actually *changing* it, perhaps in fundamental ways.

The critical point is that this type of analysis could be reproduced through essentially limitless examples. There is always room for a society to rethink its problems, rethink its solutions, and, importantly, *rethink how it prioritises the energy and resources it has available for problem solving.* If a society does this effectively it may find that it can solve all of its most important problems while reducing its consumption of energy and resources within sustainable levels (and redistributing its energy and resources when responding to new problems that arise). Doing so, of course, may produce a very different type of society.

How might Tainter respond?

One way Tainter might respond to this analysis is to argue that it seems to ignore the tendency of all societies to increase in complexity. Even if Tainter accepted, as he might well do, that there is room to reduce the energy intensity of industrial civilisation in the short term, he might nevertheless reiterate that societies are constantly faced with new problems, such that any attempts at voluntary simplification will eventually be rendered unsuccessful by the inexorable pressure to increase social complexity in response to new problems. For that reason, the costs of maintaining society will still tend to increase over the long term. Tainter might insist, therefore, that my analysis has not been able to provide any escape from the inherent tendency of civilisations to grow in social complexity until they cannot afford the costs of their own existence.

While I accept that societies will constantly be faced with new problems and that solving them will tend to increase social complexity, this is not fatal to the position I am defending. It would only be problematic if it were assumed that voluntary simplification is a passive or static form of life, as opposed to one that is dynamic and evolving. But I maintain that achieving sustainability, far from being passive or static in any way, must be a strategy that is self-reflective and constantly in flux. Again, if in places Tainter might seem to accept this point, he does not seem to appreciate what it means for his dismissal of voluntary simplification. The thought processes, behaviours, and institutions which voluntary simplification might represent cannot be static or unchanging, but must constantly respond to new circumstances and opportunities in novel ways.

Granted, if voluntary simplification meant reducing consumption and then returning to old ways of living, one can understand why social complexity would tend to increase over time, negating any initial benefits of voluntary simplification. But voluntary simplification allows for a more nuanced definition. It can and should be considered an ongoing process, in which people and societies continually seek to reduce and restrain consumption, while also rethinking how best to invest the energy and resources at their disposal. Accordingly, there is no reason to think that a society cannot be sustained, over the long term, on an environmentally sustainable level of energy and resource consumption, while still solving its most important problems (including new problems). Voluntary simplification, therefore, is not about achieving a stasis; it is about actively working on reaching and then maintaining some form of dynamic equilibrium within sustainable limits. This will not be easy, of course; but it is not impossible. And it may be the only escape from the Four Horsemen.

A second way Tainter might respond to my analysis is to say that there is already room for it within his own theory.[43] Although this would require a degree of self-contradiction, the response would seem to have some initial justification. After all, in his historical analysis, Tainter states that the Byzantine Empire (which survived the collapse of the Roman Empire in the fifth century) is an example, albeit the only one he claims, where 'a large, complex society systematically simplified, and reduced thereby its consumption of resources.'[44] At first instance, this seems to be the strategy I am defending. But after acknowledging Byzantine simplification, Tainter immediately adds that '[w]hile this case shows that societies can reduce consumption and thrive, it offers no hope that this can be commonly done.'[45] More importantly, however, Tainter points out that simplification in the Byzantine Empire was both forced – that is, made necessary by a gross insufficiency of resources – and temporary.[46] Since I am defending a strategy of simplification that is both voluntary and practiced over the long term, the Byzantine example is not evidence that voluntary simplification already fits within Tainter's theory. Rather, establishing the viability of voluntary simplification extends Tainter's theory in a way that avoids his tragic conclusions.[47]

A third way Tainter might respond to my analysis is by stating that, even if simplification were an available strategy, it will not be voluntarily embraced on the grounds that people will perceive that it is against their own interests. In fact, when considering whether voluntary simplification is possible, he states: 'I am confident that usually it is not, that humans will not ordinarily forgo affordable consumption of things they desire on the basis of abstract projections about the future.'[48] Although Tainter's position here has some intuitive force, it is far from being self-evident. Tainter seems to assume (without being explicit about it) that reducing consumption is against one's self-interest.

But that assumption, despite being culturally entrenched, is empirically debatable, and in consumer societies it is most probably false. Indeed, there is now a vast body of social and psychological research indicating that many if not most Western-style consumers are actually mis-consuming to some extent, in the sense that they could increase their wellbeing while reducing their consumption.[49] The intricacies of that research cannot be explored here, but if it can indeed be shown, as I believe it can, that large portions of high consumption societies would benefit from exchanging superfluous material consumption for more time to pursue non-materialist forms of wellbeing, this would provide further support for the argument that voluntary simplification is not only possible, but desirable. If more people came to see this, one would expect simplification to be voluntarily embraced, not out of altruism but through self-interest.

Nevertheless, while that might be so at the individual or community level, the question of whether *governments* will ever voluntarily initiate overall reductions in societal production and consumption is more challenging. After all, governments depend for their existence on taxes, and a larger economy means more taxable income, so a process of voluntary simplification is almost certainly not going to be initiated from the 'top down'. The overriding objective of governments around the world is to expand their economies without apparent limit, and continued growth requires (among other things) a citizenry that seeks ever-higher material standards of living. This growth model of progress is arguably a reflection of an underlying belief that social progress requires more energy and resources in order to increase existing standards of living and solve ongoing problems. But if the global economy has now reached a stage where the growth model is causing the very problems it was supposed to solve, as many argue it has, then voluntary simplification provides the most coherent path forward, especially for the most highly developed regions of the world.

Although the prospects of governments embracing some 'top down' policy of voluntary simplification seem very slim, it is also clear that governments create many of the structures within which social movements operate, and those structures can function either to facilitate or inhibit a process of voluntary simplification. While an examination of ways governments could facilitate such a process lies beyond the scope of this essay, the 'growth imperative' structurally built into modern economies suggests that if voluntary simplification is to emerge, it may well have to be driven 'from below'.[50]

Voluntary simplification, as I have defined it, involves rethinking problems, exploring new solutions, and reassessing how the limited energy and resources available for problem solving are prioritised. This is where the practical implications of the analysis become clearest. The task is to evaluate, personally and socially, how and where energy and resources are used and for what purposes; to isolate those areas where those resources are being wasted or misdirected; to redirect or redistribute those resources toward solving the most pressing social and ecological problems; and, where possible, reducing the overall energy-intensity of our ways of living even if this involves reductions in social complexity. If a household, community, or society does this effectively it may find that it can solve all its most important problems, including new ones, while reducing its consumption of energy and resources (or at least not getting locked into ever-increasing consumption and complexity). But this process is not about achieving some passive ecological, social, or economic stasis; it is about constantly working on reaching and then maintaining some form of dynamic equilibrium within ecologically sustainable limits. Given that presently the global economy is far exceeding the sustainable carrying capacity of the planet, it follows that voluntary simplification implies creating very different social and economic systems.

As I have argued elsewhere,[51] an ecologically sustainable society would probably need to be based on a highly self-sufficient, low-carbon economy that uses mostly local resources to meet local needs. These would be zero-growth economies that were sustained on ecologically viable levels of resource consumption and environmental impact. This implies that material living standards would be far lower than what are common in consumer societies today, but basic needs for all could be met and high quality of life could be maintained through non-materialistic sources of meaning and happiness. Embracing lifestyles of voluntary simplicity, therefore, does not necessarily mean hardship or deprivation. Rather, it means focusing on what is *sufficient* to live well, rather than constantly seeking increased consumption and greater affluence.

Should industrial civilisation continue to pursue the path of growth without limits, in an attempt to universalise affluence, it will meet the fate of all previous civilisations, with all the suffering that implies. To avoid this, what is required is voluntary simplification. If voluntary simplification is not embraced on a sufficiently wide scale to avoid social, economic, or ecological collapse, it nevertheless remains the most effective way for individuals and communities to build resilience. It would free up more energy and resources to deal with systemic disruptions. In the current milieu, therefore, perhaps the ability to withstand forthcoming shocks is the best we can hope for.

The 'Law of Progressive Simplification'

Industrial civilisation is at a point in history when it is faced with the pressing issue of whether it can afford the problem of its own existence. Like a growing number of others, I do not believe that it can, at least, not for much longer. Ongoing environmental and financial crises around the world are barely disguised metaphors for this question of affordability, and they present all of us living in industrial civilisation with the question of how best to respond to this problem – the problem of whether civilisation can afford the costs of its own complexity.

We are hardly the first to be faced with this problem; indeed, all previous civilisations have faced it. But perhaps we can be first, thanks to Joseph Tainter, to understand the dynamics at play. Perhaps we can even respond in such a way as to avoid the collapse scenario that has marked the end of all other civilisations. Prior civilisations attempted to sustain themselves and avoid collapse by continuing to increase complexity in response to new problems, but always this strategy has resulted in collapse, because eventually the energy and resources needed to subsidise increased complexity becomes unavailable. Nevertheless, this seems to be the very response industrial civilisation is taking presently, and indeed it is the one which Tainter himself recommends as the best course of action. As he puts it, 'modern societies will continue to need high-quality energy, and securing this should be the first priority of every nation with a research capability.'[52]

As I have argued, this advice from Tainter is deeply problematic, given that energy-intensive problem solving led to collapse on all other occasions in history, of which he is very aware. The advice appears more problematic still if one accepts that the world is facing a future of 'energy descent'. But Tainter's advice follows the logic of his own assumptions. While I accept that complexity generally has diminishing marginal returns, I have tried to show, albeit in a preliminary way, that voluntary simplification is actually a viable and desirable response to this challenging dynamic. In doing so, I have turned Tainter's solution on its head: where he sees the solution to civilisation's problems in further complexity, I maintain the best and probably the only solution lies in voluntary simplification.

This position is not without esteemed support. The great historian of civilisations Arnold Toynbee described the 'Law of Progressive Simplification' as a process of 'etherealization',[53] whereby humanity learns to meet its deepest existential needs with declining material and energy demands. He explained that the result is 'not a loss but a gain; and this gain is the outcome of process of simplification because the process liberates forces that have been imprisoned in a more material medium and thereby sets them free to work in a more ethereal medium with greater potency.'[54] He added that this involves 'not merely a simplification of apparatus but a consequent transfer of energy, or shift of emphasis, from some lower sphere of being or of action to a higher.'[55]

Toynbee explained this process primarily in terms of efficiency improvements via 'technical progress'[56] and the 'human control over physical nature.'[57] In my view, progressive (or voluntary) simplification ought to *include* such dematerialisation or deintensification via technological innovation, but refers more fundamentally to a socio-ethical or even spiritual approach to life that is independent of the state of technology. In other words, progressive simplification can be undertaken immediately, with or without further technological advance, and indeed, with or without biophysical pressures. We can even conceive of civilisations that embrace simplicity in advance of necessity. That is, by resisting overcomplexification as a means of *avoiding* problems, as opposed to overcomplex civilisations (such as present-day industrial civilisation) that are pressured to simplify in order to *resolve* their problems.

If humanity does not learn to embrace voluntary simplification within the present iteration of (industrial) civilisation, the minimally optimistic hypothesis I posit is that humanity will *eventually* come to see that it is the only path to genuine sustainability and flourishing within biophysical limits. Of course, given the profound seductions of complexity, the insecurities of the human ego, the grasping for power, and the limitations of the human intellect, it is possible and indeed likely that this lesson may not be learned until many more civilisations rise and fall as a result of the diminishing returns on complexity. Indeed, it is possible that humanity never learns this lesson.

However, the faith implicit to my vision of SMPLCTY is that *eventually* humanity will learn that voluntary simplification is the only path to civilisational stability and flourishing. Just as humanity (so far) has managed to avoid nuclear Armageddon for fear of mutually assured destruction, so too might our species one day learn that voluntary simplification is required for the same reason. As cultures develop this deep historical consciousness – when they see more clearly the repeated patterns of collapse occurring over and over again – I believe our species will slowly absorb this wisdom, in a piecemeal fashion, over an indeterminate timescale. This may take centuries or even millennia, but over time the ranks who come to see this truth will expand, eventually leading to the deep transformation of human society. One way or another, there will be a Great Simplification, whether by design or disaster. Thus, as John Michael Greer declares, let's 'collapse now and avoid the rush.'[58]

As opposed to a utopian fantasy or prediction, I have suggested that SMPLCTY ought to be received as an *orienting vision* that should increasingly guide human endeavour as it becomes clearer to more people that growth-orientated alternatives will always end in collapse. It designates a civilisation in dynamic equilibrium, constantly balancing and rebalancing its societal goals in relation to its sustainable (and therefore limited) flow of energy and resources. The turn to non-materialistic sources of meaning and happiness does not imply a turn away from nature, sensuous experience, or the material world, it only implies negation of practices that are unnecessarily materially and energetically consumptive (i.e., unsustainable). The questions of how much is enough, of what, and for whom, are the defining value-laden inquiries that inform the ethics and politics of SMPLCTY.

According to this view, human beings would be justified in being messengers, advocates for, and prefigurative pioneers of voluntary simplification, even if our success or validation likely lies beyond this civilisational cycle. If the cause is known to be good, then we can take solace in the fact that we are serving a noble cause bigger than ourselves – not other-worldly but of this Earth – even if many of the rewards will only accrue to future generations. But as the Greek proverb goes: 'a civilisation flourishes when people plant trees under which they will never sit.' When struggles are of profound existential import, patience can be a necessary virtue, and there is honour in being an underlabourer whose modest but necessary contribution will one day be forgotten.

As I have noted, practising simplicity in the here and now also has the fortunate consequence of building resilience today, preparing an individual, household, or community for potential conditions of collapse. Thus, it is an approach to life that is justifiable even if (as is very likely) the ethos of voluntary simplification does not expand sufficiently to avoid the collapse of industrial civilisation. In a range of related social movements (permaculture, voluntary simplicity, degrowth, etc.), the ranks of simplicity thinking and practice are expanding, albeit, for now, very slowly. It seems that SMPLCTY is an idea whose time has not yet come. But I believe that such a time will eventually come, even if it takes hundreds or perhaps thousands of years.

Although the energy and resource flows are limited within this envisioned form of life, the exploration of the good life remains unlimited, in the same way that a pianist is not limited by the 88 keys of a piano. There will never be a time when all the beautiful sonatas have been written, just as there will never be a time when all possible manifestations of beautiful lives have been lived. Human beings are tasked with creating as an aesthetic project the meaning of their own lives. Within biophysical limits and upon sufficient material foundations, we are limited only by our imaginations. This is the bounded infinity of human flourishing.

The good life according to SMPLCTY is achieved primarily through aesthetic experience, both creatively (making art) and passively (appreciating art). This is an endless creative process of infinite diversity and stimulation. As I'm using the term, art refers both to conventional objects and productions (painting, music, sculpture, literature, etc) but also the artful products created by artisans (everyday artefacts that are both useful and beautiful). Indeed, as I have illustrated elsewhere,[59] human beings are related to their own lives in a manner that is akin to the relationship between sculptor and clay, imposing on us the exhilarating but terrifying burden of applying our own aesthetic criteria to the spiritual practice of self-fashioning.

Importantly, this can be understood as a means of solving a 'problem' within Tainter's framework – the problem of how to live a full and meaningful life – in ways consistent with the 'less is more' strategy of voluntary simplification. Within industrial civilisation, the human search for meaning is pursued in ways that are violent, unsustainable, unjust, and perhaps worst of all, largely unsuccessful. We now face the prospect of collapse sometime this century. My thesis is that voluntary simplification presents a meaningful alternative to collapse, grounded in an aesthetics of existence.

Taken to its logical extreme, this aesthetic vision of the good life culminates in a mystical blurring of art and life, where humans relate to each other neither as master and slave, nor as capitalist and worker, but in the reciprocal and revolving relationships of artist and art lover. This signifies an evolution from *homo economicus* (the archetype of industrial civilisation) to *homo aestheticus* (the archetype of SMPLCTY). This can be understood as the outcome of an underlying creative process: the Will to Live, evolving into the Will to Power, and culminating in the Will to Art.[60] Through this cosmological process, the aesthetic universe seeks to experience itself through the nodes of consciousness and creativity that have emerged in the fabric of existence.

The archetypal, self-governing citizen in SMPLCTY is the poet-farmer, who lives simply in a material and energetic sense, contributes to necessary economic production and community governance in non-hierarchical conditions, and who otherwise explores the good life through creative activity and aesthetic experience. There will of course be artistic 'geniuses' whose work captures and impresses the social imagination more than others, but the poet-farmer is an ordinary creative soul who revels in aesthetic practices without need or expectation of social recognition. This civilisation democratises the poet. Art does not replace religion in such a society, but it answers the same (and perhaps some new) spiritual needs, such that the artist comes to replace the priest as spiritual advisor and existential provocateur.

Having undergone an artful descent, an ecological civilisation will discover that it is good and worth preserving. The fundamental structural requirement of voluntary simplification does not otherwise contain or delimit the forms of life that can be created within biophysical constraints. An infinite diversity of aesthetic communities may arise, loosely networked for mutual support and appreciation. Eventually *homo aestheticus* might even evolve into *homo mysticus*, a state in which the poet-farmer, who has moved through the aesthetic condition, no longer has an urge to create beyond subsistence and rather finds *Being* enough. This represents the true and only End of Art. *Homo mysticus*, like *homo aestheticus*, is not a state of life-negation but of ultimate life-affirmation. As ever more time and energy are transferred away from materialistic pursuits, we will turn to the realm of the spirit to satisfy our hunger for infinity.

Over millions of years, these aesthetico-mystical communities will live creatively and sustainably, producing and appreciating unimaginable forms of art and aesthetic experience. So many artistic geniuses will emerge that anything resembling an exhaustive 'art history' will become impossible, and egotistical hopes of being 'remembered' will fade. There will be millions upon millions of Beethovens, Shakespeares, and Goethes, etc. to enjoy – as well as aesthetic exemplars as yet unimagined. Increasingly human beings will experiment with novel ways of immersing themselves in the deep well of aesthetic resources at their disposal, as if playing Herman Hesses's 'Glass Bead Game' as a form of life.[61] As the ideal of S M P L C T Y is approached, beauty will beget beauty, and an aesthetic singularity will everywhere threaten to explode in a chain reaction of unfathomable spectacles of creativity and sensuous experience. The nature of this singularity is unknowable in advance, but it should be acknowledged as a possibility, even if we must then pass over it in silence, like all mystical phenomena.

Science tells us that at some distant point – perhaps in hundreds of millions of years – Earth will be swallowed by a black hole, destroyed by a comet, or become uninhabitable due to the heat-death of the sun. Accordingly, the human story is, ultimately, finite. Our cosmological contribution is our art – our human stories – all of which will one day be dust, blowing in the winds of a dark, cold, silent universe. After an indeterminate duration of cosmological expansion, the universe may implode into the singularity from which it emerged or expand at the speed of light, and the mysterious cosmological process might begin again, repeating this aesthetic cycle an infinite number of times, in eternal recurrence. This mystery needs and allows for no primal explanation. That the Will to Art exists at all is the marvel of all marvels.

To paraphrase T.S. Eliot, we are the music, while the music lasts.[62]

---

[1] See my previous essays in this collection, especially 'The Cosmos as a "Readymade": Dignifying the Aesthetic Universe'; 'Creative Evolution and the Will to Art'; and 'Pessimism without Despair: Suffering, Desire, and the Affirmation of Life'. The full set will be available here: http://samuelalexander.info/s-m-p-l-c-t-y-ecological-civilisation-and-the-will-to-art/ (accessed 10 May 2023).

[2] Samuel Alexander, *Prosperous Descent: Crisis as Opportunity in an Age of Limits* (Melbourne: Simplicity Institute, 2015).

[3] Samuel Alexander, *Art Against Empire: Toward an Aesthetics of Degrowth* (Melbourne: Simplicity Institute, 2017).

[4] See Samuel Alexander, 'Homo Aestheticus, the Artful Species: and Evolutionary Perspective' and Samuel Alexander, 'Giving Birth to Oneself: Ethics as an "Aesthetics of Existence"' in this collection of essays. See link in note 1.

[5] I have discussed social and political policies and institutions in my other academic work on degrowth, permaculture, and energy descent. See, for example, my four volumes of collected essays, as well as *Degrowth in the Suburbs: A Radical Urban Imaginary* (Singapore: Palgrave, 2019, co-authored with Brendan Gleeson). Although I will discuss political issues further in the final substantive essay in this collection ('The Aesthetic State'), the basic approach of this project is even more fundamental. As Aristotle once remarked, before we inquire into what the best political arrangements are, what is needed is some conception of what a 'good life' consists of. These essays are attempting to clarify the nature of the good life as an aesthetic agent in an aesthetic universe, which is a way of providing normative foundations to my political views.

[6] This phrase is borrowed from Duane Elgin, *Voluntary Simplicity: Toward a Way of Life that is Outwardly Simple, Inwardly Rich* (New York: Harper, 2010, 2nd edition).

[7] I have analysed the meaning of an 'aesthetic justification' of existence elsewhere. See Samuel Alexander, 'An Aesthetic Justification of Existence: The Redemptive Function of Art' in this collection of essays. See link in note 1.

[8] Samuel Alexander, *Sufficiency Economy: Enough, for Everyone, Forever* (Melbourne: Simplicity Institute, 2015).

[9] Erich Fromm, *To Have or To Be?* (New York: Continuum, 2007).

[10] See Samuel Alexander and Amanda McLeod, *Simple Living in History: Pioneers of the Deep Future* (Melbourne: Simplicity Institute, 2014).

[11] Joseph Tainter, *The Collapse of Complex Societies* (Cambridge: Cambridge University Press, 1988).
[12] Ibid.
[13] Joseph Tainter, 'Resources and Cultural Complexity: Implications for Sustainability' (2011) *Crit. Rev. Plant Sci.* 30: p. 33.
[14] Joseph Tainter, 'Problem Solving: Complexity, History, Sustainability (2000) *Population Environments* 22(1): p. 34.
[15] Joseph Tainter, 'Sustainability of Complex Societies' (1995) *Futures* 27(4): p. 400.
[16] See Samuel Alexander, 'Voluntary Simplicity as an Alternative to Collapse' (2014) *Foresight* 16(6): pp. 550-566.
[17] See generally, Vaclav Smil, *Energy and Civilization: A History* (Cambridge, MA: MIT Press, 2017).
[18] Marshall Sahlins, *Stone Age Economics* (London: Routledge, 2017).
[19] I have discussed the slow development of technology in pre-history in my essay, Samuel Alexander, 'Homo Aestheticus, the Artful Species: An Evolutionary Perspective' in this collection of essays. See link in note 1.
[20] See Tainter, note 13, p. 24.
[21] Joseph Tainter, 'Social Complexity and Sustainability (2006) *Ecological Complexity* 3: p. 94.
[22] See Samuel Alexander and Joshua Floyd, *Carbon Civilisation and the Energy Descent Future* (Melbourne: Simplicity Institute, 2018); Joshua Floyd, Samuel Alexander, Manfred Lenzen et al, 'Energy Descent as a Post-Carbon Transition Scenario: How "Knowledge Humility" Reshapes Energy Futures for Post-Normal Times' (2020) *Futures* 122: 102565. I am indebted to David Holmgren for the concept of energy descent. I have also benefited greatly from discussing and writing about energy descent with Joshua Floyd, including its application to Tainter's work.
[23] Robert Ayres and Benjamin Warr, *The Economic Growth Engine: How Energy and Work Drive Material Prosperity* (Cheltenham, UK: Edward Elgar, 2009).
[24] See Tainter, note 13, p. 26.
[25] See Tainter, note 15, p. 400.
[26] Joseph Tainter, 'Energy, Complexity, and Sustainability: A Historical Perspective' (2011) *Environmental Innovation and Societal Transitions* 1: pp. 93-4.
[27] Joseph Tainter, 'Social Complexity and Sustainability' (2006) *Ecol. Complex.* 3: p. 93.
[28] Ibid, p. 94.
[29] See Alexander, note 16.
[30] See Tainter, note 13, p. 31.
[31] Ibid (emphasis in original).
[32] See Tainter, note 21, p. 99.
[33] See Tainter, note 21, p. 91.
[34] See Tainter, note 13, p. 33.
[35] See Tainter, note 21, p. 99.
[36] See Tainter, note 11.
[37] See Tainter, note 21, p. 100.
[38] Ibid.
[39] See Tainter, note 26, p. 93-4.
[40] See Tainter, note 21, p.100.
[41] See Joseph Tainter, 'A Framework for Sustainability' (2003) *World Futures* 59: p. 215.

[42] See Tainter, note 26, pp. 93-4.
[43] See Tainter, note 41.
[44] See Tainter, note 13, p. 31.
[45] Ibid.
[46] Ibid.
[47] Although the term 'voluntary' suggests that simplification is purely a choice to embrace or forego, it should be noted that while simplification is currently a 'choice', soon enough it may become *necessary* due to resource or energy scarcity that may *impose* simplification upon industrial civilisation. My argument, therefore, is essentially that simplification is coming whether we want it or not, so we should 'choose' and plan for this necessity (in advance of its imposition) rather than have it imposed upon us through collapse.
[48] See Tainter, note 13, p. 31.
[49] See, e.g., Samuel Alexander 'The Optimal Material Threshold: Toward an Economics of Sufficiency' (2012) *Real-World Economics Review* 61: 2-21.
[50] See Samuel Alexander and Brendan Gleeson, *Degrowth in the Suburbs: A Radical Urban Imaginary* (Singapore: Palgrave, 2019), especially Ch. 4; and Samuel Alexander, 'Voluntary Simplicity and the Social Reconstruction of Law: Degrowth from the Grassroots Up' (2013) *Environmental Values* 22(2): pp. 287-308.
[51] Samuel Alexander, *Entropia: Life Beyond Industrial Civilisation* (Melbourne: Simplicity Institute, 2013).
[52] See Tainter, note 26, p. 94.
[53] Arnold Toynbee, *A Study of History: Abridgement of Volumes I-VI by D.C. Somervell* (Oxford: Oxford University Press, 1987), p. 198.
[54] Ibid.
[55] Ibid. See also, Fromm, *To Have or To Be?* See note 9.
[56] Ibid.
[57] Toynbee, note 53, p. 199.
[58] John Michael Greer, 'Collapse Now and Avoid the Rush' *Resilience* (6 June 2012).
[59] See note 4.
[60] See Samuel Alexander, 'Creative Evolution and the Will to Art' in this collection of essays. See the link in note 1.
[61] See Herman Hesse, *The Glass Bead Game* (London: Penguin, 1972). I return to this novel in the concluding essay in this collection.
[62] See T.S. Eliot, 'The Dry Salvages' from *Four Quartets* (1941). Available here: http://www.davidgorman.com/4quartets/3-salvages.htm (accessed 2 January 2023).

'I know of no more encouraging fact than the unquestionable ability of man to elevate his life by conscious endeavour. It is something to be able to paint a particular picture, or to carve a statue, and so make a few objects beautiful, but it is far more glorious to carve and paint the very atmosphere and medium through which we look.... To affect the quality of the day, that is the highest of the arts.'

– Henry David Thoreau

POET-FARMER: A THOREAUVIAN AESTHETICS OF SUFFICIENCY

In the previous essay I explored Joseph Tainter's analysis of the dynamics of civilisational development and collapse (see this endnote for a review).[1] When applied to today's globalised, industrial civilisation, a case can be made that we have already passed the point of positive returns on growth and complexity. Indeed, civilisation seems to be in a developed stage of decay or 'uneconomic growth', which is threatening to transform into unplanned, chaotic collapse as planetary boundaries are breached and financial systems tremble.[2] Such a descent could be driven by a confluence of any number of factors, including financial crisis, war, pandemic, resource scarcity, or the crossing of environmental tipping points.

One might think that an obvious and appropriate response to excessive complexity would be to embrace a strategy of 'voluntary simplification' – that is, creatively solving pressing societal problems while also reducing energy and resource demands. For example, cycling more and driving less would advance human health and environmental sustainability, perhaps even happiness, while also reducing energy and resource demands. Such strategies would also free up energy and resources to solve other problems. But Tainter attempts to show why this type of voluntary simplification is not usually available. He argues that solving problems typically requires energy and resources, from which it would follow that solving new or worsening problems requires *increases* in energy and resource use, not *reductions*.

In my critical analysis of Tainter's theory, I outlined why his pessimistic conclusions were based on an unduly narrow way of analysing and engaging societal 'problems'. I showed that if we rethink *which* societal problems are to be solved and in *which ways*, it is possible to adopt voluntary simplification (thus addressing ecological overshoot) while also solving key social problems (like eliminating poverty and achieving distributive equity). Of course, this would require profound shifts in the nature of the existing growth-orientated civilisation, not merely finding ways to make this civilisation sustain itself for a bit longer. I argued that a necessary part of any strategy for achieving this outcome, and escaping Tainter's tragic conclusions, is reimagining the good life beyond consumer culture, as well as building societal structures that support rather than inhibit a sufficiency-based a way of life.[3] If overconsuming and overly-complex societies were to embrace post-consumerist conceptions of flourishing, the immediate benefit would be reducing energy and material demands, mitigating environmental pressures. But it would also free up scarce resources to solve other problems that humanity faces, without necessarily getting locked into the dynamics of complexity that Tainter outlines so powerfully.

According to this logic, voluntary simplification is an alternative to collapse, and I attempted to show why, in fact, it may be the *only* alternative.[4] Furthermore, if it transpires that collapse cannot be avoided, then learning to get by with minimal but sufficient energy and material wealth remains an attractive living strategy to adopt. This is because it is likely to prepare households and communities for the prospect of *involuntary simplification*, as economies contract due to the deepening of societal and ecological crises. This suggests that voluntary simplification ought to be pursued, irrespective of whether it is likely to be widely embraced. In short, we should aim for sustainability, but may have to settle for resilience.

I maintain that initiating and successfully prosecuting a process of voluntary simplification – or degrowth – will depend on an aesthetic transformation of tastes in relation to material culture. One of the central theses in this collection of essays is that the aesthetic capacities and sensibilities of humankind can be fully explored in rich and satisfying ways, while living 'simply' in a material and energetic sense. On that basis, I am proposing that expanding opportunities for artistic expression and aesthetic experience are among the best ways of moving toward a civilisation that is environmentally sustainable, socially just, and personally fulfilling. In that light I have employed the term SMPLCTY to refer to an ecological civilisation of simple living 'poet-farmers'. These citizens would live aesthetically stimulating and diverse lives while mindfully constraining material and energy requirements.

Building on that vision of artful descent, in this essay I will turn to the life and philosophy of Henry David Thoreau to highlight an aesthetics of sufficiency that I maintain lies at the heart of SMPLCTY. Such an aesthetics underpins the living strategy of the poet-farmer, of which Thoreau is a fine exemplar. While this essay attempts to convey a material culture of voluntary simplicity mainly from an individualist perspective – from the perspective of daily experience – the social implications are unpacked further in the next essay, where the aesthetic ideas of William Morris are engaged. The final substantive essay (before the conclusion) takes the analysis a step further, into the realm of politics, by looking more deeply into the Schillerian concept of an 'aesthetic state' (essay forthcoming). First, however, attention must be given to what voluntary simplicity might look like, and feel like, as a way of life.

Poet-farmer: The simple life of Henry David Thoreau

Few individuals in history evoke images of 'the simple life' more distinctly than the poet, farmer, and philosopher, Henry David Thoreau. In 1845, when Henry was 27 years old, he left his hometown of Concord, Massachusetts, and went to live alone in the woods, near Walden Pond. There he built himself a small cabin and for two years earned a simple living mainly from the labour of his own hands. He spent his days growing his own food, writing poetry and philosophy, and sauntering through the woods, observing and recording the seemingly infinite wonders of nature in a state of prolonged fascination. It was a period of immense personal growth for Thoreau, during which he struggled productively with the question of how much material wealth – or, rather, how little – a person actually needs to live well and be free.

The main literary product of Thoreau's time living in the woods was a book called *Walden* (1854).[5] This is a dense, unclassifiable text that is part autobiography, part nature writing, and part 'simple living' manifesto, but which is now widely regarded as one of the classics of American literature. Not only that, *Walden* offers a penetrating critique of materialistic culture, one all the more piercing due to the fact that Thoreau was both a ruthless social critic and highly skilled in the art of poetic expression. This makes for engaging and often challenging reading, especially at those times when we might see ourselves in the object of Thoreau's often scathing cultural and economic critiques.

In today's era of overlapping ecological, economic, and cultural crises, *Walden* is a text that is more relevant than ever before. As well as providing early insight into the destructive and oppressive nature of many processes of industrialisation, this prescient book also warns people of the self-imposed slavery that can flow from mindlessly dedicating one's life to the never-ending pursuit of 'more'. If nothing else, Thoreau's life and writings serve as a fiery, poetic reminder that there are alternative, simpler ways to live – forms of life which are freer and indeed more fulfilling than those governed by consumerist values and practices.

Thoreau's central message, as I reconstruct it below, is that a life of material sufficiency is all that is needed to fully explore one's aesthetic capacities. In our age of ecological overshoot, I contend that this is a message deserving of the closest attention, for it suggests that energy descent futures involving planned economic contraction, or degrowth, are not inconsistent with human flourishing. Indeed, reimagining the good life beyond consumer culture presents itself as the only path available for living well, sustainably, and justly on a finite planet with eight billion people (and counting). This is not to suggest that personal practices of voluntary simplicity alone will ever be enough to produce an ecological civilisation. But it does suggest that an ecological civilisation implies voluntary simplicity, and indeed, that profound shifts in relation to material culture may need to precede the systemic changes which are also needed.

In that light, I will now review the main threads of Thoreau's life story. My purpose is not to provide a guide on how to live a simple life or to explore what structures might be needed to facilitate such a cultural shift (two subjects I've written about extensively elsewhere).[6] Rather, my new contribution will be attempting to highlight how the emergence of any post-consumerist material culture will depend on what I am calling an aesthetics of sufficiency. In other words, my argument is that contemporary *tastes* must shift with regards to material culture before there is much hope of an ecological civilisation emerging through political action. As I have suggested, a cultural or aesthetic revolution must precede the political transformation, and if it does not, any political transformation is likely to merely reproduce the old world soon enough. If this position is accepted, it should influence the question of political strategy, for it would imply that any politics of ecological civilisation might need to be founded upon an aesthetics of sufficiency. Put otherwise, a society must develop a *taste* for degrowth before there is much chance of an economics or politics of degrowth. Developing such a taste is a central task of aesthetic education.

Thoreau on materialistic culture

In order to understand what drove the young Henry Thoreau out of his township and into the woods, it is necessary to acknowledge the context in which he was living. The middle of the nineteenth century was a time when the Industrial Revolution was really taking hold in the United States. From Thoreau's perspective, his contemporaries were getting seduced by the extraordinary productive power of industry and machines, without putting their minds to the question of why or to what end they were expending all their efforts and labours – or at what cost. The railroad was the defining emblem of industrialisation in Thoreau's eyes, and he often wrote of it metaphorically, as a representation of the emerging economic system that was fast changing the face of the United States and indeed the world. 'We do not ride upon the railroad,' he asserted, 'it rides upon us.'[7]

Thoreau had travelled widely in his province, but everywhere, in shops, offices, and fields, the inhabitants seemed to him to be living lives of 'quiet desperation',[8] committing themselves to 'nothing but work, work, work'[9] in order to pay for their rising material desires. 'The twelve labors of

Hercules were trifling in comparison with those which my neighbors have undertaken; for they were only twelve, and had an end; but I could never see that these men slew or captured any monster or finished any labor.'[10] Thoreau likened people's materialistic cravings to the heads of a hydra, noting that 'as soon as one head is crushed, two spring up.'[11]

The ancient Chinese philosopher, Lao-Tzu, once said: 'He who knows he has enough is rich.'[12] Thoreau was telling his contemporaries that they had enough, but that they did not know it, and so were poor. Always wanting more luxuries and comforts, and never content with less, Thoreau felt that people did not understand the meaning of 'Economy', did not understand that 'the cost of a thing is the amount of ... life which is required to be exchanged for it'.[13] 'Most [people],' he insisted, 'even in this comparatively free country, through mere ignorance or mistake, are so occupied with factitious cares and superfluously coarse labors of life that its finer fruits cannot be plucked by them.'[14] By a 'seeming fate', there was 'no time to be anything but a machine'.[15]

And for what? People's lives were being 'ploughed into the soil for compost'[16] just to obtain 'splendid houses' and 'finer and more abundant clothing ... and the like'.[17] But as Thoreau would insist: 'Superfluous wealth can buy superfluities only'.[18] Indeed, he claimed that 'most of the luxuries, and many of the so-called comforts of life, are not only not indispensable but positive hindrances to the elevation of mankind.'[19] More concerned about accumulating nice things or climbing the social ladder than they were about their own destinies, people astounded Thoreau with how 'frivolous'[20] they were with respect to their own lives. The following passage states his position directly:

> If I should sell my forenoons and afternoons to society, as most appear to do, I am sure that for me there would be nothing left worth living for... I wish to suggest that a man may be very industrious, and yet not spend his time well. There is no more fatal blunderer than he who consumes the greater part of his life getting his living.[21]

But Thoreau saw his townsfolk labouring under this very mistake. 'It is a fool's life,' he declared bluntly, 'as they will find when they get to the end of it, if not before.'[22] It was the English poet William Wordsworth who wrote, 'Getting and spending, we lay waste our powers', and we can imagine Thoreau being wholly sympathetic to that critical sentiment. It appeared to Thoreau as if his fellow citizens were falling into the consumerist mode of living not because they preferred it to any other, but because they honestly thought there was no choice left. 'So thoroughly and sincerely are we compelled to live, reverencing our life, and denying the possibility of change. This is the only way, we say.'[23]

Thoreau was not convinced. He was of the view that 'there are as many ways [to live] as there are radii from one center',[24] and a consumerist existence was only one of the options available, and by no means the wisest choice. 'Even the life which [people] praise and regard as successful is but one kind', and 'why should we exaggerate any one kind at the expense of others?'[25] Forever the thoughtful non-conformist, Thoreau tended to believe that '[w]hat old people say you cannot do you try and find that you can',[26] and on that basis he boldly proposed that there should be '[o]ld deeds for old people, and new deeds for new.'[27] Surely, he thought, there were more fulfilling ways to live. On Independence Day, 1845, Thoreau began his living experiment out in the woods, near the shores of Walden Pond.

The Walden experiment

In the second chapter of *Walden*, entitled 'Where I Lived, and What I Lived For', Thoreau offered a direct explanation for his exit from conventional society. 'I went to the woods because I wished to live deliberately, to front only the essential facts of life and see if I could not learn what they had to teach, and not, when I came to die, discover that I have not lived.'[28] Elsewhere he said that his purpose in going to Walden Pond was to 'transact some private business with the fewest obstacles.'[29] In one sense this 'private business' was simply to write in solitude, close to nature, and away from modern distractions. In another sense, though closely related to the first, his motivation was to solve, or at least better understand, the *economics* of living well. What is the proper relationship to adopt in relation to money, possessions, and other forms of material wealth? How much is enough? What is an economy *for*? How best to earn a living? Thoreau had decided that, perhaps, the best path was to reduce his material needs and desires and to live a simple life. Simplicity of living was to be his means to the elevation of meaning and purpose – his path to genuine freedom.

Thoreau suspected that, 'If your trade is with the Celestial Empire'[30] – by which he meant, if your concerns are 'higher' than merely getting and spending – then very little is actually needed to be happy and free, provided life is approached with the right attitude. 'Simplify, simplify'[31] was to be his refrain. One should not need an impressive house, fancy clothes, exotic foods, or extravagant possessions to live well. Those things are not the stuff of true satisfaction. They are superfluities, often merely distractions. Thoreau argued that by minimising consumption people could find themselves with more freedom to pluck the finer fruits of life, in ways that may not always be obvious.

This, in essence, exemplifies the way of sufficiency Thoreau put to the test at Walden Pond, by living simply and largely rejecting the division of labour. As far as possible he grew his own food, and drank water from the pond. He cut down some trees and built himself a cabin with but one small room, and made some furniture. It was not much, but it was enough. And just enough was plenty. Thoreau did not wish to be chained to the economy, so he practised self-reliance; he did not wish to be slave to artificial material desires, so he practised self-discipline; and he did not wish to live what was not life, so he avoided wasting his precious time working to acquire more than he needed.

How much is enough?

In order to live a full and free life, Thoreau felt that one must begin by thinking seriously about what really are the necessaries of life, 'for not till we have secured these are we prepared to entertain the true problems of life with freedom and prospect of success'.[32] This passage is important because Thoreau was seeking to avoid a misunderstanding that might arise from his celebration of material simplicity. Simplicity is not material destitution, he is saying. We all have basic physical needs that have to be met (though they may be fewer than we commonly think). But once those basic needs are met, we are not obliged to dedicate our lives to the pursuit of more. Thoreau proposed that when people have obtained those things necessary to life, 'there is another alternative than to obtain superfluities; and that is, to adventure on life now, [our] vacation from humbler toil having commenced.'[33]

Thoreau was warning us not to assume that material wealth will always contribute positively to our lives, for often, in insidious ways, it will not. It is not that there is anything inherently evil about money or material things; it is just that each moment we spend pursuing such things beyond what is necessary is a moment we could have spent on some free, non-materialistic good – such as talking with friends, walking through the woods, meeting our civic duties, being creative, or just relaxing. Sometimes trading our time for money and things will be a good trade, no doubt. But sometimes such a trade will ultimately cost more than it is worth, making us not richer but poorer, and thus be a bad trade.

This can apply both at the individual level, as Thoreau highlighted, but also, as Joseph Tainter argued, at the societal level. That is, sometimes the pursuit of more energy and resources can cost more than it comes too, as the marginal utility of consumption and complexity declines and eventually becomes negative. Conversely, as I am proposing, sometimes deliberately reducing or moderating consumption and complexity through voluntary simplification can be life-enhancing. The simple life, however, is never a destination but always a process. Both individually and socially, this way of life demands constant evaluation of the question 'how much is enough?' in relation to the question 'enough for *what*?' This will need to remain a dynamic evaluation, given that the answers to both questions might shift over time.

With respect to clothing, Thoreau expressed his simplicity by reflecting on his own modest attire: 'if my jacket and trousers, my hat and shoes, are fit to worship God in, they will do will they not?'[34] It is an interesting question to consider, if not in relation to the worship of God, necessarily, then more generally in relation to the living of a passionate life. Old clothes will do, will they not? Thoreau proposed that they will do just fine. He is not glorifying the poor or prescribing to us a dress code. He is attempting to get us to reconsider cultural assumptions about the importance of material things (in this case clothing) to a well-lived life. His argument is not that one cannot live a happy and meaningful life in fine clothing, so much as fine clothing is not necessary for a happy and meaningful life. If so, he would suggest that we do not waste our freedom labouring superfluously to purchase fine clothing. Thoreau's point was that if our goals are 'higher' than materialism, acquisitiveness, and social status, we should recognise the limited need for money and possessions in our lives. '[M]y greatest skill has been to want but little,'[35] he proclaimed.

Thoreau made essentially the same point with respect to shelter. An average house in his neighbourhood cost about eight hundred dollars (at the time) and Thoreau noted that to lay up this sum would take from ten to fifteen years of the labourer's life; add the farm and one would have to spend twenty, thirty, or forty years toiling – more than half of one's life is easily spent. Would the American Indians have been wise to give up their modest but functional tepees on these terms? Thoreau had his doubts, suggesting that 'when the farmer has got his house, he may not be the richer but the poorer for it, and it be the house that has got him.'[36]

Thoreau wanted to show at what sacrifice our more 'advanced' dwellings were obtained. He suggested that, by living more simply, we might secure all the advantages without suffering any of the disadvantages. With this in mind, he went to Walden Pond with a range of hand tools, cut down some trees, and in about three unrushed months had built himself a modest but sturdy cabin. Again exemplifying his alternative mode of economic analysis, Thoreau declared that, 'I intend to build me a house which will surpass any on the main street in Concord in grandeur and luxury, as soon as it pleases me as much and will cost me no more [in terms of life] than the present one.'[37]

It appears, then, that Thoreau was perfectly content with his shelter, modest though it was. Did this not make him richer than a king who is dissatisfied with his palace? With a little more wit we could *all* be richer than kings, Thoreau implied; but, unfortunately, 'Most [people] appear never to have considered what a house is, and are actually though needlessly poor all their lives because they think that they must have such a one as their neighbors have.'[38]

Thoreau's philosophy of voluntary simplicity is neatly summed up in the following passage: 'I am convinced, both by faith and experience, that to maintain one's self on this earth is not a hardship but a pastime, if we will live simply and wisely.'[39] This is perhaps the most important lesson that he learned while living in the woods, and it was a lesson that stayed with him for the rest of his life. We might not have a pond nearby to replicate Thoreau's living experiment, and we might not want to live alone in the woods. But in an age where a minority of the global population grossly overconsumes Earth's resources while billions live in destitution, Thoreau offers profound lessons in simplicity, moderation, and mindfulness that remain applicable to the analysis of the contemporary world.

Nevertheless, when engaging the question 'how much is enough?', Thoreau insisted that we must each find our '*own* way'.[40] As noted, this is not so much a destination as it is an ongoing creative process. Thoreau was not interested in giving anyone detailed instructions on how to live a simpler life; nor did he want to save us the trouble of thinking for ourselves. Rather, he wanted to stoke the fire in our souls and inspire us with ideals. 'Don't spend your time in drilling soldiers,' he once wrote, 'who may turn out hirelings after all, but give to the undrilled peasantry a *country* to fight for.'[41] He wanted to inspire people to seek meaning in life beyond materialistic acquisition and accumulation, and he believed that doing so leads to the tantalising insight that human flourishing requires less material wealth than previously thought. Practices of mindfulness in relation to material culture can offer liberation from the false needs that are so often imposed upon us by consumer capitalism.

♦ ♦ ♦

By the time he died in 1862, Thoreau had acquired a degree of fame as a philosopher and environmentalist, although the amount of money he earned from his writing and lecturing over his entire life was minimal. Nevertheless, the fact that his books, essays, and poems barely sold was of little consequence. He had woven literary baskets of a delicate texture, and although he had not made it worth anyone's while to buy them, he felt that it had nonetheless been worth his while to weave them.[42]

Thoreau's life is a reminder that dedicated individuals can explore simpler, freer, ways of life by adopting a new frame of mind and acting upon it with creativity and conviction. Doing so may not be easy, of course, since it will involve moving in the opposite direction to where most of humankind is marching. But as Thoreau would say, 'If a man does not keep pace with his companions, perhaps it is because he hears a different drummer. Let him step to the music which he hears, however measured or far away.'[43]

An aesthetics of sufficiency

The theory and practice of voluntary simplicity has been explored at length in the scholarly literature and popular literature.[44] Over the years I have made my own contributions, both in terms of cultural analysis and in terms of political and economic analysis.[45] For present purposes, I will not restate those analyses or review the literature, but instead attempt to offer something new by examining voluntary simplicity from an aesthetic perspective. My argument is that the practices of voluntary simplicity will not be widely embraced – necessary though they may be – until new tastes are developed in relation to material culture. Moreover, in ways to be explained, I believe that those new tastes for simple living may be developed most effectively through aesthetic rather than rational means (or, better still, through both at once). In what follows, then, I will return to some of the key aspects of material culture that Thoreau confronted (e.g., clothing, housing, food, etc) and consider them from an aesthetic perspective.

An aesthetics of the self

Although my focus below will be on the aesthetics of material culture, I begin this inquiry by returning to the notion of self-creation, previously examined in relation to the work of Friedrich Nietzsche, Michel Foucault, and Richard Rorty.[46] The logic here is simple: in order to develop new tastes in relation to material culture, people educated into consumerist lifestyles might need to reshape their subjectivities through practices of 'self-fashioning'. One of the central insights of Foucault's 'aesthetics of existence' was that the self is not something to be discovered but rather something that needs to be *given form*. Notably, this insight was already well developed in Thoreau's practical philosophy of voluntary simplicity. He would have been very sympathetic to the Foucauldian ideas of 'self-fashioning' and the 'art of living', as the following passage makes clear:

> I know of no more encouraging fact than the unquestionable ability of man to elevate his life by a conscious endeavour. It is something to be able to paint a particular picture, or to carve a statue, and so make a few objects beautiful, but it is far more glorious to carve and paint the very atmosphere and medium through which we look.... To affect the quality of the day, that is the highest of the arts.[47]

Similarly, in the conclusion to *Walden*, Thoreau urged us all to 'live the life [we have] imagined.'[48] All individuals, he maintained, are tasked to make their life, even in its details, 'worthy of the contemplation of [their] most elevated and critical hour.'[49] He thought that there are as many ways to live 'as there can be drawn radii from one center,'[50] and he desired that there 'be as many different persons in the world as possible.'[51] But he also saw 'how easily and insensibly we fall into a particular route, and make a beaten track for ourselves,'[52] how easily we fall into the 'deep ruts of tradition and conformity.'[53]

This troubled Thoreau, for he thought that if we do not live *deliberately* – that is, if we only get out of bed because of 'the mechanical nudgings of some servitor'[54] – then we are just sleepwalking through life, injuring eternity by killing time. 'Little is to be expected of that day, if it can be called a day, to which we are not awakened by our Genius.'[55] Thoreau is speaking not so much to geniuses here, as to the genius (or poet) in us all. Take yourself and your life seriously, he is saying. Do not let yourself be swept along. Claim your freedom and exercise your capacity to create your own fate. Compose yourself! WAKE UP! 'Moral reform', Thoreau proposed, 'is the effort to throw off sleep... To be awake is to be alive.'[56]

As scholar Carl Bode put it: '[Thoreau] believed that his job was to become a writer but a writer in a noble Transcendentalist way – a poet first in what he did and next in what he wrote.'[57] The poet's noblest work, according to Thoreau's ambitious conception of the poet, was one's life, and poetry or prose would grow out of that life. With a slight change in the language, this could easily be interpreted as a Foucauldian perspective: ethical practice, it could be said, is the effort to transcend the subjectivities that have been imposed upon us by society and to give form to oneself through deliberate self-fashioning. To compose oneself is to be free, and Thoreau's message in *Walden* was that freedom requires (among other things, of course) a wise and disciplined relationship to material culture. This was a wisdom and discipline that he believed was largely absent from his own society, and it is easy enough to infer what his views would be on consumerist cultures today.

As outlined in the essay on Friedrich Schiller,[58] if we are to create or re-create ourselves, aesthetic education may be needed to induce the state of 'play' that is required to loosen the grip of our 'normal' sense of self. Schiller argued that in a state of play we are more open to experimenting or 'playing' with how we craft our lives. In this condition of aesthetic freedom, we are more volitionally open to trying different things, exploring different ways of living, and becoming someone new. Schiller did not believe, however, that play had any necessary implications – it didn't mean that we *would* choose differently, or if we do choose differently, play does not constrain *what* those choices would be. But playfulness is a state of aesthetic freedom which makes choosing differently possible and more likely. This is because it expands the imagination in terms of the range of lives that could be lived and leaves us less constrained by habitual ways of living. I believe that such volitional openness is a first step in transcending consumerist subjectivities – by freeing ourselves from ourselves. In short, through exposure to art and aesthetic education we are more likely to be artful ourselves. Or, as William Morris put it: 'that which most breeds art is art.'[59]

Clothing

Beyond an aesthetics of the self, how might new tastes for sufficiency manifest in relation to material culture? Let me start by turning to clothing, this being the domain of life where we express our personal aesthetics or 'style' most noticeably and immediately. The primary purpose of clothing is to keep us warm and its secondary function, at least in modern times, is to cover nakedness. That being said, those functions have been marginalised in consumer societies today, where clothing's purpose has evolved to be primarily about expressing one's identity or social status. There are powerful cultural expectations to look a certain way depending on context, and since fashion changes so quickly, there is social pressure to constantly upgrade and expand one's stock of clothing. These aesthetic expectations drive consumerism and the growth economy at the expense of a healthy environment, creating socially corrosive cultures overly focused on cosmetic concerns and status signalling.

In a post-consumerist society, the importance of high fashion would presumably be drastically reduced or even disappear. Clothing might come to be seen as an exterior shell that says little or nothing about the depth of a person's character. Moreover, in an age of ecological overshoot, spending extravagantly to always look 'brand new' would be recognised as a cultural practice that was neither necessary nor something deserving of social admiration. Accordingly, sustainability seems to imply a radical alternative to the consumerist aesthetic prevalent in affluent societies today. Along these lines, Thoreau suggested that any necessary or important work may be accomplished without adding to our wardrobes. 'A [person] who has at length found something to do will not need to get a new suit to do it in.'[60] Beware then, he wrote, 'of all enterprises that require new clothes, and not rather the new wearer of clothes.'[61] With regard to personal appearance more broadly, it can be confidently inferred that Thoreau would reject today's 'cult of youthfulness', which treats aging as a process that ought to be disguised at any cost. In a sane society, something as natural as going grey or developing wrinkled skin would be no cause of shame.

Of course, human beings have always expressed themselves through what they wear and how they present themselves in society, so we should expect that 'style' would not so much disappear as evolve in an ecological civilisation. But such new forms of style would reflect the ethics and aesthetics of sufficiency that would come to shape material culture in all domains of life. In comparison with affluent societies today, people adopting an aesthetics of sufficiency would generally have fewer changes of clothing, and happily embrace second-hand items wherever possible. Limited wardrobes could nevertheless be worn in creative ways and arrangements. This would require many people to rethink their 'image' in light of the new aesthetic, including their 'self-image', in ways that might require a deliberate reshaping of the self by the self. New clothing would be made from organic fabrics, sustainably produced, which itself would create a different 'look'. Clothes would be mended as often as necessary before being repurposed or composted, and the art of sewing might return to many households as a meaningful and pleasurable form of creative labour.

Furthermore, in an ecological civilisation, it can be surmised that clothing would be functional, comfortable, and durable, so there would be no worry about lying down on the grass if the mood called for it, opening up new opportunities for a simple and sensuous reconnection with nature. Neckties, high heels, and ostentatious displays of expensive jewellery would likely disappear as relics of a bygone era, meaning that even the 'feeling' of clothing would change, not merely the 'look'. A time would come, no doubt, when people wearing high fashion or practising 'fast fashion' would be the ones perceived as lacking style and taste. Conversely, the creative and eccentric clothing makers and stylists would be the ones socially admired and sought after. At such a time, it would be clear that a new, creative, and highly localised aesthetics of sufficiency had emerged, laying the foundations for a politics of sufficiency.

My argument is that such aesthetic shifts in relation to self and style may need to *precede* changes in political economy, given that the structures and institutions of political economy will not serve ecological ends until the outcomes of an ecological civilisation are *desired*. Put otherwise, if there is no taste for simplicity, then the social forces needed to drive changes in the political economy will be lacking. The dictum from poet Samuel Taylor Coleridge deserves restatement: we must create the taste by which we will be judged.

Housing

On the path toward an ecological civilisation, a similar aesthetic evolution might need to shape both our homes and how we furnish them. In contrast to the resource and energy intensive McMansions that are increasingly prevalent today (especially in the United States and Australia), housing in an ecological civilisation would develop a taste for 'small is beautiful'.[62] A modest but sufficient house minimises the materials and time needed for building, as well as shrinking the spatial footprint, thereby minimising pressure on urban sprawl. Most importantly perhaps, a small house reduces the energy needed to heat and cool it, especially if well designed in terms of materials, orientation, window placement, and insulation. Less space also incentivises frugality and minimalism, as there would be little room for material clutter and superfluous accumulation. The following line from William Morris perfectly reflects the aesthetics of sufficiency under consideration: 'Have nothing in your houses that you do not know to be useful, or believe to be beautiful.'[63]

According to this aesthetic, more furniture might be homemade (perhaps even the house itself); building with mudbricks or cob might become more common, changing the look of neighbourhoods; more spaces would be dedicated to home-based production (e.g., arts, crafts, and gardening) rather than merely consumption; renovations would rarely if ever be merely cosmetic; and the piano rather than the television might become the heart of the lounge. It should be clear, then, that nothing here suggests that homes in an ecological civilisation would be ugly. Instead, an evolution in taste implies that the sense of beauty and style would be very different, reflecting a humble aesthetics of sufficiency rather than the slick uniformity of modernist chic. Scarcity begets creativity.

Beyond the simplicity of one's material possessions, Thoreau thought that there is something important in the *aesthetic experience* of providing for oneself, of being self-reliant, that has been lost as a result of so-called 'modern improvements' and capitalism's extreme division of labour. He wondered whether 'if [people] constructed their dwellings with their own hands... the poetic faculty would be universally developed, as birds universally sing when they are so engaged.'[64] But, alas, he lamented, 'we do like cowbirds and cuckoos, which lay their eggs in nests which other birds have built.'[65]

'Shall we forever resign the pleasure of construction to the carpenter?'[66] Thoreau asked, noting that never in all his walks had he come across anyone engaged in so simple and natural an occupation as building their own house. 'Where is [our] division of labor to end? And what object does it finally serve? No doubt another *may* also think for me; but it is not therefore desirable that he should do so to the exclusion of my thinking for myself.'[67] Thoreau had come to believe that his contemporaries were endeavouring to solve the problem of their livelihoods by a formula more complicated than the problem itself. 'To get his shoestrings he speculates in herds of cattle.'[68] In contrast, Thoreau attempted to show that, if one were prepared to live simply and with more self-reliance, people could 'become richer than the richest are now.'[69]

Thoreau's calculus here is essentially the same as it was regarding clothing. Perhaps it would be nice to live in a palace or a mansion or even the nicest house on the block. But it must not be forgotten that the more expensive one's housing is, the more life one will probably have to spend earning the money needed to buy or rent it.[70] Furthermore, he asked rhetorically: 'what is the use of a fine house if you haven't got a tolerable planet to put it on?'[71] From this perspective, why not keep our housing modest and simple? Given that housing is the greatest overall expense in most people's lives, this is an area where we should be cognisant of the time and freedom cost of consumption. This is especially so, Thoreau argued, given that 'the cost of a thing is the amount of... life which is required to be exchanged for it'.[72]

The paradoxical insight being offered here is that by lowering the 'standard of living' (measured by consumption in housing) people could actually increase 'quality of life' (measured by subjective well-being)? Indeed, Thoreau was suggesting that by embracing an aesthetics of sufficiency and living in modest accommodation, people could literally save years if not decades of labour and thereby become 'richer than the richest are now,'[73] not in terms of property, of course, but in terms of freedom and contentment. 'If I seem to boast more than is becoming,' he concluded, 'my excuse is that I brag for humanity rather than for myself.'[74]

Food

Continuing with basic material aspects of life, I will now turn to consider food from an aesthetic perspective. One of the more perverse aspects of the industrial-consumerist aesthetic is the bizarre expectation today for visually perfect, unblemished fruit and vegetables in supermarkets. This can result in vast amounts of perfectly edible food being thrown away or left to rot on account of it being aesthetically unacceptable to the contemporary consumer. This highlights how aesthetics can have moral and political implications. Furthermore, the aesthetic demand for exterior perfection is generally achieved through industrial application of chemical pesticides and herbicides, and risks impacting negatively on the food's taste and nutrition.

In an ecological civilisation, this industrial-consumerist aesthetic would need to be transcended. A culture might emerge in which it would be considered tasteless to throw away good food if even a single person went hungry, and cosmetic blemishes would not be considered flaws but merely the inevitable result of natural, organic production. Similarly, it would be seen as bad taste to eat meat from factory farms, and in general meat consumption would be greatly reduced due to environmental (especially climate) impacts, and the heightened sensibility with respect to animal welfare. Thus the picture of an ordinary meal could begin to look very different from the highly processed, meat-heavy diets prevalent in the West and increasingly elsewhere. This would likely result in a new engagement with cooking styles, tastes, and recipes.

Given that diets would probably be healthier on account of these changes, the very aesthetic of human bodily shapes would likely transform in an ecological civilisation, with a reversal of the obesity epidemic. In terms of home production of food, the tidy but unproductive lawns and nature strips common today would be dug up and planted with fruit trees and vegetable gardens, transforming the 'look' of the suburbs and reminding people of the changing seasons. The productive permaculture garden or food forest might become new status symbols as the new aesthetics of sufficiency took root in culture, a corollary of re-localising and decarbonising the economy.

This analysis exemplifies how a shift in something as seemingly insignificant as 'taste' can have far-reaching societal implications. Personal distaste for factory farming, as well as developing taste for local organic food, might not only change the look of our dinner plates, but come to impact on political economy (e.g., the shutting down of factory farms as demand dries up), urban landscapes (e.g., more food gardens, fewer lawns), and even the human form (e.g., healthier diets, healthier bodies). Moreover, a renaissance of home gardening would reconnect people with natural systems and flows, shifting the sensuous experience of daily life in positive ways. This would help ameliorate the 'nature deficit disorder' which has been diagnosed in modern societies (a subset of what I've called the aesthetic deficit disorder).[75]

Most of these themes were prefigured in the life and philosophy of our poet-farmer under consideration, who grew most of the food he ate. Growing his own food, however, came to be something much more than a matter of physically sustaining himself. In a chapter of *Walden* entitled 'The Bean Field', Thoreau tells us that:

> I came to love my rows, my beans... They attached me to the earth, and so I got strength like Antæus. But why should I raise them? Only Heaven knows. This was my curious labor all summer — to make this portion of the earth's surface, which had yielded only cinquefoil, blackberries, johnswort, and the like, before, sweet wild fruits and pleasant flowers, produce instead this pulse. What shall I learn of beans or beans of me? I cherish them, I hoe them, early and late I have an eye to them; and this is my day's work.[76]

I am reminded here of the passage by novelist Nathaniel Hawthorne (a contemporary of Thoreau's) in which he talks with similar devotion about his own vegetable garden:

> I used to visit and revisit it a dozen times a day, and stand in deep contemplation over my vegetable progeny with a love that nobody could share or conceive of who had never taken part in the process of creation. It was one of the most bewitching sights in the world to observe a hill of beans thrusting aside the soil, or a rose of early peas just peeping forth sufficiently to trace a line of delicate green.[77]

Thoreau admitted that, since he had little aid from horses, cattle, or hired labour, or from the latest farming implements, he was 'much slower' in his work than other farmers.[78] Nevertheless, he claimed that he became much more 'intimate' with his beans on this account and that his slower more personal approach yielded a 'constant and imperishable moral.'[79] This moral, he seemed to think, was that the fastest and most efficient way of farming, that is, the way that would yield the most profit in the market, was not necessarily the best way, *all things considered*. As philosopher Philip Cafaro has noted, Thoreau 'makes a point of doing most of the work himself, rather than contracting it out to more productive specialists with more elaborate tools. He does not, he tells us, bother with "imported" fertilisers. These moves would increase his productivity, but he refuses to allow that to dictate how he will farm.'[80] Furthermore, Thoreau could have hired himself out as a day labourer and for much less effort been able to buy his food at the grocer, but he chose not to. Doing so would have left him relying on others first to hire him and second to produce and then sell him his necessaries.

But Thoreau's reasons for living simply go deeper even than securing his independence and freedom. Allowing others to grow food for him, even if it was more 'efficient' or 'economic' to do so, would also have disconnected him from the land, from direct contact with Nature, that is, from the elemental source of both his material and spiritual nourishment. And Thoreau would have no truck with that. He did not just want the beans to eat; he also wanted the *sensuous experience* of cultivating them. In 'The Bean Field' we get an insight into the nature of his labours. Being outside, he tells us, working up a sweat under the morning sun and sky, hoeing his beans in the fresh country air, 'yielded an instant and immeasurable crop.'[81] At such times, he noted somewhat cryptically, it 'was no longer beans that I hoed,'[82] suggesting, we can suppose, that he was cultivating not so much the land as his own soul.[83]

Thoreau delighted at being 'part and parcel of Nature.'[84] The chickadees became so familiar with him that at length one even perched upon an armful of wood which he was carrying, pecking at the sticks without fear. 'I once had a sparrow alight upon my shoulder for a moment while I was hoeing… and I felt that I was more distinguished by that circumstance than I should have been by any epaulet I could have worn. The squirrels also grew at last to be quite familiar, and occasionally stepped upon my shoe when that was the nearest way.'[85] Thoreau would listen to the brown thrashers as he worked his rows and would carefully observe the wildlife on the edge of his field. As he was not driven by an urge to maximise profits, and was thus in no real hurry, he could rest on his hoe and watch the hen-hawks circling high in the sky, 'alternately soaring and descending, approaching and leaving one another, as if they were the embodiment of my own thoughts.'[86] Philip Cafaro captures the significance of these and similar experiences:

> To a poet-naturalist, opportunities for such encounters, even opportunities to feel changes in the weather and mark the natural course of the day, are strengthening and vivifying. Thoreau contrasts this work with factory and office work, suggesting again that the experience lost is not made up in increased pay or productivity.[87]

Today more than ever before, this Thoreauvian calculus deserves serious consideration. But it will take some concerted imaginative effort on our part to broaden our view of things, since Thoreau suggested that the typical, entrenched urbanite, who is highly dependent on the grocer and who lives and works mostly indoors, can barely comprehend what it could even mean to be 'part and parcel of Nature.' And until we have some sense of its richness, some sense that there is another, simpler, more intimate way to provide for ourselves, we are likely to continue doing economics in the usual, narrow fashion and structuring our lives accordingly, not knowing what we have lost, or, rather, what the market economy and its division of labour has taken from us. 'This is the only way, we say.'[88]

Broader implications of an aesthetics of sufficiency

In the discussion above I considered an aesthetics of sufficiency from four key perspectives, relating to self-fashioning, clothing, housing, and food. This type of analysis could be applied to all aspects of life, some of which I now briefly note in closing. Consider, for example, the aesthetics of transport and travel. In consumer societies today, the automobile sits alongside clothing and housing as an object of consumption that is often designed and desired in order to convey wealth, success, and status. But according to an alternative aesthetics of sufficiency, the Lamborghini or Porsche would be considered a bit tacky, extremely wasteful, destructive, and contrived – certainly not something considered beautiful or to be envied or admired. There would be far more interesting and important things to focus on, for as Henry David Thoreau would say: 'Superfluous wealth can buy superfluities only.' Or, as Epicurus put it: 'Do not spoil what you have by desiring what you do not have.'

In an energy descent future, life would likely be embedded in a highly localised society, whereby people's main forms of transport would be cycling or walking. Aside from the environmental benefits, this would be a positive aesthetic innovation because it would increase the human connection with nature, keep us fit, and expose us to the elements in ways that would enrich our sensuous experience of the world. Again, this would be a remedy for 'nature deficit disorder'. With good wet weather gear and adequate lights, even cycling home at night in the rain can be a sensuous delight, as many cyclists already know. This is what might be called an 'acquired taste' – something that might seem unpleasant until you actually do it and discover its gift of gentle exhilaration.

Rather than go on holiday in homogenous luxury resorts overseas, the practitioner of an aesthetics of sufficiency would sooner take the family camping in the local national forest or beachside village, again transforming our sensuous experience of the world in ways that could enhance our lives, provided we had developed a 'taste' for simplicity, nature, and the outdoors. This could open the door to what is today called 'alternative hedonism' or 'frugal hedonism' – that is, simpler ways of living that explore the various potentials of living 'more with less'.

By creating a post-carbon way of life, members of an ecological civilisation would avoid experiencing in their day-to-day existence the worst climate impacts, signifying one of the most extreme aesthetic benefits of a sufficiency-based way of life. The wind farm would be perceived as a vista of supreme beauty, enriching the landscape, not something aesthetically objectionable. At the household level, the impression of a 'good sized' family might tend toward one child. In matters of detail, not flushing urine to save water might raise aesthetic objections from within the consumer mindset but become the 'new normal' in the conserver society of an ecological civilisation. Similarly, using a composting loo to create 'humanure' might offend the squeamish bourgeois sensibility, and yet defecating in drinking quality water might offend an alternative sensibility that emerges in SMPLCTY.

Furthermore, an ecological civilisation would likely produce vastly different urban and suburban landscapes, where advertising and cars were increasingly absent, de-polluting the visual, aural, and mental environments. Thus people would be freer to have thoughts of their own, liberated from the attention-demanding industrial-consumerist aesthetic. Even the arts themselves would doubtless evolve. The corporate production of formulaic pop music, vapid television shows, and meaningless 'spectacles' of performance art, might lose their hold on society and create cultural space for a rebirth of authentic, local art, uninfluenced by the promises or seductions of the globalised market economy.

All this, of course, returns us to the question of 'story' and its importance, both in terms of self and society. Mending one's clothes or growing one's own food within the Old Story might be considered by many to be a shameful requirement, symbolising an unsuccessful life of poverty. But within the New Story I am trying to tell of degrowth, permaculture, voluntary simplicity, and related movements, such practices would be seen and experienced as a fulfilling exercise of creativity. They would be examples of frugal hedonism – small but meaningful acts of ecological care that draw social admiration and offer aesthetic rewards.

Each element in life looks very different depending on the underlying narrative that gives those elements context. Accordingly, 'story' can be understood as the meta-aesthetic issue that shapes the 'taste' we have for various aesthetic forms, values, and practices. An ecological civilisation therefore requires stories of self and society that transcend the consumerist story. This implies a new aesthetics of existence, from which a 'taste' for SMPLCTY could emerge.

---

[1] Tainter's theory is based on what he calls the diminishing marginal returns of complexity. By this he means a process of civilisational development in which the benefits of societal complexification diminish over time. At first a society proceeds through phases of significant beneficial growth in complexification, where new institutions, technologies, and social practices emerge that solve societal problems and thereby improve the lives of most people. Thus complexification is experienced as progress. But given that the benefits of complexification seem to decline over time (owing to the lowest hanging fruit being picked first), there comes a point when further growth in complexity stops offering net benefits and begins to impact negatively on a society. Eventually all the energy and resources a society has available are invested in solving *existing* problems, meaning that when *new* problems arise, as they inevitably will, they cannot be solved. At such a point, society enters a phase of deterioration. When declines in complexity occur swiftly, as they sometimes do, this is experienced as societal collapse – or involuntary simplification. With some persuasive force, Tainter maintains that his theory explains the rise and fall of civilisations in history better than any other. See Samuel Alexander, 'Artful Descent: A Cosmodicy of S M P L C T Y' in this collection of essays. The full set will be available here: http://samuelalexander.info/s-m-p-l-c-t-y-ecological-civilisation-and-the-will-to-art/ (accessed 10 May 2023).

[2] Without attempting anything like an exhaustive review, some preliminary literature to begin with includes: Thomas Homer-Dixon et al, 'Synchronous Failure: The Emerging Casual Architecture of Global Crisis' (2015) *Ecology and Society* 20(3): 6; William Ripple et al, 'World's Scientists' Warning of a Climate Emergency' (2021) *BioScience* 71(9): pp. 894-898; Thomas Wiedmann, Manfred Lenzen, Lorenz Keyber, and Julia Steinberger, 'Scientists' Warning on Affluence' (2020) *Nature Communications* 11: 3107. See also, see the reports by David Spratt and Ian Dunlop, published by the Breakthrough Institute, which review and analyse the latest climate science. Available at: https://www.breakthroughonline.org.au/publications (accessed 20 April 2023).

[3] Most of my academic work addresses this broad research agenda. See www.samuelalexander.info (accessed 10 June 2023).

[4] See, e.g., Samuel Alexander, 'Voluntary Simplicity as an Alternative to Collapse' (2014) *Foresight* 16(6): pp. 550-566.

[5] Henry Thoreau, *Walden*, in Carl Bode (ed), *The Portable Thoreau* (New York: Penguin, 1982), pp. 258-572.

[6] See note 3.

[7] Thoreau, *Walden*, note 5, p. 345.

[8] Ibid, 263.

[9] Henry Thoreau, 'Life without Principle' in Carl Bode (ed), *The Portable Thoreau* (New York: Penguin, 1982), p. 632.

[10] Thoreau, *Walden*, note 5, p. 260.
[11] Ibid.
[12] See Goldian Vanenbroeck (ed), *Less is More: The Art of Voluntary Poverty* (Rochester: Inner Traditions, 1991), p. 116.
[13] Thoreau, *Walden*, note 5, p. 286.
[14] Ibid, p. 261.
[15] Ibid.
[16] Ibid.
[17] Ibid, p. 270.
[18] Ibid, p. 568.
[19] Ibid, p. 269.
[20] Ibid, p.262.
[21] Thoreau, 'Life without Principle, note 9, p. 636.
[22] Thoreau, *Walden*, note 5, p. 261.
[23] Ibid, p. 266.
[24] Ibid.
[25] Ibid, p. 274.
[26] Ibid, p. 264.
[27] Ibid.
[28] Ibid, p. 343.
[29] Ibid, p. 275.
[30] Ibid.
[31] Ibid, p. 344.
[32] Ibid, pp. 267-8
[33] Ibid, pp. 270-1.
[34] Ibid, p. 278.
[35] Ibid, p. 324.
[36] Ibid, p. 288.
[37] Ibid, p. 304.
[38] Ibid, p. 290.
[39] Ibid, p. 325.
[40] Ibid.
[41] From Thoreau's journals, as quoted in Leo Stoller, *After Walden* (1957), p. 123.
[42] See Thoreau, *Walden*, note 5, p. 274.
[43] Ibid, pp. 564-5.
[44] I have edited a collection of some this literature. Samuel Alexander (ed), *Voluntary Simplicity: The Poetic Alternative to Consumer Culture* (Whanganui: Stead and Daughters, 2009).
[45] See note 3.
[46] See Samuel Alexander, 'Giving Birth to Oneself: Ethics as an "Aesthetics of Existence"' in this collection of essays. The full set will be available at the link in note 1.
[47] See Thoreau, *Walden*, note 5, p. 343.
[48] Ibid, p. 562.
[49] Ibid, p. 343.
[50] Ibid, p. 266.
[51] Ibid, p. 325.
[52] Ibid, p. 562.

[53] Ibid.
[54] Ibid, p. 342.
[55] Ibid.
[56] Ibid, p. 343.
[57] See Carl Bode (ed), *The Portable Thoreau* (New York: Penguin, 1982), p. 15.
[58] Samuel Alexander, 'The Politics of Beauty: Schiller of Freedom and Aesthetic Education' in this collection of essays. The full set will be available at the link in note 1.
[59] William Morris, 'The Beauty of Life' in William Morris, *Hopes and Fears for Art: Five Lectures by William Morris*. Available at https://www.marxists.org/archive/morris/works/1882/hopes/chapters/index.htm (accessed 10 May 2023), para. 11.
[60] Thoreau, *Walden*, note 5, p. 278.
[61] Ibid.
[62] See E.F. Schumacher, *Small is Beautiful: Economics as if People Mattered* (New York: Harper Perennial, 2010).
[63] As quoted in Sara Wills, 'William Morris', in Samuel Alexander and Amanda McLeod (eds) *Simple Living in History: Pioneers of the Deep Future* (Melbourne: Simplicity Institute, 2014).
[64] Thoreau, *Walden*, note 5, p. 300.
[65] Ibid.
[66] Ibid, pp. 300–1.
[67] Ibid, p. 301.
[68] Ibid, p. 288.
[69] Ibid, p. 295.
[70] I have addressed the complicated and critically important issue of access to land elsewhere. See Alex Baumann, Samuel Alexander, and Peter Burdon, 'Land Commodification as a Barrier to Political and Economic Agency: A Degrowth Perspective' (2021) *Journal of Australian Political Economy* 86: pp. 355-78.
[71] Henry Thoreau, Letter to Harrison Blake (20 May 1860).
[72] Thoreau, *Walden*, note 5, p. 286.
[73] Ibid, p. 295.
[74] Ibid, p. 304.
[75] On the notion of 'nature deficit disorder', see Richard Louv, *Last Child in the Woods: Saving our Children from Nature Deficit Disorder* (New York: Workman Publishing, 2008).
[76] Thoreau, *Walden*, note 5, pp. 404–5.
[77] Nathaniel Hawthorne, *Mosses from an Old Manse* (New edn, 1857).
[78] Thoreau, *Walden*, note 5, p. 406.
[79] Ibid, p. 406.
[80] Philip Cafaro, *Thoreau's Living Ethics: "Walden" and the Pursuit of Virtue* (Athens, Georgia: University of Georgia, 2004), p. 98.
[81] Thoreau, *Walden*, note 5, p. 408.
[82] Ibid.
[83] The sensuous experience of a Thoreauvian life was exquisitely captured by William Butler Yeats, in his poem 'The Lake of Isle of Innisfree' which unambiguously references Thoreau's time living by the pond:

I will arise and go now, and go to Innisfree,
And a small cabin build there, of clay and wattles made;
Nine bean-rows will I have there, a hive for the honey-bee,
And live alone in the bee-loud glade.

And I shall have some peace there, for peace comes dropping slow,
Dropping from the veils of the morning to where the cricket sings;
There midnight's all a glimmer, and noon a purple glow,
And evening full of the linnet's wings.

I will arise and go now, for always night and day
I hear lake water lapping with low sounds by the shore;
While I stand on the roadway, or on the pavements grey,
I hear it in the deep heart's core.

[84] Henry David Thoreau, 'Walking' in Carl Bode (ed.), *The Portable Thoreau* (New York: Penguin, 1982), p. 592.
[85] Thoreau, *Walden*, note 5, p. 518.
[86] Ibid, p. 409.
[87] Cafaro, *Thoreau's Living Ethics*, above note 80, p. 99. Thoreau's point is not that factory and office work are not valuable. His suggestion is that the drive to maximise profits is disconnecting more and more people from the simple pleasures of contact with nature in their working lives. Thoreau is questioning whether the increased profits that arise from factory and office work is worth that disconnection from nature.
[88] Thoreau, *Walden*, note 5, p. 266. Thoreau also quotes Confucius: 'To know that we know what we know, and that we do not know what we do not know, that is true knowledge.' (p. 267).

‘That which most breeds art is art.’

– **William Morris**

DEMOCRATISING THE POET: WILLIAM MORRIS AND THE ART OF EVERYDAY LIFE

Born in 1834, William Morris was a poet, novelist, designer, printer, philosopher, activist, utopian theorist, pioneering environmentalist, romantic, medievalist, father, and husband. When he died in 1898 at sixty-two years of age, his doctor stated that the cause of death was 'simply being William Morris, and having done more work than most ten men.'[1] E.P. Thompson, in his prominent biography, described Morris's life as reflecting an evolution 'from romantic to revolutionary',[2] but it is probably fairer to say that Morris always remained something of a romantic, albeit one with a growing political sensibility. Despite coming to identify as a socialist, even a Marxist, it befits this complex and original thinker to acknowledge that he is, in a sense, beyond easy classification. This is why, as one commentator notes, everyone seems to want William Morris on their side.[3] He is claimed by socialists, anarchists, environmentalists, and artists – a testament to his social and political relevance, both then and now. At the same time, he has paradoxically become a neglected thinker today, unfairly dismissed by some as a nostalgic sentimentalist. But his aesthetic and political ideas point toward missing ingredients in most contemporary analyses of our troubled age, offering critical insight into how to understand, and perhaps resolve, aspects of the ever-deepening human-ecological predicament.

Before all else, Morris is remembered today as the leading figure – both arch-theorist and practitioner – in what became known as the Arts and Crafts Movement, which emerged in the late nineteenth century as a subclass of British aestheticism. This was a counter-movement against the trends of mechanisation in production and the intensifying division of labour within industrial capitalism, both of which Morris considered regressive shifts in the productive relations of British society. He feared that 'modern civilization [was] on the road to trample out all the beauty in life,'[4] dehumanising people by treating them as replaceable cogs in a profit-centred machine, all the while degrading the natural environment. Far from being crudely anti-technology, however, Morris was in favour of what today would be called 'appropriate technology'. He never rejected the role of machines in minimising hard, unpleasant labour – a point to which I will return. Rather, he celebrated the role of self-governed creative activity in everyday life, through which humans skillfully produced things by hand that were necessary for a good life.

Indeed, Morris' conception of the good life involved people realising themselves through the pleasurable expression of creative labour – what he broadly called 'art' – and he passionately explored this view both in theory and in practice. He conceived of himself 'not as an artist or poet in the High Romantic image, but rather as a craftsman engaged in the "lesser arts"'[5], and he believed that, in a well-ordered society, '[a]rt rather than religion, was to become the centrepiece of people's daily lives, directing their hearts and minds to lofty affairs.'[6] This was the aesthetic premise upon which he built his critique of industrial capitalism, arguing that the arts were 'necessary to the life of [human beings]'[7], that there was 'some unthinking craving for [art], some restless feeling in [our] minds of something lacking somewhere'.[8] I interpret this craving as a manifestation of the Will to Art, and the restless feeling he diagnosed as being a result of an aesthetic deficit in society.

In that spirit, this essay offers a reconstructive reading of Morris's views on art, labour, and politics. I begin by examining his broad definition of art, then review his utopian vision of an artful society as sketched in his novel *News from Nowhere* (1890).[9] This provides a foundation for evaluating Morris's theoretical views on labour, which were powerfully and eloquently presented in, among other places, his essay 'Useful Work v. Useless Toil'. This will lead to an engagement with his analysis of the so-called 'lesser arts' of craft, the importance of which he felt were being unduly diminished in an industrial and increasingly consumerist age. I conclude by exploring the political significance of Morris's aesthetic views, which will allow me to outline some of the societal implications of the preceding essays.

Morris's definition of art

To understand Morris's aesthetic views, it is necessary to grasp the inclusive way in which he defined art. In his most prominent definition (influenced by John Ruskin),[10] he declared that 'the thing I understand by real art is the expression by [human beings] of [their] pleasure in labour.'[11] This is meant to include not just the 'fine arts' – music, sculpture, painting, poetry, and architecture – but also what Morris would ironically call the 'lesser' arts and crafts. These lesser or decorative arts include the making of useful and beautiful things needed for practical affairs in everyday life, whether these be items of furniture, clothing, tools, household items, wallpaper, or even houses. He condemned the alienation of the artist from the craftsperson, of the poet from the people, and his overarching mission was to help create a society in which art would be part of everyday living.[12] In defining art as the 'beauty of life',[13] he explained:

> I must ask you to understand that by the word art, I mean something wider than is usually meant by it. I do not mean only pretty ornament though that is part of it; I do not mean only pictures and sculptures, thorough they are the highest manifestation of it; I do not mean only splendid and beautiful architecture, through that includes a great deal of all that deserves to be called art: but I mean all these things and a great many more, music, the drama, poetry, imaginative fiction, and above all and especially the kind of feeling which enables us to see beauty in the world and stimulates us to reproduce it, to increase it, to understand it, and to sympathise with those who specially deal with it. In short, by art I mean the... pleasure [which] is produced by the labour of [human beings], either manual or mental or both.[14]

Morris believed that creativity was an ahistorical 'need of a [human being's] soul',[15] and he wanted everyone to feel the same pleasure and meaning in labour that artists, as conventionally defined, feel when they are at work. '[D]elight in skill lies at the root of all art'[16], and he insisted that 'that which most breeds art is art.'[17] He felt art was the highest expression of the human spirit, a 'very serious thing',[18] and something as necessary to human beings as 'the bread we eat, the air we breathe'.[19] Indeed, he claimed that '[i]t is the province of art to set the true ideal of a full and reasonable life... a life to which the perception and creation of beauty... shall be felt to be as necessary to man as his daily bread.'[20] Art is 'above all the token of what chiefly makes life good and not evil, of joy in labour',[21] and in this light it can be understood why Morris believed that it was impossible to disassociate art from morality and politics.

In contrast to high romanticism, Morris rejected the narrow conception of 'the artist' as a rare and inspired genius, instead maintaining that every person had the capacity to create and appreciate art. Creative expression should be part of everyday life, uniting the two elements of 'use and beauty',[22] bringing us into a harmonious relationship with self, society, and nature. In short, Morris wanted to democratise the poet and the artist. Over the course of his prolific life, he developed a social and political vision based on this egalitarian vision that there is genius, poetry, and art in all human beings, as the following passage makes clear:

> what I mean by an art is some creation of man which appeals to his emotions and his intellect by means of his senses. All the greater arts appeal directly to that intricate combination of intuitive perceptions, feelings,

> experience, and memory which is called imagination. All artists, who deal with those arts, have these qualities superabundantly, and have them balanced in such exquisite order that they can use them for purposes of creation. But we must never forget that all men who are not naturally deficient, or who have not been spoiled by defective or perverse education, have imagination in some measure, and also have some of the order which guides it; so that they also are partakers of the greater arts, and the masters of them have not to speak under their breath to half-a-dozen chosen men, but rather their due audience is the whole race of man properly and healthily developed.[23]

On that basis, Morris argued that society should be structured and organised to enable this aesthetic conception of flourishing. His vision of socialist society was one in which art fulfilled people during their everyday activities, offering meaning and pleasure in the exercise of their skills and creative capacities. 'That cause is the Democracy of Art,' he declared, 'the ennobling of daily and common work, which will one day put hope and pleasure in the place of fear and pain, as the forces which move [humankind] to labour and keep the world a-going.'[24] And again, art included all meaningful and creative labour, not merely the practice of the so-called fine arts.

The act of creation was less about producing a particular product and more about feeling a particular way about the product one created; about feeling connected to the process from beginning to end. It was Morris' view that the 'aim of art is to increase the happiness of [human beings], by giving them beauty and interest of incident to amuse their leisure, and prevent them wearying even of rest, and by giving them hope and bodily pleasure in their work; or, shortly, to make [a person's] work happy and [their] rest fruitful.'[25] In a celebrated line from his essay 'Art for the People', Morris summarised his vision of aesthetic socialism by describing a society where art 'is to be made by the people and for the people, as a happiness to the maker and the user.'[26]

By contrast, in a society without art, Morris maintained, 'the progress of civilisation' would be 'as causeless as the turning of a wheel that makes nothing',[27] such that 'loss of peace and good life... must follow from the lack of it.'[28] Commenting critically on his own age, he suggested that people have 'degraded themselves into something less than [human beings]... because they have ceased to have their due share of art.'[29] Without this due share he believed true education and civilisation was impossible. His own diverse life as an artist and artisan instilled in him the insight that creative work is incredibly fulfilling, but it also highlighted how mundane and meaningless working life was for most people in the existing conditions of British society in the late nineteenth century. In *The Necessity of Art* (1963), Marxist philosopher Ernest Fischer wrote that 'the sincere humanist artist could no longer affirm such a world. He could no longer believe that the victory of the bourgeoisie meant the triumph of humanity.'[30] Morris had anticipated this view when he wrote: 'The Death of Art was too high a price to pay for the material prosperity of the middle classes.'[31]

But in this very Death of Art, Morris was to find a source of hope. People would eventually realise that their toil under industrial capitalism was diminishing their inherent creative capacities and desires, thereby reducing them to something less than fully human. At such a point of realisation, whether it arrived sooner or later, people would 'cry out to be made [human] again.'[32] Morris believed that 'only art can do it, [only art can] redeem them from this slavery; and I say... that this is her [i.e. art's] highest and most glorious end and aim; and it is in her struggle to attain to it that she will most surely purify herself, and quicken her own aspirations towards perfection.'[33]

This vision of aesthetic flourishing required people to develop a *taste* for art, to realise their innate craving for it, as a source of resistance, hope, and vision:

> it is hard indeed as things go to give most [people] that share [in art]; for they do not miss it, or ask for it, and it is impossible as things are that they should either miss or ask for it. Nevertheless everything has a beginning, and many great things have had very small ones; and since... these ideas are already abroad in more than one form, we must not be too much discouraged at the seemingly boundless weight we have to lift.'[34]

Art would flourish when people 'begin to long for it'[35], so he asked his audience: 'what finally can we do, each of us, to cherish some germ of art, so that it may meet with others, and spread and grow little by little into the thing that we need?'[36] Here we see that art, for Morris, as for Friedrich Schiller,[37] is both the *end goal* of a good society and also the *means* by which such a society could be produced. As noted above, 'that which most breeds art is art,'[38] a statement in which a theory of change is implied.

News from Nowhere

In order to understand how Morris saw his aesthetic ideas coming to fruition in society, I will now consider his most developed expression of that vision, in his work of utopian fiction, *News from Nowhere*. One way to clarify this literary engagement is to begin with an earlier work of fiction against which Morris was by and large reacting, namely, Edward Bellamy's *Looking Backward: 2000-1887*,[39] published in 1888, two years before *News from Nowhere*.

Bellamy's novel is told from the perspective of Julian West, who falls asleep in Boston, Massachusetts, only to wake 113 years later, in the year 2000, in a radically changed world. In its bare essentials, Bellamy presents a picture of a socialist society where technology and machines, as well as an efficient, centralised state bureaucracy, have essentially relieved human beings of menial labour. This automation of production allows everyone to work few hours and retire early to live a life of affluence and leisure.

Even from this summary, a few central themes can be highlighted with which Morris would take issue in his own novel. Most importantly, Bellamy's vision was based on an assumption that labour was fundamentally a 'curse' that had to be lifted in a well-ordered society. In contrast, Morris believed that autonomous and creative labour was not a curse but a blessing, and that human beings would flourish when they were free to employ their skills in the production of useful and beautiful artefacts for themselves and their community. From this perspective, which did not depend on sophisticated technology or much machinery, labour was not something to be escaped in order to live a life of leisure, but something in which human beings would find meaning in everyday life. Morris believed that the good life consists of pleasurable creative work – that is, art.

Furthermore, Bellamy celebrated a centralised state as the main political tool for an egalitarian distribution of wealth and for administering technology and production. Morris' vision, however, was of a decentralised society whereby the state had 'withered away' (to use Marxist terminology), leaving local communities to govern themselves. In short, if Bellamy's socialist vision was one of affluence, technology, leisure, and centralised politics, Morris' was one of simplicity, handcraft, creative, pleasurable labour, and decentralised politics. The further element Morris added to his utopian society was a strong environmentalist perspective, taking many opportunities to highlight the dire ecological impacts of industrial production and the contrasting ethic of (re)connecting with, and taking care of, nature. Both novels presented socialist visions, but they took very different forms because of these differing assumptions and priorities. Morris's utopia will now be considered in more detail, after which some of the theoretical foundations can be examined.

♦ ♦ ♦

News from Nowhere is told from the perspective of William Guest. Like Julian West, he also falls asleep, albeit in London not Boston, only to wake up in a new society. This literary technique of mysteriously 'awakening' in a radically changed, post-revolutionary world is an obvious reference to Bellamy's novel. While the precise date of the setting is unclear,[40] it can be inferred from various passages that it is early in the twenty-first century, well over a century after the time when Morris was writing.

The narrator, Guest, wakes up from his long, deep slumber, taking it for granted that he is in his own society, in his own home, on the banks of the Thames. After getting dressed, he goes outside and notices a boatman at a landing-stage on the riverbank, who greets him cordially. It being a hot day, Guest decides to go for a swim in the river. The water is so clean that he comments on it to the boatman, who seems rather surprised by the observation, not noticing anything unusual. Here we see the first hint of our narrator being in a different world, one in which nature is in a good state of health, unlike England of the early industrial era (or today). The boatman, who seems to be dressed in simple but finely made fourteenth-century attire, offers to take Guest down the river, and as they begin their journey Guest is surprised to see salmon-nets spreading out from the riverbank. Again, this points to the theme of environmental regeneration that will distinguish this new world from the old. Indeed, it is fair to describe *News from Nowhere* as one of the first statements of an ecological utopia.[41]

As conversation between the two men continues, Guest eventually discovers that he is in England, but well into the future, although he attempts to hide the shock of this realisation from the boatman. Instead, he pretends that his confused state is due to having recently returned from many years travelling abroad. The boatman offers to be Guest's guide for the day, establishing a central relationship through which the new society is described and explored through conversation.

Guest accepts the kind offer and reaches into his pocket to discuss terms of payment. The reader is here introduced to a radically new form of economy, for the boatman is puzzled and even humoured by the suggestion that he might need to be paid for what he describes as his business. 'I would do [it] for anybody', says the boat-man, 'so to take gifts in connection with it would look very queer.'[42] Later in the novel a similar awkwardness arises when Guest offers to pay for some tobacco and an especially well-made pipe. The reader learns that this world is one in which people give what they are able, and receive what they need, such that monetary transactions have become a relic of bygone times – a reflection of an 'extinct commercial morality'.[43]

As the novel proceeds, Guest is shown various places and is introduced to many people. It is through these interactions that elements of the new society are conveyed to readers. England has come to resemble a 'garden',[44] characterised not by large industrial cities but by a pastoral and agrarian way of life. The landscapes are scattered with small, elegantly built villages, and each house has its own garden, 'carefully cultivated, and overflowing with flowers.'[45] The streets, such that they are, are lined with fruit trees. People seem to live humble, simple, and yet happy lives in harmony with nature, free from 'sham wants'[46] and the 'horrible burden of unnecessary production'.[47]

Continuing his journey, Guest sees that the citizens of this strange, post-industrial world have found freedom, pleasure, and meaning in joyful labour, producing useful and beautiful wares of the highest quality.[48] Production is undertaken based on what the community needs and what the worker enjoys, not what the profit-centred market dictates. Given that the people of Nowhere have 'found out what [they] want',[49] they are 'not driven to make a vast quantity of useless things,'[50] and so what things they do make, they 'have time and resources enough to consider [the] pleasure in making them.'[51] Machines are employed when necessary, but in the main, the technologies of handcraft provide for most of society's needs:[52] All work which it is a pleasure to do by hand machinery is happily done without more advanced technologies.[53]

Furthermore, there is no longer a severe division of labour, such that people now have diverse working lives and interests. Unlike the alienated labour of capitalism, workers in Nowhere can see *themselves* in what they create. One character, a weaver, tells Guest that besides weaving, he enjoys printing, composing, and studying mathematics, and that he is currently writing a book.[54] Labour is so enjoyable under these non-exploitative conditions that there is even a vague anxiety in society about a scarcity or shortage of work. Work-as-art is presented as the free and harmonious expression of human creative capacity, as a central feature of what it means to live well. There is certainly no problem providing an 'incentive to work', which was historically given as an objection to socialism. We learn that 'the reward of labour is *life*'.[55] On this point, the contrast with Bellamy's 'utopia of leisure' could not be sharper.

One point of criticism that can be levelled at Morris' utopian vision concerns relations between the sexes. In one sense, Morris was clearly a social progressive in this regard, highly critical of patriarchal society. He attempted to present a society with radically different relations between the sexes, celebrating the fact that 'the men have no longer any opportunity of tyranny over the women'.[56] Nevertheless, in his utopia there remains a relatively traditional division of labour, although women are certainly not confined to domestic work. Still, we are told that '[i]t is a great pleasure to a clever woman to manage a house skilfully, and to do so that all housemates about her look pleased and are grateful to her. And then, you know, everybody likes to be ordered about by a pretty woman…'.[57] Lines like this have not aged well, but a sympathetic reading can suggest that Morris's main goal was to highlight the honour and pleasure that can be derived from keeping a home, a point which Aristotle made long ago by defending the household as the foundation of the *polis*. That may be true, but to the contemporary reader it is not clear why the art of housekeeping, noble though it is under non-coercive conditions, needs to remain gendered. As contemporary eco-anarchist Ted Trainer sometimes quips: 'A woman's place is in the kitchen… right next to the man.'

In further exposition of how social relations have evolved in the new society, Guest learns that systematised education is no more, with schools for children having been replaced with a more organic and less structured process of learning by doing. He is told that children 'often make up parties, and come to play in the woods for weeks together in the summer-time, living in tents, as you see. We rather encourage them to do it; they learn to do things for themselves, and get to know the wild creatures; and you see the less they stew inside houses the better for them.'[58] As well as formal institutions of schooling having faded away, the institution of private property has also been abolished. Because that property system created the conditions for poverty and crime, we are told that there is no longer any need for prisons either.

♦ ♦ ♦

So how did all this come about? In discussion with an elderly character known as old Hammond, Guest discovers that a revolution occurred in 1952, causing a rupture that gave birth to this new socialist order beyond the 'systematized robbery'[59] and 'organized misery'[60] of industrial capitalism. There is no longer a centralised government, and in fact there is no government at all that resembles anything like political societies in history. Indeed, the Houses of Parliament at Westminster have been turned into a dung-market. 'Dung is not the worst kind of corruption,' says Hammond, 'fertility may come of that, whereas mere dearth came from the other kind, of which those walls once held the great supporters.'[61]

The historic state is described, with a clear nod to Marx, as merely a 'committee' that served the interests of the upper classes and which deluded the masses into thinking that they have some share in the management of their own affairs.[62] In the place of top-down parliamentary rule, communities now govern themselves through participatory democracy, aiming for consensus. 'The whole people is our parliament,'[63] Hammond advises. A model of social discourse is outlined in which any disagreements are addressed through various stages of discussion and debate.[64] This resembles anarchist processes of governance, and helps to explain why Morris has drawn sympathies from diverse political affiliations beyond socialism.

A brief but sophisticated explanation is given for how the revolution occurred, prompted by Guest's inquiry into whether the transition took place peacefully. 'Peacefully?' old Hammond responds, somewhat aghast: 'What peace was there amongst those poor confused wretches of the nineteenth century? It was war from beginning to end: bitter war, till hope and pleasure put an end to it.'[65] We learn that the transition from commercial slavery to freedom was a 'terrible period'[66], involving strikes, lock-outs, starvation, and violent rioting and fighting. The working classes became increasingly organised and powerful, slowly squeezing more power and wealth from the upper classes, such that there came a time when 'the mere threat of a "strike" was enough to gain any minor point.'[67] Minimum wages were secured, coupled with a maximum price on the necessities of life.

Eventually, however, the upper classes fought back aggressively, in the hope of reclaiming their lost power. By order of the executive, thousands of unarmed workers were murdered in a gathering at Trafalgar Square. But this massacre merely provoked the 'great crash' of 1952, inducing an extreme state of hunger and disorder. This did not end the revolutionary period but genuinely ignited it, leading to a General Strike. The trains stopped running, the newspapers stopped printing, food stopped being distributed, and all at once the upper classes realised that the economy depended on the workers. Eventually this clash of interests led to two years of civil war, after which so much of the economy had been destroyed that a centralised state was no longer an affordable luxury. Thus, communities were forced to build the new world from the ground up, in their new conditions of precarious freedom.

Looking back on those times, old Hammond states that the 'motive-power of the change was a longing for freedom and equality.'[68] At first the socialist agents for change seemed to aim for little more than greater distribution of wealth, as if the same industrial mode of production, albeit under the governance of a socialist state, could be used to lift the poorest out of destitution and satisfy the masses. But Hammond dismissed this goal as merely 'improved slave-rations.'[69] After the civil war, what emerged could be described not as *more of the same* but rather, as outlined above, *less, different, and better*.

Trying to expand the political imagination, Morris's utopia wasn't about providing workers with a greater share of industrially produced wealth and maximising leisure using technology and machinery. In contrast to Bellamy, he was attempting to explore a radically new conception of wealth and a new means of producing it – through the pleasurable and meaningful expression of creative labour, that is, through art. Indeed, it is notable that art as conventionally defined (painting, music, poetry, etc), is barely mentioned in *News from Nowhere*. The insinuation is that life itself had become art, through the everyday satisfactions of creative activity and aesthetic experience. As Hammond says, what used to be called art 'has no name amongst us now, because it has become a necessary part of the labour of every [individual] who produces.'[70] In an important passage, the old man continues:

> The art or work-pleasure, as one ought to call it, of which I am now speaking, sprung up almost spontaneously, it seems, *from a kind of instinct amongst people*, no longer driven desperately to painful and terrible over-work, to do the best they could with the work in hand – to make it excellent of its kind; and when that had gone on for a little, *a craving for beauty seemed to awaken* in men's minds, and they began rudely and awkwardly to ornament the wares which they made; and when they had once set to work at that, *it soon began to grow.* All this was much helped by the abolition of the squalor which our immediate ancestors put up with so coolly... Thus at last and by slow degrees we got pleasure into our work; then we became conscious of that pleasure, and cultivated it, and took care that we had our fill of it; and then all was gained, and we were happy. So may it be for ages and ages![71]

Of course, the word utopia derives from the Greek word meaning 'nowhere' (hence *News from Nowhere*, which was subtitled 'A Utopian Romance'). Like Thomas More, Morris was using the term in full knowledge that the world he described did not exist and might never exist. This sometimes invites the accusation that Morris was being escapist, merely presenting a dreamworld or romantic fantasy that lacked any critical relationship to reality. But if such a critique is justified in relation to some utopians, it is unwarranted when levelled at Morris. By presenting a compelling vision of a better, richer, more meaningful and sustainable world, he was trying to expose the flaws in the industrial society of his time. His strategy was to induce discontent in the reader, and therefore have a political effect by agitating and energising his readers by provoking outrage, hope, and vision.

Philosopher Gary Zabel, in his book *Art and Society* (1993), defends Morris's utopian project, arguing that he understood:

> people are not puppets operated by anonymous historical forces, that they do not struggle, at least not effectively, for goals they cannot plausibly envision. Moreover, as an artist he knew that an image of the future capable of motivating action, and even eliciting sacrifices, had to have more than a purely intellectual appeal, that it had to be anchored in the most fundamental texture of people's sensuous and emotional experience. Socialists must deploy the utopian imagination in a struggle for what Antonio Gramsci was later to call 'hegemony', in which their emancipatory vision becomes a deeply rooted schema through which people interpret the details of their everyday lives.[72]

In this sense, Morris's novel can be considered a success, not *in spite of* it being based on a 'dream' but *because* of it. Scholar Clive Wilmer writes in his introduction to *News from Nowhere*: 'The image of dreaming could hardly be more significant. No longer a form of escape, it becomes the means whereby a different order is conceived and then becomes possible in the process of awakening.'[73] So *News from Nowhere* is neither a blueprint nor a prediction. It is an expression of discontent and a personal vision. As Wilmer concludes: 'It asserts the possibility of a different world. We are not expected to swallow Morris's dream whole. On the contrary, we are encouraged to dream for ourselves.'[74]

'Useful Work v. Useless Toil': An aesthetic analysis of labour

My review of Morris's novel highlighted how meaningful and pleasurable labour lay at the heart of his utopian vision, and how this sat in direct contrast with Bellamy's hopes for a society of leisure. According to Morris, creative work was not something to be escaped but to be sought out and embraced – for the reward was *life* itself. Just as Nietzsche revalued the place of suffering in a well-lived life,[75] Morris argued that labour need not be a curse if it is creative and self-directed. The social and political challenge was to maximise opportunities for the expression of pleasure in labour, that is, for what Morris called art. This led him to develop a unique form of anarcho-socialism, or what he sometimes called a 'Democracy of Art'.[76] These ideas regarding labour and art were presented powerfully in his essay 'Useful Work v. Useless Toil', published two years before *News from Nowhere*, and which certainly influenced the thematic content of the novel. Given the centrality of these themes to Morris's worldview, his arguments in the said essay, as well as in his collection of lectures published as *Hopes and Fears for Art*, deserve some attention.

Morris begins by acknowledging that nature does not provide everything for humankind (or any animal) without the requirement of labour. We must either labour or perish. This raises the questions: 'what shall our necessary hours of labour bring forth?'[77] And how can we gain hope of pleasure in our daily creative skill, hope of pleasure in using what it makes, and hope of pleasure in rest?[78] These are questions which we all ought to ask, Morris argued, for the answers fundamentally shape our lives and society, for better or for worse. Examining the nature of labour in productive relations can inform a critique of existing society as well as guide the vision of an alternative, freer one. What is being produced? In what conditions? And why?

Morris objected to the industrial economy of his own age on the grounds that productive relations were harmful both to the worker (harsh and demeaning toil) and the consumer (purchasing what were often meaningless, unnecessary commodities). One of his leading motivations in the essay 'Useful Work v. Useless Toil' was to meditate on the issue of why English society had developed in such a way that most people were working in horrible conditions, producing what were often superfluous things, only in demand by a leisured aristocracy. In one of his more acidic moments, Morris commented in words that could have been penned by Henry Thoreau, that:

> I have never been in any rich man's house which would not have looked the better for having a bonfire made outside of it of nine-tenths of all that it held. Indeed, our sacrifice on the side of luxury will, it seems to me, be little or nothing: for, as far as I can make out, what people usually mean by it, is either a gathering of possessions which are sheer vexations to the owner, or a chain of pompous circumstance, which checks and annoys the rich man at every step. Yes, luxury cannot exist without slavery of some kind or other, and its abolition will be blessed, like the abolition of other slaveries, by the freeing both of the slaves and of their masters.[79]

This is a polemical statement, of course, but if we distil these lines down to their core thesis it becomes clear that Morris is highlighting the critical connection between, on the one hand, what a society needs and desires to consume, and, on the other, the nature and extent of labour required to meet those needs and desires. The more a society or an individual desires in terms of material wealth, the more labour is required for production of that wealth, and Morris calls on us to remain cognisant of the trade-off here. Production is inextricably related to consumption, and both are value-laden categories that require people to answer: what is an economy *for*?

In other words, superfluous consumption in culture can require more labour than is socially optimal; that is, it can be uneconomic, with costs that exceed the benefits. Even more importantly, the production of luxuries can require *forms* of labour that are neither meaningful nor pleasurable. If, however, a society attains 'simplicity of life' by moderating its material needs and desires, then Morris argued that the labour required to produce necessary and desirable things will not be a curse but a pleasure. Indeed, this position isn't merely about pleasure but also about justice. 'For if our wants are few,' Morris maintains, 'we shall have but little chance of being driven by our wants into injustice; and if we are fixed in the principle of giving every [person their] due, how can our self-respect bear that we should give too much to ourselves?[80] Accordingly, if 'we attain also to the love of justice, then will all things be ready for the new springtime of the arts.'[81]

On this ethical basis, Morris built his social and political vision of a Democracy of Art. 'The chief duty of the civilised world today,' he argued, 'is to set about making labour happy for all.'[82] And his premise was that people would and do enjoy labour if they are free to produce beautiful and useful things. If there was labour that was inherently unpleasant, then Morris had two main responses: either, in these limited circumstances, use appropriate technology and machinery to do the work; or, to consider whether the costs of the unpleasant labour were really worth the expected rewards, and if not, then forgo such labour and what it would have produced.

Thus, Morris believed that politics was fundamentally about organising labour to provide for worthwhile needs – an orientation that is obviously and inescapably value-laden. It demands an answer to the questions: what 'needs' and 'desires' are worthwhile? And what should a society be producing, why, and for whom? Morris did not believe the market under capitalism was able to answer these questions properly. This is because markets are designed to incentivise the production of things that people are most able to pay for. But in a deeply unequal society like England (then and now), the market thus becomes directed toward the production of what the richest members want, not what a society more generally needs. Furthermore, in a culture that overvalues material wealth through a confusion of desire, the market is again distorted, making the workforce meet what are really artificial needs and 'sham wants'.[83]

All this will have, and is having, demonstrable ecological consequences too, given that superfluous production and consumption will tend to make excessive demands on natural resources and ecosystems, just as the waste-streams of such a consumerist-industrial society will degrade nature in dangerous ways. In *News from Nowhere*, Guest is told that the industrial era was a 'mistaken' way of living, because people tried 'to make "nature" their slave... [as if] "nature" was something outside of them.'[84] This type of mistake was problematic from an eco-centric perspective, purely on the grounds that ecosystems and wildlife are of inherent worth and ought not to be destroyed to meet the dubious needs of consumerist cultures. But even with respect to specifically human wellbeing, Morris was disturbed by how industrial society was making life ugly, turning rivers into filthy sewers, clearing ancient forests, polluting the air with sulphurous smoke, and generally making the increasingly urban environment unpleasant and unhealthy to be in. In a line that establishes his place as a pioneer of environmentalism, he asked his audience: 'What kind of account shall we be able to give to those who come after us of our dealings with the earth?'[85] In sum, Morris contended that:

> If we were only to come to our right minds, and could see the necessity for making labour sweet to all [people]... then indeed I believe we should sow the seeds of a happiness which the world has not yet known... and with that seed would be sown also the seed of real art, the expression of [individuals'] happiness in [their] labour – an art made by the people, and for the people, as a happiness to the maker and the user.[86]

Beautifying labour through the 'lesser arts'

The above was framed as an aesthetic analysis of labour. Morris argued that labour is beautiful if the worker takes pleasure in self-directed creative activity in pleasant conditions; labour is ugly if the worker is forced to produce luxuries for an overclass in conditions of squalor. Thus the *sensual experience* of work was central to Morris's worldview – both critically and in terms of his vision of an alternative society. This aesthetic of labour was also the soil in which his politics was seeded.

To deepen this analysis, I return to his distinction between the 'fine arts' (of music, sculpture, painting, poetry, and architecture) and what he called the 'lesser arts' or 'decorative arts' (such as carpentry, pottery, glassware, sewing, cobbling, embroidery, printing, etc). One of Morris's central theoretical contributions to aesthetics was his critique of how the lesser arts had been driven apart, in the industrial era, from what became the conventional understanding of art (as something limited to the fine arts). When a society comes to make this distinction, Morris believed that 'it is ill for the Arts altogether: the lesser ones become trivial, mechanical, unintelligent, incapable of resisting the changes pressed upon them by fashion and dishonesty,'[87] and the fine arts 'become nothing but dull adjuncts to unmeaning pomp, or ingenious toys for a few rich and idle men.'[88] Morris sought to dignify the lesser arts and crafts by once again elevating them to the status of art proper, given that it was through these lesser arts that human beings 'have at all times more or less striven to beautify the familiar matters of everyday life.'[89]

As noted above, human beings, like all animals, must labour or perish. In labouring for those material things that humanity needs to flourish, Morris aspired for an artful labour that expressed the innate creativity of the human spirit: 'this is at the root of the whole matter, everything made by man's hands has a *form*, which must be either beautiful or ugly; beautiful if it is in accord with Nature, and helps her; ugly if it is discordant with Nature, and thwarts her; it cannot be indifferent.'[90] Accordingly, if humanity *must* labour in order to survive and flourish, and all labour must be either beautiful or ugly, then the lesser arts ought to be celebrated as the domain where human beings can 'beautify labour,'[91] by finding meaning and pleasure in the production and use of necessary artefacts. Morris wrote: 'to give people pleasure in things, they must perforce *use*, that is one great office of decoration; to give people pleasure in things they must perforce *make*, that is the other use of it.'[92]

This reinforces Morris's egalitarian ethos, which I've framed in terms of democratising the poet. This is a view that pushes against the romantic ideal of the poet as a rare and specially gifted 'genius'. Morris maintained that 'I do not want art for a few, any more than education for a few, or freedom for a few.'[93] His aim was to make art truly popular, not merely something held in the houses of the rich or practiced only by an elite class of creatives. Like Marx, Morris did not conceive of self-expression or self-actualisation as an individual affair, but as something fundamentally social and ultimately political: the free development of each is the condition for the free development of all. The vision was of an aestheticised society in which everyone was enabled to be an artist in everyday life, through the meaningful expression of creative labour, and to enjoy art (including the beautiful products of the lesser arts) in leisure. In a lecture on this topic, Morris impressed this vision upon his audience: 'I am bidding you learn to be artists, if art is not to come to an end amongst us; and what is an artist but a workman who is determined that, whatever else happens, his work be excellent? or, to put it in another way: the decoration of workmanship, what is it but the expression of man's pleasure in successful labour?'[94]

On these issues Morris looked back to medieval times – the 'Middle Ages' – and found aspects of economic life far superior to the productive relations of the industrial society in which he was embedded. 'In those days all handicraftsmen were ARTISTS, as we should now call them.'[95] This positive view of history can surprise readers, and lead to accusations of naïve romanticism or deluded nostalgia, but Morris was prepared for this counterattack and had a response. He was, of course, perfectly aware of the profound flaws of feudal society:

> Once men sat under grinding tyrannies, amidst violence and fear so great, that nowadays we wonder how they lived through twenty-four hours of it, till we remember that then, as now, their daily labour was the main part of their lives, and that that daily labour was sweetened by the daily creation of art; and shall we who are delivered from the evils they bore, live drearier days than they did? Shall men, who have come forth from so many tyrannies, bind themselves to yet another one, and become the slaves of nature, piling day upon day of hopeless, useless toil?'[96]

It is important to recognise that Morris was not crudely calling for a return to the feudal society of the Middle Ages. Rather, he was seeking to highlight how 'industrial progress' had actually been regressive in some regards, specifically with respect to opportunities in working life for pleasure in the exercise of skill. In his essay 'The Relations of Art to Labour', Morris noted that medieval craftsmen owned their own tools and materials, and by and large directed their own working day. Morris maintained that:

> ... the more the question is studied, both through the existing remains of mediaeval art and through the records left us of the condition of the people at the time, the clearer it is seen that it is no exaggeration to say that during the middle ages nothing that was made was otherwise than beautiful; that beauty formed as essential a part of man's handiwork then as it does of nature's handiwork always. And further, that this essential beauty of handiwork was, amongst a vigorous and healthy people, the inevitable result of the workman working freely, and for no master; having, as I have said before, full control over his material, tools, and time.[97]

It may be that Morris is glossing, to some extent, the nature of working life in the Middle Ages, but resolving that historical question is not my interest and, in the end, it wasn't Morris's primary concern either. He was looking to the past to better understand his industrialising present, so that we could all move toward a better, freer, and more dignified future in which all people can have a share in art. The following passage makes his prospective mission clear: 'It is a dream, you may say, of what has never been and what will never be; true, it has never been and therefore, since the world is alive and moving yet, my hope is the greater that it one day will be true.' Hopelessness, he reminded his listeners and readers, would have locked his mouth shut, not opened it.[98]

The politics of everyday aesthetics

As discussed above, Morris felt that the productive relations of industrial capitalism were draining everyday existence of its aesthetic value, its beauty, emptying life of its art and recklessly degrading nature along the way. Beauty was not something he hoped would be restored merely to artists, narrowly defined. He was calling for a wholesale aesthetic rebellion in the name of humankind, all of whom deserve to realise pleasure and meaning in creative labour – in art. As Gary Zabel notes, leaving aside a few scattered comments on aesthetics in Marx and Engels, Morris was the first socialist writer 'to frame a theory that locate[d] art squarely within the general life process of society.'[99]

That was the foundation of Morris's worldview, upon which he built his eco-aesthetic politics. His political activity was an education for hope, an attempt to refine social and political aspirations and imbue them with greater ambitions. Like Friedrich Schiller,[100] Morris was of the conviction that a new type of human being had to precede any successful structural transformation of society, for without the former the latter would eventually degenerate into what it was trying to leave behind. Art was necessary to that transformation of character. Like Marx, Morris took the dignity of self-expression as something that could not remain 'individual' but ultimately required social and political expression. As Terry Eagleton explains:

> The aesthete... possesses more truth than the left generally imagines. The point is not to substitute art for life, but to convert life into art. Living like a work of art means fully realising one's capacities – this is Marx's ethics. It is also the basis of his politics: socialism is whatever set of institutional arrangements would allow this to happen to the greatest extent.[101]

Morris would have agreed, albeit colouring his own conception of aesthetic socialism with a far deeper shade of green than Marx ever employed.[102] In 'The Society of the Future', Morris upheld a vision of a 'society conscious of a wish to keep life simple, to forgo some of the power over nature won by past ages in order to be more human and less mechanical, and willing to sacrifice something to this end.'[103] If he were alive today, Morris would surely be an advocate for degrowth, for he believed, as the contemporary phrase goes, 'less could be more' – but not just less of the same, but less and different. He did not merely want the working classes to receive a greater share of industrially produced material wealth. He demanded a new conception of wealth and freedom. He wanted human life and society to become so infused with art that the very distinction became obsolete.

Nevertheless, Morris was certainly not blind to 'what stupendous difficulties, social and economical, there are in the way of this.'[104] Industrial capitalism wasn't going to lie down lie a lamb at the mere request of left-leaning environmentalists or political radicals. He was also aware that both his lines of critique, and his vision of an alternative society, would seem strange or even out of place in an industrial era. 'How can I ask working-men passing up and down these hideous streets day by day to care about beauty?'[105] As to be expected, he had an answer. Part of his theory of change was based on what he saw as the natural, emerging consequence of people becoming ever more alienated from their own creative natures. To his listeners he insisted that 'you will become so discontented with what is bad, that you will determine to bear no longer that short-sighted reckless brutality of squalor that so disgraces our intricate civilisation.'[106]

We see here that even his vision of aesthetic rebellion was grounded in affect as much as reason. It would be a *felt need* that would emerge and drive the transformation of society, as much as a new understanding. Indeed, the relationship here is dialectical: a new sensibility could create fertile conditions for a new understanding, just as a new understanding of things could affect sensuous experience. Thereby sensuality and understanding develop in fruitful collision, each shaping, as it is shaped by, the other.

Looking back from the twenty-first century, it is clear that Morris was premature in anticipating these affective drivers for revolt, but this error in timing implies no necessary error in approach or strategy. Even a glance at the world today suggests that simmering discontent with the status quo is everywhere beginning to boil, and thus the task of political organisers and activists is to ensure, via aesthetic interventions in culture, that this powerful social energy is directed towards considered action for justice, sustainability, and wellbeing, not used to fuel further polarisation and violence. Both pathways remain live options, even as it is almost certain that what results will fall somewhere between these extremes. Morris would remind us, however, that where along that spectrum society eventually falls is, in large measure, up to us. And in that spirit, he would urge us to see that our primary task is to 'kindle the desire for beauty, and better still, for the development of the faculty that creates beauty.'[107] With a nod to Schiller, Morris believed in the critical importance of aesthetic education, encapsulating his theory of change in his maxim: 'that which most breeds art is art.'[108]

Although Morris was arguably a better critical and visionary theorist than he was political strategist, he was not so naïve as to think that beauty could be restored to any human society merely by art and artists (narrowly conceived). As the long passages in *News from Nowhere* make abundantly clear, he knew full well that his vision of an aestheticised society needed to join forces with social and political agitators fighting the existing order, and with prefigurative activists trying to build the new world within the shell of the old. He knew that any transition to a radically new society was only going to transpire by way of crisis, hardship, and suffering. But it is no good having an effective means of realising one's political vision if the vision itself is misconceived, and that is the enduring value of Morris's radical aesthetics. He presented a compelling vision worth fighting for – an Ecological Democracy of Art. And even if you have 'built castles in the air,' as Henry Thoreau once wrote, 'your work need not be lost; that is where they should be. Now put the foundations under them.'[109]

NOTE TO READER: THERE ARE TWO FURTHER ESSAYS TO BE PUBLISHED IN THIS COLLECTION. THE FIRST IS 'THE AESTHETIC STATE: TOWARD AN ECOLOGICAL DEMOCRACY OF ART'; THE SECOND IS AN EXTENDED CONCLUSION AND REVIEW. WHEN COMPLETED, THESE FINAL ESSAYS WILL BE POSTED AT www.samuelalexander.info. IN DUE COURSE THEY WILL ALSO APPEAR IN AN UPDATED EDITION OF THIS VOLUME OR AS A SEPARATE VOLUME.

[1] See Clive Wilmer, 'Introduction' to William Morris, *News from Nowhere and Other Writings* (London: Penguin, 2004) p. ix.
[2] E.P. Thompson, *William Morris: Romantic to Revolutionary* (London: Merlin Press, 1976).
[3] See, e.g., Mark Bevir, 'William Morris: The Modern Self, Art, and Politics' (1998) *History of European Ideas* 24(3): pp. 175-194.
[4] William Morris, 'The Beauty of Life' in William Morris, *Hopes and Fears for Art: Five Lectures by William Morris*. Available at: https://www.marxists.org/archive/morris/works/1882/hopes/chapters/index.htm (accessed 10 May 2023), para. 11.
[5] See Bevir, 'William Morris', note 3, p. 179.
[6] Ibid.
[7] William Morris, 'The Art of the People' in Morris, *Hopes and Fears for Art*, note 4, para. 8.
[8] William Morris, 'Making the Best of It' in Morris, *Hopes and Fears for Art*, note 4, para. 109
[9] William Morris, *News from Nowhere*, in William Morris, *News from Nowhere and Other Writings* (London, Penguin, 2004), pp. 41-228.
[10] See William Morris, 'Preface to the Nature of Gothic' in Morris, *News from Nowhere and Other Writings,* note 9, p. 367 ('the lesson which Ruskin here teaches us is that art is the expression of man's pleasure in labour').
[11] Morris, 'Art of the People,' note 7, para. 38.
[12] Paragraphing from Jessie Kocmanova and J.E. Purkyne, 'The Aesthetic Opinions of William Morris' (1967) *Comparative Literature Studies* 4(4): p. 418.
[13] See Morris, 'Beauty of Life', note 4.
[14] William Morris, 'Introduction to Art to Labour'. Available at: https://www.marxists.org/archive/morris/works/1884/artintro.htm (accessed 10 May 2023), para. 1.
[15] William Morris 'Art and Socialism'. Available at: https://www.marxists.org/archive/morris/works/1884/as/as.htm (accessed 10 May 2023), para. 51.
[16] William Morris, 'Some Hints on Pattern-Designing' in William Morris, *News from Nowhere and Other Writings* (London, Penguin, 2004), p. 263.
[17] Morris, 'Beauty of Life' note 4, para. 102.
[18] Morris, 'Art of the people', note 7, para. 2.
[19] See Bevir, note 3, 'William Morris' p. 178,
[20] William Morris, *The Collected Works of William Morris* (London: Longmans, Green & Co, 1910-1915), Vol. 23, p. 279.
[21] William Morris, *The Unpublished Lectures of William Morris* (Detroit: Wayne State University Press, 1969), p 52.
[22] William Morris, 'Art and the Beauty of the Earth'. Available at: https://www.marxists.org/archive/morris/works/1881/earth.htm (accessed 10 May 2023), para. 1.
[23] William Morris, 'The Lesser Arts of Life' (lecture, 1882) Available at: https://www.marxists.org/archive/morris/works/1882/life1.htm (14 July 2023).
[24] Morris, 'Beauty of Life', note 4, para. 104.

[25] William Morris, 'The Aims of Art'. Available at: https://www.marxists.org/archive/morris/works/1886/aims.htm (accessed 10 May 2023), para. 8.
[26] Morris, 'Art of the People' note 7, para. 46.
[27] Ibid, para. 8.
[28] William Morris, 'The Lesser Arts', Morris, *Hopes and Fears for Art*, note 4, para. 27.
[29] Morris, 'Beauty of Life' note 7, para. 34.
[30] Ernest Fischer, *The Necessity of Art* (Harmondsworth: Penguin, 1963), p. 52.
[31] Morris, 'Art and Socialism' note 15, para. 49.
[32] Morris, 'Beauty of Life' note 7, para. 54.
[33] Ibid.
[34] Ibid, para. 41.
[35] Ibid, para. 56.
[36] Ibid.
[37] See Samuel Alexander, 'The Politics of Beauty: Schiller on Freedom and Aesthetic Education' in this collection of essays. The full set will be posted here: http://samuelalexander.info/s-m-p-l-c-t-y-ecological-civilisation-and-the-will-to-art/ (accessed 10 May 2023).
[38] Morris, 'Beauty of Life' para. 102.
[39] Edward Bellamy, *Looking Backward: 1887-2000* (Oxford: Oxford University Press, 2009).
[40] Morris wasn't merely unclear about when the novel was set; the dates upon which to base a timeframe are seemingly contradictory or inconsistent. In Chapter 2, the boatman describes a bridge, built in 2003, as 'not very old'. From this it can be inferred that the book is set soon after 2003. Readers also discover that the revolution occurred in 1952 (which I discuss later in this essay), and the character old Hammond, who is around 105 years old, was present during the revolution, seemingly as a young man, not a child. These timestamps considered together suggest the era of the book could be in the first or second decade of the twenty-first century (allowing old Hammond to be a young adult during the revolution). Given that Bellamy's novel was set 113 years in the future, we might imagine that Morris also reflected that timeline in his own book, which would be 2003. Nevertheless, in Chapter 12, it is stated that people had been living in the new society for at least 150 years, and given that the revolution was 1952, a reader might infer that the setting is early in the twenty-second century. But if that is so, old Hammond cannot have been alive during the revolution 150 years earlier, given that we are told he is 105. These inconsistencies cannot be resolved, but doing so is not critical to understanding the novel. It may have been that Morris introduced these inconsistencies as he revised the original serialised publication of the text into the book version, where some key dates were changed (e.g., the date of the revolution was changed from 1910 to 1952, no doubt reflecting Morris' pessimism about the likelihood of revolution during his own lifetime).
[41] See generally, Marius de Geus, *Ecological Utopias: Envisioning the Sustainable Society* (Utrecht: International Books, 1999), especially Ch 6.
[42] Morris, *News from Nowhere*, note 9, p. 50.
[43] Ibid, p. 74.
[44] Ibid, p. 105.
[45] Ibid, p. 81.

[46] Ibid, p. 111.
[47] Ibid, p. 124, See also, p. 127.
[48] Ibid, p. 76, p. 81, pp. 121-3.
[49] Ibid, p. 127.
[50] Ibid.
[51] Ibid.
[52] Ibid, p. 125.
[53] Ibid, p. 127.
[54] Ibid, p. 58.
[55] Ibid, p. 122.
[56] Ibid, p. 93.
[57] Ibid, p. 94.
[58] Ibid, p. 65.
[59] Ibid, p. 97.
[60] Ibid, p. 126.
[61] Ibid, p. 107.
[62] Ibid, p. 108.
[63] Ibid, p. 107.
[64] Ibid, p. 119.
[65] Ibid, p. 133.
[66] Ibid.
[67] Ibid, p. 136.
[68] Ibid, p. 134.
[69] Ibid, p. 135.
[70] Ibid, p. 160.
[71] Ibid (emphasis added).
[72] Gary Zabel, 'The Radical Aesthetics of William Morris' in Gary Zabel, *Art and Society: Lectures and Essays by William Morris* (Boston: George's Hill, 1993).
[73] Wilmer, 'Introduction' note 1, p. xxix.
[74] Ibid, p. xxxv.
[75] See Samuel Alexander, 'Pessimism without Despair: Suffering, Desire, and the Affirmation of Life' and Samuel Alexander, 'An Aesthetic Justification of Existence: The Redemptive Function of Art' in this collection of essays. See link in note 37.
[76] Morris, 'Beauty of Life', note 4, para. 104.
[77] Morris, 'Art of the people', note 7, para. 15.
[78] William Morris, *Useful Work v. Useless Toil* (London: Penguin, 2008), p. 2.
[79] Morris, 'Art of the people', note 7, para. 54.
[80] Ibid, para. 52.
[81] Ibid, para. 55.
[82] Ibid, para. 41.
[83] Morris, *News from Nowhere*, note 9, p. 111.
[84] Ibid, p. 200.
[85] Morris, *Collected Works*, note 20, Vol. 23, p. 165.
[86] Morris, 'Art of the people', note 7, para. 46.
[87] Morris, 'The Lesser Arts', note 28, para. 2.
[88] Ibid.
[89] Ibid, para. 3.
[90] Ibid, para. 4 (my emphasis).

[91] Ibid, para. 8.
[92] Ibid, para. 5.
[93] Ibid, para. 65.
[94] Ibid, para. 58.
[95] Ibid, para. 15.
[96] Morris, 'Art of the People', note 7, para. 17.
[97] Morris, 'The Relations of Art to Labour',
[98] Morris, 'Art of the People', note 7.
[99] Zabel, 'Radical Aesthetics', note 72, p. 1.
[100] See note 37.
[101] Terry Eagleton, 'Be Like the Silkworm' (29 June 2023) *London Review of Books* 45(13).
[102] That said, see the growing body of literature on Marxism and ecology, especially the work by John Bellamy Foster that is plausibly reconstructing Marx as an environmentalist.
[103] William Morris, 'The Society of the Future' (1889). Available at: https://www.marxists.org/archive/morris/works/1887/societyfuture.htm (accessed 15 July 2023).
[104] Morris, 'The Lesser Arts' note 28, para. 35.
[105] Ibid, para. 40.
[106] Ibid.
[107] Ibid, para. 29.
[108] See note 17.
[109] Henry Thoreau, *Walden*, in Carl Bode (ed.) *The Portable Thoreau* (New York: Penguin, 1982), p. 562.

www.ingramcontent.com/pod-product-compliance
Ingram Content Group UK Ltd.
Pitfield, Milton Keynes, MK11 3LW, UK
UKHW062309290726
14090UKWH00018B/975